GEORGE W. CABLE

Courtesy of the New Orleans TIMES-PICAYUNE

GEORGE W. CABLE

GEORGE W. CABLE

A BIOGRAPHY

ARLIN TURNER

DUKE UNIVERSITY PRESS

DURHAM, NORTH CAROLINA

1956

PRINTED IN THE UNITED STATES OF AMERICA
BY THE SEEMAN PRINTERY, INC., DURHAM, N. C.

For Thelma

CONTENTS

PREFACE

A PUBLISHER OF GEORGE W. CABLE'S WORKS, Roswell Smith, said of him in 1886, "He is probably one of those to whom monuments will be erected in the next generation." Cable had discovered Creole New Orleans for literature in the short stories collected as *Old Creole Days,* and in this book, along with two novels, he had brought literary realism to his region, the South, and had pioneered the use of authentic dialects in fiction. He was called the greatest Southern author since Poe, and many reviewers thought it appropriate to compare him with no one less than Nathaniel Hawthorne, Alphonse Daudet, Victor Hugo, or the great Elizabethans.

Roswell Smith knew these facts but the monuments he predicted would be erected to recognize Cable's work as a social reformer as much as his literary achievement. While memories of the Reconstruction era were still fresh in the South, Cable had launched a determined campaign in behalf of civil rights for Negroes. His efforts were met by a flood of abuse in his section, some of it astonishingly virulent and crude. He was called a traitor to the South, a bastard son attacking for personal gain the sacred institutions of his region. Yet for ten years he continued the debate, exhausting every means within his reach to bring a just solution to the great sore problem. He lectured, he wrote essays, he organized a group of prominent Southerners to publish their views.

Thus at the middle of his career Cable became embroiled in the affairs of his time as few authors have ever done. His convictions were so clear and his devotion to humanitarian reform was so strong that he turned from a satisfying campaign for prison reform and pushed his literary work to the back of his desk while he embarked on a course he knew would set him at odds with the normal spokesmen for his section. He chose this course deliberately and persisted in it against the advice of respected friends. When the cause had been lost as a practical matter, in the early 1890's, he abandoned it regretfully and channeled his reform efforts in the last thirty years of his life to home culture clubs and garden clubs in his new home, Northampton, Massachusetts.

To follow Cable's long career is to move, in the strongest of the currents and crosscurrents, from the lush days of antebellum New Orleans, through the Civil War and Reconstruction, to the subsequent era of uneasy truce in the war over civil rights. His works, the novels and tales only slightly less than the polemical essays and lectures, reflect the social questions uppermost in the forty-five years in which he wrote his books. And in those books he told stories and created characters that have made for him a distinctive place in American literature.

Because Cable put himself and his section and his times so fully into his works, it has seemed necessary to say in this biography a good deal about his books, about his surroundings in New Orleans and the South, and about the problems that agitated his contemporaries. I have dwelt at some length on the New Orleans that his parents knew and that he knew in his first twenty-five years because his major works were set in that period and were built from a combination of historical research, his own recollections, and the traditions in his family.

In 1928, three years after Cable's death, his daughter, Mrs. L. L. C. Biklé, published a volume of his letters connected by a thread of biography. She succeeded admirably in picturing her father in his family and among his associates and in revealing his personality, but she did not attempt a complete biography and did not explore the controversial aspects of his career. Fortunately there are abundant materials on which to base a full account of his life. It was his habit to preserve all letters and documents that came into his possession, as well as notes and drafts produced in his literary workshop. These materials and also his letters have found their way in great numbers into libraries and archives.

The richest holdings are in the Cable Collection at Tulane University, and it is pleasant to record here my thanks to Dr. Garland F. Taylor, who as librarian has gone far beyond the call of duty in making those materials available with the greatest convenience to me. More than a dozen other libraries holding Cable letters or other documents have given me access to them. These libraries are named in the text or in footnotes where their holdings are mentioned. I am happy to say also that Mrs. Biklé has generously opened for my use the materials in her possession, including Cable's letters to his first wife. My colleague Professor Jay B. Hubbell has read the manuscript and has made useful suggestions. Professor Floyd Stovall has read the manuscript also and Mr. Albert Mordell has read part of it. Among the others who have either given me information themselves or helped me to track down information I needed are Clarence Gohdes, Robert Cantwell, Newton Arvin, Edward Larocque Tinker, George Matthew Adams, Hjalmar H. Boyesen, Charles

Duffy, Norman Holmes Pearson, Walter Pforzheimer, the late Charles Scribner, Mrs. Margaret Cox Wright, and Miss Anna Gertrude Brewster.

My work has been assisted by a fellowship of the John Simon Guggenheim Foundation and by support from the Duke University Council on Research and the Louisiana State University Research Council. I am grateful to Mr. Ashbel Brice and his staff at the Duke University Press for informed aid in readying the manuscript for print.

GEORGE W. CABLE

CHAPTER I

AT THE FOOT OF THE GREAT RIVER

GEORGE W. CABLE was born in New Orleans on October 12, 1844. His birthplace was a rambling frame house set back in spacious grounds. It fronted on Annunciation Square and looked east toward the Mississippi River, half a mile down Race Street. The Faubourg de l'Annunciation, including the Place de l'Annunciation, had been laid out in 1815, or earlier, but for a quarter of a century afterward had remained a thinly occupied suburb at the western, up-river fringe of the city, with here and there a plantation type of home shielding a detached kitchen, slave quarters, and stables behind. In 1844, with the squares less than a third built in, the suburb was beginning its reign as the home of wealthy merchants and lawyers and doctors.

Like others in the *faubourg,* the Cable house stood in a wide lawn and was surrounded by magnolias, live oaks, orange and fig trees, umbrella chinas, and the flowering shrubs that thrive in semitropical New Orleans. It had the appearance of a one-story house, but there were rooms upstairs, with gable windows and others let into the low-pitched roof by dormers. There were fireplaces to drive off the chill of the damp winter months and large porches to catch what breeze might stir in the summer afternoons. It was a country house, generous enough in its proportions for a large, self-sufficient household. The luxuriant grounds, well kept but informal, and the comfortable lines of the house brought to mind a cheerful family in prosperous circumstances.[1] Such was the Cable family in 1844. With the birth of George there were five children, and the financial affairs were in good order.

[1] Long afterward Cable described the house and surroundings of his birth and also recalled his childhood activities in an article on New Orleans for *St. Nicholas,* XXI (Nov. and Dec., 1893), 40-49, 150-54. See also an interview with Cable in the New Orleans *Picayune,* Feb. 19, 1898.

The main facts of Cable's life appear in the volume by his daughter, L. L. C. Biklé, *George W. Cable: His Life and Letters* (New York, 1928). Another daughter, Mary Cable Dennis, has set down recollections of her father in the first half of the volume *The Tail of the Comet* (New York, 1937). In an article on "The Cable Family in Indiana," *American Literature,* I (May, 1929), 183-95, George S. Wykoff has brought together additional facts on Cable's ancestry.

The history of George's parents was one repeated over and over in the settling of the West. They had been married in Indiana, uniting families who had come from widely separated points in the seaboard states. Then they had moved farther, to New Orleans, expecting to improve their lot.

The father, George Washington Cable, had been born in Virginia, where his paternal and maternal ancestors had settled before the Revolution. Before 1830 he had moved with his parents first to Pennsylvania, where they freed the slaves they owned, and then to Dearborn County, Indiana. There in 1834 he married Rebecca Boardman, whose antecedents had lived in New England since the seventeenth century and whose parents had moved to Indiana in 1807.[2] In the first two years after George Washington Cable and Rebecca Boardman were married, they lived at Lawrenceburg, Indiana, on the Ohio River below Cincinnati. He apparently prospered, first in the cooper's trade and later as proprietor of a tavern, but the records suggest that his affairs were managed with a restless, venturesome spirit. With their daughter Emily, who had been born on December 12, 1834, they moved in 1836 to Greensburg, in the adjoining county on the northwest. There he entered business, but in the panic of 1837 he lost everything and at the age of twenty-six was ready to move again and make a new start.

In family tradition it was Rebecca who proposed going to New Orleans. The husband of one of her sisters had been a trader on the Mississippi and had brought back enticing reports of the Crescent City. But such reports could have come from many sources. Traffic on the

[2] George Washington Cable, father of the novelist, was born at Winchester, Virginia, Feb. 28, 1811, the only child of George Cable and Mary Stott. The earliest of the family in America seems to have been Jacob Kobell, one of three brothers who came from Würtemberg, Germany, early in the eighteenth century. His son, Sebastian, modified the name to Kable—a spelling which was kept in one branch of the family and appears in the name Kabletown, near Winchester. (See J. E. Norris, ed., *History of the Lower Shenandoah Valley*, Chicago, 1890.) His son was George Cable's father and the novelist's great-grandfather. A document preserved from 1816 (in the Cable Collection at the Howard-Tilton Memorial Library, Tulane University) shows that Mary Stott was one of the eleven living children of Robert and Eliza Stott, apparently of Pennsylvania Dutch extraction, who were slaveholders and had lived in Northumberland County, Virginia, at least since 1772.

Rebecca Boardman was descended from Samuel Boreman, who came from England to Ipswich, Massachusetts, in 1638 and later moved to Connecticut. Thaddeus Bordman (as the name was spelled after the second generation in America) moved with his family to New York State in the 1790's. There his son Amos, Rebecca's father (whose generation inserted the *a* in the name), married his second wife, Sylvia Noble. She was descended from Thomas Noble, one of the founders of Westfield, Massachusetts. His son and his grandson, Matthew and Obadiah Noble, were founders of Sheffield, in the same state. Ezekiel Noble, Obadiah's son and Rebecca Boardman's grandfather, was a private in the Revolutionary army.

Ohio all seemed to have its destination or its origin in New Orleans. The steamboats and the flatboats carried a wide assortment of passengers bound for Louisiana. Some were flashy, bejeweled dandies; some were hardy tradesmen; others were populous families leaving little behind, hoping for much ahead. All shared the fancy that at the foot of the great river lay the pot of gold. New Orleans held out to them both adventure and fortune. It was the fourth city in the nation; many thought it was destined to outstrip all those on the eastern coast. The perspective of history lights up weaknesses in its commercial structure that should have been discernible even in 1837, but few inside or outside the city saw them. Ahead were still two decades of plunging growth. One visitor in 1847 had no doubt that New Orleans would become "the largest city on the continent of America, and perhaps in the world."[3]

If George Washington Cable had been a farmer, he would have been drawn to the rich cotton and sugar land of the lower valley. But for a tradesman and businessman, the future lay in the city. He and Rebecca set out in 1837, traveling the fifteen hundred miles to New Orleans by the Ohio and the Mississippi. Their journey can be imagined in many of its details, for such moves were likely to follow a pattern in the leave-taking, the loading of belongings, and the visiting with strangers on the boat. Others among the families swarming in the same direction wanted to know and to be known; some had absorbing stories to tell. When the boat was pointed in to a landing, the small clearing became the stage for a scene in the high drama of migration on the river.

The second child and first son, John Edmonds, was born in Kentucky, presumably while the boat pushed down the river, as if to prophesy the new life awaiting all of them.

As was usually true, the move severed the ties of the family with friends and relatives; and though Rebecca took the children afterward for long visits in Indiana, the new home meant a new life. It was the new life in the new home that filled the family consciousness as the children grew up. When George W. Cable, born seven years after the move, reached maturity and began to write, he supplemented his own observations and his research in New Orleans history with traditions that had been kept alive in his family. Many pages in his stories and novels delineate the New Orleans he knew as a boy or his parents had known before him. His father was soon in the full swing of activities, and his fortune took the quick and dramatic turns that seem to belong to fiction.

[3] Albert James Pickett, *Eight Days in New Orleans in February, 1847* (no publisher, n. d.), p. 18.

The New Orleans which George Washington Cable and Rebecca first saw from the levee at the foot of Canal Street was a city of extremes and contrasts. The most European city in the United States, it exhibited as no other city did the new world alongside the old world transplanted. It was bilingual; and besides French other languages of continental Europe clashed on its sidewalks, its *banquettes*. There were also varieties of patois compounded of half a dozen tongues. The Creoles, tracing their lineage to the best blood in France and Spain, maintained a proud aloofness, frequenting the opera and the theater, reading the newest books from Paris, and having no more than necessary to do with the pushing, commercial *Américains*. In the waterfront saloons and in the pothouses of the "Swamp" at the rear of the city, the roistering Kentucky boatmen caroused with the polyglot tramps who had been collected from around the globe and cast ashore by the ships that came to trade.[4]

Wealth and poverty stood side by side, beauty and filth, refinement and crudeness, glamour and squalor. At one level was the precise dueling code; at another the tradition of the rough-and-tumble, eye-gouging brawls of the river men; at another the practice of stealth and the stiletto. The Creoles, the Irish, the Italians were Catholics; the evangelical Protestant churches were building and growing in the American quarter; the Negroes and mulattoes held their pagan orgies at the edge of the city and paid homage to the *voudou* queens. In one circle the manners of Paris prevailed, blended with an extravagant version of the cult of Southern "beauty and chivalry." In another circle, often in the same sector, moved the scrapings of the earth.

These divergent groups were everywhere in evidence, as were the merchants, the planters, and the professional men who had come from the states east and north and were prospering through what the Creoles labeled ungentlemanly practices. The rivalry between the Creoles and the hated intruders was openly acknowledged and at its climax. In 1836 the city had been divided into four units: three municipalities and Lafayette, the newest section in the expansion up the river. There was a mayor of the whole city, with a council, but the divisions had their

---

[4] B. M. Norman's *New Orleans and Environs* (New Orleans, 1845) contains a happy combination of facts about the city in the preceding decade and genial comment on what was peculiar to the life there. The city directories supply much information beyond the listings of residents and business houses. Other reports on New Orleans in the middle decades of the century are in Harriet Martineau, *Society in America* (New York and Paris, 2 vols., 1837) and *Retrospect of Western Travel* (Cincinnati and London, 2 vols., 1838); Edward Sullivan, *Rambles and Scrambles in North and South America* (London, 1852).

separate boards of aldermen and were all but autonomous. The conflict resolved itself slowly. When the city was again consolidated in 1852, the Creoles maintained their exclusive social position but relinquished political and commercial precedence to the *Américains*.

Whether George Washington Cable thought of himself as one of the intruding *Américains,* or was at once aware of the fight for dominance being waged in the city, he could not overlook the extremes and the overnight reversals of fortune. New Orleans had become accustomed to sudden, perverse strokes of fate. Spring floods on the Mississippi River, threatening the city or actually breaking through the levee, had been a part of the history since Bienville chose the site and built the first huts in 1718. Warm days flowered the azaleas and the oleanders but might bring yellow fever or cholera. The wealth-bearing ships at the wharves might turn smallpox into the city. When epidemics hit, all fled who could; those who could not flee stayed resignedly and buried the dead, putting what faith was possible in the current methods of fighting the diseases: firing cannon to shake the infection to the earth or burning pitch in barrels at the street corners to purify the air. Some put their trust in charms dispensed by the *voudou* queens.

The vicissitudes of life were received with the aplomb usual in boom times. A venturesome, soldier-of-fortune outlook prevailed. Affairs in the city were carried on with the same abandon the men displayed who volunteered for the war of Texas independence or for the filibustering expeditions to the south. Business enterprises were daring. The stakes were large. A few months of operating on the river might net a reasonable fortune; clearing and cultivating a tract of land granted for service in the War of 1812 might found a plantation dynasty. Gains might be swept away with even greater promptness, but to many of the plungers total loss left them where they had started a few years or months earlier —and they could plunge again. George Washington Cable must have felt a compatibility of spirit and temperament with his new home.

New Orleans had not escaped the panic of 1837, but quickly resumed its headlong expansion, as was attested by the opening in 1838 of the St. Charles Hotel, the most magnificent building west of the Appalachians. Even so, Cable did not prosper at once. In 1838 and on into the following year Rebecca was with her parents in Indiana, awaiting a better turn of events. His letters to her showed him always cheerful and bubbling with hope, but though he could write on March 20, 1839, that he had made $2800 in six weeks, he still did not direct her to come.[5] Perhaps his prosperity at the moment was something less than he implied, but his optimism was warranted, and when the 1840 census was taken, Rebecca and the children were with him again and he owned one slave.

He had become a partner in the firm of J. R. Borgstede & Co., grocers at 29 Tchoupitoulas Street, whose main business was supplying the river boats and through them the settlements reached by the river. The partnership soon had enterprises far afield. The conveyance records and the steamboat enrollments reveal in part the expanding interests. On August 20, 1839, the partners bought a griff boy named William, "a confirmed run away"; on July 17, 1841, half a block in the up-river suburb of Carrollton; on February 20, 1844, an improved lot near Annunciation Square. On June 8, 1845, they gained possession of 320 acres of land on the Bogue Falaya River, across Lake Pontchartrain from New Orleans. The conveyance records of the parish show that the land had on it a sawmill and sundry buildings. The tradition in the Cable family has it that there were investments in brickmaking also.

In 1844 Cable gained a part interest in the steamboat *Edna*. Within a year it was sold and he bought with Borgstede the *New Brazil* and the *Westwood*. The captain of the *Edna* while Cable was part owner was William Harvey Cable of St. Louis, probably a distant relative. The master of the *New Brazil* when it began operating for J. R. Borgstede & Co. was James E. Cable, a cousin of George Washington Cable's, who had the qualities of a proud Mississippi steamboat captain. He left the river in 1849 for the California gold fields.[6] The investment represented by these boats can be estimated from lists of the time showing steamboat valuations. The figures ranged up to $70,000, with the average falling between $20,000 and $30,000.[7] Cable had become a businessman of considerable wealth and corresponding prominence in New Orleans. A hint of instability, however, lies in the fact that the *Edna* and the 320 acres of land had come through mortgage foreclosure.

The third child, Mary Louise, was born in 1840, and Frances Antoinette in 1841. Though Rebecca no longer had to stay in Indiana to weather out hard times, she took the children for a visit in 1842. In

---

[5] The greatest number of letters quoted or cited in this volume are in the Cable Collection at Tulane University. One group of letters, those Cable wrote to his first wife, Louise Stewart Bartlett Cable, are in the possession of Mrs. L. L. C. Biklé. Letters in these two collections are cited without mention of location. The owners of other letters are shown.

[6] Letters James E. Cable wrote from the gold fields were printed in the *Picayune;* see the issue of Oct. 9, 1849.

[7] See *DeBow's Review,* VIII (May, 1850), 376-77.

keeping with the growing prosperity, the Cable family moved in 1844, not long before George was born on October 12, from 98 Barthelemew Street to the spacious house on Annunciation Square. In 1845 the two oldest children died of scarlet fever, John Edmonds on June 20 and Emily on July 30. They were buried at Cypress Grove, the most favored of the Protestant cemeteries. Because it was on Metairie Ridge, it had, unlike other New Orleans cemeteries, graves below ground in addition to the vaults above ground. Rebecca was at first afraid she would not love the other children after losing these. But she was not one to nurture her grief, and the effect seems to have been, ultimately, to intensify her affection for the others, deepen her religious nature, and reinforce the moral austerity her children and even her grandchildren remembered as most characteristic of her. The sixth child, James Boardman, was born in 1846.

The Cables lived on Annunciation Square until George was five years old; and though there were many moves afterward, he lived within a few squares of it until he was past forty and had written the stories and novels on which his reputation mainly rests. This first home was ideal for a boy. The largest of the open spaces that had been reserved in the city, Annunciation Square was at the center of what was called the garden district. In these surroundings and from the example of his mother he grew into an interest in gardening that remained important to him the rest of his life. As he reached the age to learn the names of the streets and his neighbors, he began to know the special qualities of the history and composition of his city—qualities which he remembered himself or knew from family tradition and reproduced in the books he wrote years afterward. Street names such as Celeste, Carondelet, St. Mary, and Nuns were a reminder that the city had been laid out by French-Catholics. Toledano Street spoke for the Spanish; Tchoupitoulas Street for the Indians; Washington, Jackson, and Fulton Streets for the Americans.

Near his home were the city's first waterworks, an iron foundry, and several of the cotton presses which exacted part of the toll New Orleans levied on the cotton trade passing over its wharves. When nearly fifty years later he wrote of New Orleans for *St. Nicholas,* the Century Company's magazine for children, he described a compress and confessed that as a boy he spent hours watching the sweating Negroes, naked to the waist, as they pushed bale after bale into the press. He saw the mansions being built in the district, urban counterparts of the plantation homes springing up along the river at Baton Rouge, St. Francisville, and Natchez. These homes and the social activities of their occupants reflected the wealth being garnered in the Merchant's Exchange, Banks' Arcade, the St. Charles Exchange, along Tchoupitoulas and Common Streets.[8]

B. M. Norman, the compiler of a guidebook to New Orleans in 1845, himself a printer in the city, surveyed the multiplying activities and then added, "This is completely a commercial community, however, and money is the universal ambition." He estimated that twenty thousand, or half of the businessmen in New Orleans, were migratory, spending only the busy season in the city. He asserted also that the city was visited yearly by ten thousand flatboatmen, whom he characterized as "an amphibious race of human beings, whose mode of living is much like that of the alligator, with whom they ironically claim relationship, but who carry under their rough exterior and uncouth manners, a heart as generous and noble, as beats in any human breast." Few Orleanians would have spoken so generously of the dreaded Kaintucks, but all would have agreed with Norman's further comments that they were as a matter of course not accepted in society and that the Creoles showed an equal coldness toward the permanent residents of the American city. He included one passage particularly to suggest the attitude in the old city toward the new: An aged resident of the Vieux Carré was asked why he did not visit the Faubourg Ste Marie, in the American sector just above Canal Street, to see some of the fine buildings there. The Creole replied: "Ah Monsieur B. dat is too much! You von varry funny fellow—I no believe vat you say—it's only von grand—vot you call it— vere de mud, de alligator, and de bull frog live?—von grand—grand— mud swamp, vere you say is von grand city, I no believe it!"[9]

Here was one representative of the Creoles George W. Cable was to delineate later on in his stories and novels.

[8] For a detailed descriptive and historical sketch of the Annunciation Square area in the 1840's and 1850's, see Henry N. Lewis, "Story of an Old Square Fashion Has Forsaken," *Picayune*, Nov. 1, 1908. For Cable's own account of the neighborhood and his boyhood activities see "New Orleans," *St. Nicholas*, XXI (Nov. and Dec., 1893), 40-49, 150-54, and "Some of My Pets," *Youth's Companion*, LXXV (Sept. 5, 1901), 427.

[9] Norman, *New Orleans and Environs*, pp. 68, 75, 79.

CHAPTER II

A BOY'S WILL

THE LATE 1840's were the years remembered most happily in the Cable family. In those years the children, Mary Lou, Nettie, George, and Jimmie, knew their father best. There was no hint yet of the reversal that soon would send him to the river for a new start and his wife and children to Indiana to live with her relatives. Now the father's gaiety and buoyancy had full reign. In the nursery he romped on his hands and knees or danced to his own music on the flute or sang a nonsensical song to the delight of even the youngest. Sometimes Rollo, the giant Newfoundland dog, was allowed a part in the fun. Their father was all forgiveness and kindness and usually left the correcting for Rebecca to do. He was jovial among his associates, frank and open and trusting. He smoked, at least at intervals, and, so family tradition has it, enjoyed a glass of wine in genial company but was always temperate. His friends liked to recall the easy hospitality, particularly at the Sunday dinners, in the home on Annunciation Square. On most Sundays there were guests.

Rebecca could hold her own in the jolly household, as illustrated by stories dating from those days. According to one, she thought her husband should wear a coat at dinner but carried her point, the story goes, only after she had appeared once for dinner with no dress over her petticoats.

One of the happiest memories the children kept in maturity was of the early-morning trips to market. Before breakfast was the time to go; the chief market day of the week was Sunday. The children's father liked to do the shopping himself, and to them nothing could have been better. Even Jimmie went, carried in the arms of the slave girl Martha. George's recollections of the experience he wrote out for *St. Nicholas* in 1893:

There is always a delightful uproar in these places in the hour of dawn; a bewildering chatter of all the world talking at once, mostly in German and French: a calling and hallooing, a pounding of cleavers, a smell of raw meat, of parsley and potatoes, of fish, onions, pineapples, garlics, oranges, shrimps and crabs, of hot loaves, coffee, milk, sausages and curds, a rattling of tins, a whetting of knives, a sawing of bones, a whistling of opera airs, a singing of the folk-songs of Gascony and Italia, a flutter of fowls, prattling and guffawing of negroes, mules braying, carts rumbling—it is great fun![1]

With increased prosperity the Cables had the luxury of additional servants; one report has it that slaves at the house on Annunciation Square numbered eight at one time. Two of them were characters in a story often repeated afterward: The children had one nurse named Jane (a "bright mulatress," according to the conveyance record, sixteen years old when bought for $600 on January 13, 1845), who made a habit of frightening them when their mother was not present. Another nurse, their favorite, was Martha (bought for $500 at the age of eleven on May 25, 1847, the same day another, Mary Anne, thirty-two, was sold for $600). Jane, it came out later, had killed her own child, and hated the kindly Martha because she knew her secret. In time Jane beat Martha cruelly. Following that, the other slaves went in a body to give Rebecca a full report, no one daring to be an informer without the backing of the others. Jane was sold down the river, as the saying was, to work in the rice fields, but she remained in the minds of the children a lively personification of evil.

When George was no longer entertained by exploring the stables back of the house, or the servants' quarters or the wash house, or by visiting the horses and ducks which his father kept, or even by watching the pigeons go in and out of their three-story house, complete with porch, high on a post in the back yard; when the cotton press and the waterworks and the sugar refinery had lost their fascination—then he went on longer expeditions. Writing for *The Youth's Companion* in 1901, he told how he would walk to the wharves in front of the old city and gaze at the sailing ships anchored there. The piles of stones the ships had brought as ballast and cast ashore held a rare fascination for a boy living "in a land where there is never a rock or a stone native to the soil," and he often went home with his pockets loaded.[2] Closer home, at the foot of Canal Street, were steamboats discharging produce from points on the rivers and bayous. Half a dozen of them docked every day, and the Negro stevedores rolled out bales of cotton and Spanish moss, barrels of sugar and molasses. Still farther up the river, along Tchoupitoulas Street, scores of flatboats were tied up, un-

[1] "New Orleans," *St. Nicholas*, XXI (Dec., 1893), 153. See also Norman, *New Orleans and Environs*, p. 135, and Pickett, *Eight Days in New Orleans in February, 1847*, p. 27.

[2] "Some of My Pets," *Youth's Companion*, LXXV (Sept. 5, 1901), 427.

loading flour and apples and potatoes they had brought a thousand miles and more down the Mississippi and the Ohio. One report for the year 1845 shows the arrival of 2,500 steamboats and 2,700 flatboats.

The greatest show of the day came at five in the afternoon, the hour of departure for the up-river packets. As the boats backed away from the wharf, churning the muddy water and emitting billows of smoke and blasts from the hoarse whistles, the levee swarmed with the audience the spectacle deserved, and everyone sensed the glamour and romance that had become part of Mississippi steamboating. The boys of New Orleans —and grown-ups as well—had their favorites among the fast, luxurious packets and never tired of extolling them. Travelers would adjust their plans to take passage with Captain Tom P. Leathers on the current model of his long series of palatial boats, all named *Natchez*. New records were constantly sought and achieved. Any trip might turn into a race, with crew and passengers cheering together. The glories and the tragedies of steamboating grew into George's childhood memories. Nearly half a century later he remembered and told of the night in 1849 when five steamboats burned at the foot of Poydras Street.[3] And when he wrote a novel about the river steamboats, *Gideon's Band,* more than sixty years later, he could draw on knowledge and impressions almost as vivid as if he had been himself a follower of the river.

Often George went fishing, at times at the lake with his father, at other times in the small drainage canals. Once three miles from home, as he recalled afterward,[4] he caught five sun perch, packed them in wet Spanish moss from the live oaks overhanging the ditch, and carried them home in a tin bucket. There, with a boy's pride in his accomplishment, he kept them in a pond more than a year. There were special occasions when the children were taken downtown. They might ride the Pontchartrain Railroad or the barges on the New Canal to the piers on the lake where the excursion boats loaded. They might at the Place d'Armes see a fireworks display, perhaps with a balloon ascension included, or Stickney's New Orleans Circus with its acrobatic and equestrian acts. Any visit to Congo Square was excitement enough in itself. Its official name was Circus Park, but anyone knew that years ago the fabulous Cayetano's Circus had performed in it, and that still earlier, when it lay outside the ramparts of the old city, it had been the one spot where the slaves might congregate on Sunday afternoon. The

[3] "New Orleans," *St. Nicholas,* XXI (Dec., 1893), 151. See the *Picayune,* Oct. 9, 1849. A fascinating compendium of information about the river boats is *Lloyd's Steamboat and River Directory, and Disasters on the Western Waters* (Philadelphia and Cincinnati [1856]).

[4] "New Orleans," *St. Nicholas,* XXI (Dec., 1893), 152.

Negroes had then appropriately named it Place Congo, for there they revived the songs and dances of their African childhood.

Best of all and beyond all comparison were the military parades on the Eighth of January, when the city put on its gayest attire to celebrate Jackson's victory over the British at the ramparts of New Orleans in 1815—or on Washington's Birthday or the Fourth of July. Then their father would be in all the glory of his uniform and office. In 1847 he became aide to Brigadier General E. L. Tracy, who commanded the First Brigade in the First Division of the Louisiana Militia. The next year he signed the order which established the First Brigade's part in the celebration of the Fourth. Walt Whitman, writing almost forty years later of his brief residence in New Orleans, recalled how the elaborately uniformed militiamen paraded that day and how New Orleans cheered the regiment of Louisiana Volunteers which had just returned from Mexico.[5] Such an occasion was to the taste of George Washington Cable, and he was one to do it justice. He was five feet eleven inches tall, handsomely filled out to a weight of 194 pounds, as one of his daughters remembered him.[6] He signed other orders, including the one directing the First Brigade to parade on the Eighth of January, 1850, but already he had failed in business, and soon he dropped out of the militia.

His office in the militia is testimony to the standing he had in the community. As a successful businessman, energetic and sociable, he took a willing part in the life about him. On May Day, 1849, he was on the committee of managers for a ball at Terpsichore Hall, a few blocks from his home. In promising "the strictest order and decorum," the managers probably had in mind that at a recent ball in the Third Municipality a mass fight had developed in which several rusty old pistols were snapped, so the newspaper reported, but fortunately none fired. Five years earlier the City Council had decreed that no weapons would be allowed in the Orleans Ball Room, and in 1850 a visitor in the city found the policemen at the ballroom door incredulous when he said he had no weapons to check—others checked six-barreled repeaters, eight-barreled revolvers, and bowie knives.[7] In 1849 the Louisiana Ball-Room held "white" balls on Thursday, Friday, and Sunday, "quarteroon" balls on Wednesday and Saturday.

[5] "New Orleans in 1848," *Picayune*, Jan. 25, 1887, in *Complete Prose Works* (Philadelphia, 1892), pp. 436-40. See also reports in the New Orleans *Crescent*, July 4, 1848, and the New Orleans *Delta*, July 6, 1848.

[6] Biklé, p. 2.

[7] Sullivan, *Rambles and Scrambles in North and South America*, p. 217.

The quarteroon, or more generally quadroon, balls were of a very special nature. To them quadroon mothers would take their daughters who had reached the age to "make an arrangement." White men danced with them and when one had made a choice, he established her in a small house on Bourbon or Rampart Street, where she provided him his second home and his second family, repeating the cycle her mother had completed before her. Visitors to the city, taken to the balls, almost invariably extolled the voluptuous beauty of the quadroon women. Locally their beauty was explained as the result of selective breeding—only those most desirable as paramours were chosen from generation to generation, and the others, along with the sons born in the system, found places among the other free mulattoes.

There is no reason to doubt that after ten years in New Orleans, if not from the beginning, the Cables felt at home and were willing to take the city as it was, though some of the local customs, to be sure, were remote from what they had known in Indiana. They found that Sunday was the best day to go to the market for produce and also the busiest day at the theaters and the racetracks, but they may have found some justice in a *Picayune* editorial of August 2, 1845. The editor noted that a multitude of races and religions were represented in New Orleans, not all of whom held the same views on the Sabbath, and he added that the churches were usually full.

George seems to have had a normal, happy childhood. His mother and older sisters could recall in later years little of precocity in his youth. They remembered that his mother had taught him geography at the age of three. He recalled himself that at nine he had set out to memorize the Declaration of Independence, on his mother's promise of a flag as reward, and that he confided to his father his intention to write a book. He had also read *Uncle Tom's Cabin,* and had wept but had "preserved no impressions from it," he wrote in the autobiographical sketch "My Politics," except an "ardent desire to marry Eva & a feeling of being widowed by her death."[8] At ten he was reading Hume's *History of England* and about then memorized a large part of *The Lady of the Lake,* which his mother earlier had read to the four children. When he first visited the Scott country, at the age of fifty-four, he remembered the poem well enough to quote line after line from memory.[9]

[8] This sketch was first written in Cable's notebook. A finished draft was made in 1889 but has remained unpublished except for brief excerpts in Biklé. Because the notebook draft contains specific details deleted in the revision, references here are to it. Both the notebook and the later draft are at Tulane University.

[9] In the diary-letter he sent home from England in 1898, in the possession of Mrs. L. L. C. Biklé. A small portion of this manuscript is included in Biklé, pp. 221-43.

His formal schooling can be outlined only sketchily. Presumably he attended the public schools, the first of which had opened in the city in 1841. He may have gone to the new Jackson Boys' School, a block from Annunciation Square. Before he was ready to start school, however, even if he entered at the age of five, as was permitted, the family had moved to Chestnut Street, between Seventh and Eighth, nearly a mile away. A move the next year to Brainard Street, between Josephine and Jackson streets, reduced the distance to the Jackson School to half a mile, and it was about as far to the public school on Clio, near Nayades Street (later St. Charles). But those moves followed business reverses, with the result that from 1850 to 1854 George spent as much time in Indiana as in New Orleans.

The causes of George Washington Cable's business failure are not clear. A cycle of cholera and yellow fever in 1848 and 1849 no doubt contributed, for thousands of residents fled the city and business all but stopped. In May and June, 1849, furthermore, New Orleans suffered the greatest flooding it has ever known. River water from Sauvé's Crevasse, a levee break above the city, flooded 220 inhabited blocks to an average depth of four feet. His failure seems not to have come at one blow, however, and it may be that the fall in the price of cotton from ten cents in late 1847 to five cents a year afterward had some bearing. Family tradition has it that the burning of two steamboats was one of the causes. In 1848 the boilers of the *Westwood* exploded twelve miles below New Orleans, killing a dozen people,[10] but that occurred a year after the boat had passed into other hands. The registration records show no transfer of title for the *New Brazil* after Cable and Borgstede bought it in 1845. The inference, therefore, is that it was destroyed, but no report of its loss has been uncovered. One case from the records of the Fifth District Court in New Orleans will illustrate how fickle trading on the river might be. Early in 1848 the owners of the steamboat *Duroc* owed the Borgstede and Cable firm nearly $1000 for supplies. A slave was surrendered and sold for half the debt. Then in April the court awarded a judgment for the remainder and ordered the *Duroc* seized. It was sold at sheriff's auction on April 22.

By the opening of 1849 the partnership of Borgstede and Cable was dissolved. Thereafter G. W. Cable & Co., a partnership of Cable and Alfred Wellington, had the Merchants' Exchange Saloon and Wine Store first at 32 and later at 26 New Levee Street. On February 26 Cable sued to collect a $500 note he held, and in March and April he gave Charles E. Alter three notes of his own totaling about $700. It seems

[10] See *DeBow's Review*, VII (Aug., 1849), 187.

likely that he was pledging his dwindling resources to finance still another venture. In May the schooner *Friendship* sailed from New Orleans with a cargo Cable was sending around Cape Horn for the California trade. Thomas Guard, an Indianian and for some years a close friend of Cable's in New Orleans, went along to dispose of the goods.[11] The venture met ill luck from the start of the voyage. What happened finally is not clear, but before the end of the year Cable's property in New Orleans was being sold at sheriff's sale on order of the Fifth District Court. Rebecca and the four children had gone to Indiana; her husband was still in New Orleans, doing nothing, he wrote her, and unable to pay his own expenses—but with good prospects.

The prospects remained good, as always with him, but in the remaining years of his life he had little more than prospects. Yet the misfortunes did not dampen his exuberance. In his first letter to Rebecca in Indiana on May 5 he wrote in his headlong hand:

> The place of parting soon is said
> It was in New Orleans
> The cause is plain—Oh dreadful fate
> It was for want of *Means!*

At the end of the same letter:

> When first we were united "Bec" we dreamed of naught but bliss
> And when our vows were sent above we sealed them with a kiss
> And now when fortune shuns our door and fancy turns to truth
> Let's take that same old kiss again which we enjoyed in youth
> For now when years have rolled away & we have children *four*
> Please give them all a kiss for me—to *you* I send a score.

Almost every letter contained love jingles; one was entirely in verse.

Still he found no work. He would move to Cuba, he wrote Rebecca on May 27, 1850, if she would consent. Walking in his sleep on July 17, he fell from the upstairs gallery, dislocating his shoulder and breaking his leg above the knee. The next five weeks he spent in the care of Dr. Warren Stone at the Canal Street Infirmary, or Maison de Santé. He sent for his family and they reached New Orleans in September. He held an appointment as notary public at Banks' Arcade from 1850 to 1852, but much of that time he spent on the river, irregular work sufficing only to keep the household going. In 1853 came yellow fever in such a scourge that this year became the absolute for comparing all later epidemics. Before mid-summer Rebecca had taken the children to Columbus, Indiana. Her husband was first on the river but returned

[11] Letters from Guard to Cable are at Tulane University.

to New Orleans in July. In the late summer the fever gripped the city with a fierceness beyond all past experience. In August the death rate had mounted to three hundred a day; the Young Men's Howard Association, founded in 1837 to administer relief in times of epidemic, had at one time five hundred orphans in its care. Cable once saw seventy-four bodies lying above ground at one cemetery with no one to dig graves. He spent the late summer with a friend at Biloxi; Rebecca borrowed from relatives the money she had to have.

Finally, on October 5, he had work on a steamboat and soon could send Rebecca twenty dollars. His spirits rose at once: he was making money fast, he wrote; prospects were better than in four years; he expected to make $2000 that season, though at the moment, ironically, the boat was lying on a sand bar of the Yazoo River above Vicksburg, waiting for rain and higher water. Once he sent a gold dollar for each child. George's first letter to his father, written out on his slate and copied by his mother, was rewarded with another gold piece around. In this letter he wrote, "I would like very much to know what business you are in also when you are coming after us for we are so lonely without you that it makes us very unhappy." In his second letter he wrote, "Pa how glad we would have been could you have come, as you anticipated but we hope the time is not far off that you will be with us."[12] In May, 1854, Rebecca made traveling suits for the children, but instead of instructions to come she received a dispatch and then a box of groceries for the coming weeks. She dreamed of her husband often, she said, always "clean, cheerful & happy." She hoped though he would "leave off the filthy weed and not taste a drop of the critter." A few weeks later he informed her for her "gratification" that he had quit the filthy weed and the critter.

The weeks dragged on. The children walked to the post office every day and returned droopy if there was no letter from Pa. Rebecca's resources and her spirits were both near bottom. She had cut herself a coat from one of his, and she could make out in most ways, but she must have a little money. At the end of the letter she asked him to plant at the tomb in Cypress Grove Cemetery "two running roses, a white and a yellow of the best kind; also the English Ivy." On November 1, 1854, Cable at last sent for his family, ending their final sojourn in Indiana. They returned to the neighborhood where they had lived formerly— first on Melpomene Street near Hercules; a year later on Seventh Street near Magazine, two blocks from the house they had occupied on Chestnut Street. This was the family residence until after New Orleans had

[12] These letters are printed in Biklé, pp. 9-10.

fallen to the Union forces six years later. Through 1855 Cable remained on the river, but after that he was never able to work steadily. In the summer of 1856 he was at Pass Christian hoping to regain his health. In the next year he was a deputy constable and after that became a marker at the customhouse. He died of chronic diarrhea on February 28, 1859, and was buried at Cypress Grove Cemetery.

The children remembered their father chiefly from the prosperous years of the 1840's. Their early recollections of their mother focused on the years of adversity beginning in 1850. George once wrote of those years: "By exertions that seemed like a daily and nightly self-destruction, prolonged through years, she cared for her husband through his failing days and kept her children clothed, sheltered and in school."[13] Resourceful and coolly determined, she proved equal to emergencies as they arose. Once when she was on a steamboat and cholera broke out, she nursed the victims. When there was not money to buy clothes, she sat for days in the tailor shop of a friend learning to make her husband's cast-off clothes into trousers and coats for George and Jimmie. At another time she contracted to make pillow slips, expecting to turn out fifty a day.

Actually young George's recollections could not reach far back of 1850. But the years of poverty and uncertainty came at a time to leave clear impressions. In the years after the family was reunited in 1854 his father probably took on for him the character of a Greek dramatic hero, half-tragic, half-pathetic in his struggle against the will of the gods. In that drama his mother emerged as the one able to thwart, at least in part, the perversity of fate.

It would be a mistake, though, to think of George as a prematurely aged youngster depressed by the family misfortunes. As he afterward remembered his years from ten to fourteen and wrote of them in a children's piece, "Some of My Pets," for the *Youth's Companion,* they were filled with a normal boy's interests and activities. When he was twelve, he and Jimmie had the excitement and tribulation of keeping rabbits and bantam chickens and had a mongrel dog, Fannie, who grew from a fluffy ball into a faithful playmate of the two boys and was still in the family when George left to join the Confederate Army.

George missed few of the amusements boys found in or near the city. "Children love New Orleans" was the thesis of an account he wrote long afterward for *St. Nicholas.* The happy, reminiscent mood of this sketch leaves no doubt that he was telling of what he and Jimmie did almost fifty years earlier. They played cowboy with lassos, flew

[13] Biklé, p. 11.

lantern kites at night, played the Creole lads' game of "noyas," which consisted of throwing peach seeds into a hole in the ground. They had squirt guns made of joints of bamboo cane and blow-guns which the Choctaw Indians made from six feet of cane and sold at the markets. They trapped songbirds and went fishing at the lake. If George's activities differed in any way from those of his playmates, it was only that he was fonder of birds and flowers, that he observed more closely the fish in the canals hovering over their nests or the coloring of the sky or the effect of fireflies at night or the brilliant coloring of the four-o'clocks.

Though the Cable family made their home in 1854 in a familiar part of the city, they could notice changes. They learned that the new city government occupied the hall at Lafayette Square, formerly the seat of the Second Municipality, that as this symbolized, the center of political and commercial power had moved across Canal Street into the American sector. They found also that the public schools had continued to expand. There was a Girls' High School at Magazine and Second streets and a Boys' High School on Laurel Street near First. Both were only a short walk from home.

With the death of his father, George's schooling ended abruptly. He was fourteen years and four months, so slight of stature he could have passed for half as old. He had demonstrated an uncommon ability in mathematics and composition and had written for the school paper, *The Spirit of the Times*. All in all, though, no one would have called him qualified to take over the support of his mother and two sisters and younger brother.

CHAPTER III

IN THE REFINER'S FIRE

AT HIS FATHER'S death George left school and stepped into the position his father had held at the customhouse since November, 1857. He was marker at Private Bonded Store No. 7. George began work, according to one report, without official appointment but with the approval of kindly superiors who knew how urgent were the needs of the family. Going abruptly from the schoolroom and the playground to man's work, he held the job until the war closed the warehouses more than two years later. The family stayed on at the house on Seventh Street, the five members drawn into a tight unity of understanding and assistance, standing together against difficulties and looking hopefully for better days. Jimmie stayed in school, and Mary Louise, nineteen years old, soon was teaching. George kept up his studies in spare time, for as he afterward wrote, study had come natural to him since childhood.

As North-South tensions mounted through 1859 and 1860, orators and newspapers in New Orleans kept the public in step with developments. One of the most authoritative voices of proposal and prophecy was that of Benjamin Morgan Palmer, pastor of the large and wealthy congregation at the First Presbyterian Church. In his Thanksgiving sermon on November 29, 1860, he talked on the subject that was uppermost in his listeners' minds. "The abolition spirit is undeniably atheistic," he asserted, though it might disguise itself, like the French Revolution, in the cloaks of human rights and reason. He continued with a cry that rang through the church—and through the blood of his listeners long afterward: "We will not shrink even from the baptism of fire. . . . Not till the last man has fallen behind the last rampart shall [our trust] drop from our hands."[1] From other pulpits also came the biblical defense of slavery and suggestions of means that might be necessary to preserve it. One morning late in January, 1861, the minister at Trinity Episcopal Church prayed, not for the President and Congress of the

[1] Included in T. C. Johnson, *Life and Letters of Benjamin Morgan Palmer* (Richmond, 1906), pp. 206-19.

United States, but for the "governor and people of this commonwealth and their representatives in convention assembled." The Louisiana Secession Convention had just passed the ordinance of secession.

At the announcement of the secession ordinance on January 26, cannon and church bells sounded in New Orleans. There were rockets and lights and bands and parading soldiers through the next week, reaching a climax on February 4 with the news that Jefferson Davis had been elected President of the Confederacy. On February 12 the newly designed state flag was unfurled at Lafayette Square, and on Washington's Birthday came a still greater crescendo in the parades and the speeches. After the fall of Fort Sumter in April the fire companies began military drills; the governor asked business houses to close at two o'clock in the interest of the afternoon formations. The legislature chose Major General John L. Lewis, under whom George Cable's father had served in the militia, to command the growing state militia. Threats of what "we would do" gave way to reiterations of what "we will do." Everyone knew that one gentleman could whip ten shopkeepers, and in the immediate context loose definitions of the words were acceptable.

And so it was in New Orleans as it was throughout the South, but with more dash and color. Even young girls talked "blood and thunder," so one woman recorded in a diary which George W. Cable later edited and published,[2] and young brides were tearfully happy to send their husbands away to war. Then in late spring the oldest companies left for Virginia. The war had ended work at the customhouse, and where George Cable had been employed bayonets were being made. In the flurry of business that followed secession, finding other work was not difficult. He became cashier for H. Block & Co., wholesale grocers on Common Street, where Henry Block, now in partnership with James M. McCandlish, had kept a store a dozen years earlier when George's father was in business a few blocks away. Through these months George's mind filled with the details he was to recount afterward in the historical sketch "New Orleans before the Capture" and with almost equal faithfulness in two of his novels, *Dr. Sevier* and *Kincaid's Battery*.

July brought reports of the first battles in Virginia. Slowly the war took on the aspect of reality, though it was still far off. Daily there was less hope of an early close. By September of 1861 a barely perceptible gloom had settled over New Orleans. Month after month

[2] The diary of Dora Richards Miller, published as "A Woman's Diary of the Siege of Vicksburg," *Century*, XXX (Sept., 1885), 767-75, and "War Diary of a Union Woman in the South," *Century*, XXXVIII (Oct., 1889), 931-46; and in *Strange True Stories of Louisiana* under the second title.

the ships had lain at anchor below the city, waiting for the blockade to be lifted, but it had been strengthened instead. By the opening of 1862 the initial spurt of business had passed. Warehouses were quiet; shipping had disappeared except for one or two steamboats a day from the bayous or the rivers out of reach of the Federals. Most of the steamboats, the proud river packets among them, were tied up to rust and rot along Slaughterhouse Point.

So nearly everyone of military age was at the front that the few who remained were often asked why they had not gone, and saw the question on the countenances of others who did not ask it. Older men drilled in the Confederate Guard, at Coliseum Place, where George Cable and his schoolmates had played ball not long ago; and on the deserted levee in the old city Creoles marched to commands in French learned in French manuals. George learned from guarded remarks of his employers that, contrary to what the newspapers said over and over, the defenses of the city were anything but adequate. Sometimes when business was slack, he would walk across Canal Street and, climbing to the unfinished top of the customhouse, would look out over the city, remembering the doubts he had heard whispered in the store. On April 9 thousands stood on the streets or leaned from the balconies to see the corpse of General Albert Sidney Johnston, a casualty of the first day at Shiloh, escorted from the Jackson Railroad station along Canal Street and St. Charles to the City Hall. One of the soldiers accompanying the body, now a hardened veteran, was a former schoolmate of George Cable's.

The move against New Orleans came by the river, from below. When the news reached the city on April 24 that the Federal ships, commanded by D. G. Farragut, had passed Forts Jackson and St. Philip and were steaming on up the river, fire bells called the home-guard to their posts; schools were dismissed; the streets filled with people. Left alone in the store where he worked, George Cable locked the doors and joined the crowds at the levee, three blocks away. Cotton emptied from the warehouses for burning on the levee turned the night into lurid day. Ships moored along the levee were fired and cut loose. Confusion, fear, helpless wringing of hands increased with the hours of the night. Many finished their packing and were ready to flee at daybreak. Frenzied mobs were in the streets all the next day. George saw a man, apparently guilty of no crime except bewilderment, strung up to a lamp post on Common Street and then cut down by a squad of the Foreign Legion. His employers having fled from the city, he closed the store and went back to the levee and milled with the crowd as

Farragut's ships rounded Slaughterhouse Point and anchored off the landing at Canal Street. Later in the afternoon he joined a mob in Common Street, many of whom were armed, as they followed two Union officers to the City Hall, yelling with the lustiest of them, "Hang them! Hurrah for Jeff Davis!" After five days of tangled negotiations in which no terms had been reached Farragut decided to occupy the city on April 29. George Cable was one of the sullen mob in Lafayette Square when Marines from Farragut's command lowered the state flag at the City Hall. He was as proud as anyone, he wrote afterward, that the invaders had been obliged to lower the flag themselves.

The hauling down of the flag at the City Hall closed one period in the history of New Orleans; the disembarking of General Benjamin F. Butler's troops on May 1 to occupy the city opened another. In the next half year George witnessed a sequence of events which Orleanians were to remember with stronger feeling than the arrival of Farragut's ships. History has recorded Butler as an administrator of some ability and a scoundrel of considerable proportions. To the Orleanians he was simply Beast Butler. George continued to work as a clerk and cashier, for a time in the store of W. A. Violett & Co., dealers in groceries and provisions in a building between New Levee and Fulton streets. A silent partner in the company was William C. Black, who was to be George's employer and friend for a decade after the war.

George asserted years later that at this time he shared the thoughts and feelings of his neighbors in New Orleans. There can be little doubt, in fact, that the Cables were among the most ardent Confederates. They shared the common resentment of Butler's General Order No. 28, the notorious woman order, which directed his soldiers to treat any woman scorning them as a woman of the street plying her trade. Like others they resented also Butler's raising money through assessments, his brother's profiteering and allegedly his own, his measures to force loyalty into the churches and schools, and especially his hanging of William B. Mumford, a private citizen who with others had hauled down and mutilated a United States flag raised at the mint while negotiations for surrender were in progress. George could remember at least once marching in the front rank of a mob that might have committed just such an offense as Mumford's.

General Order No. 62 of September 24 made specific demands on the Cable family. All eighteen years of age or over who had formerly been United States citizens and had not taken the oath of allegiance must take the oath by October 1 or register as enemies and declare their property. Penalties were fine, confiscation of property, and imprisonment. Nearly 68,000 had taken the oath by October 21, about 28,000 of them after the issuance of this order. Rebecca Cable refused to take the oath and on September 30 declared herself an enemy of the United States, and so did Mary Louise and Antoinette. George was twelve days short of his eighteenth birthday; Jimmie was sixteen. In December, registered enemies, not including men of conscription age, were permitted to leave New Orleans, not to return. The Cables stayed on until the following spring, and then were ordered to leave. On May 26 Dr. Walter Bailey, the family physician, certified that Rebecca was too sick to travel, and she remained several months, keeping Jimmie with her.

Mary Louise and Antoinette, George wrote afterward, "were banished, these two harmless girls of 22 & 20, into the starving Confederacy, almost absolutely penniless."[3] Taking him along as their little brother, in short pants, they left by boat for Mandeville, on the north shore of Lake Pontchartrain. At night they camped out, as tradition has the story, and ate the lunch Rebecca had packed for them. Inside their loaf of bread they discovered a pistol which she had kept in spite of Butler's order of August 16, 1862, confiscating all weapons and offering cash rewards and emancipation to slaves who reported weapons in the possession of their masters. Next day they met a party of Confederate soldiers, who by good fortune included New Orleans friends, one a beau of Nettie's who had been an associate of Mumford's in removing the flag from the mint. The soldiers had an ox wagon, the tradition runs, and could help the refugees along the road to Mississippi. They crossed the state line into Pike County and settled in plantation homes near Summit. Rebecca and Jimmie joined them in October, and they all continued to "visit" in Pike County and at Crystal Springs, sixty miles farther north. The plantation where George stayed, Oak Grove, was six miles from Summit. There were forty slaves and only one white man, the sixty-year-old head of a family which, even with his sons and sons-in-law in the army, still numbered ten members. It sheltered a series of refugees from 1862 until past the close of the war. Since the regular schools had been closed, Mary Louise was soon teaching, and she remained at Oak Grove until the end of the war.[4]

On October 9, 1863, George Cable left the plantation and near Summit enlisted in the Confederate cavalry. He recalled long afterward

[3] "My Politics."

[4] Dora Richards Miller had been on this plantation in October and November, 1862, and had recorded the life there in her diary. As he did with other such references in editing the diary for publication, Cable changed the plantation name from Oak Grove to Oak Haven.

that when the enlistment officer, a Lieutenant A. Smith, asked, "You solemnly swear you are nineteen years old?" and had an affirmative answer, he added, "You'd better say nine."[5] Lacking three days of his nineteenth birthday, George was five feet five inches tall and weighed about a hundred pounds. He joined Company J of the Fourth Mississippi Cavalry, Colonel C. C. Wilbourn's veteran regiment, in a brigade commanded by Brigadier General Wirt Adams.

During the autumn of 1863 there were only minor engagements in Mississippi. After Vicksburg had fallen on July 4 and Port Hudson four days later, the Confederate infantry was withdrawn east of Jackson. Grant and Sherman were in Tennessee engaging Bragg at Chicamauga and Chattanooga. Admiral Porter was patroling the Mississippi, supported by garrisons along the eastern shore. General William H. Jackson's division of Confederate cavalry, operating between the Mississippi and Pearl rivers, had Adams's brigade in the rear of Natchez and two others farther north covering Vicksburg. The mission of Jackson's cavalry was to harass the river garrisons, destroy river shipping, prevent the Federals from drawing supplies from the country, and protect the railroads and other arteries of supply.

On October 9, the day George enlisted, a detachment of cavalry under Major Harry Eastman marched from Vicksburg against the Confederate regiments to the south. Near Rocky Springs the next day Eastman met a detachment of Adams's cavalry commanded by Lieutenant Colonel Robert C. Wood. After a lively exchange at Alfred Ingraham's plantation, Wood retreated toward Port Gibson, once forming his men behind a thicket at the top of a hill, and again behind an embankment at a turn of the narrow wagon road. The Union cavalry stopped three miles from Port Gibson. Returning along the road, Eastman saw nine Confederate dead, half a dozen dead or wounded horses, and abandoned cartridge boxes, saddle bags, blankets, hats, and coats.

It seems likely that Cable was in this skirmish, for one of his messmates remembered thirty-five years afterward that on the same day, his second in the army, he received a slight wound.[6] Furthermore, he had joined his company at Gallatin the day before, not far from the scene

[5] Cable to Charles Scribner, October 11, 1901, in the archives of Charles Scribner's Sons. Cable's experiences in the cavalry have been spliced together from his letters, his autobiographical writings, the records of his service he preserved, and the letters of his family and his comrades. These facts have been fitted into the history of his unit as it can be traced in *The War of the Rebellion: A Compilation of the Official Records of the Union and Confederate Armies* (Washington, 1880-1901) and various histories of the cavalry action in the region in which he served.

[6] W. H. Pascoe to Cable, Feb. 20, 1898.

of the encounter. If he was present, he had a quick introduction to just the kind of fighting he would see in the next several months—darting in to strike a vulnerable spot and out again, always avoiding a direct engagement, for as a rule the enemy was in greater numbers. This abrupt initiation and his wound must have made him more readily acceptable to the soldiers of the Fourth Mississippi, many of whom had gone through the Tennessee campaign of the preceding spring and had fought before Vicksburg through the summer. Almost at once he assumed a position that none of the soldiers could have expected of the frail clerk when he reported for duty. With habitual cheerfulness he encouraged his comrades, the wounded and the disheartened alike, after a futile or a costly raid. So, at least, some of them remembered after thirty-five or fifty years. They also remembered him kneeling amid the confusion of camp, keeping his promise to his mother that he would pray for her every night.[7]

During the first weeks Cable was close enough to visit his family occasionally. His mother and sisters made his uniforms and kept him so well supplied that he drew no clothing from the quartermaster until eighteen months after his enlistment. They also made a jacket or a shirt now and then for one of his messmates. He corresponded with former schoolmates and friends, one of whom was Bettie Coleman. The Lloyd R. Coleman family, neighbors of the Cables in New Orleans, had fled first to Mississippi and now were at Newbern, in northwest Alabama, to stay until the end of the war. The letters from Bettie suggest more than a casual interest on his part and perhaps no more coy reserve than was to be expected on her part. Once she wrote that she had received only eight of the twenty-one letters he had sent. She recalled the evenings he had spent with her and her sisters in New Orleans, and the playing and singing in which he had been the leader. She would not send the photograph he requested, for she was sure he did not really want it, but would enclose for Nettie one of the new songs she had learned.

To the end of the year the cavalry units kept up the game of cat and mouse with the Union forces, and every few days there were skirmishes. Adams had two secret missions: to protect a signal station midway between Natchez and Vicksburg for communicating with the Trans-Mississippi Department, and to maintain the eastern end of a ferry service sending arms to the western bank. At the plantations of "certain traitors" he would burn the cotton and the buildings and remove

[7] See J. A. Covington to Cable, Feb. 21, 1898, and Dec. 28, 1903; and A. Richardson to Cable, Jan. 2, 1914.

the slaves; next he would set up his ten artillery pieces and fire on the river boats.

Cable became toughened to the saddle in these first months; he gained assurance that his constitution would hold up. As a matter of course he never wrote his mother now or later of dangers or hardships, but he regularly argued down her fears that life in the camps would be too hard for him. When his squad had stopped one day at a plantation in Louisiana, the owner voiced the impression that many probably had when they saw him. After asking whether this boy was actually in the army and being assured he was, the planter exclaimed, "Great Heavens! Abe Lincoln told the truth—We *are* robbing the cradle and the grave."[8] By February of the next year, however, Cable had grown bronzed and wiry and was ready for the solid month of riding and skirmishing he would have during Sherman's Meridian raid.

At the end of January Adams was ordered to the east bank of the Big Black River opposite Vicksburg, where Sherman had assembled a force superior to any the Confederates could draw up to oppose him. After two days of forced marching, Adams was in position when the Federals moved out of Vicksburg. "All the blue bonnets were over the border," Cable wrote afterward. At four the next morning, February 4, Adams dismounted two regiments of cavalry, one of them the Fourth Mississippi, before the enemy advance. They held their ground until three in the afternoon, and then retreated across Baker's Creek bridge. The next morning the Fourth Mississippi was again dismounted to fight as infantry, and forming the rear guard at Clinton the next day, it suffered heavy volleys from the flank as it moved forward on the road to Jackson.

It was probably in this attack that George Cable became separated from his regiment. Or he may have been in the part of Wilbourn's Fourth Mississippi Cavalry ordered to conscript duty late in January, and so may have missed the fighting to this point. Whichever the case, at nine o'clock that night he and a captain of cavalry rode together approaching Jackson. Three times that day they had been obliged to swing south in an effort to get ahead of the fighting, but the smoke of the battle advanced as fast as they did, for the fighting covered twenty miles during the day. Cable reached his command only at the end of the next day, beyond Pearl River where the Fourth Mississippi had taken position in the rear of the retreating infantry. But before this, he had acquired a new mount. At the edge of Jackson he and his

[8] Recounted from Cable by C. M. Clay, "George W. Cable," *Critic,* I (Oct. 8, 1881), 270-71.

companion had discovered a riderless horse which afterward fell to him when they cast lots and replaced the "wee, slim, white-footed bay pony, all hair and dandruff and bones," which he had brought into the cavalry with him. The new mount was Sandy, whose history he recounted years later for the *Youth's Companion* in his article "Some of My Pets."

On February 7 Cable's regiment took up the fighting where it had left off two days before, but now still greater odds were with the enemy. Only forty of the Fourth Mississippi had yet reassembled, and replacements brought the number to only a hundred. Adams engaged the Federals at Lake Station, Decatur, and Chunky Station, and then withdrew east of Meridian to cover the Confederate retreat on into Alabama. After destroying the mills, shops, warehouses, and railroads around Meridian, Sherman turned back toward Vicksburg. On February 18 the Confederate cavalry at Meridian began a forced march northward to support Bedford Forrest, who was preparing to meet a cavalry force under General W. Sooy Smith. Four days of riding brought Cable and his comrades to West Point, where Forrest had chosen to engage the Union cavalry, but Smith was already in retreat. They began a headlong march to overtake Sherman and on February 27 were at Sharon, north of Canton, again on the flanks of the Union army. Two days later the Confederates began skirmishing as the Union columns resumed the march toward Vicksburg, and they kept up the attacks through the cold, rainy days until the last of the army crossed the Big Black on March 4.

In the one month of the Meridian raid George Cable had ridden about 700 miles, 300 in one forced march, the remainder in skirmishing on the fringes of a vastly superior force. He was wounded on February 29.[9] As the Federals moved out of Canton on that day, Adams's brigade took position on their left flank. When Cable's squadron charged a detachment of Illinois infantry ambushed in a lane, he was wounded in the left armpit. The wound was dressed in the house where Sandy's former rider, a Confederate scout, had been nursed and had died—thus it was that George learned the rest of Sandy's story which he told later. It seems likely that the house was A. J. Montgomery's at Madison Station, between Jackson and Canton. Not long

---

[9] The date of Cable's wound was determined in this way: in a letter of Dec. 3, 1913, William H. Pascoe, a comrade of his, recalled that Cable was wounded in the skirmish in which Captain Magruder was killed. The *Official Records* of the war reveal that Captain J. M. Magruder of the Fourth Mississippi was mortally wounded on February 29. In a letter to his wife on Jan. 12, 1885, Cable recalled how he had suffered from "that bloody, ragged hole in" his "poor swelled back & stiff arm and not a little from the vile smell of that sloughing wound."

afterward his mother was with the Montgomerys; apparently she had come from Summit across the path of the recent fighting. George made a quick recovery and was soon back in camp. On March 10 he was assigned to the quartermaster's department, where he would be relieved of hard riding while his wound healed.

Rebecca stayed at Madison Station and in the summer was joined by Nettie, but Mary Louise said she could not honorably leave her teaching at Oak Grove to join them. Rebecca and Nettie became accepted members of A. J. Montgomery's household, as did George also, for he visited there often in the following year. They came to be intimate also with the Lafayette Montgomerys and others—a directory of 1861 lists nine Montgomerys in Madison County, all planters. George was able to visit his mother and Nettie at intervals until the end of the war. In June Wirt Adams's brigade, now commanded by General Henchie F. Mabry, was ordered to Forrest's command, too late to have a part in Forrest's victory at Brice's Cross-Roads on June 10 but in time for the battle in which he was defeated by General A. J. Smith near Tupelo on July 14, and it was in Forrest's second engagement with Smith near Oxford at the middle of August.

On September 22 Cable drew his pay and reimbursement for the use of his horse. Sandy had been stolen, probably after the fighting around Oxford. Dismounted cavalrymen might expect abrupt transfer to the infantry, but Major F. A. Beck, the brigade quartermaster for whom Cable was clerk, relieved his immediate need by agreeing to lend him a horse whenever they were in the field. In the succeeding weeks Cable shuttled back and forth through the northern half of the state with the troops or on individual missions for the quartermaster, often stopping at Madison Station.

His brother James was now a Confederate cavalryman in the regiment collected by Colonel Benjamin D. Lay in the first half of 1864 and stationed in southwest Mississippi. George felt a guardian's concern for the young soldier, who was eighteen, slight of stature, and troubled by weak eyes. In a letter of November 26 he wrote: "So Jim, take care of yourself, be a good soldier, study army regulations, *read your bible, say your prayers without fear of comment,* write to us often, keep up your spirits, don't fall in love nor the enemy's hands, and let cards alone." Within a week George learned that Jim was at Oak Grove with Mary Louise. A raiding party had surprised the entire district command where Jim was stationed and those who escaped capture, including the district commander himself, did so by taking to their heels separately. Greatly distressed, George wrote on November 29. First of all, Jim must get back to his command, even if he had to set out on foot to find it. Now that they were both dismounted, they should ask to be transferred so as to be together. "I will be with you," he wrote, "and hand in hand, & shoulder to shoulder we will bear each other's toils, & share each other's pleasures." Soldiers were entitled to transfer to a Louisiana command if they were serving in a unit from another state, as both of them were, and a friend from New Orleans, George Lyman, would help them get into his regiment, the Twenty-Second Louisiana Heavy Artillery, then at Mobile. But after a time in the hospital Jim was designated for limited duty and was assigned to a cotton agent in Meridian. George stayed on with Major Beck.

In the first months of 1865 the Confederate units in Mississippi, now only fragments, could not oppose even small Union forces raiding in the state. Militiamen of the state might be called up, but there were no arms for them. The number of deserters multiplied. The citizens suffered at the hands of both sides: dismounted cavalrymen took horses wherever they could find them; the Federals foraged almost the length of the state. In March there was not money to pay the soldiers.

If George had thought one year or two years earlier, as some had, that the Southern cause was lost, the letters he wrote his mother gave no hint of it. And if he had lost hope for the cause, his course would have been no different—there was never a question as to where he owed his loyalty, and he was determined to be a good soldier. From the beginning of the war he had seen but few Confederate successes. He had seen Farragut's ships anchor before helpless New Orleans; he had been pushed both ways across Mississippi by Sherman's juggernaut of the Meridian raid; his regiment had barely missed Forrest's victory over W. Sooy Smith in February, 1864, and over Sturgis the following June, but had been present at the series of defeats the Confederate cavalry suffered later in the year. More recently he had seen the whole state of Mississippi pillaged at will; he had seen deserters shot before the assembled troops but knew that others were deserting.

Early in March all the infantry units in Mississippi were sent to the Carolinas to oppose Sherman, leaving Forrest's cavalry of six thousand men the only Confederate force of any consequence in the state. At the middle of the month Wirt Adams was ordered to West Point, where Forrest was preparing to meet a raid General James H. Wilson was ready to launch from northern Alabama. Adams's cavalry reached West Point on March 30, after almost two weeks of marching in the mud. George had written his mother on March 20 that he had a tent to sleep in, and had added: "Poor soldiers! why should I be so much more comfortable than many who have breasted the storm of war from the beginning?" The others slept under "shebangs," made of stretching blankets across a sapling bent over to the ground or a pole supported by a forked stick at each end.

On April 2, in the last battle of the war, Forrest met Wilson at Selma, Alabama, and was defeated. Adams's cavalry was at Selma, but George was not. No longer to have the use of Major Beck's horse, he had finally requested transfer to the artillery at Mobile and was waiting in West Point for action on his request. In a long letter to his mother on April 8 he wrote:

I know that you and Nettie are in such good hands and hearts that nothing less than the enemy can hurt you. What right we have to such kind friends is more than I know, but we must strive to keep them whether we deserve them or not. . . . I have been so marvelously fortunate as to be boarding for only 1.50 per day, being just one tenth of the current rate. More! A lady over the way sent over to the tent & urged me to draw my rations, send them to her house, & eat my meals for nothing. Moreover the woman is poor. Her husband, too, asks me to accept the kind offer, but I have plenty of money & cannot eat up the dinners of her little children. If I had made arrangements to stay, I would have carried out the plan we at length agreed on—to teach her little children when I came home to supper. The tears came thick in her eyes when she said that her little ones might one day be in distress and I be able to assist them. This is not a bad world after all—it only has its failings which we must humor and overlook. . . .

After the defeat at Selma Forrest brought his broken ranks to Gainesville, Alabama. Mobile fell early in April; Lee surrendered at Appomattox Courthouse on April 9. Cable had begun clerking for Captain T. Ellis and he clerked also for Major J. P. Strange, adjutant of Forrest's cavalry the length of the war. With the staff and attachés he arrived on April 14 at Forrest's headquarters in Gainesville.

Always diligent in self-education and self-improvement—studying mathematics and Latin and practising drawing whenever he could in the camps, and reading the Bible regularly—Cable was aware of the advantages he had as a clerk. His close friends were still his messmates, but at headquarters he associated with men of greater accomplishments, Major Strange, for example, and Henry Ginder, Forrest's lieutenant of engineers, and in a small way Forrest himself. At Gainesville he was one of "them clerks" Forrest asked for a dozen times a day. As he recounted the occurrence years later in the pages of *Current Literature* when he was its editor,[10] he was the clerk Forrest chose to write out the papers freeing his slaves, presumably some of those he had brought with him at the beginning of the war. As the slaves were called into the room one at a time, Forrest asked each to state whether he had been a good master. The answers were all affirmative. Then as each paper was ready, Forrest signed it and called another slave.

Even though in Gainesville only three days before returning to Macon, Mississippi, George made friends in the town, as was his custom wherever his unit camped. He played his guitar for some young ladies who taught him new songs in turn. After his departure he wrote to them, and in a few days one replied for her two sisters as well as herself—they wished their "Minstrel Boy" were back, for they missed "those tender, touching, harmonious notes" of his guitar. Twenty years later one of the sisters wrote to ask whether George W. Cable, the noted author, was their minstrel boy.

Cable was thinking of home, now that the end had come—the main street in Gainesville reminded him of Prytania Street; a steamboat making a landing on the Tombigbee River brought back home more vividly than anything he had seen for two years. He feared his mother's courage might fail, but "I should remember," he wrote her on April 16, "how all my life I have seen you suffer & be strong." "You must really make Mary Louise come up to Madison this summer," he added. "The way times are now, I think it is highly desirable & necessary that we should be as little scattered as possible. . . . These are the 'Times that try men's souls,' and my constant prayer is that when ours are tried they may go through the ordeal as gold thro' the refiner's fire."

The months in the Confederate cavalry had greatly accelerated the maturing which had begun at the death of George's father. The responsibilities he had assumed as a boy of fourteen had been multiplied by the opening of the war and later by the scattering of the family. He had adjusted himself to life in the cavalry, and as much as conditions allowed, had cared for his mother, his sisters, and his brother. He had made friends among his comrades and had won both their respect for his abilities and their gratitude for his kindness and sympathy. He had adjusted himself calmly and rationally to the milieu of courage, suffering, and death.

More conspicuously perhaps, the war had developed and fixed his habits of mind. His comrades remembered afterward the sympathy

[10] XXII (Aug., 1897), 101-2. This account of the incident is reprinted in my article "George W. Cable's Recollections of General Forrest," *Journal of Southern History,* XXI (May, 1955), 224-28.

and the encouragement he had given them. It became his habit to face things as they were, and to look beyond to whatever hope remained. Acquainted with disaster since 1850, especially since 1859, he was prepared to look beyond the loss of a battle, the loss of a campaign, finally the loss of the cause for which he had fought, to the necessity of going on with whatever was left. In writing to his mother, he never echoed any regret for failures. Rather he took them as facts from which to start. What was important to his mind was hope, supported by determination to achieve the best outcome possible. It was this attitude that had prompted him to keep up his studies in camp. It was this attitude that kept him free of bitterness or resignation at the end of the war and turned him instead to charting a future for himself and his family.

Forrest surrendered on May 4. On May 6 his cavalrymen began leaving for home, paroled prisoners of war. Three days later, at Gainesville, Forrest wrote his farewell message to his troops. Before the end of the month George Cable was in New Orleans, at work.

CHAPTER IV

SWORDS INTO PLOWSHARES

THE DEFEAT of the Confederacy had been certain so long that to many the day of surrender brought less grieving over the lost cause than relief that finally the end had come. George Cable had thought only hazily beyond mustering-out day, but he was homesick for New Orleans and by going at once could have transportation and subsistence furnished. There was enough of regret and uncertainty and urgency, however, to sober his delight in returning home. His hopes for reuniting his family and making a new start were centered in New Orleans. With no home there, no clothes but his gray uniform, no money but his soldier's pay in worthless Confederate notes, he must find work, at a time when business was undergoing a confused redirection into peacetime channels.

He became an errand boy in the tobacco house of F. Van Benthuysen on Magazine Street and once was sent with a message to General E. N. Banks at the headquarters of the Department of the Gulf. Enraged to see the Confederate uniform worn in his presence, Banks asked, "Don't you know that there is a law that forbids you to wear that uniform?" As Cable remembered the incident, his reply was, "Yes, sir, I know that, sir. But I remember an older law which I am bound to regard, which forbids a man to appear without any clothes at all, sir."[1]

The streets were full of people; trade was beginning to flow again. If he could have thought only of himself, he might have stayed on at odd jobs while waiting for an opening. But the war had strengthened the sense of mutual dependence that had existed in his family since the death of his father, and George had predicted that their greatest test would come when the fighting was over. And so when he returned to Mississippi in the summer and began clerking in a store in Kosciusko, he was taking the best way to hold the family together. Jim could work with him, and they would be less than fifty miles from his mother and Nettie, still with the Montgomerys in Madison County.

Though he expected to be in Kosciusko at most a few months, George managed to have a full existence, as had been his habit in the

[1] Biklé, pp. 24-25.

cavalry. After long days in the store there was time to study and to finish a drawing, "The Empress of Fashion," which was praised by a local art teacher. He attended the services of the Mississippi Synod of the Presbyterian Church, which met at Kosciusko in October, and when he and Jim were hosts to a delegate in their room, "Sans Souci Shanty," it was cause for regret, he wrote his mother, that he had not drawn John Bunyan rather than the Empress. He had the trust and affection of his employer, G. D. Bustamante, and after he had left for New Orleans, one lady always felt like crying, she said, when she came to buy something and did not find him in the store.

What could be saved from his salary of fifty dollars a month was laid away against the time when the family would be together again and would remember the poor, as he said, while his mother would make biscuits under her own roof. Once when he considered making a small speculative investment, his mother sent him two gold pieces which had been among his first earnings in 1859, but like her he believed in nest eggs and so after all could not venture the gold pieces.

George kept up his efforts to return to "New Orleans la Belle," and he was there in early December, the luckiest son in the world, he said, for within five days he had offers of five jobs and was urged to take a room rent free. He began clerking for Lloyd R. Coleman, who had fled at the fall of New Orleans and had just returned to his business as cotton and commission merchant in Union Street. At first George lived with the Colemans on Orange Street, where they had been his neighbors before the war. "If I only had you here & wasn't in love," he wrote his mother, "I'd be just as happy as a lark." The object of his love seems to have been Bettie Coleman, his employer's daughter, whom he had showered with letters while he was in the army. She gave him a volume of Milton's poems on Christmas. In answering a teasing reference his mother had made to his love, he wrote on January 18, 1866, "I like it—keep on—say something else funny." To a friend in Kosciusko he wrote he was to be married the next year.

It had been George's habit to write cheerfully to his mother and sisters, even at the darkest moments during the war, but now every letter reflected an exuberance that was obviously genuine. He went to Dr. Palmer's services at the First Presbyterian Church, as he had done before the war, and he enjoyed the programs of study, reading, and singing of the Young Men's Weekly Prayer Meeting. Whenever he could afford it, he attended a concert; opera performances were to begin again and promised to be better than ever. Jim was in the city, and so was Nettie, the bride of James Cox; Mary Louise came for a while also, and though she had to leave again to teach school, she went this time only to Madisonville, on the north shore of Lake Pontchartrain. George expected higher salaries and lower rents soon; then he could bring his mother to the city.

The work was lighter than at Kosciusko and he found the cotton business pleasant, "but I cannot help striking higher, & trying for an honorable profession," he wrote his mother on January 26. "May the world regret me when I die!" "The Empress of Fashion" had come from Kosciusko to hang over the mantel of the Colemans' parlor, and he had begun a drawing of Robert E. Lee.

Of one thing George was sure: His heart was "set on the old Crescent City." James Cox could not tempt him to join in a new mercantile business at Greenville, Mississippi. Early in 1866, however, he saw a way to enter a profession by becoming an apprentice to a railroad construction engineer in Texas. Before the end of February his mother hastened from Mississippi to see him, but he did not leave until early July, and then not for Texas but the Atchafalaya River instead, where he was to begin as rodman with a surveying party. He seems not to have wavered in his decision to become a surveyor, but the letters he wrote home suggest that he was more interested in the other surveyors and the river and the swamps than his new profession. He was pleased and perhaps surprised to find that he could stand the July heat, and he felt at ease shouting "like a ship captain in a hurricane, from sunrise to dusk." He had inherited enough of his mother, he said, to enjoy the hard work, and soon he would be made chief flagman.

The surveyors had begun work where the Red River flows into the Mississippi and the Atchafalaya begins its course southward to the Gulf of Mexico. After two weeks they had followed the Atchafalaya to Cow Head Bayou, and George was happy that next they would run a line from Red River Junction along the Mississippi south to Baton Rouge. He had seen enough for a lifetime, he said, of white herons, sandpipers, alligators, sickly cotton and corn, empty houses, mud, and cottonwood brakes. But at the mouth of Red River on July 23, malarial fever struck the party. He was prostrated for weeks. His apprenticeship as an engineer was at an end; in fact, it was two years before he could resume steady work, six years before the effects of the fever were entirely gone.

When he was well enough to travel, he went to visit in Mississippi, happy to combine flight from the steaming late-summer of New Orleans with a visit among the Montgomerys and other friends of the war years. In the next two years his family moved twice, first to Jackson Avenue and then to St. Andrew Street, still within a few blocks of all the houses they had occupied in New Orleans. By 1868 George had returned to work. Again he considered joining James Cox in Greenville; again the attraction of New Orleans was too great. He began as accountant for William P. Converse, Jr., a commission merchant in Poydras Street. In the next three years he was accountant for two cotton firms, A. Henderson Peale and Company and then Scott, Cage and Company, and was secretary of the Orleans Oil Works Company. His efficiency and dependability won the tolerance of his employers when he was incapacitated by the lingering effects of the fever, which showed up most often in his weakened eyes.

What had been the course of his previous love affair is not recorded, but likely his long illness was one obstruction. In February of 1869 he became engaged to Louise Stewart Bartlett, and on December 7 they were married by Dr. Palmer at her home on Magazine Street. He was twenty-four and she two years younger. Though they had grown up as neighbors, they became acquainted only after they were grown. Her father, William Allen Bartlett, who traced his ancestry to the *Mayflower,* had come from Connecticut to New Orleans as a young man and there had married Louisa Burling Stewart, of Northern descent also.[2] Louise, the second child and first daughter of the family, had dark hair, slight build, and delicately cut features. She had innate poise and dignity of bearing and a sober disposition. From the day of their marriage she shared his seriousness of purpose and became the devoted encourager and assistant in all his work.

George Cable was no more satisfied with the career he had fallen into than he had been four years earlier, though his success had been enough to discourage thought of starting anew in another. His study had brought a measure of satisfaction, but his was a nature to demand a way to use the fruits of his study. He could not read history without relating it to the present and seeing in it guides for shaping the future; he could not study the Bible or hear a sermon without relating the precepts to himself and his community. Similarly his reading stirred in him an urge to write. From the days when he wrote for his high-school paper and helped edit it, he had liked to write and had felt some satisfaction in his efforts. His letters of the war years and afterward, often interlarded with whimsical drawings, are clearly from the pen of one aware of style and pleased at the effects he could gain. The poems of his courtship may have been to his mind only pretty testimonials of

[2] See the obituary notice of Louise Bartlett Cable in the *Daily Hampshire Gazette* (Northampton, Mass.), Feb. 29, 1904.

his love—foolish lines he later called them—but they were prompted no doubt by the same urge which produced the drawings earlier.

Almost every issue of the New Orleans dailies carried some unsolicited contribution; the Sunday papers as a rule had several. Poems were heavily in the majority. Before the end of 1869 George Cable was a contributor and had joined other members of a literary club in a plan to write a weekly column which his friend C. Harrison Parker had agreed to print in the *Picayune.* When copy was not forthcoming from the others for even one issue, Cable filled the space himself. Thus began on February 27, 1870, the column headed "Drop Shot," which he wrote weekly for eighteen months and daily for a month of that time.[3]

Masquerading as Drop Shot, Cable appeared some ninety times, his pieces averaging slightly more than a column in length. In total, this writing discloses much about its author's mind and activities; it is in effect a log of his development during almost two years in which he was feeling his way toward a beginning in serious authorship. If there is less spontaneity and less intimacy than would appear in a private journal, there is an offsetting gain in responsibility of content and care of execution. He wrote in effect a sequence of personal essays on endlessly varied topics with no limitations as to matter or manner except those imposed by his own judgment or his reticence.

At first the author was little more than an alert citizen commenting haphazardly, often superficially, on local matters. A year and a half later his topics were mainly literary; he had reached some bases of literary judgment, had recognized the usable materials lying about him, and had begun gathering and refining those materials. A third of what he wrote proposed to be serious creative work, and there is much speculation on literary aims and methods. A scholarly bent and a rigid self-discipline are evident throughout, as is also a growing concern for righting the wrongs in the world about him. Indeed, the column reflects unmistakable lines of development in its author.

The matter of the essays ranges from the real to the fanciful, the trivial to the momentous, the solemn to the ludicrous. One day there might be a mock-serious discourse on woman's dress; one day a descrip-

---

[3] During March and April, 1870, the column was missing on three Sundays, but thereafter, except for four weeks late in that year, it appeared every Sunday until July 9, 1871, when the author, always anonymous, bade farewell to his readers. From Feb. 21 to March 19, 1871, "Drop Shot" appeared also in the five week-day issues. On Aug. 20, 1871, the paper carried "A Letter from Drop Shot—in the Woods Somewhere," and on three Sundays of the following year, Feb. 11, 18, 25, the column was revived. A summary of Cable's term as columnist appears in my article "George Washington Cable's Literary Apprenticeship," *Louisiana Historical Quarterly,* XXIV (Jan., 1941), 168-86.

tion re-creating the feeling of a summer night in the Crescent City; one day an analysis of rhyme and refrain; one day a poem on the ruins at Spanish Fort; and the next a senseless letter in illiterate jargon. Experimentation shows in almost every column. The author's habit was to converse with his readers, raising questions for speculation, speaking tentatively at times and quite positively at others.

The columnist ran but little to autobiography, but did reveal something of his day-to-day routine: the ride to the office on the horsecars, the duties of a clerk in a cotton house, the confusion in the *Picayune* composing room. He told of the shrubs he brought from the woods to his garden, a steamboat ride to Biloxi, an August vacation by the Gulf; he wrote of high-school debating and editing a school paper, recalled from his youth. The portrait that could be pieced together was of a man who, in addition to his regular work and study and writing, found time for a happy existence, normal in most respects but distinguished by an unusual interest in flowers and trees and birds, and a discriminating awareness of the people, the speech, and the activities of the streets.

Cable dealt repeatedly with local affairs—as an observer who found them interesting or as a reformer attempting to persuade. Though reluctant to commit himself at first, he did not hesitate later to pass judgment on any issue that he broached. True, his remarks on lotteries, public amusements on Sunday, venal politicians, the public schools, and Negroes in the horsecars—all warm controversial topics at the time— were often indirect and guarded, but he had something to say on all of them. To make concrete his plea for artistic and cultural betterment, he wrote in behalf of a quarterly for New Orleans, a literary society, an art gallery, a lecture series, and the teaching of music in the schools.

Much of the comment aimed beyond the local, attesting a breadth of interest, though perhaps no wider knowledge than could be drawn from the newspapers and magazines to be found at the *Picayune* offices. On woman's rights Cable was noncommital, but he conceded, with the whimsy typical of his column, that women had a right to more of the virtues, more cultural accomplishments, more sensible dress. He lamented the dearth of worthy authors, the vogue of worthless and harmful reading, the mad pursuit of money, with the accompanying sacrifice of higher accomplishments. Dances he called "stupid hops," and he had no kinder word for "those profoundly silly stage tricks and worse spectacular displays of the day"—not intended to include normal stage plays, apparently. Though it is right to see in these judgments a zeal for moral and social reform, it is right also to note that such attitudes might be expressed any day on the editorial page of any local newspaper.

Cable asserted twenty years afterward that in the early 1870's he had no views at variance with those his neighbors held on the problems of the South, and with inconsequential reservations these writings bear out his assertion. His strictures on Yankees and his general attitude on sectional matters appear normal for the Deep South at the time. A proposal to make religious training compulsory in the public schools he considered an attack on Catholics and Jews and an example of Northern oppression. He objected that separate horsecars were not provided for the Negroes—though his concern seems to have been less to aid segregation than to save the blacks from embarrassment and abuse.

Significant as anything else in these writings is their evidence that the author found the things around him worth writing about—the melée at the station as the variegated populace embarked for summer resorts, quiet days by the seashore, evenings on the balconies of the Vieux Carré, an old fort and the ruins of an early Jesuit indigo farm. A paragraph in the last column he wrote, February 25, 1872, suggests that he was ready to begin working the mine of early local history:

Louisiana's brief two centuries of history is a rich and profitable mine. Here lie the gems, like those new diamonds in Africa, right on top of the ground. The mines are virgin. Choctaw legends and Spanish adventures may be found overlying each other in profuse abundance. Only one man, if I know aright, has culled among these nuggets. The historian of Louisiana . . . in following the annals of colonization, has uncovered the mines of romance. But the half, I am sure, has not been told.

The historian mentioned was Charles Gayarré, who in the next dozen years was to have an important but contradictory association with Cable's writings.

Cable mentioned over fifty authors and quoted from many of them, mainly poets, because he thought most on poetry, he said. Poe, Tennyson, Milton, Shakespeare, Longfellow, Byron, Scott, Hawthorne, and Bacon he named most often. Some of his comments are serious attempts at appraisal, and taken together they reflect a considerable literary acquaintance. Swinburne and Poe were overspiced with poetic tricks, but he could commend Poe's "bewildering harmony" and his "marvelous melody." To him Walt Whitman was one of the heavier workers of the machine age. In these views, no doubt sincere, he echoed the popular judgment which gave Whitman no quarter and qualified all estimates of Poe on account of the facts of his life.[4] As a rule Cable was more questioning than dogmatic and spoke as an apprentice poet rather than a critic; he was searching for principles to govern his own versifying but always spoke apologetically of his efforts.

He printed sixty-odd poems of his own, most of them serious in purpose but many of them nonsense rhymes concocted of puns, conundrums, parodies, and countless novelties of thought and method. Some were praised locally and he reprinted two at the request of his readers. "The Arrival," a whimsical poem on the birth of his first child, Louise, he saw reprinted eleven times within a year. As it continued to appear afterward, frequently altered and attributed to other authors, he enjoyed asserting his claim to the poem with a feigned show of hurt at the literary theft. For example, he wrote on September 2, 1897, to one who had said in print it was his impression that the author of the poem was George Cooper:

Will you allow me to give you my impression. I have an impression that it was coopered by quite another George. My impression is that it was written by myself twenty-seven years ago on the occasion of the birth of my first child. If you can't take my word for it I can show you the child.

I am not a frequent versifier and I never should have prized this bit if it had not immediately upon its first publication (in the New Orleans Picayune) begun a mad career of getting stolen. Like Helen of Troy, and others. . . .

Let me tell you, even the humblest poet "will turn." And I am bound to say that I wish my conscious or unconscious trespassers would give this much stolen trifle a respite. Zounds, man! have I done nothing else worth stealing? It's mortifying![5]

The poem was included in at least three anthologies.[6]

---

[4] See Lafcadio Hearn's denunciation of Whitman in the *Times-Democrat*, July 30, 1882; in Hearn's *Essays on American Literature*, ed. Sanki Ichikawa, with an introduction by Albert Mordell (Tokyo, 1929), pp. 91-95. Hearn explained to Whitman's friend W. D. O'Connor that his printed judgments were due in part to what he knew was acceptable in the newspapers. See Elizabeth Bisland, *The Life and Letters of Lafcadio Hearn* (Boston [1906]), I, 271.

[5] A copy of this letter is at Tulane University. The *Christian Union* of New York, VIII (Nov. 12, 1873), 397, printed the poem, considerably altered, as "A Strange Sail" by Fred Layton. See Biklé, pp. 166-69, for Cable's bantering protest. The *Times-Democrat* printed the poem on December 24, 1882.

[6] In Slason Thompson, ed., *The Humbler Poets* (Chicago, 1885), it was attributed to Mortimer M. Thompson (Doesticks). The error remained in a new edition of 1889 but was corrected in the edition of 1899. The poem appeared under Cable's name in Carolyn Wells, ed., *A Parody Anthology* (New York, 1904), p. 72; and Mary Elizabeth Burt, ed., *Poems That Every Child Should Know* (New York, 1904), pp. 152-53. It is included in Biklé, pp. 168-69.

Though Cable did not escape altogether the shallow conventionality that blighted newspaper verse in his time, he more than once satirized such verse. A moral slant usually appears in his poems, often in morals drawn in the manner of Bryant or Longfellow from incidents or natural phenomena. Several of the poems have the ring of sincerity in their humanitarian plea. Such a poem is "The Children of the Poor" (May 1, 1870), which is more than suggestive of Thomas Hood and reflects the author's increasing social awareness. Below are three of the thirteen stanzas:

> You can hear their voices faintly
>   Against the window cast,
> Like a recollection calling from
>   A wild and painful past. . . .
>
> For there's not a sight so painful
>   In the reach of heaven's grace,
> As a look of sad experience
>   Upon an infant's face. . . .
>
> Shall we sit and sigh, contented
>   To reach a languid hand
> To those whom waves, less cold than we,
>   Fling dying on the land? . . .

Perhaps the best are nature poems, several of which evidence restraint, sobriety, finish, and an uncommonly discriminating observation. Others are more apparently personal. On July 10, 1870, he printed a poem he had written after visiting Cypress Grove Cemetery, where his father and sister and brother were buried. "To Louise," in his column the next week, was a love lyric sent his fiancée June 25 of the year before when he was at Plaquemine to give his eyes a rest.

In the later issues, Cable took the role of urging the public back to thoughtful reading in the standard genres, back to that "inward inquiry so shamefully out of style." Then in his farewell column, he recommended the reading of such established authors as Taine, Scott, Tennyson, Milton, Emerson, Malory—but not to the exclusion of new authors. He recommended also the reading of novels, saying that like the parables of the Bible they may teach moral precepts. Though he had grown up in a home which held the distrust of novels common among strict Presbyterians, and though he was unswerving in his religious observances, he had reasoned his way to accepting novels.

In one essay (February 26, 1871) Cable said Bret Harte's story "The Luck of Roaring Camp" had hardly been surpassed in its type. In another he drew a comparison between Mark Twain and Josh Billings (July 17, 1870). Though he concluded with a slight preference for Billings, because he found both wit and good sense in every sentence, his remarks show that he understood Mark Twain as few readers did in 1870. He valued satires like "The Beef Contract" and the descriptive portions of *The Innocents Abroad* as highly as the frog story. Cable's own bumpkin character Felix Lazarus, who appeared now and then in his column, was modeled after Billings and at first employed misspelling and other strained illiteracies which made the kinship obvious. But in this essay he objected to Billings's forced illiteracies, as he did also to those in Will Carleton's farm ballads; and whenever he introduced Felix afterward, he injected a good measure of homely astuteness into his malapropisms and puns, but he dropped misspelling and other tricks of the humorists. He had tried his hand at the more extravagant devices and had discarded them for the more restrained humor of character and incident.

Cable became convinced while writing his column that his talent did not lie in poetry. He published fewer poems in the late issues and said he doubted that he should try anything except comic rhymes (December 4, 1870). His interest had shifted to prose description and the didactic essay. All along he had experimented in prose as well as poetry, and in the last few columns directness and seriousness largely crowded out the puns, the tortured expressions, and the striving for cleverness. He used little dialogue but in several pieces showed himself adept at reporting the actual dialects of New Orleans. In luxuriance of description "A Phosphorescent Sea" (August 21, 1870) would not be out of place beside passages Lafcadio Hearn was to write, in *Chita,* for example, eighteen years later.

The last few issues of the column hint that Cable was ready to give it up, for his interest had turned to subjects inappropriate to it. He included descriptions of the city and the swamps. He quoted a visiting artist who called New Orleans the most picturesque city in America except Quebec; he cited a historical incident to prove that the records of early Louisiana held all the materials a poet or a novelist could ask. During his eighteen months of experimenting he had grown rapidly. He had read widely and with a purpose and had sharpened his observation, and he had gained assurance that he was ready for serious work.

That assurance was in no sense false. His writings for the column are remarkable most of all for their excellence—given the scant literary experience that lay back of them. Without the benefit of even a complete high-school education and loaded from the age of fourteen with the duties of a soldier and a breadwinner for a family, he had managed to read enough to write with astonishing maturity about books and authors. In effect his only practice with his pen earlier had been in letter writing, but the earliest of his letters had shown uncommon ease and effectiveness in the turning of thought and language. His correspondents found his letters delightful or merry or heartening, as they often said. He had a natural inclination toward study and composition, but the quality of his first extensive writing, in his newspaper column, grew from ambition and devoted self-teaching as well as natural aptitude.

Before closing his column, Cable had spent a term as journalist full time. The success of his column had won him by early 1871 a reporter's post on the *Picayune*. He left his accountant's desk and considered himself launched as a journalist.

Some of the reporting was to his liking—the Mardi Gras celebration for example. Masked parades on Shrove Tuesday had appeared in New Orleans nearly fifty years earlier, but only since the war had they become fully established; and in 1871 the Mistick Krewe of Comus staged its most elaborate parade and ball since its organization fifteen years earlier. The subject of the pageant, Spenser's *Faerie Queene,* was supposed to be as close a secret as the membership of the Krewe, but well before Fat Tuesday it had been betrayed by purchases of the poem in the bookstores. Cable's report opened with a poem of his own and occupied two full pages on February 22 and again the following Sunday. He wrote at length on Spenser and the poem and had enjoyed the research for his report no less, apparently, than the spectacle itself, but he relished the unrestrained mirth in the streets. He was a proud local son giving full play to a notable event in the life of the city. At the middle of May he had another welcome assignment—to accompany Horace Greeley in and about the city during his first visit to the South. His sympathetic presentation of Greeley in his reports and in "Drop Shot" was in keeping with the policy of his paper, for Greeley had won a measure of acceptance in the South by supporting amnesty for ex-Confederates; and a year later, when the *Picayune* was even more directly the spokesman of the local Democratic party, it supported him in the presidential campaign.[7]

Another of Cable's assignments did bring him, however, into some disagreement with the editorial policy. In reporting the meetings of the Teachers' Institute, he first denounced the carpetbagger superintendent for not allowing segregation in the meetings. Then his resentment cooled and he drew back from the first position while the other newspapers

[7] *Picayune*, May 16, 17, 18, 21, 1871.

kept up the clamor. His employers were displeased, he wrote afterward, at his slight defection but took no particular cognizance of it.[8]

What caused Cable to leave the newspaper is not altogether clear. It is certain that refusal to report a theatrical performance was involved. According to his friend George E. Waring, who had his information directly from Cable, it had been agreed that he would not be required to report the theater and he refused when asked to do so once because other reporters were not available.[9] Cable was not satisfied, however, with this explanation as it was repeated in print afterward and in 1889 wrote out a fuller statement in the autobiographical sketch "My Politics":

I was naturally and emphatically unfit for the work of gathering up and throwing down heterogeneous armloads of daily news. I had neither the faculty for getting more news, nor the relish for blurting out news for news' sake after it was got. Had I possessed these equipments in any excellent degree, I need never have lost my place because—as has been printed of me— I would not violate my conscientious scruples, or, more strictly, the tenets of my church, by going to a theatre to report a play. The fact is I had no strong reportorial value in me to offset this somewhat vexatious scrupulosity.[10]

"I disliked reporting," he told a reporter for the *Picayune* on January 5, 1909: "in fact I disliked it so thoroughly that I made an absolute failure. I never failed so in anything else in my life."

When it was intimated that his resignation would be welcome, he left the *Picayune* in the summer of 1871 and began work for William C. Black and Company, cotton factors on Common Street. Black, as a partner of W. A. Violett, had been an employer of his before the war and was to remain his friend and employer until his death in 1879.

The last issues of the "Drop Shot" column leave no doubt that the author was ready to abandon it, and reporting as well. That his aim was now above journalism is shown by the fact that a few weeks after leaving the *Picayune* he was ready with the manuscript of a book, built mainly of selections from his column. It would print about 120 pages, of which 40 would be verse. "The work takes the form of a story," he wrote on October 31 to Charles Scribner & Co., the only one of the three publishers he approached who cared to see the manuscript, "with scenes laid in and about New Orleans, involving descriptions of scenes & seasons especially characteristic of the place, and portraying three or four personal characters representative of classes peculiar to this com-

[8] "My Politics."
[9] "George W. Cable," *Century*, XXIII (Feb., 1882), 602-5.
[10] Quoted in Biklé, pp. 39-40.

munity." Though he offered to bear the full cost of two thousand copies, the manuscript was rejected as being too fragmentary. In thanking the editor, he concluded, "after a while, when more at leisure, I am going to try to send you something that *will be published.*"[11] This manuscript seems not to have been preserved, regrettably, for it was his first attempt at extended narrative and it would show the local characters he chose to include. One was no doubt the bumpkin Felix Lazarus; perhaps one was a Creole and another a mulatto.

As it turned out, Cable was not through with newspapers. To the editors, he afterward said, he was still their talented fellow townsman with the facile pen. At the middle of January, 1872, when the *Picayune* changed hands, he agreed to contribute regularly again but not as a staff member. Alva Morris Holbrook, who had been with the paper for thirty-three years, sold out to a stock company of 224 members, who wanted to make the paper more than ever before an organ of the Democratic party. Little news was printed now except of local politics, because, the editor said, nothing else was of comparable importance. By the first week in January, as a matter of fact, the struggle between the two factions of the Radical party was so tense that anarchy and violence threatened hourly. United States marshals, at the behest of George W. Carter, Speaker of the House and a leader of the customhouse faction, arrested Governor Henry Clay Warmoth, the lieutenant-governor, and members of the legislature on a charge of conspiracy. The rump legislature then met and expelled other members. In the days following, two antagonistic legislatures met in the city; Federal troops were drawn up outside that of the Carter faction and outside a saloon where it met in caucus; the armory at Jackson Square was raided by a mob.

Such were the times in which Cable revived the "Drop Shot" column on February 11, 18, and 25, and also began on February 14 a weekly series on "The Churches and Charities of New Orleans." His plan was to write on the most historic of such institutions in a way to support the campaign for local reform and also, he wrote in the initial article, to redeem New Orleans in the opinion of outsiders. He wrote as a proud citizen telling with reverence and restraint the early history of his city. The articles took him back to the founding of New Orleans, for the Ursuline Nuns, the subject of his second essay, came in 1723, five years after Bienville's first settlement, and in telling of the St. Louis Cathedral he was led back to the first house of worship. He found much that was stranger than fiction, he said, and only reluctantly passed over

[11] Letters to Charles Scribner & Co., Oct. 17, 31, Dec. 11, 25, 1871; Jan. 19, 1872; in the archives of Charles Scribner's Sons.

it. The nine accounts are clear recitals, varied in presentation, a happy fusion of current with historical facts.

The series ended on March 17, no doubt on the editor's decision, for the subjects of other articles had been announced and Cable later said he wrote all that were desired. The fruits of the research were ultimately great. In the records at the Cabildo, which had been the seat of colonial government, at the Cathedral, and at the City Hall he had discovered both an abundance of materials and an interest of his own that was to give direction and shape to his entire literary career. He found a history overflowing with daring and heroism, romance and tragedy, much of which had not yet been sifted from the bundles of yellowing documents and the crumbling newspapers. He found also and began collecting ready-made stories.

To oblige his friend C. Harrison Parker, Cable reviewed books in the Sunday issues,[12] and in carrying out another assignment for the *Picayune* late in the summer, he aligned himself as a local reformer. He was asked to attack the Louisiana Lottery Company "with all the virulence" he chose. The two editorials he wrote showed him the force he could command for such purposes and also what reverberations might ensue.[13]

The Louisiana Lottery Company was a formidable opponent. It had been chartered by the state legislature in 1868, when the annual license fee of $40,000 was so welcome in the treasury as to offset public disapproval, but sentiment had increased against it as people realized that it was tax exempt and had an absolute monopoly. Under the astute direction of its president, Charles T. Howard, the company had bribed enough members of each legislature to protect its charter, and by employing its tremendous financial resources, it had won a measure of public favor. It gave eagerly to charity, more than once providing large sums to relieve suffering from floods when the state treasury had no such funds to appropriate. The ex-Confederate generals P. G. T. Beauregard and Jubal Early, at reported salaries of $30,000 a year, presided at its major drawings and spoke in its behalf when the occasion demanded.[14]

[12] Among them were George Calvert's *Goethe* and Henry Abbey's *Ballads of Good Deeds,* both reviewed on July 14, 1872.

[13] For this and Cable's subsequent reform efforts in New Orleans see my articles "George W. Cable's Beginnings as a Reformer," *Journal of Southern History,* XVII (May, 1951), 136-61, and "George W. Cable, Novelist and Reformer," *South Atlantic Quarterly,* XLVIII (Oct., 1949), 539-45.

[14] See Berthold C. Alwes, "The History of the Louisiana State Lottery Company," *Louisiana Historical Quarterly,* XXVII (Oct., 1944), 964-1118; and Richard Henry Wiggins, "The Louisiana Press and the Lottery," *Louisiana Historical Quarterly,* XXXI (July, 1948), 716-844. Neither work mentions the struggle between the *Picayune* and the

Another means of lessening opposition was by keeping the city news-papers silent. To this end, Howard had bought $10,000 in stock in the company which took over the *Picayune* in January, 1872. He paid only one-fourth down, obviously holding the remainder back to force the company to keep an agreement that the paper would "lay off" the lottery. On March 1 the board censured the editors for suppressing a recent grand jury report castigating the lottery company and demanded the remaining $7500 Howard owed. But the board vacillated in its policies until changes in its membership brought a stiffened attitude. The new president was Dr. D. Warren Brickell and another member was William C. Black, the first Cable's family physician and the second his employer. It was then that Cable was asked to attack the lottery.

The first of his articles was the leading editorial on August 11, the second was a front-page editorial two weeks later. Bribes paid by Howard to members of the legislature, Cable wrote, had secured passage of a bill which even Governor Warmoth had allowed to become a law without his signature. He characterized the lottery as "a heinous offense against society," a "crying sin, this subtle poison, that so cankers the morals of the rising generation," phrases he applied to the lottery without much change years later in his story "The Taxidermist." The news-papers, the pulpits, and individuals were called on to condemn the lottery managers and everyone associated with them. Following a meeting of the stockholders at which Howard received no satisfaction, he entered on September 6 a libel suit for $20,000 against the publishing company. Cable was not named in the suit, having written anonymously, and so had no part in the further proceedings unless to help write the *Picayune's* editorial defenses and its new attacks on the lottery. The controversy raged in the columns of the paper for something over two weeks; but on September 19 a new editor, R. B. Rhett, took office and there was no further mention of the lottery. Howard's victory was complete. No newspaper of the city, in fact, was able to hold out for long against the lottery from its beginning in 1868 until 1892, when its career was ended by the decision of the United States Supreme Court holding the Federal antilottery statute of 1890 to be constitutional.

As a matter of fact, the *Picayune* was in no position to carry on a war with the lottery company, or to invite any adversaries it did not have already. The election of November 4, 1872, intensified rather than diminished the political uncertainty. The candidates of the fusion ticket

---

lottery in 1872, for which the facts given here have come mainly from newspaper re-ports of the time.

supported by the Democrats were first declared elected, but then came the notorious war of the returning boards, opened by a Federal court in New Orleans and ended, at least temporarily, by a decision of the United States Supreme Court and President Grant's approval of the resulting action. The original returning board was declared illegal; another was established and supported as it recanvassed the returns and reversed the findings of the first board. With the help of Federal troops the officers designated by the new board took office, but the struggle continued on all fronts, most fiercely in the newspapers. The *Picayune* was of course in disfavor with the state administration thus counted into office, and it showed no inclination to seek favor of Governor Kellogg and what it habitually called his "bayonet legislature." One entanglement followed another. Rhett resigned the editorship on October 22 and the paper was in the hands of Holbrook again before the end of the year.

The assault on the lottery company must have looked to Cable afterward like a thrust at an unassailable foe who grew even stronger in the struggle. Still, he could have some satisfaction in the position he had taken in a cause supported by hundreds of the most respected men of the city. He also had learned something about reform efforts that would be useful to him later.

He continued to write occasionally for the local papers, even after he had published stories in the national magazines: once whimsical verses signed Drop Shot,[15] a children's story signed Felix Lazarus at another time,[16] later a poem signed Damon.[17] For years afterward in fact he sent pieces to the newspapers now and then, comments on occasional topics or the whimsical verses he liked to write the rest of his life. On July 4, 1872, he wrote his mother he was being paid for letters he wrote for the *Picayune,* but they are not readily identifiable. The paper printed a dozen or more articles, however, from late 1871, when he ceased to be a reporter, until 1874 that appear to show his hand. One such article, published on December 24, 1871, is "A Life-Ebbing Monography," which recounts from old records the story of a white man who opened a vein in his arm and inserted the blood of a fair mulatto so that he could then legally marry her. The description of the scene, the turn of the language, the indirection in such phrases as "the year eighteen hundred and something beyond," the avowal that there is no

---

[15] "Closing-Out Sale," *Picayune,* Sept. 8, 1872.

[16] "The Rhyming Spider: Felix Lazarus to the Children," New Orleans *Morning Star and Catholic Messenger,* Jan. 11, 1874.

[17] "The Locomotive," New Orleans *Sunday Times,* May 10, 1874. This poem was kept among newspaper clippings of other pieces known to be Cable's.

moral, "neither wisdom nor beauty in this tale, but it is true"—all suggest that Cable wrote it. It seems, in fact, to belong to the ancestry of two of the stories of the next few years, " 'Tite Poulette" and *Madame Delphine*.

At the same time Cable had a writing schedule which looked beyond the newspaper pieces. At least by 1872 he had begun writing the stories he was to publish in *Scribner's Monthly* during the next few years. In writing to his mother on August 20 of that year while she was visiting in Indiana, he said: "My papers have somehow taken a form which must make a book if they are fit to make anything." What he meant is not clear. He no doubt had in mind the newspaper writings he had assembled the year before, and he may have thought of adding historical sketches and true stories to fill out the portrait of New Orleans he had intended earlier. However that was, he had adopted a routine which in the next ten years enabled him to do his literary work while filling a post in the counting room.

He rose early, wrote an hour or two before breakfast, and at the end of the day studied and wrote as late as his eyes would allow. When his eyes were overtaxed, his wife or his friend Norman Walker of the *Picayune* staff or someone else read aloud the books he had for review and the history of Louisiana, which now was essential to his writing. While his wife was spending the summer with her mother on the Gulf coast, where their second daughter, Mary Boardman, was born on August 23, 1872, he made solid use of the long, hot days. On week-end visits with his family he wrote for the *Picayune*. From early July until the new cotton crop was harvested in the fall, work was light at the office. Then he might read or write at his desk or might slip away to the archives or the newspaper collection at the City Hall. Even so, he said he was a month behind with his writing.

At Carnival time in 1873 an editor of the *Picayune,* E. C. Dill, asked Cable to report the parade of the Mistick Krewe of Comus again. "While I was engaged in getting the advance information," he recalled nearly forty years afterward, "I met some men from Scribner's Monthly."[18] One of them was Edward King, whom Cable afterward liked to call his discoverer.

[18] Interview in the *Picayune,* Jan. 5, 1909.

CHAPTER V

"JADIS"

EDWARD KING remarked afterward, when he was called the discoverer of George W. Cable, that rather "Cable discovered himself, and would have dawned upon the world had there never been any 'Great South' scribes in New Orleans, to hear his mellifluous reading of his delightful sketches."[1] Cable was always eager, though, to credit King with introducing him to the Eastern publishers.

King came to New Orleans early in 1873. With an illustrator, J. Wells Champney, he was beginning eighteen months of travel on which to base a series of articles on "The Great South" for *Scribner's Monthly Magazine*. While recording voluminous facts, King also interpreted and judged. He came south with an open mind, inclined to be sympathetic, and before leaving Louisiana had decided he could recommend the South to the sympathy and generosity of his Northern readers, and to their sense of justice. He and Champney were delighted with New Orleans. They found in the Vieux Carré much of what they had both seen in Europe, but they saw more than carnival and gaiety and romantic past. In fact King broached most of the questions the people had uppermost in their minds. He opened his article: "Louisiana to-day is Paradise Lost. In twenty years it may be Paradise Regained. . . . It is the battle of race with race, of the picturesque and unjust civilization of the past with the prosaic and leveling civilization of the present." The former aristocrats, of the plantations and of the city, Creoles and Americans, told him of property worth half its former value, of the lack of capital for even the meagerest rebuilding, of interest rates from thirty to sixty per cent, of confiscatory taxes. A prominent Creole historian, Charles Gayarré, obviously, told him that "among his immense acquaintance, he did not know a single person who would not leave the state if means were at hand."

All were eager to explain that the former slaves would not work, that one state legislature had included fifty-five Negro members who could not read or write. Of the populace King wrote that "each and

[1] Biklé, p. 51.

every foreign type moves in a special current of its own, mingling little with the American." Again, "It is also astonishing to see how little the ordinary American citizen of New Orleans knows of his French neighbors; how ill he appreciates them. It is hard for him to talk five minutes about them without saying, 'Well, we have a non-progressive element here; it will not be converted.' Having said which, he will perhaps paint in glowing colors the virtues and excellences of his French neighbors, though he cannot forgive them for taking so little interest in public affairs"[2]—as if King had read books of Cable's not yet written. But he had talked with Cable and others, both Creoles and Americans.

What King's papers accomplished cannot be said exactly. Readers of the articles—in the magazine from July, 1873, to December, 1874, or in the thick volume of the next year, or in the two printings in England—found in them the first extended treatment of the South under the Reconstruction government. Looking backward from 1914, Cable wrote to F. L. Pattee that he thought the papers had no effect on the Southern literary awakening, that the two were merely coincidental.[3] Yet the papers prepared readers and editors for literary use of Southern materials and thus opened the way for Southern writers. Within the next ten years every important magazine made some effort to encourage writing in and about the South. The effect of the "Great South" undertaking on Cable's literary fortune was direct.

King found in Cable an abundance of both facts and interpretations. To Cable the visitors represented high literary and artistic accomplishment, though King was only twenty-five and Champney thirty. After leaving a factory to become a newspaper reporter, King had been to Europe twice, had published a book, was a contributor to *Scribner's Monthly,* and talked eagerly of the fiction and poetry he was writing. Champney's beginning had been similarly modest, as a wood-engraver's apprentice, and later he had been twice to Europe for study. They visited in Cable's home and bounced his two children on their knees. They went with him to the Cotton Exchange, met his employers, and caught his enthusiasm for the old city. On the eve of their departure, he read them the stories he had been writing and laying away, known only within his family. They were so impressed with the stories and his modest dedication to his writing that they were certain he deserved help in making a start. King, the voluble spokesman of the pair, took some of the stories away with him and in the following months kept up a stream of letters to his new friend, who had agreed to supply

[2] Edward King, *The Great South* (Hartford, 1875), pp. 17 ff.
[3] In Biklé, p. 47.

additional information for the Louisiana articles and to read proof on them.

King had taken with him "Bibi," the tragic story, in broad outline a true story, of an African prince in American slavery, a story no one outside the author's immediate family had read. On March 25 it already had "waltzed away to New York," to Richard Watson Gilder, associate editor of *Scribner's Monthly,* but its fate was not settled for weeks. In the letter King wrote on that day he added: "Fear not, O Cable, for your fame is sure if you continue to make Bibis." And on April 24, " 'Bibi' rode me as a nightmare last night." On May 9 he wrote again: "Bless you, my dear friend, if they don't print it, someone else will. But I am jogging their weak memories. I am deluging them with reproaches. . . . But I am only a worm crawling before the Scribnerian throne. Still, I plead poor Bibi's cause. . . . My heart goes out to you earnestly in your striving; and all the more because I know you will succeed."

King's pleading and his reproaches did not save "Bibi." Gilder rejected it on May 19, as other editors were to do afterward, all perhaps for the reason given by George Parsons Lathrop, at the *Atlantic Month-ly:* "on account of the unmitigatedly distressful effect of the story."[4] Rejected a second time by Gilder on January 2, 1875, after it had been revised and he had held it a full year, the story was not published until it became the episode of Bras Coupé in Cable's first novel, *The Grandissimes.*

Meanwhile another story was on its way to the Scribnerian throne. King had taken " 'Sieur George" with him also, and after returning it for revision he forwarded it early in May and himself reached New York toward the middle of July, in time to make a direct plea to Gilder, as he had planned to do for "Bibi." A week later, July 22, he wrote Cable: "The battle is won. 'Monsieur George' is accepted, and will be published in *Scribner.* . . . I read the story myself to the editor, who liked it; it trembled in the balance a day, and then Oh ye gods! was accepted! I fancy I can see you waltzing around the office of the venerable cotton brokers, shouting the war-cry of future conquest! Courage!"[5] King's skill in reading the Creole dialect may be doubted, but not his relish for it. Like Mark Twain, William Dean Howells, and others afterward, he spoke in Creole, he said, and he scattered Creole expressions through his letters.

King's efforts did not lessen after " 'Sieur George" had been ac-

---

[4] In Biklé, p. 48.
[5] In Biklé, pp. 46-47.

cepted. For several years he was Cable's unofficial agent in New York, arguing his case in the Scribner office, forwarding rejected stories to other editors, and urging him to work slowly, submit nothing below his best, and especially guard his health. He recommended Cable to other editors, and in Paris six years later persuaded the editor of the *Parisian* to make him an offer for some of his writings.[6] It was King who first urged him to move east, to write a novel, and to consider translating his stories into French. But as important as his tangible assistance or his advice, was the exuberance of his encouragement. "I am now ready to admit . . . that you are a genius," he wrote late in 1873. "Now I hope you will labor up from this level, and never, like Harte, drop below it! Still you have the satisfaction of knowing that there are but few who can touch the level where you stand now. Be strong! O my friend—BE STRONG!!!" A few months later, "One who has so thoroughly the artistic feeling should always make his methods as artistic as possible. How you grow!"

Robert Underwood Johnson, who was assistant editor of *Scribner's* in 1873, wrote long afterward that it was "a fresh and gentle southwest wind that blew into the office" when "'Sieur George" arrived and that the editors believed in Cable from the start.[7] Though Gilder had rejected the first story and needed two months and King's pleading to persuade him to accept the next, after reading it in proof he wrote the new author on August 29:

I feel moved to say that "we" hope you know that you have the makings of one of the best story-writers of the day. All you want to do is to appreciate yourself. You will do much better than "'Sieur George". . . . Go to work in good earnest and high faith in yourself—work as religiously as if you had already Bret Harte's reputation—& perhaps you may have one as lasting.[8]

Those who read "'Sieur George" at the Scribner office in the spring of 1873 or in the October number of the magazine were introduced to old New Orleans, which they were to know in the following years as Cable's province. They were led along the *banquettes* of the French Quarter, under the balconies balustraded with intricate iron-work; they stopped to peer into the flowered courtyards or caught teasing glimpses through the sap-green shutters that might be cautiously ajar but never open wide; they paused, as it were, across the street from a dilapidated old house and heard from the author an enchanting tale of *jadis,* once

---

[6] C. S. Wasson to Cable, April 4, 1879.

[7] *Remembered Yesterdays* (Boston, 1923), p. 122.

[8] In Biklé, p. 49.

upon a time, when the house and the street had known better days. A reviewer in the *Picayune* of October 5, 1873, when the story had just appeared in the magazine, said that local readers would recognize it at once "as a genuine story of New Orleans."

'Sieur George lived at the corner of Royal and St. Peter streets in a house which Lafcadio Hearn found still resisting change ten years after the story was published and which is pointed out today as 'Sieur George's House,[9] but Cable placed it no more exactly than "in the heart of New Orleans." It is a story of the olden time; street names are of less moment than the "gray stucco peeling off in broad patches," giving "a solemn look of gentility in rags, . . . like a faded fop who pretends to be looking for employment," the "masses of cobwebbed iron," the "square court within, hung with many lines of wet clothes, its sides hugged by rotten staircases that seem vainly trying to clamber out of the rubbish."

The story is told with the indefiniteness appropriate to a street where decayed old men or dark-eyed young women slip through half-opened doors, leaving the observer to wonder what is inside and what stories the mildewed walls could tell. For fifty years 'Sieur George came and went, known by no other name to the reader or to the landlord, Kookoo. The author wanders in and out of the old house, reporting a snatch of conversation or a glimpse of the hair trunk always kept in the rooms, telling of 'Sieur George setting out for the Mexican War, or climbing the stairs with a faltering tread. With such indirect touches the thread of the story is unwound: 'Sieur George has spent fifty years losing and attempting to regain his own fortune and that entrusted to him which should have gone to support a friend's daughter left to his care, and later a granddaughter. His disintegration has paralleled the decay of the house, and finally when he can no longer pay the rent he is glimpsed picking his way to the bounds of the city, where he will sleep in the tall grass. He has always meant well, has intended the best for the daughter of his friend and later her daughter. At the last he has a new combination and is sure that with ten dollars he could win. The hair trunk full to the brim of worthless lottery tickets has taught him nothing.

The *Scribner's* editors thought the story confused, and in deference to their objections several sentences and a final paragraph were added after the first printing. They expected a plot with definite complica-

---

[9] In an article on "The Scenes of Cable's Romances," *Century*, XXVII (Nov., 1883), 40-47, Hearn identified and described the landmarks of Cable's writings published to that time. 'Sieur George's and seven other houses still standing and associated with Cable's stories are described in Stanley Clisby Arthur's *Old New Orleans* (New Orleans, 1936).

tion, suspense, and resolution, and so were hardly prepared for a story achieving its effects through lightness of touch, half-revelation, and suggestion. Readers of Nathaniel Hawthorne's stories had met the same difficulty. In fact, the method of "'Sieur George" is reminiscent of Hawthorne in the location of the action in a hazily defined past, real in atmosphere rather than circumstantial details, and in the reliance on hints and speculation instead of direct assertion. And too, the trunk of lottery tickets recalls Hawthorne's chest of worthless currency in "Peter Goldthwaite's Treasure." Though Cable's attention was not mainly on plot, he was yet uncertain what methods were most suitable to his purposes and what liberties he might take in constructing a story. In consequence "'Sieur George" employs artificial concealment and contrivance of plot that suggest an author attempting to stay within a narrative method unsuited to his materials.

Yet the reader is not troubled by the half-heard conversations and the glimpses of the hair trunk, for with the first sentence he enters a fairy land of *jadis* and is caught up by the gentle movement of the story, as if loitering on the streets of the old city, stopping here before a courtyard, there before a shop window, and yet urged on to see what is next. The air of anticipation grows as the story takes turns as unexpected and as revealing as those in the narrow streets—twenty years passed, or 'Sieur George appeared in full regimentals, off to Mexico, or he climbed the stairs with a baby in his arms. The sense of expectancy, the surprise at every step, the effects felt but hardly noticed hold the reader's interest.

"'Sieur George" is in a style which in every sentence, especially in the abundant figurative language, reflects the author's fondness for whimsical turns of thought and expression. If this trait seems at first strained, after a page or two its delicate, ironic turns become integral to the place and the action of the characters. The trunk and the house and the street become symbols, not subtle in themselves, but subtle in the handling and in the way their meanings enter the reader's awareness. The flavor of the dialect is unobtrusive but unmistakable in its effect. Through the simple French phrases and the occasional Gallicized pronunciations the reader is reminded that the people are French and talk in French, but the best effects come from such expressions as "he addresses to him a few remarks," by which the language is suggested without a burdensome transcription.

After Cable's first story had been accepted, his editors asked repeatedly for others. In the next three years he submitted ten more stories, of which six were published in *Scribner's,* three were rejected and apparently destroyed, and one was published in *Appletons' Journal.*

The second story, "Belles Demoiselles Plantation," in *Scribner's* for April, 1874, avoids the hiatuses of plot and the straining for suspense of "'Sieur George," and it has excellences only partly realized in the first story. It concentrates on the essentials and yet is richer in suggestion. Lafcadio Hearn thought it the most singular of Cable's stories.

The plot is of the simplest and is only the vehicle for the character study. It tells of Colonel De Charleu and Old De Carlos, each descended in a slender line from the count who came to Louisiana long ago an agent of the French king. De Carlos, descended from a Choctaw woman, the count's wife for the nonce, and with other undesignated mixtures of blood, clung to his inheritance, a block of dilapidated buildings in the heart of New Orleans. De Charleu, of purest blood, had inherited the most beautiful plantation in Louisiana, where he lived with his seven daughters. Wishing to build also the finest house in the city and forgetting in cavalier fashion that the plantation was already mortgaged to De Carlos for more than it was worth, he proposed to buy his distant relative's property. De Carlos would not sell but would make an even exchange, for thus he would not relinquish his claim, as he saw it, on the original count's blood. An exchange was unthinkable to De Charleu until he discovered that the river was eating inexorably toward his house, and then he agreed. As both looked on, the noble mansion slipped into the river, taking with it the seven beautiful daughters. In De Charleu's periods of consciousness before he died a year later he insisted the trade had not been completed; his kinsman of Choctaw blood, his faithful nurse during the year, insisted they had traded. Loyalty to blood finally would not allow either to cheat the other.

The character trait at the center of the story is generalized for the Creoles as a whole, to the displeasure, understandably, of some of them who read the story: "One thing I never knew a Creole to do. He will not utterly go back on his ties of blood, no matter what sort of knots those ties may be. For one reason, he is never ashamed of his or his father's sins; and for another—he will tell you—he is 'all heart.'" Pride of descent and loyalty to blood are as strong in De Carlos, Injun Charlie as he is called, as it is in De Charleu, surrounded by his *belles demoiselles* and boundless splendor. De Charleu says once, "And we had both been bad enough in our times, eh, Charlie?"—not with the facile implications that would be expected in Bret Harte, but simply to testify to the bonds between them. He has no compunction for the luxurious idleness of his life, for "his name was fame enough."

The delicate relations between the two kinsmen are revealed in a touch here and a hint there. They converse in English, which hobbles and stumbles from unfamiliarity, as a reminder that intimacy is impossible. Neither uses profanity in the presence of the other for the same reason. Yet they discover in the presence of calamity the loyalty each owes the other.

In the glimpses of the *demoiselles,* dancing past the windows or smothering their papa in kisses, Cable approaches the portraits of young Creole women that were to ornament his later stories. The women in "'Sieur George" stay far in the background; here they flit in and out of the story, figures of grace, frivolity, and charm. The French they speak is refined, of course, and is suggested by a few French phrases and locutions, but when they mention Injun Charlie, they switch to English—"something is going to took place"; "too blame clever, me, dat's de troub'." Cable was exploring the use of dialect. He had learned that without burdening the reader he could give the flavor of the Creoles' speech in either French or English. His inclination was to strive for the literal accuracy of full transcription, but he realized that some compromise must be made, and his editors cautioned him to simplify the dialect.

The original of the Belles Demoiselles plantation was tumbled down and overgrown in Cable's time, but as in the story, it had been passed down through generations of one family, unnamed, he says, because "the old Creoles never forgive a public mention." Lafcadio Hearn found it a few years later still recognizable from Cable's description, though on the opposite side of the river, and he saw evidence that it would in time meet the destruction Cable had postulated for it.

The third story printed, "'Tite Poulette," in *Scribner's* for October, 1874, was probably one of the first Cable wrote and possibly a reworking of the sketch in the *Picayune* entitled "A Life-Ebbing Monography." Along with "Bibi," it grew from his sympathy for the Negro race as he had become aware of it in the early history. In narrative method it suggests "'Sieur George." There is less reliance on half-revelation for suspense, but there is some of the same kittenish playing of revelation against concealment, as when we are told that the wigmaker whispered something about Madame John. The passage continues: "She was the best yellow-fever nurse in a thousand yards round; but that is not what the wig-maker said." Still, this whimsicality has an unexpected appropriateness. The glimpses of characters or of shadowy interiors and the accidentally overheard remarks are the threads from which the fabric is woven that has a clear, simple design when completed.

The story suggests in a few quick touches the essentials of the system under which the quadroon women lived in early New Orleans. Zolli, white as a water lily and black-eyed, had been taken by her mother to the quadroon balls. There she had met Monsieur John, who had treated her generously and at his death had left her well provided; but after loss in a bank failure she and 'Tite Poulette, white as she and vastly more beautiful, have made their living by occasional dancing lessons and a little needlework. Now 'Tite Poulette "has seventeen," as the admiring young Creoles say, an age when she should, as the cycle demands, attend the balls and there make an arrangement. Madame John, forced to dance at the Salle de Condé but careful to keep 'Tite Poulette away, dreams of a white marriage for her and decries bitterly the law which prohibits it. But the young woman has no protest—"God made us. He made us just as we are; not more white, not more black."

The full meaning of their purgatory is realized only when Kristian Koppig, a Dutch clerk, declares his love and begs 'Tite Poulette to marry him. She stands immobile except for the flow of tears and the words, "It is against the law." Then, in a turn which the reader does not expect but through fleeting hints has been prepared to accept, Madame John produces papers to prove that 'Tite Poulette is not her daughter but was left to her when her parents died after landing from Spain. In the dignified beauty of the two women, the bitter protest of Madame John and the resigned acceptance of 'Tite Poulette, the story is a moving plea for the quadroon caste. The author apparently wished not to identify the system with the Creoles solely. Though the manager of the Salle de Condé is Monsieur de la Rue and the bewitching "smiles and grace, smiles and grace" at the ball are French, the system belongs to the time and place, not to one part of the population.

The action is set in real houses on Doumaine Street—one of which is known today as Madame John's Legacy—and the coming and going on the narrow sidewalks lends a compelling sense of actuality. Koppig is an awkward piece of stage furniture, but he is useful to the story as a source of humor and as a newcomer to the scene who can speak from an unencumbered conscience. It is with the two women, the first women Cable drew full-scale, that he achieves his greatest success. Through glimpses of their faces at the window and snippets of their dialogue, he suggests without full delineation their feelings and their speech "in the unceasing French way."

"Jean-ah Poquelin," published in May, 1875, impressed Cable's editors as the best he had yet written. It was a favorite with Mark Twain, who liked to read aloud the Creole-English of the title character.[10] It illustrates what H. H. Boyesen later told Cable was most valuable in his books, the portrayal of two civilizations in conflict. The Creole and the American civilizations are suggested, in essence, as they stood delicately balanced at the point where the future course was faintly discernible. The old and the new are side by side: Jean's decaying old house on the bank of the abandoned canal and the straight gravel road bordered by new cottages. To balance Jean, with his mysterious past of smuggling and slave-trading, is White, an efficient young clerk. Jean is one of the old Creoles who, one of the Americans says, "would liever live in a crawfish hole than to have a neighbor."

But there is more to the picture. The development company which finds Jean's padlocked enclosure in its way has no motive but profit. The members of the party who threaten Jean are drunk and have no more commendable motive than to torment him because he prefers to be left alone. When they realize, finally, that he has died at the end of seven years of caring for his half-brother, a leper, and has guarded the isolation of his house in order to save him from the Terre aux Lépreux, they stand uncovered and stunned at the climactic moment when the black mute shoulders Jean's coffin and turns down the path through the swamp to the land of the lepers, followed by the leper-white brother.

"Jean-ah Poquelin" shows Cable maturing in his fictional method. It has his usual compression and heightening through suggestion and quick turns, but there is greater naturalness than he had yet achieved. The author stays outside Jean's padlocked grounds, maintains that point of view, avoids speculations by secondary characters. The impact of the final revelation is breath-taking, though the reader then realizes that details earlier have pointed to the outcome. The dramatic intensity is the greater for the dignity—and the horror—of the tableau at the edge of the woods. "Jean-ah Poquelin" left no doubt that a fiction writer with uncommon dramatic power had appeared.

The story has a substantial base of actuality. In his boyhood Cable had seen the streets pushed from the high ground near the river into the swamp back of the city. When he wrote the story, plantation homes still stood in swamps that had once been indigo or sugar cane fields. Jean's house seems to have had as a model that of a "childless, wifeless, companionless old man," "Doctor" Gravier, which early in the nineteenth

[10] Howells wrote after almost half a century (*The Great Modern American Stories*, New York, 1920, p. xi) that he could not read this story "without hearing the voice of Mark Twain in reading its most dramatic phrases with his tragic pleasure" in the defiance of the old slave-trader. Howells made a similar comment in *Literary Friends and Acquaintance* (New York, 1900), pp. 403-4.

century stood on the bank of Poydras Canal. Cable described this old man in his article "The Great South Gate," later a part of *The Creoles of Louisiana,* and Hearn, who surely checked his surmises with the author, suggested that both the house and Gravier appear in the story.

"Madame Délicieuse," printed in August, 1875, is one of the most delicate, most whimsically gay of Cable's stories. Its plot is airy and offsets in charm anything it may lack in plausibility. Old General Villi-vicencio's disowning his son because he would not become a soldier is convincing only because this is a story of long ago and the General personifies archaic Creole pride and imperiousness. The love affair of the son and Madame Délicieuse is fantasy, but it is acceptable, for before it is revealed, the reader is at home in the remote *jadis.*

The setting is on Royal Street, appropriately, for Madame Délicieuse and the General belong at the center of the Vieux Carré. But the street and the houses are less important than in "'Sieur George" or "'Tite Poulette"—the atmosphere is set rather by the bevy of Creole ladies on a balcony waving handkerchiefs and receiving kisses thrown by the veterans of 1815 marching in an Eighth of January parade. An election in which a few days later the old and the new will measure strength, a threatened duel that descends into farce—all is keyed to the conniving and coaxing of a clever and beautiful woman to bend a haughty old man to her will. When all is resolved amid embracing and kissing and they pass out into Royal Street, they are met by the rare odor of orange blossoms.

The story is almost entirely in dialogue; the language is French, of course, and is rendered in good English except for occasional archaisms and French idioms. The characters are Creoles of refinement, admirable and lovable in all their foibles, and a reviewer in the New Orleans *Times* of June 1, 1879, thought they could not fail to please the Creole readers. The General belongs to a past which refuses to admit that it is past, but his hatred of the *Américains* and his love of the old order are as natural to him as breathing and do not deny him kindness, gen-erosity, and fairness any more than his pride keeps him from acknowl-edging finally the bravery of his son.

In several respects the "Café des Exilés," in *Scribner's* of March, 1876, differs from the other stories. The characters are refugees with multi-farious backgrounds, brought together by their homesickness and their purpose of smuggling arms to the Antilles. There are two threads of the plot and a storyteller is employed who recounts what he has been told by the chief character. Yet it is recognizably a Cable story.

Again the story is built solidly into its background. The Café des Exilés, actually on Rampart Street, was moved to Burgundy in the story, and the refugees from Cuba, San Domingo, and the other islands came directly from history. The story focuses on four characters and leaves the others, each with his particular confused past, to form a back-drop for the rivalry of two of them for the love of Pauline, daughter of the owner of the Café. There are instances of double or triple areas of understanding, depending on how much the different characters know of the rivalry for Pauline and the plans for smuggling. Cable obviously enjoys working out the intricate complication, but he does not employ intricacy for its own sake; he succeeds, rather, in narrating a story of conspiracy and intrigue with a directness that sacrifices nothing of suspense. The dialect is troublesome more than in any of the earlier stories, for the dialogue includes varying mixtures of Irish, French, Spanish, and Italian, but after a page or two the reader begins to feel at ease with the speech.

Of all Cable's stories "Posson Jone'" had widest and most distinguished commendation in his lifetime. It answered for Charles Dudley Warner the question of realism against idealism: it showed him that actual life, even low life, can be heightened to gain an idealistic effect.[11] Edmund Gosse, reading it in England, saw in its delineation of races and nationalities sure promise of a great novelist.[12] It is ironic that these judgments were passed on a story which had been hawked from one editor to another before it found a publisher. Rejected at *Scribner's*, it went to the New York *Times*, the *Galaxy*, and later *Harper's Magazine*. H. M. Alden, editor of *Harper's*, returned it on July 28, 1875, with the comment: "The disagreeable aspects of human nature are made prominent, & the story leaves an unpleasant impression on the mind of the reader." The stories in *Harper's*, he added in a letter of August 9, "must be of a pleasant character &, as a rule, must be love-tales." Finally "the little parson story," as Gilder called it, found a place in *Appletons' Journal* for April 1, 1876.

"Posson Jone'" does not have the delicacy or the rich suggestion usual with Cable. It is broad comedy, presented in bold strokes of extravagant action and characters that approach caricature. Yet nowhere did he demonstrate a surer hand, and nowhere did he achieve more truly delightful effects. Posson Jone', the giant bumpkin preacher from the West Florida parishes, in New Orleans on business with five thousand dollars belonging to "Smyrny" Church, could not encounter a more

---

[11] "On Mr. Cable's Readings," *Century*, XXVI (June, 1883), 311-12.
[12] A review in the *Saturday Review*, LII (Aug. 20, 1881), 238.

antithetical person than Jules St. Ange, nor one who would welcome the encounter more. For Jules and his body servant Baptiste are out of funds. The episodes are hilarious in which Jules and the parson visit gambling parlors and saloons and then, when Jones has become drunk, attend the buffalo and tiger fight at Congo Square. Jones talks in a stream of "lingual curiosities" of the backwoods which barely exceed in curiousness Jules's own manipulations of the English language. The scene at Congo Square, where Jones preaches to the throng and then hugs the tiger to his chest and pursues the buffalo, talking all the while of Daniel in the "buffler's" den, leads as a matter of course to the scene of Jones in jail and another at Bayou St. John as he embarks for home, a saddened Christian ("which I hope I can still say I am one"). Jules has arranged his release from the *calaboza* and now offers to replace, with his own winnings in a card game, the money of Smyrna Church which has mysteriously disappeared. Jones refuses, and as he kneels on the boat vowing his humility before God, Colossus, his slave, returns the lost money, which he slipped away earlier for safekeeping. Jules, impressed by the "so fighting an' moz rilligious man as I never saw," pays his debts with his winnings and goes "to his father an honest man."

The supporting materials are in keeping with the broad comedy. The time is soon after 1800, when the streets are filled with Kentucky flatboatmen, sailors from the ports of the world, and refugees from the West Indies. Congo Square, back of the old palisaded city, the site of the slave orgies of dance and song and of Cayetano's famous circus, is the scene of the tiger and buffalo fight. The characters of Jules and Jones are as clear-cut as any others Cable drew in his stories, and at the level of the servants the contrasts between the two worlds represented are effectively reinforced.

These seven stories had reached the publishers by November of 1875. After that Cable sent nothing for three years. The pay for the stories, about seventy dollars each, was negligible in relation to the time they required. He had been able to finish them only by hiring an assistant in his office and holding himself to a killing schedule. Furthermore, not all of his work had been accepted. Two stories, "Dr. Goldenbow" and "Hortensia," were rejected by *Scribner's* in the fall of 1874, at least partly because, Cable said afterward in "My Politics," they had political implications. Another, "Ba'm o' Gilly," was rejected the next year. These stories seem not to have been preserved. Cable had reached a pause. It had been his hope to leave the counting room and give himself wholly to literature, but he could not unless he found a way to make writing pay better.

Before submitting the last of these stories, he visited his publishers in July. He took the leisurely voyage on the steamer *Juniata,* which made a call at Havana. This stop supplied him with details for the Cuban background of "Café des Exilés," which he submitted to Gilder later in the year; and apparently it bore fruit also in a pleasant love story of the sort Alden wanted for *Harper's.* Rayburn S. Moore has pointed out that the story "Don Joaquin" in *Harper's* for January, 1876, though published anonymously, was assigned to Cable by current reviewers of the issue and in the index to the magazine prepared in 1893.[13] The story suggests Cable in its careful execution and in some of its phrasing, but it is facile rather than significant in any respect. The fact that Cable never acknowledged "Don Joaquin," apparently, and that none of his friends writing about his early years as an author ever mentioned it leaves little doubt that he wanted to disown it.

Reaching New York, Cable put himself in the hands of his publishers. *Scribner's Monthly Magazine* was then less than four years old, a late addition to the Scribner publishing house. The editor was the poet and novelist Dr. J. G. Holland, who had first conceived the undertaking and had launched it with the support of his close friends the elder Charles Scribner and Roswell Smith, a successful lawyer and business man who at the age of forty was attracted to publishing because he saw in it a means of furthering the religious and philanthropic work he had become interested in. In his wish to promote through the magazine better understanding between the North and the South, Smith had conceived of the "Great South" undertaking, and he continued to think of the South, he once wrote Cable, November 14, 1882, as "struggling under a burden almost too grievous to be borne." The periodical *Hours at Home* was drawn in at the outset and its editor, Richard Watson Gilder, became associate editor. Though Cable never met Holland, he felt the weight of his personality through others at the Scribner offices, and in 1889, eight years after Holland's death, he published a short tribute in which he dwelt chiefly on Holland's practical religion.[14]

---

[13] " 'Don Joaquin,' a Forgotten Story by George W. Cable," *American Literature,* XXVI (Nov., 1954), 418-21.

[14] "A Word About Dr. Holland," *Christian Union,* XL (July 25, 1889), 100. In a privately printed volume, *A Memory of Roswell Smith* (1892), Cable summed up the life and character of his friend. Histories of the Scribner firm and the Century Company and of the magazines they published, together with sketches of the staff members associated with Cable, are contained in the following volumes: Robert Underwood Johnson, *Remembered Yesterdays;* William Webster Ellsworth, *A Golden Age of Authors* (Boston, 1919); Samuel C. Chew, *Fruit Among the Leaves* (New York, 1950); Roger Burlingame, *Of Making Many Books: A Hundred Years of Reading, Writing and Publishing* (New York, 1946).

The enthusiasm for Cable's stories had spread through the staff at *Scribner's,* and after his visit in the summer of 1875 he was adopted into the company. Several members of the staff besides the editors formed the habit of adding personal notes to routine letters, often in phrases imitating his Creole dialect. It was as if each felt responsible for his personal and literary fortune. These friendships were among the strongest Cable ever had. Roswell Smith became the most intimate friend of his life outside of New Orleans; the younger Charles Scribner and Robert Underwood Johnson, the assistant editor, were his close friends the remaining fifty years of his life. Yet of all those in the organization it was Gilder who did most in shaping his literary work; in the next two decades Gilder was his most constant and, as he called himself, his severest critic.

Gilder was himself a voluminous writer and an influential figure on the literary and artistic scene. Hamlin Garland once wrote that Gilder "lived in the constant hope of discovering genius in every mail."[15] Though he did not recognize Cable's worth in the first mail, he soon was calling him a genius in one letter after another.

It was Gilder's habit to edit Cable's manuscripts all the way to page proof, declaring often that he regarded Cable's abilities so highly he was unwilling to print anything short of his best. In a memorial after Gilder's death Cable wrote: "He spoke with a fidelity which every now and then was unflattering and rigorous. He had no time to waste in mistaken tendernesses."[16] Attempts to make over their betters, as Gilder put it once, were customary at *Scribner's* and Roswell Smith assured Cable in 1882 that in ten years he had not seen an instance in which the effect of the close editorial supervision had not proved salutary. On January 4, 1874, almost at the beginning of their acquaintance, Gilder wrote Cable, "You are always so considerate, so willing to try to understand the editorial impertinence that— I like you. . . . You are a genius, and that is a rare article. Being a genius, you might claim the right of being grouty & cussed which you are not." Though Cable for the most part followed his editor's suggestions, at times he argued back and occasionally he refused to give in.

Gilder's concern for the excellence of his friend's work was unquestionably genuine, but no less genuine was the concern to make Cable acceptable to his own views and the editorial policies of the magazine. That much of the shaping he did was for the best is evident, but it is also evident that he was cautious and oversensitive to the limitations a family magazine such as *Scribner's* must impose on its authors.

Gilder kept in mind the editorial purpose of promoting reconciliation between the sections, "of helping to develop a Southern literature," as Roswell Smith put it, "and holding out a helping hand to our brethren at the South." King's "Great South" papers fitted into this purpose, but Cable's story "Bibi" did not, for it dealt in an unforgettable way with the question of slavery and by implication with the aftermath of slavery. Very probably too Gilder found in the story a stronger realism and more unpleasantness than suited his taste. He must have felt some reluctance, as the wording of his second rejection suggests he did, in turning down a story which had ridden Edward King like a nightmare and impressed his assistant editor, Robert Underwood Johnson, as a "powerful Victor Hugo-like episode." Looking backward from old age, Johnson suggested that Gilder declined "Posson Jone'" because of a fear that Dr. Holland would object to the drunken parson in it.[17] Gilder's confused statement in returning the story to Cable on November 16, 1874, supports this inference. There is a twofold irony in the decision on "Posson Jone'": it proved to be one of Cable's most generally praised stories, and in the next few years Gilder thought direct moralizing his greatest literary fault.

Though Gilder did not say, as Alden said for *Harper's,* that a story must be pleasant, he repeatedly urged Cable to avoid the unpleasant. He found a figure of speech in "'Tite Poulette" unpleasant; he would print "Café des Exilés" if he could "omit a touch or two of horror," and he added, "Write something intensely interesting—but without the terrible suggestion you so often make use of." It is tempting to speculate on the kind of fiction Cable would have produced if from the time he first submitted "Bibi" onward his work had been judged by an editor less fearful of the unpleasant and the touches of horror.

In his first letter to Cable, August 29, 1873, Gilder exhorted him to be always clear, and he regularly asked for more directness of method and language. As a matter of fact, he wrote several times asking to have a character identified or an incident explained in a manuscript he was reading. Often he seems to have asked for an obviousness that would have destroyed Cable's narrative art, but at times he was right in concluding that indirection and vagueness were troublesome out of proportion to the effect achieved. Cable's method had much in common

---

[17] *Remembered Yesterdays*, p. 123. In an article "Mrs. Grundy and Richard Watson Gilder," *American Quarterly*, IV (Spring, 1952), 66-72, Robert Berkelman argues convincingly that Gilder was less squeamish than most other editors of his time.

with Nathaniel Hawthorne's, but perhaps his fault lay in attempting to apply Hawthorne's method at times when his materials demanded the forthrightness of realism. In fact, Hawthorne had the same difficulty in adapting his method to the tales he set in the everyday world of his own time.

In the matter of dialect Gilder learned from Cable—and admitted as much. He found it difficult at first but after the method had been explained to him he was delighted to realize that it enabled Cable to achieve one of his best effects—the flavor of the speech without the burden of a difficult transcription. "Your broken French is capital," he wrote on March 31, 1875. "It is something more than dialect—it is drama." Gilder's editorial caution is understandable, for Cable was employing difficult dialects, in contrast to the conventionalized forms that had appeared in fiction before him. Furthermore, the admissibility of dialect at all was to be debated for years yet.

Gilder's letters were usually a balancing of compliment and complaint. The slight pruning and revising he wanted for the first stories became more urgent and more drastic requirements for the later ones. He thought "Madame Délicieuse" one of the best stories he had ever read, but he added in a letter of March 31, 1875, "You bother me. Your conception of character is strong—artistic—your style is bright & witty —your plots are generally good—your field is all your own—and I consider your stories a great acquisition to the monthly—but you lack in the capacity to edit yourself. This is the only thing that makes me fear for your literary future." Of the same story he wrote on June 7, "Given the same subject there is not another man in the country could have done it so well—except, possibly, Bret Harte." It may be that such mixed judgments were just what was needed to drive Cable to his best work. Apparently Gilder thought so.

Perhaps Gilder's editing of Cable can be summed up as an attempt to adapt him to a widely circulated magazine without sacrificing his distinguishing excellence. Cable believed as he said many times that stories are found rather than made and always preferred "true stories" of the kind he mined in early history. Such stories were hardly adaptable to the neatly rounded plots he was urged to build. Gilder no doubt sensed the excellence, the strength of the stories, but one wonders whether he understood just wherein the excellence lay. It is as if he weighed each new story on scales calibrated only in degrees of suspense, surprise, and climax; as if he could feel the merits but had no standard for appraising a piece of fiction making more effective use of anticlimax, as usually conceived, than climax, or proceeding with such a quiet, yet emotionally charged movement as to draw its suspense from sources not taken account of in the critical canon of the time. Gilder's handicap in reading "Jean-ah Poquelin," for example, is suggested by the fact that he had twice named Bret Harte to encourage Cable to do his best work.

The influence exerted on Cable's literary development by the *Scribner's* editors, especially Gilder, was undeniably great. They gave him a reputable medium of publication and constant encouragement. They gave him warm friendship and advice on problems ranging from what to read to where to live. They urged him to edit himself and to work slowly; they maintained a sympathetic, tolerant attitude, and Gilder's criticism touched on some of his chief faults. The value Cable himself put on the supervision is recorded in the tribute he wrote after Gilder's death, looking back to the early years, past the intervening years when he had not found Gilder's criticism acceptable. It concludes: "To me, let me testify, he was a shaping, guiding influence, noble, invaluable, and endearing. He must have been so to a multitude of others."[18]

[18] *Century*, LXXIX (Feb., 1910), 635.

CHAPTER VI

A PAUSE

CABLE returned from New York in the summer of 1875 believing his stories could be brought out in a volume and convinced that only through books could he realize anything from his writing. Harper & Brothers declined to undertake a volume of his stories, as did Scribner also, even after he had proposed to furnish a list of 500 subscribers. D. Appleton & Company held out some hope if the "miscellaneous sketches" could be strung together on some thread. On Gilder's advice again, Cable let the matter rest there.

He was still determined to write and was no less eager to improve than four years earlier when he sought criticism from an editor who had declined to publish his gathering of the newspaper pieces. After seeing a notice of "Jean-ah Poquelin" in the Boston *Literary World* that questioned the accuracy of the dialect, he wrote the editor on May 31, 1875, "I assure you that scarce a day has passed since the publication of 'Jean-ah Poquelin' that I am not told by persons who have been accustomed to hear the 'dialect' from their earliest days, and many of whom speak it, that I have rendered it capitally. Though it does not absolutely prove anything I will add that I am a creole myself, living today in sight of the house where I was born."[1] The false assertion that he was a Creole testifies, at least, to his eagerness to defend the dialect and his certainty of its accuracy. The editor was correct, he wrote, in saying that he betrayed inadequate training, and he added, "I wish to be understood as sincerely seeking information & instruction, . . . for I intend to write some more creole sketches."

He asked criticism from his friends also and advice on books to read, for he realized he had not read enough. Gilder recommended Hawthorne, Turgenev, the French fiction writers, and Bret Harte. Turgenev, then enjoying an accelerating vogue in America, was recommended by others also, and more than once Cable had seen his own

---

[1] In the Berg Collection at the New York Public Library. A few sentences from this letter appear in John D. Gordon, "First Fruits . . . ," *Bulletin of the New York Public Library*, LV (Dec., 1951), 596-97.

stories compared to Hawthorne's. His seriousness in following Gilder's advice is suggested by the fact that when a friend, N. Picard, visited him during the next month, they read Turgenev and Mériméé together, while his mother sat by, as Picard said afterward in a letter of June 22, 1874, "to lend to the scene that indefinable sense of peace and happiness & repose." Picard said also: "Your quiet energy & patient perseverance under the most trying circumstances, will serve me as a model whereby to shape my entire future career."

The trying circumstances Picard mentioned were just as real in the Cable household as the happiness and repose. From 1870 to 1877 Louise bore five children and at intervals her health failed. In a note of despair not usual with him, Cable once wrote his mother, November 1, 1873, "I am in a narrow place. My poor wife's feeble frame stands like a sunken wreck right in the channel of all my plans for our mutual comfort and happiness." Frequently, though, Louise made time to help with his literary work, reading aloud or writing for him when his eyes gave way. The reading aloud was one of the pleasantest rituals in the family and often was shared with neighbors and visitors. Picard heard such a reading, as King and Champney had done earlier when Cable read from his own manuscripts, and as many others, including Lafcadio Hearn and Mark Twain and Joel Chandler Harris, were to do afterward.

In these years Cable was never free of the kind of financial difficulties he had known since the death of his father, and he faced them with his habitual cheerfulness. To his mother, who was with Mary Louise at Hammond late in 1874, he wrote on November 27 in the same phrases he had written often from the army camps ten years before: "Keep up spirits; don't be *too* gay; and we'll all come out straight in the end and laugh at this." A year later he wrote the children: "When I hear that you are enjoying the pleasures of the sea-side, I am so delighted that I open my sleeve slyly and laugh right into it till it is as full of laugh as a bath-house. I have a hole in the elbow for this very purpose. A man named *Pauvreté* (Poverty), a Frenchman, made it for me for nothing."[2]

From their marriage to the completion of their house at 229 Eighth Street in 1878, George and Louise moved almost every year, from Standeau Street to Louisiana Avenue to Delahaise Street to Constance Street. The houses they rented must have a room for his mother but none could be spared for a study.

Saturdays and Sundays during the summers he spent at Ocean

[2] Sept. 2, 1875; printed in *The Cable Story Book*, ed. Mary E. Burt and Lucy L. Cable (New York, 1899), p. 167.

Springs. Sitting on the front porch facing the Gulf, he shared with Louise his week's experience and talked over his hopes and plans, or he wrote a book review or an editorial for the newspaper. On Sunday he took the children to the little wooden church where their grandmother Bartlett played the organ. The grownups played croquet under the pines back of the house, or the men fished, or all went bathing, the children racing out the pier and across the hot sand. Or he took the children for a walk along the beach or through the woods back of the house, stopping to gather shells or pick flowers, to notice the shape and coloring of a leaf, to identify a bird by its song.

For all his absorption in his literary work, Cable could not forget that his living came from the counting-room. His writing had been possible only because he was willing to sacrifice himself, but the kindness of his employers had contributed. They were as indulgent, he said, "as proper discipline of the counting-room could be strained to allow," permitting him to slip away when work was slack and to hire an assistant to work under his supervision. Even when a slip of his pen cost the house three hundred dollars, he later recalled, he found their forgiveness ready.[3]

The senior of his employers was William C. Black, for whom he had clerked before the war and since leaving the *Picayune*. A Virginian who had moved to Mississippi and then to New Orleans in the 1840's, Black was one of the most respected men of the city and the holder of many public trusts. At a desk within arm's reach of his, Cable was daily for almost a decade associated with the most prominent men of the city. He was proud of being a good accountant and afterward liked to allude to his efficiency. He became manager of finances and of the accounting department; and when Black became chairman of the Finance Committee of the New Orleans Cotton Exchange, he became secretary of that committee and treasurer's clerk of the Exchange.

Cable felt something of a founder's concern for the Cotton Exchange and soon was a stockholder. Founded in 1871, a year later than the New York Cotton Exchange, the exchange supplied the uniformity and stability needed for the volume of business passing over the wharves of New Orleans, and within two years it was the world's greatest spot cotton market, handling from one-fifth to one-fourth of the annual crop. Its first superintendent, who soon became secretary also, was Henry G. Hester, a close friend of Cable's. He was a man of imagination and courage, and when he retired to emeritus status after sixty-three years in office, the exchange was almost literally of his making.[4]

---

[3] See "My Politics."

[4] For the history of the Exchange, see James Ernest Boyle, *Cotton and the New Orleans Cotton Exchange* (New York, 1934).

The effect of associating with such men as Hester and Black must have been to draw Cable closer to the thinking of the respectable businessmen, almost all of whom were conservative Democrats such as his colleagues had been on the *Picayune*. It is not surprising that he was aware of the strife and the currents of thought around him, but rather that his opinions did not remain the same on all public issues as those held by his friends. His own statements make it clear that by 1875 he had veered far from the position of conservative Southerners on the question of the Negro. That vexing question had appeared in his earliest stories and in the next dozen years was to demand more and more of his thought and effort. His fullest account of the development of his social and political views is a sort of intellectual autobiography, "My Politics," written in 1889 but not published.

It was not until several years after the war, he wrote in "My Politics," that he began to think for himself or to question any of the attitudes prevailing in the South. During the war he had been unquestioningly for slavery, secession, the Confederacy, and Jeff Davis. Hearing "The Bonnie Blue Flag" sung a year after the surrender merited an exclamatory report in a letter to a war comrade. He was elated when candidates of the "old non-submission party" were elected in 1865 and when New Orleans the next year re-elected Mayor John T. Monroe, who had defied Farragut and Butler at the fall of New Orleans. A street riot on July 30, 1866, left two hundred killed or wounded and set a pattern of force and violence which was to continue through much of the decade of military rule ending in 1877. Such events were of a nature to reinforce the attitudes and feelings that had been strong in his family throughout the war.

Louisiana suffered under the most corrupt carpetbagger government in the South, except perhaps that in South Carolina. At one time two governments existed side by side; legislatures derived their authority from Federal troops drawn up in the streets; troops were used to seat and maintain judges, who in turn rendered decisions supporting carpetbagger control from the governor down to precinct constables; the President of the United States, the Congress, and the Supreme Court were aligned to protect the officials against the verdict of popular elections; twice the citizens of New Orleans fought Federal troops. On these issues Cable thought as his friends thought and was never tempted to support the Radical governments—though in such a course he could have followed the example of an ex-Confederate general in New Orleans, James Longstreet. Yet the questioning turn of his mind led him to ask whether there was not some way out of the chaos. Recognizing that every anchor of the Southern political and social structure had broken loose, he began in those caustic years, he said afterward, to think for the first time.

It became a habit of his to search for logic and consistency. Late in the war, for example, he was troubled when he learned that the Confederacy was threatened with secession of its own member states, was in danger of being destroyed by the application of a principle it was still fighting to establish. Similarly he was disturbed to hear Southern spokesmen saying after 1865 that the right of secession had been settled negatively by the sword, for how could the sword settle a matter of right? Accustomed to hearing slavery defended in the political forum and in the pulpit alike, he heard it said now either that slavery was wrong or that it was at least anachronistic in nineteenth-century America. In his search for bearings, he went to the Declaration of Independence and the Constitution, and to the Bible as well. The bulwarks in the Biblical defense of slavery, such as St. Paul's letter on Onesimus, he found shaky at best. What then of the whole pyramid of race philosophy in the South? If the Negroes had been victims of a centuries-old wrong, was not the society guilty of that wrong morally obliged to make retribution even at great cost?

At first he had questions rather than conclusions, and he was too practical to forget the realities confronting the South. Since childhood he had thought of the Negroes as menials capable of loyalty and affection but also of cruelty, bestiality, and corruption. More recently he had seen them venal in public office, either of their own intention or through the manipulation of corruptionists, as when in a half-Negro state legislature they voted the wishes of carpetbaggers and scalawags standing around the chamber. He became convinced of one thing: the return to stability and decency was being retarded by the inclination of the best Southerners to stand aloof while public affairs fell into the hands of the inept and the corrupt. He had not himself taken the oath of allegiance at first.

In reporting the unsegregated teachers convention for the *Picayune,* he had puzzled over the rightness of the Southern attitude and also the need for segregation as a practical matter. Shortly afterward he was assigned to report the annual examinations in the public schools, including the unsegregated high schools. Observing Negro teachers in some of the rooms and Negroes and whites "standing in the same classes and giving each other peaceable, friendly & effective competition" left him convinced, he wrote in "My Politics," that "the day must come when the black race must share and enjoy in common with the white the whole scale of *public* rights and advantages provided under American government," and that therein lay the only real solution to the difficulties confronting the South.

While Cable's opinions were forming on this issue, he felt an increasing concern for the affairs of his community and a conviction that he must dedicate part of his effort to philanthropic ends. In this dedication his wife joined. She was prepared by her upbringing to share alike his strict adherence to the tenets of the church and his missionary zeal for social improvement. In a debating society he had joined others who were groping for bearings in the currents and cross-currents of the time; at every turn he found institutions and attitudes solidly built on the past. The study of local and national history thus became integral to his struggle toward conclusions on current issues. Evening after evening he met with C. Harrison Parker and Henry G. Hester upstairs at the office of the *Price Current* to read and discuss George Bancroft's *History of the United States.*

From the early 1870's onward Cable saw events increasingly in the light of his humanitarian concern for the Freedman. It was in that light that he wrote "Bibi" and " 'Tite Poulette" and at about the same time he was disturbed by notes he detected in the newspapers and on the streets: there was whispered talk of a race war and of a black peasantry; there seemed to be a steadily rising antipathy for the Negroes, a willingness to lay on them total blame for the malfeasance of the Radical Party. The Democrats, on whom the future of the South must depend, held to a "masterly inactivity," in his phrase, as if to say they would participate only if the old order were restored without change except for technical emancipation.

His was the type of mind to demand that the Freedmen have actually the public rights granted by the Thirteenth and Fourteenth Amendments, and on the practical level he could see no real objection to unsegregated professional meetings or unsegregated schools or the appointment of a mulatto, a graduate of the Ecole Polytechnic of Paris, as mathematics teacher in the unsegregated Boys' High School. But in all these instances his views were antithetical to those generally declared about him. Then, in 1875, came the expulsion of the colored pupils from the Girls' High School. On that occasion, as he recorded in the story of "The Haunted House," one of the *Strange True Stories of Louisiana,* a mob went to the storied old house at the corner of Royal and Hospital Streets, questioned the pupils one after another, as the awed teachers stood by, and expelled all who had—or could not prove they did not have—a tinge of Negro blood. Afterward a mass demonstration in Lafayette Square protested against the mixed schools.

Cable's twofold resentment of both the aim and the means of the action swept him into his first public utterance on the Negro question— a letter in the *Bulletin* of September 26, 1875, signed "A Southern White Man." Starting from the assumption that good comes from open discussion of public questions, he went calmly about building the case for unsegregated schools, or rather the case against the mob interference with schools which he believed had been operating satisfactorily for the children of both whites and blacks. Briefly he refuted the usual charges against the mixed schools. The time permitting contact in the schools was almost a negligible particle in a child's full time; under slavery there had been no fear that a white child would be harmed by contact with his colored playmates—or the contact at the breast of his colored nurse. School regulations could be depended on to remove any child, white or black, whose contact would be harmful. And besides, association in school, beyond the strictly formal activities in class, would always be a matter of personal choice, as it would always be with whites only, among whom no one would argue there is ever any near approach to equality. It follows naturally in his argument that properly qualified Negro teachers should be acceptable in the mixed schools. The proponents of separate and equal schools must prove, furthermore, that the cost would not be impossibly great.

On the school tax he spoke more positively than on anything else. "This ought never to be considered an expense. It is an investment, and the most paying public investment that is made. It is every citizen's interest to have the masses educated. Inestimably more expensive will it be for us to refuse to provide for, or for us to hinder, the elevation of the many thousands among us, whose dense ignorance and incapacity is today the greatest incubus that lies on the material interests of the State." As for race antipathy he believed in it more strongly than the opponents of mixed schools, he said, for he had faith that the Caucasian race would "preserve its purity without the bolstering aid of mass meetings, or the expulsion of well-behaved children from the schools where they are now attendant without injury to any person concerned." And finally, if there is race superiority, "the lesson it teaches is magnanimity, not scorn."

The editor, Page M. Baker, accompanied the letter with a refutation equally long. After assuring his readers that the writer of this "plausible and ingenious argument," the producer of this "heretical seed," was really a Southern white man, he marshaled his arguments, though mainly in sweeping statements. "The only condition under which the two races can co-exist peacefully is that in which the superior race shall control and the inferior race shall obey. . . . African proclivities are towards savagery and cannibalism. . . . For our part we hope never to see the white boys and girls of America forgetful of the fact that negroes are their inferiors." Baker was the appropriate spokesman for the attack on mixed schools, and it was no doubt for that reason that Cable picked out the *Bulletin* for his letter. Baker had brought his paper to a frenzy on the issue, and had supported the mass meetings and the expulsion of colored children.

Eager to drive home his points, Cable wrote a reply, which Baker refused to print, as did A. M. Holbrook for the *Picayune* also, and it remained unpublished.[5] While "pleading the right and usefulness of free discussion," he introduced matters and used phrasing more likely to antagonize than to convince most readers of the newspaper. His impatience showed through, for Baker had done no more than appeal to ancient prejudices. A final thrust shows how far his resentment had dulled his sense of effectiveness in argument: "New Orleans has suffered from the 'foul contact' at least as little as from the fragrant proximity of the somnolent sons of Gascony whom she never dreamed of cramping into special, equal, separate accommodations."

Whether Cable believed the subject of segregation could be debated publicly in New Orleans in 1875, he must have realized that references to the sons of Gascony and to the "lacteal argument," as Baker called it, would infuriate many who would have listened to arguments less accusing. When he laid the rejected letter away, he noted what Baker had said in refusing it—that if he kept it ten years he would be ashamed he had written it. His own prediction was that in ten years the entire South would have come around to his views. The events of those ten years did not prove him a prophet, but in 1875 there was good evidence, at least on the surface, the developments were in the direction he was pointing. The Freedmen were voting and the unsegregated schools had raised no difficulties within themselves. There had been an indication two years earlier of how far the public attitude might swing toward granting equal civil rights.

In a move to conciliate the Negroes enough to win their support for the Democratic party in the next election, a committee of fifty white men, including General Beauregard, joined with fifty colored men in New Orleans and drew up a platform which was adopted in an open meeting of June 16, 1873. The platform was a remarkable document to be sponsored by businessmen representing most of the large concerns

[5] The manuscript is at Tulane University.

of the city and to be endorsed by the Catholic archbishop and even the *Picayune,* organ of the conservative Democrats. It acknowledged equal rights in the schools and other state, city, and parish institutions, in all resorts and travel facilities, among stockholders and employees of companies, in landowning, and in the holding of public office. In effect it recognized complete civil equality and pledged the coalition party to oppose all race prejudice and violence. Though the movement at no time gained the support elsewhere in the state it had in New Orleans, its failure was due more to poor management apparently than anything else. At a mass meeting on July 15 a statement was read from eight prominent Negro politicians saying they would help vote the carpet-baggers out of office when their rights had been attained within the Democratic party. Whether this hint of distrust was intended or was warranted is difficult to say, but once it had entered as a wedge, the two factions were quickly sundered. The movement was dead two weeks later.[6]

When Cable wrote his letters to the *Bulletin* two years afterward, he of course remembered the willingness to end segregation and guarantee civil rights to the Freedmen, and in this context his two letters can be better judged. If such concessions could be made in practical politics, the question must be debatable still, and referrable to ethical as well as practical considerations. Yet Cable did not argue the question of Negro rights in print again for another decade. He did not wish to antagonize friends such as A. M. Holbrook, Page Baker, and William C. Black. He loved and revered Black too much to wrangle with him, but often at their adjoining desks when business was slack, they skirted the fringes of the question. When the exchange had reached a certain point, Black would say, "I'll have you know that this is a Democratic counting-room, sir"; Cable would take his hat and walk out without replying. Yet he was ashamed, he wrote in "My Politics," for not speaking out against a strengthening system which he thought violated the ground principles of the American government and ethical principles as well.

For three years after 1875 Cable sent nothing to his publishers. When they requested more stories, he gave them hope but no promises. He was reading and he was planning a novel. Edward King and no doubt others had suggested that he write a novel. As he recalled in the essay "After-Thoughts of a Story-Teller," published in 1894,[7] his great-

---

[6] See T. Harry Williams, "The Louisiana Unification Movement of 1873," *Journal of Southern History,* XI (Aug., 1945), 349-69.

[7] *North American Review,* CLVIII (Jan., 1894), 17-18.

est encouragement came from J. Dickson Bruns, a distinguished associate of Timrod and Simms in Charleston earlier and himself an author
of considerable accomplishment. He recalled, without naming him, how
Bruns, his family physician, had called from the door of his office,
"Begin it! Never mind how it's to come out; you have abundant in-
vention; trust to that." Still later, in a letter to his wife of March 23,
1903, he spoke of Bruns as "my most important adviser in matters of
literary effort when I most needed friends." What Cable needed to set
him to work in earnest on the novel was the spur that came in a correspondence which Hjalmar Hjorth Boyesen, professor of literature at
Cornell University, opened on February 17, 1877.

While visiting New Orleans seven years earlier, Boyesen had been
overwhelmed, he wrote, by the materials lying ready for a novelist.
Then when he read "Belles Demoiselles Plantation," he was confident
the right author had arrived, and now Gilder told him Cable was writing
a novel. His own favorite of the stories, "Madame Délicieuse," he knew
almost by heart; when he read it to his students, they heard it with
tears in their eyes. "I only wish to hasten the day," he wrote, "when
our whole public shall recognize your exceptional merit,—your genius."
Cable answered with a summary of the novel he was writing and had in
a reply of March 17 exclamations of the magnificence of the material and
assurances that success would be his only for the taking. The two men
did not meet until four years later, but in those years they exchanged
photographs and long letters in which each intoduced himself in intimate terms. They wrote chiefly of their literary interests and activities,
Boyesen taking the lead and directing the correspondence mainly to
Cable's work.[8]

As Boyesen revealed himself in these letters, he was a man of enveloping enthusiasm, effusive in his praise, urging his new friend on with the
same devotion he gave to his own writing. In America since 1869 and
at Cornell since 1873, he had contributed verse, fiction, and criticism to
the magazines and had published three books. He told of his own ambition and his financial burden as a way of bolstering Cable's courage.
On January 20, 1878, he wrote: "At the very threshold of your career
you convinced me that you had a great future before you, if you chose
to reach out your hand & grasp it. I believe so yet. . . . Fame has already
marked you for her own. . . . I have felt a strong affection toward you

[8] Most of the letters exchanged between Cable and Boyesen are printed in an article
of mine, "A Novelist Discovers a Novelist: The Correspondence of H. H. Boyesen and
George W. Cable," *Western Humanities Review*, V (Autumn, 1951), 343-72.

hitherto, because I believed in you, because your individuality as revealed in your work attracted me irresistibly."

From New Orleans Cable reciprocated the warm feeling and grew
more confiding, as in a letter of January 3, 1878:

My dear Mr. Boyesen, I have just that discontent—I keep up just that
champing of my bit that you, I know, would want me to indulge in. I
ought to be writing. A man ought to keep invested the talents of gold
that God has given him as well as the talents of silver. I can write better
than I can do anything else. Business is distasteful to me. I love literature;
I'm no Samson in it, it's true; but so much the more it doesn't follow that
I should have my eyes punched out & go to grinding corn in this Philistia
of a country. . . . If it wasn't for one single thing I should be altogether comfortable—the black sheep in my flock is my ambition. I drug it with every
possible opiate; I get it to sleep, I jog along with it muffled up in my bosom,
I think I have peace, when—here comes a letter from Gilder or yourself,
and—it takes me weeks to get the brat quiet again.

Boyesen's first work, which William Dean Howells printed in the
Atlantic Monthly in the early 1870's, was romantic fiction reflecting the
nostalgia he felt for his native Norway. After coming under the influence of Turgenev and the French novelists, he grew unhappy with the
contrived fiction which, as he and Howells and Mark Twain came to see,
often had no more commendable goal than to amuse young women.
Now his respect was for novels probing human problems in real life.
When he recommended Turgenev as a model for the handling of social
problems, Cable's reply was that he had already learned much from
Smoke and must read others of Turgenev's books.

Cable agreed with Boyesen in condemning artificially contrived plots,
in demanding the plot be only the vehicle for bringing the problem of
the story into strong relief, for giving logic to the portrayal of typical
characters in real situations. On March 6, 1878, he wrote:

The great problem of a novel should be something beyond and above the
mere puzzle of the plot, something great and thought-compelling, that teaches
without telling, that brings to view without pointing, that guides without
leading and allures without fatiguing, through the dimness and shadow and
uncertainty of a new path out at last upon the illimitable savannahs of God's
sweet, green nourishing truth. Excuse me; I don't want to say anything
great, and I couldn't if I wanted to, but when you talk about the story-teller's
mission in such trumpet tones I can't help prancing a little.

What do you think of one of these novels that smell of the moral like
very small houses do of the dinner that is cooking in the kitchen? Don't
they make you restless? Everybody eats dinner, and dinners ought to be

cooked in every house; everybody ought to be moral, and novels ought to have a moral effect; they ought to nourish the soul as viands do the body; maybe you don't believe it but I believe it. However, I don't propose to permit any novelist through the medium of his novel, to hold me on his lap and spoon his morals down me to the limits of distention!

As they thus exchanged views, Cable and Boyesen moved toward greater certainty on the aims, materials, and means most worthy of the novelist —at the time when Howells, Mark Twain, and Henry James were likewise maturing as novelists and were acknowledging similar obligations to truth and reality and subtlety of method.

One of the things Boyesen did with a will was praise Cable in the Scribner offices. In the summer of 1877 he talked of Cable's novel to Dr. Holland, and by January 8 of the next year he had convinced Blair Scribner that Cable was "a great man" and had induced him to publish Cable's stories in a volume. Cable learned from Gilder that his friend had "actually bribed" Scribner by guaranteeing the publishing costs. Boyesen had not wanted Cable to know what he had done, and he never had any doubt that the book would pay out.[9] In accepting such generosity, Cable had moments of uneasiness, as when Boyesen wrote that his students at Cornell would buy a hundred copies of the volume. "I shudder—," he replied on January 14; "if you love me don't offer *anything* that *ever* I do to *anybody* except on its intrinsic merits. You will excuse me for appearing to suspect such a thing; it's such a common occurrence down here, and *therefore*—besides all better reasons—because I am a Southerner—I would like the handful of people that make up my little world to be assured I am nobody's widow."

"If I could get just twice what I have been getting for my writings," Cable wrote Boyesen a few days before learning his stories would be published, "I could arrange to write, easily & quickly enough." Now, with the hope of realizing something from the stories while writing the novel, he could think again of literature as a career. His salary came from three sources: Black's cotton house, the New Orleans Cotton Exchange, and the National Cotton Exchange. At different times he had proposed to drop a portion of his work and give the time to writing, but each time his salary had been raised. In 1876 he had bought two lots on Eighth Street, and lacked only two years, he wrote Boyesen in 1878, of paying for the house he had built on them. "I dare not coquette with my commercial arrangements," he said, "be it ever so daintily."

Uncertainties of health, moreover, had reduced his literary output to

[9] See Boyesen's letters in the Scribner archives.

nothing. In spite of a month's vacation in the spring of 1877 and a round of "cod-liver oil, whiskey, iron, arsenic, and—awfullest of all—friends' multitudinous medical advice," he wrote Boyesen on April 27, he had no health through the summer. Another vacation later and the coming of fall weather were more effective; and he continued to recover, even with the longer hours, often extending to midnight, brought on by the new cotton crop. But he did not do an hour's literary work from March to December, and before the end of the next year disaster in the form of yellow fever had struck in such a way as to upset whatever hopes he had.

New Orleans had known yellow fever since 1796, and perhaps earlier, though the epidemics before that year were not identified as the dreaded fever. From then on it returned with varying fierceness almost yearly. In 1832 it teamed with the cholera to take off over 8,000 from the population of 55,000. The greatest of all the epidemics, which Cable's father witnessed in 1853, accounted for 11,000 deaths between the first of June and the first of October. Though the death rate in 1878 was only slightly more than half that of 1853, that year still holds its place as the second most disastrous in the history of the city.[10]

At the opening of 1878 there reigned in New Orleans an optimism not known for two decades. On June 6 the Board of Health said the health had never been better. Already, though, two crew members from the *Emily B. Souder* had died of yellow fever within a week after it had tied up at the wharf. By July the *Picayune* was demanding that the Board of Health report the extent of the epidemic, for the attempted secrecy had strengthened the rumors. When the Board made the figures known, the exodus began, thousands taking the contagion with them into the interior.

Business stopped. Terror gripped the city. Music was forbidden; the church bells were silenced; sawdust was spread in the streets to deaden sounds. Ice was scarce and trebled in price. The Young Men's Howard Association raised over a million dollars for the stricken; money and supplies came from Northern cities and from Europe. October 9 was declared a day of fasting and prayer. The newspapers urged the refugees not to return. Everybody was impressed by the blindness of the treatments employed—quinine and castor oil for the victims,

---

[10] Cable dealt historically with yellow fever in New Orleans in an article entitled "Flood and Plague in New Orleans," *Century*, XXVI (July, 1883), 419-31, which in revised form appeared in *The Creoles of Louisiana*, 1884. For an intimate view of the disease in the city see Theodore Clapp, *Autobiographical Sketches and Recollections, during a Thirty-Five Years' Residence in New Orleans* (Boston, 1857).

lime spread in the streets and gutters, sheets saturated with carbolic acid hung in the rooms or in the yards, barrels of tar burned and cannon fired in the streets. The official total was nearly four thousand deaths, but everyone knew there were more, for many families were not attended by doctors and did not record their dead. The Board of Health did not declare the epidemic over until November 20.

On October 17 Cable wrote Charles Scribner: "Death has been thinning the ranks of my kindred and of my own family and household." On the same day he sent Gilder a fuller account, and on November 5 he wrote Boyesen, then traveling in Europe following his marriage on June 27, a calm but moving narrative which concluded: "It looks as if we had had trouble; but I assure you, such is the terrible behavior of this fever in some houses that we are, by comparison, subjects of congratulation, and can, ourselves, sincerely say, 'God has been good to us.'" For six weeks death had hung over his household as the yellow fever attacked his wife, his four children, the family of his sister Nettie, and the families of his wife's two sisters. Nettie's husband, James Cox, to whom Cable went as a nurse, died first. Cable's son George died and was buried in stealth lest the other sick children learn of it.[11] There were other deaths among the relatives, but the rest of Cable's own family survived.

His gratitude to his neighbors and the Howards and his pride in the heroism he saw daily were balanced by resentment at the failure to take the steps common sense dictated. Quarantine of incoming ships was not enforced for business reasons; the newspapers and even the health authorities and the doctors owed such allegiance to commerce that they refused to acknowledge the presence of yellow fever or cholera until it had become epidemic; medieval drainage and sewage disposal made the city barely sufferable on account of the odors in the rainy summer months. The whole experience stayed fresh in his mind and was reflected in half a dozen of the books he wrote afterward.

The death of James Cox in September left Nettie penniless with three children. She had studied art but was by no means prepared to make a living. Cable moved her at once to a house across from his on Eighth Street and Rebecca moved in with her. With "Ma's room" in his own house converted into a study, he had for the first time a place to work away from the quarters of his family. He must have the room, he said, for he had lost two months of golden moments from his novel.

Publication of the volume of stories had been set first for April, 1878,

[11] Burial was at the Lafayette Cemetery Number 1, probably for the reason that it was closer than the Cypress Grove Cemetery.

but was postponed to the fall, and then to the next spring. The delays reflected the publisher's lack of faith in the book, though the second was explained as due to the purchase late in 1878 of Armstrong's interest by Blair and Charles Scribner, sons of the first Charles Scribner, who had died in 1871. Cable was himself not sanguine about the book, he wrote Boyesen January 14, 1878, "but whisper it not to Miché Scribner!" His stories had created something of a local sensation, at least, when they first appeared, but the latest of them had been in print over two years. The editors accepted his proposal to bring "Posson Jone'" from *Appletons' Journal* to join the other six stories but did not follow his suggestion of arranging the stories chronologically and giving a date to each appropriate to its historical orientation. To his mind the exact historical context he had given them was important. Nor was his idea accepted of heading each story with one of his old Creole songs "gathered with great difficulty & strangers to printer's ink." The songs waited another seven years to know print.

Cable made only the barest revisions in the magazine pages, except for a few additions in "'Tite Poulette" and "'Sieur George" for greater clarity. Boyesen had warned him on January 30, 1878, that "So delicate a production as for instance Madame Delicieuse, which still haunts my memory with its odor of orange flowers, will bear very little handling." The search for a title, with Boyesen and everyone at the Scribner office taking part, lasted more than a year and ended only a month before publication. Cable's first suggestion, *"Jadis,"* would have had both a literal and a suggestive appropriateness—but only in New Orleans. For with it and others of the titles he proposed, "Créoles du Vieux-temps," "Hammock and Fan," "Under the Cypress and Orange," and "Spanish Moss" among them, the overtones would be lost on anyone not knowing the peculiar local connotations of the words or the special associations of a hammock and a fan on a New Orleans summer afternoon, or the meaning of the ageless cypress tree and the odor of orange blossoms on the Southern breeze, or the effect of gray moss draping the low, horizontal branches of the live oaks. Finally the publisher proposed "Old Creole Days," a happy choice because it hints at the time, the place, and the people of the book without giving it away as a collection of stories.

Old Creole Days was issued on May 17, 1879. The author was to receive 10 per cent royalty on all copies beyond the first edition of a thousand, which Scribner said was "unusually large for a collection of stories." He set to work himself promoting the sales in New Orleans, distributing circulars and forwarding orders from the book stores. "It has been a matter of pride with me," he wrote on June 5, "to secure them a hearty welcome home & that is fairly well done already. There is scarcely a copy in town for sale today." A month later 250 copies had been sold in New Orleans—"very remarkable and altogether unprecedented," Scribner said. On August 15, three months after publication, the first thousand had been exhausted and a second edition was going to press.

Cable had received abundant criticism of the individual stories from friends such as King, Champney, Boyesen, Bruns, and Picard as well as his editors. One of his most valued literary advisers was Marion A. Baker, brother of Page Baker, who was his lifelong friend and perhaps his closest friend in New Orleans. On a trip east in 1872 Marion Baker took one of Cable's poems, "The Morning Glory," and tried to place it in *Appletons' Journal.* From then onward he read Cable's manuscripts as they were written, gave him detailed criticism, and was a constant source of encouragement. As literary editor of the *Times-Democrat* after 1881 he never missed an opportunity to show his high regard for Cable's work.

Except for *L'Abeille,* the French-language newspaper, which continued disdainful of the stories, the New Orleans papers spoke proudly of the native son who had distinguished himself in a larger area. They treated *Old Creole Days* as the most important book yet written locally and one of the greatest books in American literature. The reviewer in the New Orleans *Times* wrote on June 1:

The writings of Mr. Cable may be ranked with those of any American prose writer, not excepting those of Nathaniel Hawthorne, which they in many respects resemble, and in some respects excel. . . . In the delineation of female loveliness there is hardly an American author who can be compared favorably with Mr. Cable. He is more of an Alphonse Daudet than a Charles Dickens, although in his conceptions and style he resembles both.

The local reviewers touched particularly on what the Creoles were known to resent: the portrayal of their group character and the representation of their speech. The *Picayune* said, in a tone maintained throughout its review: "These charming stories attract attention and commendation by their quaint delicacy of style, their faithful delineation of Creole character, and a marked originality. The careful rendering of the dialect reveals patient study of living models; and to any reader whose ear is accustomed to the broken English, as heard in parts of our city every day, its truth to nature is striking." In its review the *Times* faced the matter more directly and more fully:

He chooses his materials for his character sketches, like the real artist, and gives us the Creole, not perhaps as the upper crust think Creoles to be, nor as that upper crust would like them to be, but just as they are, just as you, I and a hundred others have met them on rue Royale, in the Cathedral, at the French Market and elsewhere in the old town. So true is the author to this idea that some of the pictures sting, and, with the sting, draw forth the critic's remonstrance, which remonstrance is the true criticism of the merits of the picture. . . . [Yet he] treads upon the Creole toe only accidentally, as it were, while on the road toward his subject, . . . and he loses no opportunity to make due allowance for those same foibles of which he is speaking, and to bring out into as strong a light as possible all the noble and chivalrous traits for which the Creoles are distinguished.

Newspaper reviewers outside New Orleans were no more restrained; any reservations they had were buried, as a rule, among such statements as this from the Boston *Courier*: "We not only have no hesitation in pronouncing their author a genius with special captivating endowments, but we feel it an imperative critical duty to so declare him." Reviewers in the magazines gave *Old Creole Days* more detailed criticism. Writing in *Scribner's* Charles DeKay, brother of Gilder's wife, used the word "charming" like a refrain and of "Jean-ah Poquelin" said, "The man who can write such a story is no mere talented writer; he is a genius in his way." Edward Eggleston, in the *North American Review* of November, found mistiness that at times leaves the reader to guess out "a half-told riddle," but he pronounced Cable faultless in handling scene and character and motivation and in his use of dialects. A reviewer in *Appletons' Journal* for September was delighted with the realism of detail. Edmund Gosse, writing in the *Saturday Review* of London two years later, August 20, 1881, when three of these stories had been published in England with *Madame Delphine,* declared that "Posson Jone'" alone established Cable as "a novelist with new powers and a brilliant promise." The mass of people in that story, he said, are drawn with a skill "such as no writer of modern times, except Flaubert, has displayed."

Perhaps the most understanding criticism appeared in the *Atlantic Monthly,* January, 1880. The author found the stories as fresh and vivacious as Bret Harte's had been at first but more human and delicate. He realized that the race prejudice and the race clashes lying at the center of these stories produce a natural interplay of laughter and tears.

Cable's "mastery over mongrel dialects," the reviewer continued, "is something marvelous." The stories are first of all dramatic, at times overdramatic, he said, and in summary, "One and all have an ardor, a spontaneity, a grace of movement, a touch of fire, which are severally present as elements, and summed up in that rarest of endowments, an original and delightful *style*." We wait, the review concluded, to see whether Cable can sustain a full novel with the exhilarating interest he achieves in the stories.

The reviewers of *Old Creole Days* did not agree on the merits or the faults singled out, but they all sensed that it was a significant addition to American fiction. Some saw in it mainly new materials which would be worked as the mining camps of the West had been exploited by Bret Harte and his disciples. Some realized that the confusion of peoples and languages in New Orleans invited an intricacy of character delineation and a probing of social forces not suggested in Harte's West, that in writing of mixed blood Cable had opened up highly challenging areas for the novelist. They were delighted with his Creoles, leading their Gallic existence in a semi-tropical city bathed in an Old-World atmosphere. Some of them recognized that he had brought realism to the South, that he had an observant eye and an ear attuned to the infinitely varied speech he heard on the streets, that for all the indefiniteness and strangeness he cast over his world, it was nonetheless a real world accurately recorded alike in details and general tone. He was the first—they were aware though not all were ready to call this a virtue—to give his characters real speech, finely reported in its details of intonation and syntax as well as in pronunciation and grammar. Few if any realized the extent to which his had been the pioneer's task in determining an acceptable use of dialects in fiction and in working out a satisfactory orthography.

Cable's readers found that some of his incidents clung in their memory; they liked to talk in his Creole patois; they spoke of the charming characters he had added to American fiction—the word "charming" seemed essential to any comment on his stories. Many of them recognized the effects of his delicate Gallicized style, which maintains a balance between the light and the serious and turns to whimsicality just short of excessive sentiment.

The seven stories of *Old Creole Days* were the products of experiment conditioned by editorial criticism, the author's reading, and his own evolving theories of fiction. What were their direct literary antecedents is not easy to say. The author wrote Boyesen on March 6, 1878: "You would laugh to know how little fiction I read. . . . And now I feel that to have studied certain men's methods would be of unknown value to me." The studying he had done since leaving high school had been mainly in mathematics, surveying, the Bible, and American history. In his home Shakespeare, Milton, Tennyson, and the poetry of Scott and Poe had been read, but little fiction because it was not acceptable in strict Presbyterian homes. While writing the "Drop Shot" column, for the first time he made a place in his schedule for reading as distinct from studying, and the literary references and discussions in the column reflected some acquaintance with Scott, Dickens, Kingsley, Hawthorne, Victor Hugo, and Bret Harte. His statement to Boyesen was no doubt overmodest, partly because it was made to a professor of literature. Another statement made forty years later in a letter of July 21, 1914, to F. L. Pattee,[12] who was writing his *History of American Literature since 1870,* must be closer to the truth. He recalled that before he began to write he had read some French authors, Hugo, Mérimée, and About, but had read Dickens, Thackeray, Poe, and Irving more. The most fruitful of his reading, however, had been in "the old *Relations* of the priest explorers and much other French matter of early historical value." From these and early newspapers and documents came the provocation to write his first stories because, he said, "it seemed a pity for the stuff to go so to waste." There was no end to the materials, he thought. He could write more and could learn to write better—if he had the time.

[12] In Biklé, p. 47.

CHAPTER VII

"THE GRANDISSIMES"

CABLE had been at work on a novel more than two years before *Old Creole Days* was published. It was wanted for *Scribner's Monthly* and as a book later it would draw royalty from the first copy. On January 9, 1878, Gilder proposed scheduling it to follow serials by Boyesen and Frances Hodgson Burnett. But poor health had kept Cable from the manuscript almost a year and he could not commit himself. Six days earlier he had written to Boyesen: "But wait! First, I shall—I *will,* God willing, finish the work I have commenced. Second, only give me time to finish pay'g for my pretty little house—a couple of years or so—and I am determined then to make room among my occupations for the delightful one of authorship." After Gilder's proposal had reopened the question of his future, he wrote Boyesen again on January 14:

If I decide to respond yea, I must make engagements looking to the pursuit of Authorship as a profession, if nay, it is to turn to mercantile pursuits *for life.* There is no trifling with the issue; it is on me & must be bravely met. On either side I see an urgent group of as noble friends as ever a man could proudly call his own.

Again he compromised, agreeing only to make what speed he could. He hired an assistant in the counting-room as he had done in writing the stories. By mid-August he had submitted manuscript enough for three installments. The October *Scribner's* announced the novel for later serialization, and Gilder suggested that the payment be $1000, the same Boyesen was being paid for *Falconberg,* but he invited Cable to say so if he thought he should have more. The chapters already in New York were returned, and Cable began the months of revising which continued down to galley proof of the last installment. Early in February, 1879, he had reworked the first installments. On March 4 Gilder approved the work and advanced $500; four days later he sailed for a year in Europe, leaving Robert Underwood Johnson to see the novel through the magazine. The serialization began in November, 1879; the novel appeared in book form twelve months later, simultaneously with the last installment.

After reading Cable's outline for the novel, Boyesen wrote him on March 17, 1877, that it was "going to be the kind of novel which the Germans call 'Kulturroman,' a novel in which the struggling forces of opposing civilizations crystalize [*sic*] & in which they find their enduring monument." *The Grandissimes* bore out Boyesen's prediction. In it two civilizations clash and also two races, or rather two attitudes toward the Negro race in America. The novel is set in the first year after the Louisiana Purchase, when the Creoles were slowly acknowledging that they belonged to the United States and must live with the *Américains* who were moving in among them. When Cable was writing, three-quarters of a century later, that clash had disappeared from the political and commercial realms but persisted in social and cultural intercourse. The clash over the Negro had not subsided but had become more acute since emanicipation, for with that stroke, as Cable thought, all possessing Negro blood had received the same freedom without rights which had belonged to the pariahs of 1803, the free men and women of color. Thus he was writing of the two problems which to his mind had dominated Louisiana history from the purchase to his own time.

He planned his story on a scale to include richly assorted materials from that history. The entire social scale, from the slave newly arrived to Creoles tracing their ancestry to the proudest French and Spanish explorers, is presented in a sequence of episodes, often tense dramatic scenes, which expose widely different facets of life in the old French and Spanish city becoming American. The cession brought to a climax the clash between the European and the American, the old and the new, enacted in the romantic old city of quadroon balls, duels, *voudou* worship, African dances in Congo Square; of multitudinous family reunions on *grandpère's* birthday, generations-old family rivalries; of yellow fever and floods. For all the remoteness and glamour, the book succeeds in giving the whole a convincing actuality. The houses and the streets are suggested rather than described, public events of the time are but hazily reported, but nothing of reality is lost. The effects of the cession on the courts, on office holders, and on land titles, the growing stream of immigrants, the failure of the indigo planters and their switch to sugar cane after Etienne de Boré had shown the juice of the cane could be crystallized—such is the historical backdrop before which the characters work out their destinies.

The method is dramatic from the first paragraph. The characters are sparingly introduced and are left to reveal themselves, often in scenes well enough defined for stage production. From this method, which Cable like Howells and James had learned from Hawthorne and Turgenev, derive both virtues and faults in *The Grandissimes*. It taught him to avoid Thackerayan self-obtrusion and to make the characters sustain themselves through the action. Thus he could let the characters draw their own fine line between the intensely dramatic and the sensational, as was natural to them but would not be easily done by another method. More than one scene, in fact, is saved from melodrama only by the firm hold the characters themselves maintain on the action. He knew them—in their prototypes of his acquaintance—as extravagant in action, gesture, and speech and accustomed to wear their emotions at the surface. For years he had stored up on scraps of paper and in his memory their gestures, their turns of phrase, their songs, their ways of thought.

Yet the dramatic method in fiction may become artificial, as Howells came to realize. The threads of Cable's plot are as intricately interwoven as are the relations within the multitudinous Grandissime family, and he was tempted into the hinting and half-revealing that had marred some of his early stories. He had learned to hold suspense more through the natural evolution of character and action, and less by the artificial narrative devices he had used in " 'Sieur George," for example, but the reader still finds himself occasionally having to recall hints and splice together evidence at an effort out of all proportion to what is accomplished. Still, such elements add the whimsicality that is so appropriate to the characters and so essential to the balance maintained between the real and the fanciful.

Though Cable thought of *The Grandissimes,* in agreement with Boyesen, as a study of moral problems existing in a particular social order, it is first of all a novel of character, and in the characters lies his greatest achievement. Almost every one of his characters was new to fiction, except as he had already drawn similar ones. Their novelty and originality was easy to achieve; the difficulty lay rather in giving them adequate roots in actuality. Of these characters Cable insisted, as he did of others in his books, that they were copied from models. When asked a year after the book was published whether he had a model for Aurore Nancanou, the bewitching, mercurial young Creole widow whom William Dean Howells thought one of the great heroines of fiction, Cable replied, "Oh, she is the closest I have made—my very best portrait."

As to the original of Honoré Grandissime, the Creole of *sang pur* who undertook with cautious heroism to win his people to a course which would right the wrongs of the past, especially wrongs to the slaves and free quadroons, he told the same inquirer: "I have known him for years. I met him only last week in Canal Street."[1] This remark for print did not name the original, but in a letter to his wife of June 8, 1887, Cable identified Honoré as Adolph Schreiber, a Creole, his name notwithstanding, a member of a prominent New Orleans family, and a former employer of his. Still later, in "After-Thoughts of a Story-Teller," 1894, he said all the prominent characters in the book except Clotilde, Aurore's daughter, were drawn from models. Aurore's model had once been his next-door neighbor.

Though specific testimony is wanting about others of the characters, Agricole Fusilier, for example, the unflinching champion of the old Creole order, or the tragic Honoré Grandissime, f.m.c. (free man of color), half-brother of the pure-blooded one of the same name, Cable probably drew them from originals he knew well. Palmyre, the mysterious, beautiful mulatto sorceress, seems to have come straight from life, but Raoul Innerarity was likely fabricated from traits Cable had seen in various young Creoles. The care with which he filled in details of even their speech is suggested by his response when a reader of the novel in manuscript questioned whether Clemence, the Negro *marchande des calas,* born in Virginia and brought to Louisiana, would plausibly speak both French and English; Cable replied that her speech was factual and also plausible. Her dialect, her gossip, and her songs he had heard on the streets or at the French Market since childhood.

The action of the story revolves about Joseph Frowenfeld, a newcomer to New Orleans whom circumstances invited to observe and take part in events which make up the story. The author employed the words and actions of this character, supplemented by their reflection in Honoré Grandissime, to express his own views on the problems raised in the book. But the final portrait did not satisfy him. A year after finishing the novel, he wrote William Dean Howells that he had failed to portray Frowenfeld's goodness artistically.[2] Actually Frowenfeld is less a failure and less an incomplete man than Robert Underwood Johnson implied when he argued that more human frailties must be added. It is true, he lacks the warm humanity of Aurore Nancanou, for example, and the ingratiating foibles of Raoul Innerarity, and the heat and stubbornness

---

[1] Charles M. Clay, "George W. Cable," *Critic,* I (Oct. 8, 1881), 270-71.
[2] Oct. 8, 1881; in Biklé, pp. 72-73.

of Agricole Fusilier, but any deviation from his course would have altered the character Cable meant to portray. As Honoré Grandissime approaches the same goals, he loses also the humanity which others of the characters, even those most sketchily drawn, have in such abundance.

Cable said in "My Politics" ten years after writing *The Grandissimes* that he had intended all the political implications anyone had read into it, that he could not have failed to reflect the problems which then commanded so much of his thought. In the first years after the purchase he saw parallels to many of those problems. Loyal Confederates after 1865, no less than the Creoles in 1803, were obliged to switch their loyalties to a hated government which was to them a usurping force from outside. Both saw threats to their rights and their traditions. To Cable, at least by 1879, no less than to Frowenfeld and Honoré Grandissime, the old and cherished way of life, admirable as it was in some respects, held inequities which the new government would remove.

Cable had written Boyesen that a novel must teach but must "teach without telling," but he had difficulty following the principle. Believing that slavery had been a wrong and had been bolstered by defenses stemming ultimately from greed, he saw in his novel a means of exposing the wrong and the hypocrisy of thinking which had supported it. In the early drafts he employed auctorial asides and long dialogues of his characters to discuss slavery and the position of the free quadroons. In the successive revisions he dropped almost all the asides and shortened the dialogue, but the novel is still a powerful attack on the traditional Southern attitude toward the Negroes. The conventional assertion that the slaves were "the happiest beings on earth" is mentioned, in all its irony, by several of the characters. The life of decrepit old Clemence, hobbling along the street and singing of the pies she sells, is one refutation. Her death dramatizes all the hopelessness of her existence in one scene—after her frantic plea not to be hanged at the edge of the swamp, she is told to run and is shot in the back. The f.m.c. half-brother of Honoré Grandissime is a quiet but impressive epitome of the near-white mulattoes' lot. Educated in Paris, he has wealth left him by his Grandissime father, becomes a business partner of the white Honoré at a time when his financial strength saves the property of the other Grandissimes. He drifts quietly in and out of the story, never sitting in the presence of the whites, being attacked when he fails to remove his hat, and drowns himself finally when he despairs of winning the beautiful quadroon Palmyre, who nurses a hopeless love for the white Honoré.

But it is in the story of Bras Coupé that the cause of the Negro is most impressively presented. It was the story originally called "Bibi," Cable's earliest attempt at fiction, written as he said out of sheer indignation when he first came across the old Black Code for the governing of slaves.[3] In it the regal bearing and spirit of a prince are joined with savage hatred, superstition, and fear. It marshals a sequence of events which include the betrayal of Bras Coupé's love, his months as a fugitive in the swamps, his capture in the midst of voodooistic orgies, his punishment in accordance with the Black Code, including hamstringing, his pronouncement of gargantuan curses which appear to take form in actuality, and his stern death after he has lifted the curses on the plea of the widow of his owner, who has, symbolically, laid her baby in his arms. The story is stark realism in spite of the romantic elements inherent in the materials and the characters. The author remains outside the narrative, allowing the weight of the story itself to accent the moral judgment. The blame is not laid to any individual. Full penalty is not exacted and Bras Coupé is treated kindly whenever circumstances and the code permit. Chance is partly responsible, but slavery and its supporting code stand convicted—so indirectly that the Grandissimes do not hesitate to tell the story among themselves but also so hauntingly that their minds return to it even after a dozen years. Though it occupies two chapters at the center of the book, it is not felt to be a digression, for to the Grandissimes it is no less important in the present than in the past. It demands to be told, and on one day, fittingly on the day of the *fête de grandpère,* it has three tellings. And so to the end of the book it appears in the thought and speech of the characters like a chorus pronouncing a judgment none of them can escape.

The Bras Coupé story was compounded of materials and in a manner typical of Cable's fiction. It was his habit in the early 1870's "to talk with old French-speaking negroes, not trusting to the historical correctness of what they told me, but receiving what they said for its value as tradition, superstition or folk-lore." One of them, a porter in William C. Black's office, told him the story of Bras Coupé.[4] Cable had been studying the distinguishing traits of the African tribes represented among the American slaves. His chief source was two thick volumes by M. L. E. Moreau de Saint-Méry, *Description topographique, physique, civile, politique, et historique de la partie française de l'ille Saint-Dominique,*[5] in which Lafcadio Hearn found the Creole proverbs and other

[3] "My Politics."

[4] See Cable's account of how he came to write the story written out for his daughter Lucy, Feb. 12, 1899; printed in part in Biklé, pp. 179-80.

[5] Philadelphia, 1797-98.

lore that so fascinated him. Moreau's characterization of the Jaloff tribe lent credence and details to the story he had heard.

After the story had been published, Creoles of Cable's acquaintance vouched for its authenticity. In all likelihood he knew other versions differing enough among themselves to warrant any liberties a narrator might take. In the New Orleans *Item* of October 27, 1880, Lafcadio Hearn wrote the history of "The Original Bras-Coupé"[6] as he had it from Alexander Dimitry, the Creole scholar who had given Cable a "Dirge of Saint Malo" and may have told him also of Bras Coupé. Louis Gottschalk, the world-renowned Creole musician, had heard one version of the story from his grandmother and in 1881 narrated it in his autobiography.[7]

Continuing the practice of instructing their betters, as they phrased it, the *Scribner's* editors supervised *The Grandissimes* more closely than any of the stories and proposed changes with such urgency that the novel as finally published contained touches from the editors' hands which the author accepted only reluctantly. The debate over the manuscript reflects the editors' policies and views and also the prerogatives they assumed in dealing with an author. It shows what the novel was as Cable first planned and wrote it, and in the editorial suggestions he took and those he rejected it suggests the influence his editors exerted in shaping his literary production.

After reading part of the manuscript, Gilder wrote on August 5, 1878, that he and Dr. Holland found it "a fresh strange & entertaining as well as a pure & healthful romance," with "some capital touches—palpable hits." He was apparently satisfied with the didactic import, for he said it would no doubt help "to bring about the days of a better understanding and a more cordial feeling." There is no reason to believe that if he had not left for Europe he would have been any less strict with his editorial pencil than formerly, but Robert Underwood Johnson, with less experience and less assurance, was more cautious, surely, and as a consequence challenged the manuscript on matters that greater experience would have taught him to accept as originality of matter and method. "You must remember," Johnson wrote on February 11, 1880, "that my reputation as an editor is involved as well as yours as a writer." With the support of two assistant readers he urged greater clarity, fewer digressions, less preaching, and fuller characterization. For almost two years batches of manuscript went back and forth between New Orleans and New York. Almost every sheet of the manuscript

[6] Included in Hearn's *Essays on American Literature,* pp. 58-61.
[7] *Notes of a Pianist* (Philadelphia, 1881), p. 105.

finally used by the magazine typesetters has the readers' comments on the back, often with initials to identify the reader making each note; and some of the sheets, held over from an earlier draft, show a running correspondence between the author and his readers, for it was Cable's habit to comment on the suggestions whether he accepted them or not. Another batch of sheets, rejected entire or heavily revised and copied anew for the printer, have also been preserved.[8] These sheets supplemented by the author-editor correspondence chart the struggle to get the novel into final form.

One of Johnson's assistant readers was Irwin Russell, a native of Port Gibson, Mississippi, the author of "Christmas Night in the Quarters" and other poems in which he pioneered in the use of plantation darkies speaking their own dialect. He had appeared in *Scribner's* first in 1876 and when he arrived in New York in December, 1878, had become a protégé of the editors. He thought well of the novel as a whole and in one or two instances supported Cable against the other readers. But he objected to many details of action or speech as incorrect or "monstrous" or "very improbable." He offered corrections to Cable's description of an attack of yellow fever, relying on his own observations when he stayed beside his father, a doctor, during the epidemic of 1878. But Cable's observations had been equally intimate and their differences were perhaps only such as could be expected at a time when the disease was regarded with a mixture of awe and superstition. Cable found few of Russell's corrections acceptable. One detail which Russell found "preposterous to imagine" Cable defended as both "from life and plausible." A phrase that had been substituted, Cable remarked, might be better rhetoric but was not the phrase the Creoles used.

Russell knew the plantation Negroes of Mississippi and apparently did not realize the vastly different speech and customs that prevailed in New Orleans. He did not know as Cable did the distinctive quadroon system of New Orleans and so often made marks pointing toward a more conventional view of relations between the two races than he found in the manuscript. "Alteration is imperatively required," he said of the scene in which the quadroon Palmyre embraced the white Honoré Grandissime at his return from ten years of schooling in Paris. Cable replied with an extended refutation and concluded, "I must beg you not to omit it."

The other reader was Mrs. Sophia Bledsoe Herrick. The daughter

[8] The printer's copy is in the Harvard University Library. The rejected pages are in the Yale University Library. Additional readers' notes on separate sheets are at the Tulane University Library.

of Albert Taylor Bledsoe, champion of the Southern cause in the twenty years following Appomattox and editor of the *Southern Review,* she had lived in Mississippi and Virginia and had edited the *Review* a year after her father's death. She joined the *Scribner's* staff early in 1879. Her notes on Cable's manuscript had none of the positiveness and impatience of Russell's. She seems to have been well enough satisfied for the book to keep the author's views on slavery and the race question, whether she agreed with them or not.

On the back of several sheets of the manuscript all three readers and the author enter the debate, as at the opening of Chapter XXI. The passage in question states that Frowenfeld had observed that the civilization around him "kept the flimsy false bottoms in its social errors only by incessant reiteration." Then Raoul is made to remark, as if in illustration:

"I t'ink, me, dat hanny w'ite man is a gen'leman; but I don't care if a man are good like a h-angel, if 'e har not pu'e w'ite, *'ow can* 'e be a gen'leman?"

Russell came first, on the reverse of the sheet:

This will scarcely do. No man in that part of the county ever for one moment entertained the idea: that a man with the least tinge of Negro blood could be a gentleman—or recognized as an equal by the commonest white man. Mr. Raoul would never have thought of uttering such a truism (from his standpoint).

Next came Mrs. Herrick: "This seems to me in the main a fair criticism." Then Johnson: "Better omit as marked." Cable had the final word: "The above is a mistake. The old false beliefs of pro-slavery were only sustained by these incessant reiterations. I heard them myself from my earliest childhood, up." He kept the passage with only slight revision. At another point, early in Chapter XXVI, is the statement that here and there in a section of New Orleans a half-ruined colonial villa stood in the author's time among hovels and junk-yards and foundries—stood "like one unconquered elephant in a wreck of artillery." Russell called this "too bad a simile to pass." Johnson noted, "I am not sure about that." Cable closed the matter, "I would rather this elephant were left unconquered."

By the time the first installment appeared in November, 1879, Russell was in New Orleans, where he and Cable became slight acquaintances and where he died on December 23.[9] Johnson and Mrs. Herrick

[9] In a letter to Robert Underwood Johnson on Jan. 24, 1880, answering an inquiry about "poor Russell" after his death, Cable wrote, "He persecuted me with allusions to

continued almost another year. They questioned the use of the patois
songs, some of which were then omitted, and troublesome French
phrases as well. Cable's responses to their suggestions show an eagerness to profit wherever possible and also a firmness in holding to what
he considered best. They make clear also how solidly his writing was
founded on history and sure observation. One of Johnson's notes asked
whether a particular passage was not "a little too sublimated for the
general reader." In arguing against one of the figures of speech, he said,
"The *Atlantic* won't have 'kicking up a dust.' . . . Really, this is too
violent to be pleasant reading." Enough of the notes are of the same
tenor to suggest the weight and the direction of the editorial persuasion.

Johnson cautioned Cable against his disposition to "leave the novel
and go pamphleteering," and the revisions made in consequence were
surely gains for the artistry of the novel. On August 2, 1879, he said
that if the Negro problem were to be handled, "it must be *dramatically*
and not philippically. If you were not the *best dramatic novelist* now
writing there would be some excuse for this." On one matter Johnson
was most insistent, but to little avail. Convinced that Frowenfeld lacks
human warmth, he picked out a scene in which he is insulted by another character, Sylvestre, but keeps control of himself, stands "like a
cliff," and then walks away. In a sequence of letters Johnson begged
Cable to let Frowenfeld "knock Sylvestre over." He cited the frailties
of Hugo's Jean Valjean and other literary characters, and later he wrote,
"I implore you to let him knock Sylvestre over and indicate his own
manhood, even if he repents in sack cloth and ashes!! . . . Do pare his
goodness down to digestible proportions." After another month, on
September 19, "I wake up of mornings with the prayer that you will
let Joseph's passion get the better of his judgment in the encounter with
Sylvestre, who would look 'a so beautiful' at full length." And later in
microscopic writing, in brackets at the bottom of a letter, ". . . if possible [let Joseph knock Sylvestre down.]" Cable stood his ground,
though he did bring Joseph to the point of raising his fist and had the
bystanders plead with him that Sylvestre was drunk.

With the last serial number in print and with Gilder back from
Europe, Johnson could take a new perspective on *The Grandissimes*. He

---

one or two trivial favors I had done him & I avoided him." (In Mattie Russell, "George
Washington Cable Letters in Duke University Library," Duke University *Library Notes,*
No. 25, Jan., 1951, p. 3.) To a later query from William M. Baskervill Cable
answered on October 23, 1896, that Russell "had poetic genius" but because of his ad-
diction to drink "was a dreadful revelation of how low intellectual beauty can fall."
(In the Joint University Libraries at Nashville.)

was proud to have been its editor and could write on January 20, 1880,
"I admire every brave word you have said in the Grandissimes about
slavery and I often think how much it must have cost you." E. C. Stedman pronounced the Bras Coupé episode "the biggest thing of its kind
in American literature." Frank H. Scott wrote from the business office
on April 24, "Bras Coupé has taken hold of our memories with a much
more tenacious grip than ever did Uncle Tom." Another friend in New
York, Allen C. Redwood, quoted Sidney Lanier on September 14 as saying that Cable was the only man who had mastered the sounds of dialect.
In a letter to his brother Clifford on September 24, 1880, Lanier wrote:
"Have you read Cable's book, *The Grandissimes?* It is a work of art,
and he has a fervent and rare soul."[10] As Lanier first planned his lectures on the novel at Johns Hopkins University the following year,
The Grandissimes was to be discussed as an example of the novel in relation to the complexities of character in modern life.[11]

William Dean Howells stated his enthusiasm in private and in print.
After reading the book, he wrote the author:

I found it thoroughly knit and perfectly clear, portraying a multitude of
figures with a delicacy and unerring certainty of differentiation that per-
petually astonished me. It is a noble and beautiful book, including all the
range of tragedy and comedy; and it made my heart warm towards you while
I had the blackest envy in it. Deuce take you, how could you do it so
well?—Aurore is one of the most delicious creations I ever knew. My wife
kept reading me that first call of Frowenfeld's on the Nancanou ladies till
I was intoxicated with their delightfulness. Oh the charm of their English!
We speak nothing else now but that dialect.[12]

Howells wrote John Hay a year later: "There is no more charming
creature in fiction than Aurora Nancanou."[13] And twenty years later
he wrote in *Heroines of Fiction* that in all fiction he knew of no equal
to *The Grandissimes* "for a certain blend of romance and reality, which
does no wrong to either component property."[14]

Reviewers in the national periodicals greeted *The Grandissimes* with
enthusiasm. Some welcomed it as a relief from the stock plantation romances coming out of the South; others saw in it an "escape from the
tepid and perfumed atmosphere of the artificial over-refinement" common

---

[10] *Centennial Edition, Sidney Lanier* (Baltimore, 1945), X, 252.

[11] Aubrey Harrison Starke, *Sidney Lanier: A Biographical and Critical Study* (Chapel
Hill, 1933), p. 413.

[12] Oct. 2, 1881; in *Life in Letters of William Dean Howells,* ed. Mildred Howells
(New York, 1928), I, 302.

[13] March 18, 1882; *ibid.,* I, 312.

[14] New York, 1901, II, 240.

to the fiction of the time. They remarked on its fresh, dramatic treatment of materials new to American literature. They applauded the care,
the minute observation, and the sound research which lay back of the
book but which, most of them agreed, did not obtrude on its pages. They
spoke of its captivating story, its poetic vein, its rich portraiture of
characters and setting, its luxuriance of metaphor.

Boyesen, reviewing the book in *Scribner's* for November, 1880, called
its author "a literary pioneer, . . . the first Southern novelist (unless
we count Poe a novelist) who has made a contribution of permanent
value to American Literature." The *Atlantic* (December, 1880) considered Cable "an artist and a man of large imagination." To W. C.
Brownell, writing in the *Nation* of December 9, he was "a literary artist
of unusual powers," "a born story-teller," and his appearance in the
South at that time was "almost to be called sensational." The reviewer
in the November *Appletons' Journal,* seeing in the book fulfilment of
the promise in *Old Creole Days,* dispensed superlatives liberally: "story-
teller of the first rank"; "a picture of an epoch"; "has literally created a
people, an era, and a place." To this reviewer the book was significant
for its treatment of the subtle effects of slavery on the whites, especially
significant because written by a Southerner.

In noting the parallel the book implies between the time of its setting
and the post-Civil War years, the *Atlantic* of December remarked on
Cable's "profound sense of the larger laws of history" but added that he
was "too sincere an artist to push this parallel." This reviewer thought
the episode of Bras Coupé integral to the novel and "magnificently told."
To Brownell, in contrast, it was too grim and unpleasant for good taste,
and it argued "in behalf of a cause already won." Brownell voiced the
same squeamish view which had caused several magazine editors to re-
ject the Bras Coupé story, but it is perhaps surprising that he thought
the cause of the Negroes and quadroons, as the book postulates it, had
been won.

Several of the reviewers agreed in the flaws they picked out—Frowenfeld's role, for example, as manipulator of the action and spokesman for
the author. Brownell found in the other main characters a vividness not
usual in current novels, but he found the minor characters enshrouded
in a mist allowing them only a hazy reality. Boyesen thought the action
lags after the Bras Coupé episode; the *Atlantic* reviewer objected to the
"half-followed clews" and the author's habit of "eddying about his point."
The author of a short review in the December *Harper's* found the dialect
novel and curious enough to amuse the reader for a while but tedious in

the total effect. The *Atlantic,* in a quoted dialogue, normalized the speech to save the reader trouble but did not condemn the dialect altogether. Most of the reviewers found some difficulty in the dialect but liked the flavor it imparts to the book.

Except for *L'Abeille,* the New Orleans newspapers reiterated their pride in Cable's achievement and with some reservations defended *The Grandissimes* against what everyone knew were the Creoles' objections. Lafcadio Hearn's review in the *Item,*[15] one of the several pieces he wrote on the book for the local papers, made a special cause of answering those understood charges. Because of his own interest in them he especially welcomed the Creole songs and music which were included. Through a vagueness that is artistic, he said, New Orleans and the characters become more than real in the novel—they assume the force of half-remembered matter. "Its paintings are not always flattering to native eyes; its evocation of dead memories will not be found pleasing." But, he added, "we cannot perceive that the merit of the romance is at all marred." He was confident the Creole characters were true to fact, except that he doubted any Creole would ever hold the radical social views Cable had given the Honoré Grandissime of *sang pur.* Anticipating objections to the prominence voodooism had among Cable's characters, Hearn said, "We believe it to be, or at least to have been, a serious and horrible reality; and we know of most intelligent families among our French-speaking population who share this opinion."

Though the reviews were generous as a rule, occasional notes in them nettled Cable's literary skin, which was yet tender, he wrote Scribner on October 2. His particular reference was to the *Democrat* of a week earlier, which had accorded him the highest praise, saying:

> The creations of this novelist are in reality *not* creations. They were and are living, breathing men and women, transferred from actual life to his pages, made immortal by their repeating everyday speech and manners, and the tinge of genius thrown into every character. . . . As for the ladies Nancanou, there can be but one verdict—they are perfectly *delightful!* . . .

But the reviewer thought that in picturing the f.m.c. Cable had prostituted his talent to expediency, the demand of the Northern press for something condemnatory of Southern "intolerance." The book would appeal most, he feared, to the readers of *Uncle Tom's Cabin.*

Cable knew some of the Creoles harbored resentment that had not

[15] Sept. 27, 1880; included in *Creole Sketches,* ed. C. W. Hutson (Boston, 1924), pp. 117-23. Hearn wrote on *The Grandissimes* for the same paper also on Dec. 26, 1879, and Jan. 13, 1881.

been voiced openly. Then late in 1880 appeared in New Orleans an anonymous pamphlet from a fictitious publisher which purported to speak for all the Creoles. Its abuse was so scurrilous that Cable's friends at the Scribner house feared his life was in danger. Gilder wrote, "If you ever think it wise to come north you know where you will find friends." Entitled *Critical Dialogue Between Aboo and Caboo on a New Book; or A Grandissime Ascension,* it is a dialogue between the spirit of a Creole of the book and a descendant of his family in 1880. It charges that Cable, prompted by a "disguised puritanism, assuming the fanatical mission of radical reform and universal enlightenment," has slandered Creole ancestry, has ridiculed the beautiful and the revered for profit from "the prejudiced and inimical North"; that blinded reviewers, even in New Orleans, so lauded the book that the author had garnered both fame and fortune. The pamphlet strives for cleverness through crude exaggeration and vulgarity. Cable is likened to a "buzzard, glutted with carion, lighting heavily on a consecrated shrine," to a jackal disinterring "a cherished corpse"; he is a "Great-Liar," a dwarf driven by a "lust for gain," and has consorted with the voodoo queen Mari Lavo (Marie Laveau) and with Miss Zizi, the most beautiful of the Negresses, to beget a numerous progeny. He has destroyed the Louisiana of Chateaubriand and Longfellow, and his offense is greater because he is a native of New Orleans, an "unnatural Southern growth, a bastard sprout."

The author of the lampoon was the Creole poet-priest Adrien Rouquette, who may have been inclined to anonymity because he had been more than a casual acquaintance of Cable's and a close friend of Lafcadio Hearn. His biographer finds the pamphlet out of keeping with the man and can account for it in no way except as an expression of what he took to be the views of many Creoles.[16] He wrote poems himself in the Creole dialect and probably was not incensed at Cable's attitude toward the Negro, for he had remained a Union supporter through the Civil War, had taken the oath of allegiance at the fall of New Orleans, and until about 1876 had written for the Union newspapers published locally. It seems likely that Rouquette, highly romantic in his own literary tastes, resented most the realistic treatment the Creoles received in *The Grandissimes.* The unexplained termination of his friendship with Hearn in 1880 may have been due to this attack on Cable.

Lafcadio Hearn had become Cable's staunch advocate in the local press. Theirs was one of the strangest of recorded friendships, for they were

[16] Dagmar Renshaw LeBreton, *Chahta-Ima: The Life of Adrien-Emmanuel Rouquette* (Baton Rouge, 1947), pp. 319 ff.

at remote poles in background, way of living, outlook, and many of their beliefs. Yet they had enough bonds of common interest to support one of the longest friendships of Hearn's career. Their relations are not easy to trace, but it is clear that they were closely associated through several years, respected each other, planned literary collaboration, and helped each other whenever possible. The fact that they later became at least partially estranged is not surprising, for it was Hearn's habit to believe his closest friends had turned against him.

Hearn's sojourn in New Orleans was one of his several distinct interludes in different quarters of the globe. Following his birth on one of the islands of Greece he lived in Ireland, France, New York, Cincinnati, and after leaving New Orleans, in the West Indies, again in New York, and finally in Japan. His ten years in the city gave him his first respectable livelihood, generous friends, and an opportunity to reach beyond journalism and establish himself in literary authorship.[17]

Hearn must have met Cable soon after coming to Louisiana in 1877, for in the following year he wrote H. E. Krehbiel, music editor of the New York *Tribune,* about the novel Cable was writing and about his own helping to collect the Creole songs that were to be included in it. He would rather be in New Orleans in sackcloth and ashes, he said, than to own the whole state of Ohio, and he could readily see that Cable alone was writing of the real, albeit the strange and romantic old City. They shared an interest in the storied old houses of the French Quarter, its conglomerate population, its speech, and its songs. They shared their books; they helped each other locate out-of-the-way volumes on early local history or the hybrid languages of the Caribbean. They exchanged messages, Hearn writing in purple ink and usually without reference to date, and Hearn visited Cable on Eighth Street to meet other literary guests or to hear a new manuscript read. They went for summer vacations at Grand Isle, along with Marion A. Baker or James B. Guthrie, a lawyer and lifelong friend of Cable's.

The common ground between Hearn and Cable was primarily their interest in the Creole dialects and the related lore. Both were scholarly and together they sought whatever help they could find in books. It was not much they found—most of the printed studies of Creole speech and traditions had been made in the West Indies and so left a gap to be bridged in any study they might base in Louisiana. Their need for bolstering each other is suggested by a remark printed in *Lippincott's Magazine,* March, 1868, about a collection of slave songs: "It was hardly

[17] For Hearn's life, see Vera McWilliams, *Lafcadio Hearn* (Boston [1946]), and Edward Larocque Tinker, *Lafcadio Hearn's American Days* (New York, 1924).

worth while to try to perpetuate this trash, vulgarity, and profanity by putting it in print." In employing dialect in his stories, Cable had met reluctance in both editors and readers. Yet there was the example of Louis Gottschalk's success with his adaptations from the Creole folk music, and by 1878 Krehbiel was eager to have the songs collected for publication.

Hearn often wrote in the newspapers about Southern or Louisiana writings, and he made opportunities to speak of Cable favorably. Some of the views he printed are so close to Cable's as to leave little doubt that during the visits he paid on Eighth Street two or three times a week they exchanged literary opinions and found much to agree on. In writing on "Southern Novels" for the *Item* of November 26, 1879, Hearn stated views that Cable had already practiced and was to enunciate later:

In all we find the same kind of "gush," the same floriated English, the same adoration of "titles" and "noble blood" and other antiquated nonsense, and they all end in the discovery that some young American is the legitimate son or heir of some member of the English nobility. . . . Southern writers of real talent do not write for a district or state, but for the country at large; they are not shoddyites; they do not write books advertised as "Southern novels."[18]

Basing one essay on the wish stated in the New York *Times* that there were more Cables, Hearn wrote, "It must be remembered that Cables do not succeed by chance, but by dint of such untiring steadfastness of purpose as few are blessed with." In writing of "Successful Literature," Hearn cited Cable as the best example in New Orleans: "He has dressed up local scenes and incidents in the attractive garb of imaginative fiction, thus rescuing the facts from obscurity, and weaving strange stories as charmingly real as they are romantically ideal. In this way he has within a few years won for himself a position which none will hereafter dare to question."[19]

[18] Included in Hearn's *Essays on American Literature,* pp. 42-43.

[19] See other essays by Hearn in the *Times-Democrat,* May 26, 1881; Dec. 31, 1882; and April 15, 1883; reprinted in *Essays on American Literature,* respectively, pp. 73-75, 104-7, 112-17.

CHAPTER VIII

FACT AND FICTION

THE EDITORS of *Scribner's Monthly* were so pleased with *The Grandissimes* that they paid the author a bonus of $500. They had wanted a story to print while the serial was running, and hoped for another novel to begin in 1881. The pay for Cable's stories had been raised from eight to ten dollars a magazine page, and he could draw liberal advances. But nothing new appeared until May, 1881, when *Madame Delphine* began as a three-number serial. It was published as a book in July, and Frederick Warne brought it out in London in a volume with three stories from *Old Creole Days.*

Cable wrote the story, so he said in the preface to an edition of 1896, because of a letter he received. An anonymous quadroon had read " 'Tite Poulette" and said, as he paraphrased her letter, "If you have a whole heart for the cruel case of us poor quadroons, change the story even yet, and tell the inmost truth of it. Madame John lied! The girl was her own daughter; but like many and many a real quadroon mother, as you surely know, Madame John perjured her own soul to win for her child a legal and honorable alliance with the love-mate and life-mate of her choice."[1]

Cable thought *Madame Delphine* his best story, and in the 1896 preface he wrote, "I have a notion I shall always be glad I wrote it." He felt that it told the truth about the quadroons as " 'Tite Poulette" had not done and that it succeeded through Père Jerome in making virtue real and human as he had not done with Frowenfeld. He clearly had the earlier story in mind when he wrote this one. Madame John and 'Tite Poulette are here Madame Delphine and her beautiful daughter Olive, who has been brought up as white by her father's sister. The white lover

[1] The preface reports also that he began the story after his first trip north, though what he says about it fits the second trip instead. Yet he no doubt meant the first trip, in 1875, for the manuscript was finished before the second, and the earlier date would place the inception of the story soon after the two letters he wrote the newspapers on segregation. The long interval before he finished the story may be explained by his unwillingness to write for the pay he received and some reluctance to argue the cause of the quadroons as directly as he planned in the story.

of the daughter is not the slow-witted Dutchman of the early story but a Creole, Ursin Lemaitre Vignevielle, a man of the world, a pirate in fact turned philanthropic banker. 'Tite Poulette was actually not Madame John's daughter, but when Madame Delphine swears that Olive is not her daughter and therefore is free to marry Vignevielle, she lies. Her attitude has become clear earlier. To the explanation that the law has been made to keep the races apart, she asks: "From which race do they want to keep my daughter separate? She is seven parts white! The law did not stop her from being that." When she has told Père Jerome of the perjury she has committed, and has died in the confessional, he exclaims, "Lord, lay not this sin to her charge!"

The author keeps the reader at a distance from Vignevielle, the character who roughly parallels Kristian Koppig in the earlier story and Joseph Frowenfeld in the novel. It is Père Jerome who shares the stage with Madame Delphine. He is a kindly priest with an understanding of human frailty and human transgressions which was impossible to Frowenfeld. A jovial companion of his friends from boyhood, he voices early in the story the precept which develops in what follows: for Vignevielle's going astray his family, his friends, and the whole of society are in part responsible. From then to the final episode in the confessional the precept remains with the reader though it is barely mentioned again; and its application to the quadroons is the more forceful for being unstated. The responsibility of society for their fate is made abundantly clear by Olive's timid acceptance, her mother's protests, Jerome's understanding, the uncompromising law, and the equally uncompromising background characters.

The date of the action is about 1820, when Orleanians had lost but little of the "disbelief in the custom-house" they had in the days of the Lafittes, and when the beautiful, silk-clad quadroons at the balls "wore, withal, a pathos in their charm that gave them a family likeness to innocence." Yet the first pages describe—or better, suggest—the lower end of the Rue Royale in Cable's own time. The region has settled into "a long sabbath of decay"; the "batten shutters . . . are shut with a grip that makes one's knuckles and nails feel lacerated." If one stops to ask across the street from Madame Delphine's house, he will probably get even now the all-explaining answer, "Dey's quadroons." Descendants of the quadroons who once were fabulously beautiful in the letters and diaries of visitors to the city now sit inside their close-fenced gardens, "staring shrinkingly at you as you pass, like a nest of yellow kittens." Thus Cable approaches the time of this action, sixty years back, introducing the same kind of "palpable imaginable *visitable* past" which Henry James later spoke of in his preface to "The Aspern Papers," a past in which the strange and the familiar can be held in delicate balance. He saw old New Orleans as James saw Venice, in an "afternoon light" which limned some objects with utmost clarity and left others in shadow.[2] He achieved a reality which is the more real for the enveloping haze, the tone and atmosphere, for example, of a warm New Orleans night perfumed with the night-blooming jasmine.

The story is leisurely and as delicate as anything Cable ever wrote. Revelation comes through glimpses here and there, but with more naturalness than in the earlier stories. With a touch of suggestion, a figure of speech, an ironic turn of thought, a hint of feelings only half expressed, the reader is gently led through events that leave an effect as delicate as the odor of orange blossoms but also as haunting and unforgettable. The dialect is not burdensome but there is enough for flavor. Cable was consciously meeting objections *The Grandissimes* had raised: He did not indicate consistently the Creoles' special pronunciations, as of *r,* and he made it clear that when they switched to English they were using an unfamiliar tongue; he pointed out that in familiar conversation the Creoles, Père Jerome among them, might lapse into the patois which was most natural to the quadroons, but he used only occasional phrases to suggest the speech.

Harper's, apparently still concerned mainly with pleasant love stories, found space only to list *Madame Delphine* as "moderately worth reading," but other journals gave it full reviews. Robert Underwood Johnson, who reviewed it for the *Critic* of July 16 and also *Scribner's* for September, 1881, called it better than *The Grandissimes,* "direct evidence of genius" and suggestive of nobody except for "a rare whiff of Victor Hugo." Cable's stories would have been provincial in the hands of Mrs. Stowe or Richard Malcolm Johnston. "We do not recall anything in American fiction outside of Hawthorne," he continued, "that exhibits so many of the literary qualities which go to make for a novelist an enduring reputation." The reviewer in the *Nation* on July 21 thought the story "wonderfully true and real" but not as great as *The Grandissimes* or as powerful. Edmund Gosse, in the *Saturday Review* of London on August 20, applauded the "rich and musical prose" but would have preferred greater simplicity. The editor of the London *Athenaeum* said on August 13 it would be well if the English novelists would bestow as much pains on their work as Cable.

[2] *The Novels and Tales of Henry James* (New York, 1908), XII, x.

Johnson, who had thought Frowenfeld a bundle of unreal virtues, pronounced the characters of the new story "unmistakably human" and individualized at a time when most characters of fiction were barely distinguishable. He said Cable had "subdued his theme to a distinct undertone of a story which owes its main interest to characterization and action." The *Nation* said the story could be appreciated no matter what the reader's views on slavery; Gosse could not isolate the moral from "the warmth and perfume of the tropical city." The reviewer in the *Nation* objected that the patois had been explained with too much contrivance; Gosse and a reviewer in the London *Spectator,* quoted in the *Critic* of September 10, said the speech could be easily learned and was well worth the effort. Similarly the writer in the Boston *Literary World* of July 30 lauded the "inimitable skill" of the dialect.

Satisfying as were these reviews on both sides of the Atlantic, in which Cable found himself compared with Victor Hugo and Flaubert, he knew that close at home other considerations than artistic merit would weigh in the evaluation. A short notice in the *Picayune* of July 24 was wholly favorable, but one by Hearn in the *Democrat* of the same day illustrates the demurrers that were entered locally. Hearn spoke of Cable as belonging to the first rank of American novelists and of *Madame Delphine* as his masterpiece. Parts of the story he thought had never been excelled in America. But he considered the broken English tiresome, and he questioned the use made of it. Conceding that whites of his acquaintance used the patois in speaking to children and servants and that mothers often chided their children for using it in the presence of strangers, he still doubted that Père Jerome and his cronies would lapse into it, or even that Madame Delphine would use it. A final statement, that Cable employs the patois to good effect, suggests that he was aware of both the general disapproval of dialect in fiction and the Creoles' displeasure at finding anything but perfect speech put into their mouths.

An editorial in the *Democrat* of September 11 illustrates further the sort of external considerations that might enter into Southern newspaper criticism. An essay on "Southern Literature" reprinted a few days earlier from *Scribner's* had said that the two writers who had "brought most performance and promise to American letters" during the preceding five years were Cable and Frances Hodgson Burnett. The editor's concern was to refute the statement in the essay that the institution of slavery had fostered in the Old South a provincial rather than a universal literature. On the contrary, he argued, if the Southern system had continued, it would have produced literature of high quality. Reaching a climax, he alluded to writers of the old leisure society, of whom he named only Charles Gayarré, and declared that their works "will live when the names of even such brilliant writers as Mrs. Burnett and George Cable are forgotten."

Before *Madame Delphine* was off his hands, Cable had added a new task to the many he already had, one which had some attraction for itself and offered a way of mending the breaches in his financial walls. Colonel George E. Waring, Jr. came to New Orleans early in 1880 to collect social statistics for publication with the Tenth Census of the United States. After reading *Old Creole Days* on the train down, he sought out its author and appointed him local assistant. In April Cable began forwarding data to Waring's home in Newport, Rhode Island. The work lasted fourteen months, and the pay averaged slightly less than $100 a month.

Waring respected his assistant's ability and like Edward King earlier developed a warm interest in his personal fortune. He was eleven years Cable's senior and an internationally prominent agricultural and sanitary engineer. His acquaintances included editors and publishers, for he wrote for the *Atlantic* and *Scribner's* and was the author of half a dozen books. He and Cable could recall that they had been cavalrymen in opposing armies in Mississippi during the spring of 1864. Cable's main task for the census, to supply current information, was not uncongenial, for he had a businessman's interest in commerce and industry and was alert to community affairs. As he turned up information on drainage, sewage disposal, and yellow fever, he found that Waring echoed the demand for reform he had voiced in his writings since his days as a journalist.

In September, 1880, Cable paid his second visit to New York. From his arrival by steamer on the thirteenth until he started home a week later, his friends kept him in a holiday whirl. He was entertained by Gilder, Robert Underwood Johnson, Roswell Smith, Mrs. Herrick, Johnson's assistant in the editing of *The Grandissimes,* and others. At the Century Club he met Boyesen for the first time. These were all like old friends, though some of them he had not met before.

Back in New Orleans Cable set out on November 12 to visit the Acadian country in southwest Louisiana, for he had been commissioned to write up the Acadians for the *Tenth Census*. These descendants of the Nova Scotian exiles, scarcely known outside their settlements, had a history and a civilization worth reporting. He had observed them first while surveying on the Atchafalaya River in 1866; in 1869 he had taken a vacation among them; and ten years later he had returned in the company of Allen C. Redwood, an illustrator for *Scribner's Monthly.*

Redwood, a veteran of Jeb Stuart's Confederate cavalry, preferred Southern subjects and had come to New Orleans in May, 1879, brimful of enthusiasm, hoping especially to illustrate Cable's stories. The friendship which began between them lasted more than twenty-five years. They prowled through the old city and held "seances & confabs," as Redwood called them, on *The Grandissimes,* then in manuscript. He was no less sure than King and Champney had been before him of Cable's literary future. "If you don't ruin that small body of yours by undue libations of chicory tea & excess of Sunday-Schools," he wrote on August 26, 1879, "you are bound to go far or I'm no prophet." With Cable as his guide for the first few days, Redwood set out on June 6 for six weeks of sketching among the Acadians. After Cable had returned to New Orleans, Redwood was commissioned to report to him such observations as he could employ in some Acadian stories he was already planning. Cable asked the editors to let Redwood illustrate *The Grandissimes,* but they thought the expense greater than the gain.

When Cable returned to southwestern Louisiana in 1880 to collect information for the census, he took the new railroad directly to New Iberia and in the following weeks he traveled the length of the Acadian country. He stayed with families he had known earlier and with new acquaintances; he attended church services, dances, family reunions. In seventy-five closely written pages of a notebook he recorded the kind of information he would need for the census report and for the stories he contemplated: historical and current data, peculiar phrases, customs, and beliefs; anecdotes, traditions, and character sketches.[3] He admired the simple virtues of the simple people but lamented their backwardness. On every hand he saw need for the leadership he was to envisage for them in his Acadian stories a few years later.

The Acadian material was not included in the census after all, but Cable had gratifying freedom in writing the report on New Orleans. It was Waring's plan to preface the current statistics on each city with a short sketch of its history. Cable began writing a history of New Orleans from its founding to the Civil War. In the notebook he had used among the Acadians he assembled the facts, noting carefully his sources in the English and French historical accounts, newspaper files, and archival documents. The questions he jotted down to be an-

[3] This notebook is at Tulane University.

swered, the weighing of one authority against another, and the index of
his notes testify to his seriousness in the undertaking. When Waring
saw the history he was unwilling to shorten it, though it was three times
as long as the parallel histories of Boston and Chicago. The few dele-
tions he made were mainly to soften Cable's strictures on the moral state
at different periods in the history. The report on New Orleans was
issued in the spring of 1882 (dated 1881) and was included later in the
complete *Tenth Census.*

The phrase Waring once used to describe himself as a horseman, "a
heavy weight and a rough rider," might be applied to his other activities
also. He was daring and experimental as an engineer, and it was with
the same daring that he undertook to advance Cable's interests. Early
in their acquaintance he told Cable to stand ready to switch to a publisher who would pay better. Then on January 6, 1881, he relayed from
his friend J. R. Osgood of Boston, at first not identified, an offer of
$3500 for serial and book rights to his next novel, plus 5 per cent royalty
on book sales. Unwilling to leave his friends at the Scribner company
precipitously, Cable wired them of the offer and by the middle of the
month had sold them the serial rights for $3500, $1000 of which was
advanced at once.

The staff of *Scribner's Monthly* were especially eager not to lose
Cable, for just then they were withdrawing from the book publishing
house to continue independently. A stock company of half a dozen
from the other firm bought out Charles Scribner's interest in the magazine and most of Dr. Holland's, whose declining health had forced him
into virtual retirement. Roswell Smith, the chief stockholder, became
president of the new Century Company, as it was named. After October
the magazine would be the *Century Scribner's Monthly Magazine,* and
after another year "Scribner's" would be dropped.

The divorcement was not without ill feeling, particularly between
Roswell Smith and Charles Scribner, and it was a delicate matter for
Cable to keep his friends in both camps. The misunderstanding within
the earlier company had arisen in part from disagreement as to whether
the magazine branch should publish books. Now Scribner feared he
might lose Cable's future books to the new company, which intended
to begin book publishing and soon had spoken for Cable's future work.
Meanwhile, Waring sought an offer from Osgood for book rights to the
new novel. But no commitment was made until Cable was east in the
summer.

He had planned a visit to New York. Then on a sudden decision,
hoping a summer in New England would benefit his wife's health, he

wired his friends of the Century Company to find a place for her and the four daughters, now aged four to eleven. Elated at the opportunity to help, they engaged room and board in a farm house in Franconia, in the White Mountains of New Hampshire; and at the first of June, after a brief stop in New York, Cable established his family there for the summer.

He returned to New York and on June 4 began sitting for the portrait which the Century Company had engaged Abbott H. Thayer to paint and which was used as the frontispiece in the *Century* of the next February. In the same issue appeared an invited article on Cable written by Colonel Waring and based largely on information supplied by Marion Baker. Thayer's portrait accentuates the expanse of Cable's forehead, his delicate nose, and his full dark beard flowing into his collar. But the artist's chief study was the eyes. The sparkle, hinting of mischief and good humor, which is prominent in most of Cable's photographs, has been subdued into an expression of kindness and sympathy. To Cable's associates his eyes reflected a keen intellect, a ready wit softened by geniality. Thayer saw in them chiefly human sympathy and compassion.

After meeting William Dean Howells and visiting him at Belmont, Cable went on June 11 to Hartford to visit his wife's relatives the Bartletts. It was there that he had the chief treat of what he called the greatest holiday of his life. Charles Dudley Warner and George Warner took him in hand and made his stay in Hartford a perfect ovation, he said. They wired to Mark Twain, then beyond New Haven. He came, with Olivia, on the first train, and at a luncheon Cable had his first taste of the wild fun which always accompanied Mark Twain. He had a long talk with Harriet Beecher Stowe, who was full of praise for his writings and eager to talk about the South. Before leaving for New York on the fourteenth, he met Joseph Twichell and others at a brilliant dinner.

The following week in New York was anticlimactic and not altogether pleasant, for his relations with his publishers were not yet cleared up. At Waring's home at Newport earlier he had met J. R. Osgood and had contracted for the book rights to the novel he was writing but with the reservation that either Scribner or Smith might have it instead by equaling Osgood's terms. Neither Charles Scribner nor Roswell Smith could meet Osgood's offer, 22½ per cent royalty, with an advance of $1000 on the completion of the manuscript, but both were satisfied with their expectations of publishing his later works. Scribner was to issue *Madame Delphine* within a few weeks, and before leaving New York,

Cable had contracted with the Century Company for another work. He suggested turning to further use the history of New Orleans he had written for the census. The Century editors agreed to publish the history in seven magazine articles and later as a book. Waring approved the plan, even of having the serialization precede the issuing of the census.

When Cable took the train home on June 20, he concluded the longest and the most satisfying visit he had yet made in the East. Three publishers were vying for his work, but in a way to strengthen rather than weaken his relations with all of them. Mark Twain and Howells and the Warners had received him warmly and in New York a dozen friends had welcomed him like a member of their closest circles.

Back in New Orleans on June 23, he dropped into the welter of endeavors and responsibilities that had become habitual with him. He finished a term of grand jury duty that had begun in April and as secretary wrote the report which was submitted on June 29. Lonely as he was for his family, he reiterated in the letters he wrote almost every day that he would not for anything have them in New Orleans. As for his own health, he had gained seven pounds in the spring and had reached a remarkable summer weight for him of 103 pounds; in August he had dropped to 99.

His main work was on the history for the census. Except when the finance committee of the Cotton Exchange met, he had to be at the office only an hour or two a day. The rest of each day, until ten at night, he spent at his desk in his lonely house. Once or twice he took his sisters and Nettie's children on the cars to West End or Spanish Fort, where Orleanians went to catch the afternoon breezes from Lake Pontchartrain. The Bible class on Friday nights, Dr. Palmer's or Dr. Nall's sermons, and his Sunday school brought the usual satisfaction. Occasionally James Guthrie or Marion Baker stopped to see him in the evening, or George Henry Clements, a young artist, came by for criticism of his drawings. A Creole himself, Clements spoke out freely among his friends and in letters to the papers in defense of Cable's portrayal of the Creoles. He afterward gained some prominence and, living in the East, remained a warm friend of Cable's.

Another evening the old Baron Ludwig von Reizenstein might drop in to tell of a new butterfly he had found and to lament that he had mutilated the specimen in catching it. After arriving from Germany in 1849 Reizenstein had first written fiction and social criticism for the local

German press[4] and afterward had turned mainly to scientific study.[5] He presented Cable with a case of moths and butterflies. The two men shared a common interest in the natural world around them, each with his own purpose. One of the discoveries he called to show Cable was a large moth not previously reported on the North American continent. Cable vouched for his "bug-hunter" to the *Scribner's* editors[6] and helped the baron write up his discovery. The article was published in October, 1881. Reizenstein named the moth *Smerinthus Cablei,* in honor of his friend, who he said was "so much identified with Louisiana as a citizen and litterateur." Cable wrote Johnson, "I will try humbly & gratefully to do my duty as a godfather." Others of the Baron's discoveries were not accepted for the magazine, but two years later, no doubt with the help of intercession from Cable among his newspaper friends, he began a long series of articles for the *Times-Democrat* on the insects and birds of Louisiana. He died in the fall of 1885, but he remained clear enough in Cable's mind to take form fifteen years later in his story of "The Entomologist."

The summer of 1881 was the longest time Cable had yet been separated from his family. He made time to write the children separately, and to his wife he poured out his heart like a young lover—he reread her letters written during their courtship; he recalled the day she had come down the stairs to become his wife. Yet he would not let himself be depressed; the mountains would renew Louise's health. He could name others with irremediably worse fates than his, and he could invoke pleasant recollections, as he did on July 19:

> Let me see: how many sweet memories can I call to your mind tonight? Do you remember the day I first saw you on Walker's bluff, with your blooming cheeks and your broad brimmed hat? That is the kind you must wear when you come home. . . . Well, again: Do you remember the night we all went up to Carrollton and stood on the river bank & afterward walked over to see the Keeners? Do you remember the night we dropped in at St. Paul's church to hear the choir practicing? Do you remember that happy night—the time we rode in a carriage to Louisiana avenue with my mother? Do you remember the foolish lines beginning—"I have been to the wood-

---

[4] For an account of Reizenstein's first years in America, see Robert T. Clark, Jr., "The German Liberals in New Orleans (1840-1860)," *Louisiana Historical Quarterly,* XX (Jan., 1937), 137-51.

[5] See the *Times-Democrat,* July 8, 18, 1883.

[6] To R. U. Johnson, April 12, 1881; in my possession. Other letters touching on the Baron's moth, Feb. 16 and 26, 1881, are included by Mattie Russell in "George Washington Cable Letters in Duke University Library," Duke University *Library Notes,* No. 25 (Jan., 1951), 1-13.

land"—Sent to you from Plaquemines? And ever so much more sweet nonsense? Or are those things too idle to be cherished?

The family physician, Dr. Bruns, had advised that Louise leave the mountains by September 10, but she demurred, remembering how steaming New Orleans could be in the early fall. The manner of Cable's reply on August 26 was not unusual with him:

MADAM:

You saucy minx I have your curly-tailed, pug-nosed letter of the twenty-first. So you will not come home when I call you, eh! If I get any more sauce from you I shall write you not to come home at all—that I have made other arrangements.

Several weeks of hot weather after the 16th of September! You're crazy! Why, it is so cold here now that the cannon down at the barracks all have breeches on. The ice is a foot thick in the ice houses & the ice-cream is all frozen in the freezers.

You never saw such a time. Melancholy days have come, the saddest of the year. I am afraid there will be no figs or blackberries this year. Hurry home before the peach crop in our back yard is ruined. The peaches are dropping from the limb. The cakes in the confectioners' window are all frosted, and people seem actually indisposed to venture out even with sleighs. The hotels and restaurants keep fires up in their kitchens nearly all night, and even at home the water in the vessels on the stove has to have fire kindled under it to make it boil.

Yours nevertheless,
G. W. CABLE

P.S. You may remember me; I used to board in the same house with you in N. Orleans.

G. W. C.

Louise carried her point, and after visiting her relatives at Hartford she took the train for New Orleans on September 20.

By the time Cable's family reached home, he had decided finally to cut loose from business and leave himself nothing "for offense or defense," he said, but his "grey goose quill." Thus he closed a debate which had been with him several years. The death of his revered employer William C. Black late in 1879 had brought him close to a decision, but the partner, Robert Y. Black, continued the business and announced that Cable would remain in charge of "the finances and general affairs of the counting room." Asked for advice on that occasion, Scribner noted that *Old Creole Days* had made "an unusual beginning for a book of short stories," but it had sold only 1200 copies in six months and the royalty was yet only twenty dollars. Dr. Holland thought Cable might expect $2500 a year from his pen, but Johnson said his own family of three had expenses of that amount in New York. The final composite advice was for him to hold on to his salary of $1400 in the cotton house, write as much as he could, and see how his literary prospects would look later on. Cable closed the matter for the moment by writing Johnson on January 24, 1880, "Have served two masters so long that one might make me lonesome." But he added: "I wish I had a chance to write another novel. I believe I know how to do it now. . . . I am ready now with a good theme & a good plot & only want *time.*"

This decision could be only temporary. The trip east in the summer of 1881 opened up such alluring avenues for literary work and his commitments to his publishers were so demanding that he could not postpone his break with business. On October 1 he submitted his resignation, to take effect on December 1. Now he would have the time he had so yearned for, and he hoped to live by his pen. Sales of *The Grandissimes* had been disappointing, only 2900 in the first five months, but both it and *Old Creole Days* were still selling. The *Century* editors had suggested that he give them something on the Acadians and that he write on Albion Tourgée's novels dealing with the Old and the New South. Another proposal had come from Charles Dudley Warner, editor of the American Men of Letters series. Cable agreed to write the volume on William Gilmore Simms and had the understanding among all concerned that he might first make two magazine articles from the manuscript. Similarly the editors offered to print in the magazine anything that might grow out of the prison reform work he had begun following his grand jury term. Solicitations from other sources lent further encouragement. The *Critic,* then in its first year, asked for contributions, and *Our Continent,* a projected weekly magazine, offered high rates for a serial novel. There had been an inquiry about dramatization of *The Grandissimes* and two requests for permission to translate it for German publication. A French translation of *Old Creole Days* had been authorized, and one volume of the stories had been brought out in London. His publishers cautioned him not to expect much from abroad but worked tirelessly in his behalf.

In the summer of 1881 Cable abandoned a small business venture he had made on his own. He had set up an agency the year before to handle books and magazines at 194 Gravier Street, chiefly through the importing branch of the Scribner firm, and to take subscriptions to *The Encyclopaedia Britannica*. Returning home in June, he was confronted with a loss of $700 due to "confusion and falsifications of ac-

counts and the peculations" of his employees. He declined Scribner's
offer to share the loss.

On December 2 the Board of Directors of the Cotton Exchange
adopted a resolution commending Cable's long services. His friends in
New York were glad he was free from business but not all were optimistic. Roswell Smith, who had become his most intimate friend
among them, was solicitous—and discouraging: "For you to come to
New York would be to remove you from the atmosphere, & the types,
from which you draw and must ever draw your best inspiration. . . .
You cannot live alone by literary production, & there must be a salary
somewhere—& somehow." Colonel Waring was pleased and optimistic:
". . . you need not fear, with a little prudence at the outset, that literature will float you along handsomely." Other encouragement soon came
in an invitation to write the article on New Orleans for the *Britannica*.

Yet, what he had was mainly expectation, depending on what his
writing would pay, and in the following months he met such abundant discouragement that he again sought a supplemental income.

CHAPTER IX

THE GREY GOOSE QUILL

IT WAS WITH satisfaction for the business career behind him and a cautious optimism for the literary career ahead that Cable closed his accountant's desk on the last day of November, 1881, and for the first time gave the black sheep, his literary aspiration, a favored place in his flock. Two weeks later he had pushed the novel to the back of his desk to begin revising the history of New Orleans. This plan was acceptable to his friends in the Century Company, though they had advanced $1000 on the novel, for they assumed as he did that the history would be ready soon for both serial and book publication. As it turned out, though, both works had long, disheartening histories before they were in print.

Alexander W. Drake, art editor of *Scribner's* formerly and now the *Century*, was ready to start an illustrator to work for the history. Cable's effort to throw the assignment to his Creole friend George Henry Clements had failed, and Joseph Pennell came to New Orleans in January to make the illustrations. Twenty-one years old, Pennell had already proved himself to Drake, especially in illustrating an article on "Old Yorktown" (October, 1881) by the young Virginia writer Thomas Nelson Page. He was so excited over his assignment that every mile of his trip south was an adventure. At his arrival he wrote Elizabeth Robins, his fiancée, "if New Orleans is anything like the pictures Cable has drawn—it will really be a paradise for me." At eight in the morning he and Cable set out, first to find a room on St. Peter Street, then to breakfast at Madame Antoine's, and afterward to visit the landmarks of the French Quarter recognizable from Cable's stories. The next day he fell into a pleasant routine, sketching all day with no lunch but a banana or a cake he bought from some wrinkled old black woman on the street, and then luxuriating in his dinner with wine at Madame Antoine's. "This is really living down here," he wrote.[1]

[1] For Pennell's sojourn in Louisiana and his notes on Cable, see his autobiography, *The Adventures of an Illustrator* (Boston, 1925), pp. 86-100, and Elizabeth Robins Pennell, *The Life and Letters of Joseph Pennell* (Boston, 1929), I, 49 ff.

He went to Eighth Street on Saturday nights and at other times when there was someone for him to meet. Cable took him to see Charles Gayarré and Lafcadio Hearn; to Chalmette where Jackson had met the British; across the river to Algiers where plantations operated, to outward appearances, just as before the war; to the parish prison; to see a voodoo priestess; to the scene of a levee break below New Orleans. Late in April they took the yacht *Sappho* for a "marooning party" among the bayous and inlets and down the chain of Gulf islands to the mouth of the Mississippi. Forced by the weather to pull up alongside an uninhabited island for the night, they shot alligators and pelicans and ate gumbo which the French captain of the yacht made by his own recipe. Then Cable sang Creole songs and told, among others, the story of the flood at Last Island, which Lafcadio Hearn first heard from him and later elaborated into the prose gem *Chita*. Past the Chandeleurs Islands and Eads Port and Pilot Town and ready to turn northwest toward Barataria Bay, the marsh and bayou world of pirates and smugglers half a century earlier, they still had bad weather and so left the schooner to catch an inbound steamer to New Orleans.[2] Cable brought back descriptive notes made on scraps of paper with his future writing in mind.

Pennell's enthusiasm grew daily for the materials he had discovered for painting, so he said, just as Cable had discovered them for fiction. Though he met some of the Creoles through Cable, he could only observe them from a distance. "But alas I am entirely barred out," he wrote at the time, "for Cable the only 'Americain' down here who knows them is the most cordially hated little man in New Orleans, and all on account of the *Grandissimes;* and so he can do nothing with the better class." But to Pennell it was enough to draw the buildings and patios and ironwork that were before him everywhere in the Vieux Carré. "I am trying and with some success," he wrote Drake, "to get Cable from his restorations as he calls them and showing him that the material around us is of more value than anything we can make up." He planned further collaboration. For one thing, he made a dozen full-page etchings of the houses in Cable's stories, and when he was back east early in May they were accepted for publication in the *Century* along with a paragraph on each to be written by Cable. But they were not published in quite that way. Another scheme was for him and Cable to tour the West Indies early the next year and supply the *Century* with an illustrated travel account. The editors approved, and Cable was tempted but finally decided not to go. He proposed that Hearn go in

[2] The excursion was reported in the *Times-Democrat*, April 27, 1882.

his place, but the editors chose to cancel the tour. Pennell sailed for
Europe instead to illustrate Howells's articles on Tuscany for the
Century.

Like King, Champney, Redwood, and Waring before him, Pennell
had grown at once into admiration and affection for Cable. Their meetings afterward were the occasions for joking and hilarity, and they corresponded occasionally, Pennell often recalling his visits on Eighth Street
and their Sunday mornings at church, illustrating every sheet with appropriate sketches. In his autobiography, *Adventures of an Illustrator,*
written almost half a century later, he recalled pleasantly his collaboration with Cable and said it was as interesting as any work he ever did.

At the end of April Mark Twain came to New Orleans. He had
decided to revisit the Mississippi and to supplement the earlier magazine
articles "Old Times on the Mississippi" with enough chapters to make
a volume. Early on April 28 he arrived with a stenographer and James
R. Osgood and spent the day driving through the old city. He wrote
in *Life on the Mississippi,* published the next year:

> The party had the privilege of idling through this ancient quarter of New
> Orleans with the South's finest literary genius, the author of "The Gran-
> dissimes." In him the South has found a masterly delineator of its interior
> life and its history. . . .
> With Mr. Cable along to see for you, and describe and explain and il-
> luminate, a jog through that old quarter is a vivid pleasure. And you have
> a vivid *sense* as of unseen or dimly seen things—vivid, and yet fitful and
> darkling.

In the late afternoon they drove to West End by the swamp road
and dined on a veranda at the edge of Lake Pontchartrain. They had
as the chief dish "the renowned fish called pompano," Mark wrote,
"delicious as the less criminal forms of sin." The next afternoon they
attended a mule race held to raise funds for the Southern Art Union,
of which Cable was elected an honorary member a few days later.
Mark said he enjoyed it more than any race he had ever witnessed—
except of course a steamboat race. He liked the drilling of a feminine
"broom brigade" at the Washington Artillery building, but he thought a
cockfight, the first he had ever seen, an "inhuman sort of entertainment." On Sunday he heard Dr. Palmer at the First Presbyterian
Church, just as he used to do, he told a reporter.[3] Perhaps Cable took
him to other services during the day at his own church on Prytania

---

[3] *Ibid.,* April 29. From April 27, the day before their arrival, this paper reported
fully the activities of the visitors. Chapters XLI-LI of *Life on the Mississippi* contain
Mark Twain's report of this visit to New Orleans.

Street, for Joseph Pennell recalled years later that Mark had said of his Sunday with Cable, "I got nearer to Heaven than I hope I ever shall again." But early Sunday morning Joel Chandler Harris had arrived from Atlanta to join the group, none of whom had met him before. On Monday afternoon the party was gathered in Cable's study. It was a picture to remember, said the *Times-Democrat* the next day. The fragrance of roses drifted through the open window. On Uncle Remus's knee was a child of three, and around him were Cable's other children and Nettie's. Uncle Remus would not read his stories aloud, and so Mark and Cable, after reading each something of his own, had to introduce Brer Rabbit and bring the occasion to a climax with the Tar Baby story.

The gathering was continued through the evening at the home of Cable's friend James B. Guthrie, with a dozen other guests added. Guthrie read from Shakespeare, and his two children gave the balcony scene from *Romeo and Juliet*. Mark Twain read from *The Innocents Abroad* and added unpublished accounts of his travels in Europe. On the following evening, after Harris had departed, Major E. A. Burke, state treasurer and manager of the *Times-Democrat,* was host at John's Restaurant, where the pompano was again served, in "his last possible perfection," Mark said. Again the music, song, story, and repartee continued until nearly midnight. The newspaper reported that Mark liked especially Cable's dialect songs.

Mark Twain departed on May 6, a passenger on the new *City of Baton Rouge,* of which Horace Bixby, his old teacher in the pilot house, was captain. In the *Times-Democrat* of the next day was a report signed "Tableau" of a young man who managed to get an introduction to Mark Twain just before the boat left the dock and said, "I have read all of your writings Mr. Twain, but I think I like the Heathen Chinee the best of them all." There may have been others present who knew how Mark Twain stormed when he was thus confused with Bret Harte but it is easy to believe that Cable had a hand in getting the incident reported if not indeed in staging it, especially in view of the fact that he retold it twenty-three years later when he rose in his turn to speak at the banquet in New York celebrating Mark Twain's seventieth birthday,[4] and alluded to it after another five years at the memorial service for Mark Twain held by the American Academy and the National Institute of Arts and Letters.[5]

[4] Reported in *Harper's Weekly,* XLIX (Dec. 23, 1905), 1888-89.
[5] See *Proceedings* of the American Academy and National Institute, New York, [1911], III, 22; reprinted with other papers read at the memorial service in an issue of the

That Mark Twain had enjoyed his stay in New Orleans he made amply clear in *Life on the Mississippi*. He was kinder in describing the city than was his custom. He pronounced Harris "the only master the country has produced" in writing Negro dialect. Cable, he said, "is the only master in the writing of French dialects that the country has produced; and he reads them to perfection," and in the portions Cable had read from the new novel he was writing he found the same mastery of German dialect. Cable and Harris merited his praise especially because they did not write "in the Southern style," which he liked to credit to the vogue of Sir Walter Scott. But he had expressed earlier his admiration of Cable's writing. After reading *Madame Delphine*, he had written the author on July 17 of the year before, "the charm of it, & the pain of it, & 'the deep music of it are still pulsing through me. I could echo Howells's strong admiration, now, if he were here." At another time, March 7, 1882, Howells wrote Cable: "Yesterday I was at Mark Twain's and we read aloud from the Grandissimes. . . . Clemens and I went about talking Creole all day." And years afterward Howells recalled Mark's rapture when he first read *Old Creole Days* and especially "the thrilling force" with which he read from "Jean-ah Poquelin."[6]

At the middle of June, six weeks after Mark Twain's visit, Waldemir Kowaledsky, professor of law and national institutions at the University of Moscow, called on Cable, bringing an introduction from Boyesen, to whom he had been recommended, in Boyesen's phrase, by no less a man than Turgenev. He found Cable playing with his children in the yard. As they rode the cars to the lake for a swim, Kowaledsky told of the European literary scene and of his acquaintance with Turgenev. Cable introduced his guest to Creole acquaintances on the beach, remarking that one and then another were living types of his characters. Kowaledsky visited in Cable's home, bought his books, and was convinced that he had met one of the greatest American novelists. After returning to Russia he wrote for the *Viestnik Evropii* of the following May a detailed account of his visit to Cable, after the same journal had carried a translation of "Belles Demoiselles Plantation" in its March issue. He

---

Academy Notes and Monographs series, 1922, p. 75. For other details of this visit of Mark Twain's in New Orleans, see my article "Notes on Mark Twain in New Orleans," *McNeese Review*, VI (1954), 10-22.

[6] *Literary Friends and Acquaintance*, pp. 403-4. The letters from Mark Twain and Howells are at Tulane University. The Mark Twain letters to Cable have been printed in Guy A. Cardwell, *Twins of Genius* (East Lansing, Michigan, 1953); the Howells letters in Kjell Ekström, "The Cable-Howells Correspondence," *Studia Neophilologica*, XXII (1950), 48-61.

discussed Cable as belonging to the literary family of Turgenev, in his combination of artistry and realism and his total lack of affectation.

Extreme as were Kowaledsky's compliments, his article proved embarrassing to Cable when the *Critic* of July 28, 1883, printed a translation. For one thing it illustrated the antagonism of the Creoles for Cable by saying that he had been proposed by the French consul D'Abzac to the Athénée Louisianais, a society founded in 1876 to foster the preservation of French culture in New Orleans, and had been denied membership, and also that the president of the Athénée had refused in Kowaledsky's presence to shake hands with Cable. A Creole claiming to be in position to know, Henri Pene Du Bois, wrote to the *Critic* of August 25 denying the truth of these statements. More seriously, however, the article attributed to Cable an assertion that Boyesen was a learned man but not an artist. In a letter to the *Critic* on August 7, printed also on August 25, Cable denied any recollection of making the assertions and added unreserved statements of his respect for Boyesen's mind and work and his gratitude for the early encouragement Boyesen had given him.

There can be no doubt that Kowaledsky's article had at least a slight cooling effect on the friendship of Cable and Boyesen, but before it appeared, their correspondence had almost ceased, naturally enough, since they met at intervals in New York, where Boyesen had joined the faculty of Columbia University, and since Boyesen's encouragement was less appropriate than it had been in 1877. Almost from the opening of their friendship, furthermore, Boyesen had sensed, as he clearly indicated, that Cable wrote somewhat reluctantly, in part because of the press for time, no doubt, in part apparently because he was unable to compliment Boyesen's writings as freely as their relations seemed to demand, and also because after they had met he found himself drawn less to Boyesen than formerly. Even so, there is no indication that their mutual respect actually lessened, or that Cable ever appreciated less heartily than he had indicated in writing to the *Critic* the generous recognition Boyesen had given him in the beginning of his literary career.

Another visitor in June, 1882, was Oscar Wilde, who came to lecture at the Grand-Opera House and drew in the local press the same sarcastically unfavorable comment he encountered elsewhere on his tour. When he was entertained at the salon of Mary Ashley Townsend, a local literary favorite, Cable was invited with the assurance that Wilde admired his works and wished to meet him. Wilde wrote him from Galveston on June 20 setting a date on his return trip for the "expedition" they had planned, possibly in search of a voodoo dance, which he had read about in Cable's books and wished to see. The Cable children remembered that he came to Eighth Street, with his long hair, velvet coat, and knee breeches. One of them remembered too that after his departure a neighbor referred to "that fool Oscar Wilde." Cable's reply was, "He's no fool."[7]

At the opening of 1882, Cable's first year without a salary, he and his friends at New York realized he must make every stroke count if he hoped to live from his pen. Throughout the year, however, he shunted so much of his energy into a local reform endeavor that his pen had by no means a fair trial at supporting him.

On his trip east in June of the preceding year, while still secretary of the grand jury, he had taken a commission from the mayor, Joseph A. Shakespeare, and had inspected the Boston city jail, the state prison at Concord, and the insane asylum at Hartford to gain ideas that might be used locally. The comparison he thus gained made him the more astonished at conditions in the local public institutions, and in no mincing words the report he wrote for the jury (printed in the *Democrat* of June 30) described conditions in the jails and the asylum, for which he said the public could not escape the blame. The jury had accomplished something by calling the attention of officials to particular abuses, but it was being discharged with the worst of the horrors yet untouched, and its report would be ignored, as had been true of many others before it. "Against such treatment of matters of vital public concern," his report concluded, "this grand jury begs leave most respectfully to enter its protest before this honorable court, the city administration, the public press, and the community at large."[8]

This sentence pointed the course Cable would take. He first enlisted James B. Guthrie and the two other friends to draft an ordinance setting up a self-perpetuating, nonpolitical Board of Prisons and Asylums Commissioners whose purpose would be to study public institutions and propose improvements. Approved by Mayor Shakespeare and grudgingly by J. V. Guillotte, Administrator of Public Works and Public Buildings, who had authority over the insane asylum and who was sensitive because of a recent scandal involving the male attendants in the women's wards, and supported by the newspapers, the ordinance was passed early in November. To assist the ordinance to pass, Cable had listed himself and five others, a physician among them and his friends Adolph Schreiber and Perry Nugent, as willing to serve on the com-

[7] Dennis, *The Tail of the Comet*, p. 34.

[8] For this and Cable's other reform work in New Orleans, see my article "George W. Cable's Beginnings as a Reformer," *Journal of Southern History*, XVII (May, 1951), 136-61.

mission. Later they withdrew and fifteen other members were appointed, with Hugh Miller Thompson, pastor of Trinity Episcopal Church, as chairman. Cable believed the commissioners would be as ineffectual as newspapers and special committees had been in the past unless they had a constituency who would feel an obligation to support them. For his next step he gained a powerful ally; Major E. A. Burke, editor of the *Times-Democrat* and state treasurer, employed him to direct his paper's campaign for prison reform, and to write on the subject. The issue of Christmas Day carried two articles by Cable and an editorial which said that the considerable progress already made was "the outcome of the laborious and for a long time unaided efforts of Mr. George W. Cable." As explained in one of these first articles, Cable proposed to organize a large citizens' group without dues or specified duties except to support the commission. As a token of the backing already assured, a list of some twenty-five members was appended, among whom were Charles Gayarré, S. S. Prentiss, E. A. Burke, the Reverend Hugh Miller Thompson, C. Harrison Parker of the *Picayune,* and H. G. Hester and Thomas L. Airy, secretary and president of the Cotton Exchange. The title of the second article in the same issue, "Our Vice Mills and Jails for the Aged and Insane," suggests the slant and the vigor of the attack.

When the Board of Prisons and Asylums Commissioners met to organize on January 2, Cable was asked to report on his earlier investigations and to outline a procedure to follow. The board voted to commend his work and to endorse his plans. Everyone was invited to join the supporting organization who had any interest in seeing improvement, and on January 8 there were almost two hundred members. The newspaper supplemented its endorsement of Cable's program by reporting almost daily some outrage at the jail or the police stations which underscored the need for public intercession. Until the citizens' group was formally organized in March, Cable published an article every two weeks, each accompanied by an editorial recommending it. Once the editor compared him to Charles Dickens and Charles Reade and added, "We shall not give up this question until the monstrous wrongs that Mr. Cable has demonstrated are corrected and set right." The seven articles were a pitiless exposure of local conditions given perspective by reference to conditions the author had seen elsewhere and to theoretical treatments published in Europe as well as America. Their accusation was less against the officials of the institutions than against public apathy. In writing of the parish prison he alluded to matters that would soil the page if he recorded them, and of the insane asylum he said there were rumors of an inside history that would "bring the blush to the cheek of a murderer." He marshaled horrifying details of facilities and management, but his main thesis was that the public was responsible and was itself ultimately the sufferer.

The Prisons and Asylums Aid Association was formed at Grunewald Hall on March 7. Its list of some 250 members reads like a directory of the city's most prominent doctors, ministers, journalists, and business-men. W. R. Lyman, president of the Crescent Insurance Company, was elected president; Cable, secretary; Adolph Schreiber, one of the vice-presidents. The constitution and aims, adopted as Cable had drafted them, envisaged not only better buildings and better care of the in-mates, but also houses of industry and juvenile homes and employment aid for released prisoners. A further purpose was to assemble and dis-seminate information on existing conditions elsewhere and on develop-ments in institutional management.

Cable served without pay, but funds were raised to hire an assistant secretary, Dr. I. T. Payne, who earlier had written on prison reform for the *Picayune*. They collected information from all the parishes of the state, most other states, and several foreign countries; they became stu-dents of subjects ranging from prison architecture to juvenile delin-quency. At the monthly meetings of the executive committee Cable reported on the work, proposed further action, suggested policies, and presented ordinances he had drafted, with the aid of lawyers in the asso-ciation, for submitting to the city council. The membership of the asso-ciation met only once a year; its committees made proposals to the appropriate officials, and supplied the newspapers with material for reports and editorials.

It was the bludgeoning publicity in the papers which gave force to the whole program and caused matrons to be employed at the asylum and in the police department and sanitation to be improved at the public institutions. But these were only the by-products of more serious accomplishments, such as removal of one of the orphanages from a swamp to higher ground and the allocation of $200,000 for a new parish prison. But the greatest achievement was the closing of the municipal insane asylum, which Cable called "a chamber of horrors," the "abode of unutterable and innumerable miseries," and the removal of the inmates to new quarters provided by the legislature at the state asylum in Jackson.

When the association held its first anniversary meeting on January 8, 1883, it could be proud of its accomplishments and encouraged for the future, Lyman said in his address as president. But the knowledge of what the conditions had been remained discomforting. Hugh Miller

Thompson, speaking in effect for the local churches as well as the Board of Commissioners, sounded a note that had occurred repeatedly in Cable's articles of the year past—he could only condemn a society which produced the inmates of the prison and the asylum and then provided for them in the manner exhibited in New Orleans. For all his modesty in lauding the work of others and giving credit to the newspapers, Cable's listeners knew the greatest credit belonged to him. He was pleased with what had been done, though much of what was attempted had been defeated, as he wrote later in "My Politics," by a "ring of sheriffs, deputies and their confederates, whose pockets were directly involved." The reform work of the year had meant a sacrifice to his literary work, but he had undertaken it knowingly and as he announced the program for the future he gave no hint of slacking off. He continued to write for the *Times-Democrat* on specific matters as they came up, and during 1883 he drafted and pushed through to adoption several ordinances, including one for complete regulation of prison management.

Instead of coasting with the program, as might have been expected of a man with his need for remunerative work, Cable found himself drawn deeper and deeper into similar commitments. He was on the library committee of the Southern Art Union; member of the Louisiana Historical Society from its chartering in 1877, he worked in its program to collect and preserve local records. On one day he was asked to help organize three civic groups, and in the launching of one of them, a conference of charities, he addressed two meetings, served as chairman of the committee on organization and later on the board of directors. Besides the local success and the local acclaim, other circumstances encouraged him to continue the work he had begun. He was made a corresponding member of the New York Charities Aid Association and on August 15, 1883, was elected to the American Association for the Advancement of Science. He visited prisons and asylums whenever he went east, and in New York on March 26, 1883, he talked on prison reform before the Congregational Club. From meeting Morris K. Jesup and William E. Dodge two weeks later and finding that they, surrounded by such wealth as he could scarcely comprehend, shared his devotion to benevolent work, and from visiting with them the 5-Points House of Industry and the congregation of the poor at the Cooper Institute, he drew added assurance.

But the work already done only impressed Cable with the amount that remained. Questionnaires he sent to all the parishes of the state revealed that the Orleans parish prison had its equals elsewhere. Of greater importance, however, he came to realize that improving the parish jails was only nibbling at the thin edges, for the reports he had assembled from state penitentiaries told—or rather hinted at—a far more shocking story, that of the leasing of convicts in the South to private contractors. In September, 1882, he was invited to address the National Conference of Charities and Correction at the 1883 meeting in Louisville. Believing the occasion demanded taking his campaign to a larger area and against a greater evil, he accepted the invitation and included writing the address among his other tasks for the next year.

In the early months of 1882 Cable met only discouragement on the revised history of New Orleans and his novel. By the middle of the year the history was being rounded into a form acceptable to his editors, but the novel had many months yet of revising and rewriting.

The editors of the *Century* were at no time enthusiastic about the history articles, but saw them primarily as a means of increasing Cable's income. When they saw the manuscript in February as it had been revised from the census volume, and when they saw it again in April, further revised, it would not do. It was accurate history but lacked the picturesqueness, the lightness, the humor, the characterization which his readers expected. Cable was willing to compromise on the revision and the editors agreed to run six articles, but apparently only after Colonel Waring had acted again to benefit his friend, for they had received a request from J. R. Osgood to be allowed to publish the entire history as it had appeared in the census report. The disagreement between the author and his editors was simply that he considered the work a history and valued most its completeness and accuracy, whereas they had the needs of a magazine in mind and wanted him to single out the odd and the picturesque for elaboration in the manner of his fiction.

The articles, each with its separate title, ran in the *Century* from January to July, 1883, skipping May. They were illustrated by some fifty of Pennell's drawings. Book publication, in the fall of 1884, was by Scribner rather than the Century Company as first planned. In passing from the original manuscript to the census report, to the magazine series, and finally to book form, the history underwent sweeping alterations. Waring cut out the meticulous documentation and part of the interpretation. For the magazine Cable sacrificed the connecting portions and made independent essays on the Creoles as they were confronted by war, flood, and plague. In further revision for book publication, he defined the Creoles more fully; he restored the account of the Battle of New Orleans which had been omitted from the magazine, and thus had a continuous history of Creole New Orleans from the founding to the Civil War, supplemented by chapters on the city at the time he was writing. Thus *The Creoles of Louisiana* became finally a delineation of its subjects by the most thorough student of their culture they had yet had.

Cable once said he welcomed this opportunity to chronicle the past of the Creoles so that he could make clear his feelings toward a people he had been accused of maligning in his fiction. The successive revisions show, in fact, a conscious effort not to be unjust or unkind. In the final version he took care to cite their virtues and to balance their faults with shortcomings of the Anglo-Americans, in historical perspective or in his own time. In a concluding section written for the book he had the obvious purpose of displaying the special accomplishments of the Creoles, crediting them with mollifying their earlier faults, and he hoped they would never lose their individuality or allow the encroaching Anglo-American civilization to destroy their character, manners, and culture.

A Creole not oversensitive might find, actually, that Cable came closer to violating accuracy through sympathy than through severity, but there was still room, to be sure, for a Creole to be displeased if he insisted on unqualified reverence for his ancestors. For even while praising the earlier Creoles for their assistance in the American Revolution, to cite one instance, his greatest praise was for the later, Americanized Creoles. Actually his strictures on the *Américains* were no less severe, and in the matters he found worth heaviest condemnation both shared responsibility. But Cable felt no need to placate the Anglo-Americans and so left them to shoulder heavy responsibility for the backwardness of his own time.

The Creoles of Louisiana received only brief notices in the national magazines, in which as a rule it was welcomed as an accurate history of the people Cable's readers had already met in his fiction.[9] In New Orleans the prevailing note was of compliment. At the time the census report was issued in 1882, an editorial in the *Times-Democrat* on April 10 dealt principally with the Creole angle and asserted that Cable understood the city thoroughly, "not only its history, but its social life, its people and all its peculiarities." The newspapers announced each installment in the magazine and congratulated the Creoles for having such a masterful and sympathetic historian.[10] The *Picayune,* for example, on January 11, 1885, said, "Reading this book one cannot doubt the fondness and affection, whether returned or not, of Cable for the Creoles." Edward Everett Hale, who had met Cable on a visit to New

---

[9] See George Parsons Lathrop in the *Book-Buyer,* I (Dec., 1884), 277-79.
[10] See the *Times-Democrat,* Dec. 8, 1882; Jan. 3, 17, 28, Feb. 19, 1883.

Orleans in 1876, wrote chiefly about this book in an article in the *Critic* of September 12, 1885, "Mr. Cable and the Creoles." He said: "If his Creole friends are not satisfied this time, both with the historian and the history, they must indeed be hard to please."

On one episode of the history, however, Cable was challenged. His assertion that General James Wilkinson was guilty of conniving in the late 1780's to deliver territory of the United States to Spain was attacked in the *Times-Democrat* of April 15, 1883, by James Wilkinson, descendant of the general. Wilkinson's language and his charges, unencumbered with documentary support, were the severest yet aimed at Cable outside the editorial columns of *L'Abeille* and the *Aboo and Caboo* lampoon. Cable replied in the same newspaper on May 13, supporting his position chiefly by references to Gayarré, "that accomplished Creole gentleman and Spanish and English scholar," who had written "the best history of our state extant." Gayarré felt obliged to step in after Wilkinson had said in a rejoinder that his history showed the "greatest bias and prejudice." In long articles on May 20 and June 3 he adduced the full evidence of the Spanish documents. A query in his first article seemed to reflect a pique on a different score. "Why wait," he asked, "before taking offense, until Mr. Cable had copied my statements and republished them as his own?" Cable was distressed, even though he believed his high esteem of Gayarré was returned so genuinely that no accusation was actually intended. He wrote to Marion Baker on May 21 explaining how generously he had cited Gayarré in footnotes of his original manuscript and also in a particular declaration of indebtedness, all of which the editor had deleted. He asked Baker to broach the matter to Gayarré, who seems consciously then to have made amends, for in the second article his phrase was that Cable had quoted rather than copied from his history. Cable had expected no resentment from Gayarré, it is clear, and if Gayarré felt a pique, as apparently he did, he chose not to indicate it directly. Ironically both Gayarré and Cable were aligned in this instance against an American's charge that Cable's mission was to "pander and please" Northern readers—a charge which Père Rouquette had made earlier in his role of spokesman for the Creoles.

CHAPTER X

REFORMER AND READER ON THE NATIONAL STAGE

THE TUG-OF-WAR over the Creole history in the first half of 1882 paralleled a similar but longer and more painful struggle over the novel Cable was writing. The novel underwent much more drastic rebuilding than anything he had yet written; at one time Gilder was close to rejecting it outright and Cable considered turning to a different publisher.

When *The Grandissimes* was just beginning its serial run, Cable had proposed carrying some of the characters over into one or perhaps two more novels, but his editors discouraged the plan, for he seemingly would keep the f.m.c., and hence would extend the threads that had been most questionable in his first novel. Some months later he talked to Allen C. Redwood of building a story, probably a novelette, about the Orleans Parish Prison, employing a plot told him by Dr. D. Warren Brickell, colleague of Dr. Bruns and also physician of the Cable family. But he had made little progress by 1881, when he contracted for publication of a new novel.

The book was written—and rewritten—between late 1881 and the end of 1883. The fact that those years encompass the period of the author's prison reform work goes a good way in explaining the evolution and the nature of the book. At the opening of 1882, a month after he had left the counting-room, the manuscript reached New York, a novelette called *Bread*. To Gilder fell the task of writing for the editors on February 1, 1882, candidly and sorrowfully, as he said: It was a tract, "a 'demnition grind' without plot or artistic reason for being," loaded with moral obviousness. Disappointed as he was, for he seemed to doubt that Cable could redeem the story, Gilder added, "My dear fellow—I care more for your work than for any other writer of fiction who has written for this magazine"—a superlative indeed, since the comparison included not only Frank Stockton, Joel Chandler Harris, and Edward Eggleston, but also William Dean Howells, Henry James, and Mark Twain. The next day he wrote again, "Your recent exertions in the way of reform had to be worked off, I dare say, or worked up—in a book.... This is a study—of the question of charity."

As Gilder saw the new story, it violated the principles Cable had framed earlier in his letter to Boyesen—it smelled of the moral as small houses smell of dinner cooking in the kitchen, it attempted to spoon morals down the reader to distention. And it would have been surprising, in view of Cable's devotion at the time to social reform, if that devotion had not shown unfittingly through the fabric of his novel. Still, editors as uncomfortable as Gilder and Johnson in the vicinity of unpleasantness were hardly the best to pass on Cable's realistic studies of race antagonism, poverty, and penal barbarism. In his reading of *The Grandissimes* Johnson had seemed to want the impelling story without the iron-sinewed handling of social and moral problems which supplied its strength. Similarly Gilder seems to have wanted the charm of Cable's characters and dialect without the discomforting problems which would give them a reason for being in fiction. Allen Redwood, Marion Baker, and James Guthrie had reminded him that his literary talent was rarer and more valuable than his talent for organizing reform, but they never seriously attempted to dissuade him from his course. They knew that with the support of the most respected men of New Orleans he was accomplishing remarkable social reform, and that he would not pass up any means of advancing that cause. They knew also that the power of *The Grandissimes* and *Madame Delphine* rose in part from the humanitarian zeal that lay back of the pages.

Roswell Smith, himself devoted to idealistic reform through practical means, did not try to guide Cable away from didactic fiction. It was he who put in a word to save the new story. Though president of the Century Company, he apparently never questioned Gilder's decisions, but in this instance he interpreted Gilder's criticism so as to give Cable encouragement. In less than three weeks Cable was ready to rewrite the book, and when Gilder had the first installment again, this time entitled *Dr. Sevier,* he wired Cable, "Richard's himself again," and followed with a letter of enthusiastic praise. Gilder's enthusiasm and haste were no doubt prompted by Cable's letters to him and Johnson, while Roswell Smith was in Europe, saying that he was considering a change to another publisher; he mentioned specifically an offer of Albion Tourgée of the new weekly *Our Continent* to pay $7500 for a serial novel. But the novel was still a long way from the typesetters.

On June 28, 1882, a few days after Washington and Lee College had awarded him the honorary degree of Doctor of Letters, Cable delivered the commencement address before the literary societies at the University of Mississippi. His eight hundred listeners at the little town of Oxford could know from his first sentences that they were not to hear the usual harangue of sectional chauvinism and platitudes and that he did not expect them to accept all his ideas readily.[1] Speaking on "Literature in the Southern States," he said that because of the institution of slavery, "that crime against heaven and humanity," Southerners in the decades before the Civil War isolated themselves from outside thought and literature, and in the reading even of English books stopped at the year 1800. In consequence of this isolation and of the assumed obligation to defend slavery, only a few writers reached any stature. The fault lay in the slave society, for accomplishments in other directions, in politics and law, for example, left no doubt that ability was present.

It was "with tenderness and filial reverence," he affirmed, that he spoke of the South's "melancholy mistake." And when he came to speak of the period after the war, he spoke even more deferentially, for he must disturb the very hearthstones of his section:

Venerating the past as I must; honoring the graves of our fathers as I do; cherishing the memory of the intellectual giants whose bones lie under our sods, . . . what I would say then I say humbly and reverentially; it is this:—

When the whole intellectual energy of the southern states flew to the defence of that one institution which made us the South, we broke with human progress. We broke with the world's thought. We have not entirely in all things joined hands with it again. When we have done so we shall know it by this—there will be no South. . . . Let us hasten to be no longer a unique people.

The past generations, he continued, "would demand—they would have a right to demand, that, starting where they made their last camp, we should leave their unconscious errors behind and make new discoveries farther on, in justice and liberty and duty and all excellence, humbly mindful that they who shall come after us must do the same for us." But, "Have we the courage to be inconoclasts in our own homes?" As if to test for the answer, he named some ideas that must be pruned away:

The plantation idea is a semi-barbarism. It is the idea of the old South with merely the substitution of a negro tenantry for negro slaves. . . . Landlordism kept the South poor one century, and just as sure as it survives it will keep her poor another.

The idea of caste must also be sloughed away.

Why?—tell us why we should not send that unmanly and inhuman tyranny

[1] This manuscript speech, at Tulane University, is printed in my article "George W. Cable's Revolt against Literary Sectionalism," *Tulane Studies in English,* V (1955), 5-27.

back to India and Africa? Why should not that which we still call the "southern mind" rise to the moral dignity of distinguishing between man and man by such rules only as bear the strain of clear, conscientious logic? Why should we, who are given minds, still expatiate upon our *instincts* and go on holding our unproven *"therefores"* at the expense of our fellow-creatures and in the face of the world's best enlightenment? Is that the "southern mind"? Is the "southern instinct" not cunning enough to snuff out the stupid wickedness of exalting and abusing our fellow humans class by class and race by race instead of man by man?

To the question "Who—if not the intelligent—are to rule?" he answered,

All! All are to rule. That order of society is best, and that order of society only is American, where the intelligent are so hemmed in with the unintelligent that they cannot afford to let them rest in their unintelligence. . . . We cannot suppose that our community could hold a servile race in domestic subjection for a century and a half without producing a more lasting effect on the master race than a few subsequent years of partial change could dissipate. The statement is almost axiomatic. Hence search should be made for the flaws that must in that long period have crept into many of our views and into our temper. And who should we expect to do this? Certainly not outsiders. Certainly ourselves.

Back in New Orleans Cable wrote Mark Twain on June 29 that there had been "frequent interruptions of applause" and he was "said to have scored a decided success." He was told when he left the stage, he noted afterward in "My Politics," that five years earlier he would not have been allowed to speak as he had done of slavery and caste and the plantation system. For his listeners included the governor and the chief justice of the state, and the parents who attended were mainly plantation owners in the home state of Jefferson Davis, who was then defending the Lost Cause in print. The fact that his utterances were not generally challenged in the press but were highly commended in some papers testifies that his sincerity and his closely reasoned presentation were respected—perhaps also that the South was less sensitive to such criticism than it became a few years later.

Perhaps through Marion Baker's concern to make the speech wholly acceptable locally, the report in the *Times-Democrat* on June 29 passed lightly over Cable's strictures on caste and the plantation system and the effects of slavery on the ruling class. The same paper quoted other journals showing that the address was reported and praised editorially in the region. Editors at Oxford and Jackson called it one of the finest ever delivered at the university. The *Memphis Appeal* wrote on July 1: "He speaks with the independence of a brave thinker and pleads eloquently and sensibly. . . . Conceived in the right spirit—a thoroughly patriotic one—. . . [the speech] will encourage merit and rebuke assumption and ignorance." The Boston *Literary World* of July 15 applauded the call for a national rather than a sectional literature, and added after summarizing the address that Cable's words were "not limited in their application to the South alone."[2]

At the first of August Cable spent two weeks with his family at Ocean Springs and later in the month he went with Marion Baker to Grand Isle. On September 19 he entrained for New York, going by way of Chicago to stop over with his brother James, who was employed there in a railroad office. In New York he settled for a month in a room on West Twenty-Second Street and discovered that he could turn out work at a rate he had not found possible in New Orleans. He liked to walk on the streets in the evening and in the early morning to ride the ferry to the New Jersey shore and back. Among the letters he wrote on Sundays were long ones to his Sunday school at home.

The fate of the new novel had to be determined. Several evenings he read the manuscript to Gilder and had more encouragement than in the months past, but he had the torture of asking for money. He must have a monthly income. "If you were a little 100 pound man," he wrote Louise, "with a wife and four children dependent on your health and wits, do you think you'd worry? You couldn't afford to; you'd *have* to keep cool." He missed some sleep, he confessed, but it was in his nature to write, "Let us hope, & be bright, grateful to God, frugal, contented, living on what we have—not hope for."

[2] Notes on this address constructed by David H. Bishop from the recollections fifty years afterward of four men who were in the audience report that Cable could not be heard in the back of the hall and that the chancellor of the University, General A. P. Stewart, interrupted him to ask for attention; also that after Cable had concluded, the Rev. C. K. Marshall, of Vicksburg, rose to rebuke him for his anti-Southern views and in particular his disparagement of old-style Southern oratory ("A Commencement in the Eighties: George W. Cable's First Public Address," *Southwest Review*, XVIII, Jan., 1933, 108-14). The divergences among the four men's memories and also the reports in the newspapers of the time throw doubt on their dependability. Furthermore, Marshall was on the program to make awards to two students for declamation and quite plausibly spoke on S. S. Prentiss, whom he had known, and on the methods of oratory. This speech may have been remembered as a rebuttal to Cable, but since he had not criticized Southern oratory and in fact had named Prentiss in praise, it seems likely that after fifty years the four men reconstructed the occasion in the light of the Southern attitude toward Cable later when he had become the champion of Negro rights. In an article on "The First Public Address of George W. Cable, Southern Liberal" (*Washington University Studies*, N.S., Language and Literature, No. 20, 1951, pp. 67-76), Guy A. Cardwell has discussed the importance of this address in relation to Cable's literary and social work, having at hand not the address itself, however, but the article by Bishop and the reports in the *Times-Democrat* and the *Literary World*.

When Roswell Smith had agreed to monthly advances and Cable had $250 to send home he directed that $150 of it be used to pay his subscription to the church debt and that part of the remainder be used to pay the rent on the house across the street. He could see a way now to pay his taxes and the interest on three loans and to get through the next year, but it would be on advances. An unexpected prospect came late in the month: Gilder took him to Baltimore to meet President Daniel Coit Gilman and arrangements were begun for a series of lectures at Johns Hopkins University the following spring at a fee of about a thousand dollars.

Still, neither the work nor the financial worries spoiled his pleasure during the month in New York. It was a tonic to see Pennell, Osgood, Champney, Waring, and Boyesen, in addition to Scribner and the staff of the Century Company. He spent a Sunday at Mrs. Herrick's at Bergen Point again and he dined with the Boyesens. He was present when the Author's Club was formed and there or elsewhere met E. C. Stedman, Brander Matthews, Noah Brooks, Lawrence Hutton, Mary Mapes Dodge, editor of *St. Nicholas,* George Parsons Lathrop, and Teakle Wallis, the Baltimore poet. At the Gilders' he met Joseph Jefferson, then midway in his career of almost forty years playing Rip Van Winkle on the stages of America and Europe, and had a three-hours' conversation with him on the theater which Gilder thought the most interesting he had ever heard. One evening, when Jefferson and Mme Modjeska and her husband were guests, the talk was on Shakespeare. Another time John Burroughs was present to tap his own knowledge of birds and to welcome Cable's account of the mockingbird.

Beyond all comparison, though, were three evenings with Clara Louise Kellogg, the operatic soprano. The company on the first evening, at the Gilders', included the artist Walter Shirlaw and the editors of the *Critic,* Joseph and Jeanette Gilder, but when conversation had given way to music, Miss Kellogg and Cable shared honors. Accompanying herself on the banjo, she sang Negro melodies. His Creole songs "Pov' Piti' Momselle Zizi" and "Ah! Suzette" took her fancy, and the steamboat roustabout "Rock Me, Julie, Rock Me" she had him sing over and over. The second evening he described in a letter home on October 21:

Spent a glorious evening yesterday with the 4 Gilders, Johnson, Ed Holland, Lathrop, and Clara Louise Kellogg. Ah, me! Ah, me!! Such singing! . . . She acted as she sang. . . . O my girl! what a sight it was. . . . She sang again some negro melodies. Then they had me sing my Creole &

African things. Some came back that I had forgotten. She sang "Hey, Yea, roll a man down."

Well, well, I feel as though I had spent the night in fairy land.

The third evening was at Miss Kellogg's home. She sang Cable's songs in similar gatherings, Gilder reported, after Cable had gone back south.

Before starting home on October 27, Cable paid a quick visit to Hartford and Boston, on which Mark Twain reported to Howells, then on his way to Italy:

Cable has been here, creating worshipers on all hands. He is a marvelous talker on a deep subject. I do not see how even Spencer could unwind a thought more smoothly or orderly, and do it in a cleaner, clearer, crisper English. He astounded Twichell with his faculty. You know when it comes down to moral honesty, limpid innocence, and utterly blemishless piety, the Apostles were mere policemen to Cable; so with this in mind you must imagine him at a midnight dinner in Boston the other night, where we gathered around the board of the Summerset Club; Osgood, full, Boyle O'Reilly, full, Fairchild responsively loaded, and Aldrich and myself possessing the floor and properly fortified. Cable told Mrs. Clemens when we returned here, that he seemed to have been entertaining himself with horses, and had a dreamy idea that he must have gone to Boston in a cattle-car. It was a very large time. He called it an orgy. And no doubt it was, viewed from his standpoint.[3]

The final arrangement with President Gilman was for Cable to give six lectures from March 5 to 16, 1883. In giving an address on January 8, his annual report to the Prisons and Asylums Aid Association, he tested his timing and his delivery. With the encouragement especially of Roswell Smith he was thinking of the lecture platform to supplement his income. Smith thought lecturing the best paid literary work he could hope to find and had already proposed to Osgood that they get Cable an appointment to lecture at the Lowell Institute in Boston.

The Johns Hopkins lectures were on "The Relations of Literature to Modern Society"—a large subject, Cable said, but he found "the ocean as easy to swim in as a pond." The six titles were:

(1) The Necessities from Which Literature Springs.

(2) Its Influence on Man's Public Life.

(3) Its Operations and Effects in the Private Life.

(4) The Attitudes of Modern Society toward Literature.

(5) The Reciprocal Duties of Literature and Society.

(6) The Literary Art and the Artist.

[3] Nov. 4, 1882; in *Mark Twain's Letters*, ed. A. B. Paine (New York, [1917]), I, 426-27.

Cable was disappointed with his performance in the first lecture, though he had held the perfect attention of an audience overflowing into the aisles of the largest auditorium available, Johns Hopkins Hall, which was made to seat 250 for the occasion. He studied the lectures "dreadfully hard," he wrote Louise, and he prayed that he might "speak to the profit of souls as well as minds." At the end of the series he felt he had finished the greatest effort of his life. The press reports were favorable. "Coming after James Russell Lowell, Francis J. Child and other scholars from the great Eastern centres of learning," one reporter said, "it is the more gratifying that Mr. Cable should have scored a greater success before a Baltimore audience than either of his distinguished predecessors."[4] The Baltimore *Sun,* March 20, considered his lectures on the level of those delivered earlier by Lowell and Sidney Lanier.

More tangible evidence of success came in the invitation to stay over and give a reading from his books on March 19. "For the first time in my life, I ask you," he wrote Louise, "are you not proud of your old boy? Here I hold the hall *full* every other day for two weeks on a general subject not of momentary interest, and before the term is up am appointed (by request out of the audience) to add another evening to the six."[5] This time people stood jammed even in the vestibule beside the stage and others were turned away. When Cable sat down at the end of an hour, Gilman rose and said, "That's nothing, go on." The program had been announced as readings in Creole dialects illustrated by "historical and linguistic comments." Except while he read the scene of Bras Coupé's death, the house was in almost incessant laughter. When he turned to Gilman, seated on the platform, and asked in the words of Colossus as he read "Posson Jone'," " 'Ain't dat so, boss?' " the house "roared and applauded to the echo," he wrote home. To Mark Twain he wrote the next day, in a manner which was natural to him and which he regularly fell into in writing to his friend of solemn jest, "It's touchingly gratifying to hear them laugh & applaud where nothing funny is intended." "Since the days when Charles Dickens read his own droll stories," the Baltimore *American* said the next day, "it is doubtful whether any novelist has appeared before an American audience so well prepared to interpret his own writings as Mr. Cable." The same reporter spoke of Cable's hearty praise of the

[4] *Times-Democrat,* March 25, 1883.

[5] In a short note on these lectures, "George W. Cable Becomes a Professional Reader," *American Literature,* XXIII (Jan., 1952), 467-70, Guy A. Cardwell mistakenly concludes that the number was reduced to five, and also that Cable read twice more before leaving Baltimore.

Creole society and another remarked on "his perfect command of the Creole dialect."[6]

President Gilman wrote for the *Critic* of March 24 his own glowing report of the lectures and particularly the reading:

The author's exact reproduction of the various dialects with which he has made us familiar, his simple, unaffected and yet truly dramatic gestures, his pithy illustrative sentences, and his own keen enjoyment of the scenes he was portraying, were delightful. He was as natural, modest, and free as if he were talking upon his own balcony to a company of familiar friends. . . . His comments on the historical and actual Creole society were so appreciative and commendatory that the most sensitive Creole could not take offense at his photographic pictures.

Besides Gilman and several of the faculty, others in Baltimore entertained Cable, among them Teakle Wallis. At the dedication of a tablet to Sidney Lanier Cable spoke briefly. He found time to talk with some of the students, to attend church and Bible class, and to visit an insane asylum in the interest of the Prisons and Asylums Aid Association.

Roswell Smith had already enlisted Cable's friends to sponsor an experimental lecture at Hartford. Mark Twain managed the local arrangements and wrote advance notices in the Hartford *Courant*. The formal invitation carried sixteen signatures, headed by Mark Twain's and Charles Dudley Warner's.[7] Cable first suggested a lecture on "Creole Women," but after the success of his reading in Baltimore, Warner and Mark Twain urged him to repeat it at Hartford as the surest way to gain favorable publicity.

On his way north Cable stopped at New York on March 22 to prepare for his Hartford appearance and to address the Congregational Club on prison reform, as Roswell Smith had arranged. At New Haven, where he went with introductions from President Gilman, he found himself again in the role of a celebrity and met the president and half a dozen professors of Yale University and also the distinguished surgeon Francis Bacon. After he had talked, on his first visit to Bacon's home, of the prison reform work in Louisiana, Mrs. Bacon exclaimed, "O, Mr. Cable, come to Connecticut and teach us how to reform." Thus opened a long friendship with the Bacons.

At Hartford he was the guest of the George Warners. There were enough miscarriages in the plans to let Mark Twain do the storming he enjoyed. Once when he was striding up and down the room scolding,

6 *Times-Democrat*, March 25, 1883.
7 Printed along with Cable's acceptance in the Hartford *Courant*, March 27, 1883.

Cable said, "I didn't come over here to torment you before your time." The reply was, "O you're not tormenting me; only give me room to swear." Cable added in telling of it to his wife on April 3, "But he did not swear—much." Events went as planned, however, and Unity Hall was crowded for the reading on April 4. J. R. Osgood had come from Boston, Waring from Newport, Gilder and Roswell Smith from New York. On the stage were Osgood, Gilder, Waring, Charles Dudley Warner, and Mark Twain presiding. Afterward Mark gave a dinner party at the Hartford Clubhouse for the visitors, with Joseph Twichell included. On the next day Cable read to a woman's group, the Saturday-Morning Club, being introduced again by Mark, and on the following day to a group of fifty-five at Warner's home. The Monday-Evening Club honored him at a luncheon.

The visit was handled as the coming-out party it was intended to be. Notable people were conspicuous and there was ample publicity. The *Courant's* account of the reading at Unity Hall had a note of reserve and yet conveyed the intensity of the impression Cable had achieved. He began as if "talking with friends in a drawing-room, in a fine and small voice, but sweet and penetrating." The *Courant* continued:

Talking a little, reading a passage, moving about the stage and occasionally indulging in dramatic strokes of gesture and attitude, he made appear, little by little, the charm and grace of the women he wished us to know. The process by which he did this cannot be indicated in a notice, so delicately and by imperceptible touches of the portraits he was drawing, did he bring out the real character and the life of the people. His reading is so absolutely simple that we hesitate to apply the word dramatic to it, and yet the effect was dramatic. . . . We saw as we had hardly seen in reading his writings how exceedingly subtle is his method, how delicate and refined is his color and drawing. . . . In the dialogues, especially in the Creole dialect, which is so musical on his lips, he held his audience almost breathless under the spell he wove so quietly and without apparent effort. The entertainment was in its character so simple and unostentatious that it was not until the reader had finished that the audience began to realize the delicate creation, the charming unfamiliar picture that the author had conjured out of the air.

Still, Cable was not altogether satisfied. At first he thought Mark's "huge horse fun" in introducing him at Unity Hall had thrown him out of key, but he later thought differently and was glad for Mark to introduce him the day following at the Saturday-Morning Club. This time Mark represented him as an impostor and concluded, "He will now read you one of his *stories,* not to call them by any harder name. But if any of you are offended at his pernicious utterances you have only to rise in your place & I'll stop him at once." The reading was "Posson Jone'," and Cable thought it the greatest success he had ever had. Mark Twain recalled that he had seen Bayard Taylor, William Dean Howells, Bret Harte, and Henry James before that club but had never seen the audience so worked up and drawn out. Gilder, perhaps forgetting in his enthusiasm that he had rejected the story for *Scribner's,* said Cable must read it in Madison Square Theatre.

The reading paid Cable $125. In keeping with the main purpose, his friends supplemented their praise and assurance of future success with criticism of his performance: He needed greater volume for a large auditorium and he must work his own comments into his reading more smoothly. Smith arranged to publish in the *Century* for June a short article by Charles Dudley Warner "On Mr. Cable's Reading," which was altogether complimentary, though it did say that the delicacy of his manner and materials made him most effective before small audiences. Warner added that the scene Cable had read from *The Grandissimes* might be taken as "a fascinating model for all apprentices in the art of fiction" and that "Posson Jone'" "seems to be the most important addition that American literature has received in many years."

On the train to Newport for the week end with Waring, Cable wrote his mother, "A new future appears to be opening before me. To *us* the brown winter of the past seems just ready to give birth to a green & roseate spring, and if it be so I rejoice that you have been spared to share it." It was of Mark Twain that he had most to say in writing his family. On April 5 he apologized for repeating so much of the "horse fun" in his letters: "It sounds good enough when it's first said, & I enjoy it greatly." Of the luncheon with the Monday-Evening Club he said, "It was the maddest, merriest three hours—the wittiest uproar that *ever* I heard in my life." Another incident, recounted in his letter of April 5, suggests the give-and-take that had grown habitual between Cable and Mark Twain. Cable had said in Mark Twain's presence that the minister he had heard in the morning made a few cursory remarks before opening his sermon:

"What! not right there in church?" he asked with a look of grave astonishment.

I regarded him with loathing pity.

"My conscience, Clemens, have you sunk to that?"—He drew up his poor legs into the arm chair & groveled in it—"Yes"—(abjectly)—"Yes, I got down at last to puns! You may take that one to Charlie Warner with my love." I complained that I had seen so many handle that one that I didn't know whether it was his or whose.

—"That's *so*. It's a *beau*tiful antique."

The future Cable saw opening up before him depended on the income he hoped the platform would yield. In New York he began voice training under Franklin Sargent to give a matinee reading at the Madison Square Theatre on April 23. The staff at the Century Company went in a body to hear him and offered their criticism, that in his effort to be heard in the large hall he lost the richness of tone and the variety of inflection so effective before a smaller audience. The New York *World* of the next day and the *Critic* of April 28 commented to much the same effect. With his new purpose in mind and with the determined self-discipline that was his habit, Cable used every occasion to test and improve his platform delivery, when he visited the 5-Point House of Industry with Morris Jesup and spoke to the children, for example, and when he addressed a group meeting in New Orleans on May 15 to organize a conference of charities. A better occasion came on June 15, when he gave the commencement address at the University of Louisiana, soon to be called the Tulane University of Louisiana.

The newspapers noted that this was Cable's first address before a general audience in his home city. Speaking on "The Due Restraints and Liberties of Literature," he took up the discourse where he had left off at Oxford a year earlier. Granting that any writer must rely on his environment for materials and cannot escape compulsions from the thought and attitudes about him, still any literature must aim to be national. The speaker was no doubt thinking of his own relations to his city and section and wished to claim for himself specifically the freedom he had postulated a year earlier for new Southern authors. Will we demand of a new writer, he asked, "that he shall bow down to our crotchets and whims? . . . Will he not be expected to practise certain amiable and cowardly oversights and silences in order to smooth the frowns of sections and parties and pacify the autocratic voice of ruling classes or established ideas?" Writers "must be free; free to study principles for themselves; to present and defend truth; to assert rights; to dissolve and sublimate and re-crystallize all that is best of old and new; to rectify thoughts, morals, manners, society, even though it shake the established order of things like an earthquake." We must "throw our society, our section, our institutions, ourselves, wide open to their criticism and correction, reserving the right to resent only what we can refute." Writers

will write about their own state, their own town, possibly even their own little neighbors; but they will never conceive of their audience as less than their entire nation.... The stroke of their pen must now and then cross out some notion that some one loves better than truth, and they may from certain quarters even be denounced as turbulent overturners of order, as mischievous innovators and disturbers of the peace; but . . . they will rest in quiet assurance, that sooner or later, society will pay into their bosom its gratitude, its love and its honor.

The address was a ringing call for a literature and an attitude toward it that the South had not known for half a century. A good deal of its sentiment can be found in the writings of Henry Timrod and William Gilmore Simms earlier and of Sidney Lanier at the time, and in the editorials Joel Chandler Harris was printing in the Atlanta *Constitution*. It seemed to Cable, as it apparently seemed to newspaper editors who commented on this address and the one of a year earlier, that much of the freedom he demanded would be allowed future authors. To him, it is clear, the right course was to assume the freedom and to push ahead, though cautiously perhaps for a while, as though there were no question of its being granted. In addresses and essays during the next two years he was to follow that course—and to test the amount of such freedom he would be accorded.

An even more important occasion, both for trying his platform wings and for turning his reformer's zeal to the whole South, came on September 26 when he addressed the National Conference of Charities and Correction at Louisville on the Convict Lease System. This address, which appeared in the *Century* the following February, showed Cable a master of polemics. The strength of his feeling on the subject showed through every paragraph, and yet he supported his contentions with utter lucidity, directness, and reason. He had marshaled statistics but introduced them in just the quantities needed to drive home his points without overweighting his discourse. Telling contrasts were ready at hand. The printed essay opens with a brief description of an ideal prison and its management and proceeds to recount the horrors of the prisons in the twelve Southern states employing the lease system. The reader is not allowed to forget the contrasts in death rate, escapes, and ultimate effects on the prisoners and on society as well. The presentation is mainly objective, relying on the reports of prison officials, but his own phrases accentuate the conclusions. At points irony served his purpose well, as in quotations from prison chaplains or from managers boasting of the profits the leases had turned into the state treasuries.

It was Cable's purpose to enlighten and arouse the public, and he was sure that when the facts were known widely the leases would be terminated and the system abandoned.

The address and the essay won approval in most quarters, for its appeal was to justice, decency, and the public good. The report in Henry Watterson's Louisville *Courier Journal,* quoted in the *Times-Democrat* a week later, set the tone for editorials in the South and in the *Tribune* and the *Times* of New York:

Mr. Cable is the ablest writer the South has had since Poe, and ranks as a novelist with Howells and James. . . . He reads unusually well, and throws a fire and intensity into his reading that one would hardly think him capable of from his slender frame. His paper lasted two hours, and it is safe to say that during that time not a man but kept his eyes fixed on the speaker. It is needless to say that the Southern author received an ovation. He was applauded time and again, and at the conclusion of the reading there was a storm of hand-clapping.

Cable was made a vice-president of the National Prison Association. "Nothing I have ever written," he noted a few years later in "My Politics," "has gained me so many friends among the best people of the South." But the accusations in his address were strong. The sordid picture was drawn state by state. Half the average population of the Texas convict wood camps died in the course of two years; the Georgia penitentiary had a convict serving a twenty-year sentence for hog-stealing; any sentence over ten years was almost sure to be in fact a life sentence. He condemned the view that prisons should pay their way and urged, furthermore, that all the leases, "brutal and wicked compacts," be terminated at once—"There is no honorable way to remain under them." The lessees and responsible public officials and legislators might protest, as indeed some of them did at Louisville and afterward; citizens of the twelve states might resent the comparisons with Northern states. Still his statements could not be ignored whenever the convict leases were discussed afterward. In the Louisiana legislature of 1884 Cable's name came repeatedly into the debate on the penitentiary bill and passages were read from his Louisville address. One of the senators defending the lease and wishing to discount Cable's arguments, characterized him, the *Times-Democrat* reported on June 27, as "a Quixotic moral reformer, who, mounted upon the ass of public credulity, rode against the immovable windmills of fixed institutions."

After visiting the Louisville Exposition in the company of James B. Guthrie, who had come from New Orleans with him, and addressing the Boys' High School, Cable proceeded to New York. His purpose was only to arrange for a few readings later in the platform season, but as it turned out he stayed east three months and in that time received more distinguished attention than ever before and proved himself an astonishingly successful platform reader.

The Mallorys at the Madison Square Theatre took him up at once. They wanted him to write a play, and they encouraged him to resume his voice training. At first he was reluctant, and after he had begun lessons with Sargent again he predicted—just what happened a few years later—that "some smart reporter will by & by be saying that I have trained away my naturalness." He went daily to the Madison Square Theatre and with Sargent stationed at the back of the empty hall, he blazed away at the empty seats. "Good practice," he wrote Louise on October 21, "may have to do it some o'these days when the seats ought to be occupied."

He had learned the year before that he could turn off work in the city. On October 6 he finished the last chapter of *Dr. Sevier,* which was to begin in the *Century* the next month. He revised *The Grandissimes* by cutting out part of the dialect for a new edition, and Scribner brought out new issues of *Old Creole Days* and *Madame Delphine.* By the end of October a paper on the Acadians was finished; Gilder liked it but preferred to see it made into three or four stories. This work was possible, though, only because Cable stuck to a routine that gave foremost place to his writing and preparing for reading engagements. Sundays were of course kept for attending church, writing letters, including those to his Sunday school in New Orleans, walking, and visiting with his friends. As a rule he went also to mid-week services. He was not content to go in company with his friends who were regular church-goers, but he liked especially to invite those like Sargent who did not attend regularly. More than once he walked on Sunday through the tenement sections of the dock area on the North River.

Invitations came constantly, many of them from unexpected quarters and very flattering. His fame for prison reform work brought numerous people who like Jesup listened with admiration when he talked on the subject. Along with countless new acquaintances he saw King, Champney, Pennell, and Waring, all of whom delighted in remembering their visits to New Orleans. They inquired about the members of his family, including the fifth daughter, Isabel, born in the summer. He enjoyed Boyesen's company more than ever before—the recent article by Kowaledsky apparently had been forgotten—and he and Roswell Smith never seemed to tire of each other. He met Krehbiel, Lafcadio Hearn's friend, music editor of the *Tribune*. Often he was at the Gilders' and sometimes met others there, as on October 29 when Andrew Carnegie and Matthew Arnold dropped in and after they had gone Jefferson came from his play to join Saint-Gaudens, Burroughs, Cable, and several others already present. "O! then we had a good time," Cable wrote Louise the next day. Jefferson "has taken to me with special emphasis. We sat down together at once and had it good. . . . It was a night to remember all one's days." Another day he wrote, "Gilder is—everywhere—the sweetest, gentlest, manliest, most interesting fellow I see."

The question of the theater had been gradually forcing itself on him. There had been proposals that *The Grandissimes* be dramatized and that he himself write a play, and now he found himself often with actors and theater managers. As a matter of course he had accepted the condemnation his church pronounced on the theater; both his and his wife's families held the same strict view. But the love of consistency was paralleled in his mind by a devotion to logic and reasonableness, and so when the question demanded an answer, he set about it in the rational manner that was his habit. He promised his wife he would not write a play without talking it over with her first, and he asked his mother to pose all the arguments she could against the theater. "I am not trying to see how far I can go in that direction without going wrong," he wrote from New York on October 21, "but I am anxious to know how far I may have been already wrong, & what I ought to teach others to do and not do." Another time he wrote, "I am not seeking opportunity to jump the fence of moral proprieties; I am trying to settle a great moral question." No doubt his hours with Joseph Jefferson did much to win him over. But his conversion was slow. He talked with three ministers on the subject; he borrowed books and read them; he talked with theater people he respected. Finally he saw his first play in the company of Roswell Smith, "one of the noblest and most active Christians" he had ever known. Then he saw Jefferson in *The Cricket on the Hearth*. "If it isn't as pure & sweet & refreshing & proper a diversion as spending the same length of time over a pretty, sweet, good story-book, then I'm a dunce." Conceding still that most plays are trashy, he thought it more sensible to provide or encourage good ones than to indulge in blanket denunciation.

The embarrassment on money matters was no less than the year before. In the summer he had borrowed $1100 in New Orleans that was now called back and so was borrowed from the Century Company. Actually he could not keep all his debts in mind. The best he could do was to pay the interest when it was urgently demanded and to seek postponement in other instances. His plan was to gain enough from his readings before Christmas to meet the most pressing demands. His friends were working in his behalf—Gilman in Baltimore, Pennell in Philadelphia, Osgood in Boston, Smith and others in New York. He hoped to read two or three times in each city in auditoriums seating about a thousand.

He began the season before a drawing-room audience of a hundred on November 21 at Springfield, Massachusetts, where the *Daily Republican* said he reminded one of Dickens and was "capable without doubt of equaling that magician" in his reading. He went next to the new Chickering Hall in Boston on November 26, 28, and December 4. At Boston he found more distinguished acclaim than he had ever had. William Dean Howells, Oliver Wendell Holmes, and others equally notable endorsed him in the newspapers; Charles Fairchild, J. R. Osgood, and Howells entertained him. Edward Everett Hale, whom he had met in New Orleans seven years earlier, invited him to stay in his home and would hardly accept refusal. John Greenleaf Whittier called at his room in the Adams House and said, "I've read every line thee ever wrote, and I knew thee would be a great writer as soon as I saw thy first productions." He was a guest at the St. Botolph Club when Matthew Arnold was entertained; he attended a reception for Lawrence Barrett; and on November 27 Howells honored him at a reception attended by nearly a hundred guests. The whole of literary and social Boston seemed to be paying him tribute.

The press was more than favorable. An interview of over two columns in the *Herald* of November 28 treated him as truly a celebrity and included a biographical account he had given the reporter. The interview proved embarrassing to him, actually, for Whittier had come to call while the reporter was with him, and the printed report quoted at length from what Whittier had said. When Cable wrote to apologize, the poet replied graciously and invited him to visit at Oak Knoll.[8] The *Evening Transcript* spoke on November 30 mainly of Cable's inimitable rendering of the dialect, but by December 5 it had dropped the last shred of reserve:

It was exquisitely unique. We cannot say it equalled or surpassed something else, because we have never had anything at all like it, and in itself it was simply fascinating. If we insisted on a comparison, indeed, we should be obliged to go back to the actors of the Shakespearian era. . . . Mr. Cable's dramatic instinct is not only unerring, but he is also a consummate actor. . . .

[8] For the details of this incident see an article of mine, "Whittier Calls on George W. Cable," *New England Quarterly*, XXII (March, 1949), 92-96.

The man's sympathetic adaptability is marvelous, and the musical quality of his ringing voice is in perfect accord with this mental flexibility.

The reporter spoke at the same pitch of everything in the program. The songs, "a curiously mingled medley of French troubadour grace and wild African fervor," made one forget he was "in prosaic Boston." He knew no other Irish woman character in literature as successful as Mrs. Riley in *Dr. Sevier*. The same paper had already, on November 26, pronounced his "the most unique case of indigenous literary genius America has yet produced." He could be compared with no one but Hawthorne and stood more or less on a level with him.

The Boston engagement allowed Cable to give the series of readings he had in mind for the larger cities: On the first night he read "Jean-ah Poquelin" and "Posson Jone'"; the second night entirely from *The Grandissimes;* and finally from *Dr. Sevier,* which had begun in the November *Century.* At the first reading the house, seating 450, was not quite full; the second was to a full house; at the third seats were sold on the platform and many people were turned away. And before he left the city, two return engagements had been scheduled. His success as a reader was assured.

In New York on December 6 he addressed the Nineteenth Century Club on "The True Literary Artist," using mainly the sixth lecture of the series at Johns Hopkins University. Beginning the next Monday, he read on seven consecutive days, skipping Sunday, at New Haven, Boston, Cambridge, Springfield, Boston, Baltimore, and Brooklyn. Everywhere he found full houses, delighted audiences who remained in constant laughter, flattering press reports, and new and old friends showering him with attention and compliments. Tickets for the Boston reading on the eleventh, a matinee, were sold out in a day's time, five days in advance. To his retiring room after a reading and the encores, would come a procession of local literary people—Francis Parkman, J. T. Trowbridge, T. W. Higginson, Elizabeth Stuart Phelps, and Horace E. Scudder once in Boston, for example—smearing him over with flattering speeches, he said, "but it brushes off when it is dry—at least I hope it does." The Springfield *Republican* could account for Boston's idolatry of Cable only by the fact that he had invented a new pleasure.

The other cities he did not captivate so thoroughly, but only in comparison with Boston could they seem unenthusiastic. He had learned one sure trick to "lift" an audience. At Boston on the eleventh when he read from *Dr. Sevier* Narcisse's question to Mrs. Riley, "if you can baw me two dolla' and a 'alf," he turned and addressed Susan Coolidge, one of the fifteen seated on the stage. The house roared.

Here was success he had not dreamed of. He wrote Louise on November 24:

As my dear Narcisse says, "—You'd think I was a Major Gen'l, in fact, an' I don't like that, you know."

O no. We don't like attention, do we? It makes us pout, eh? We're not vain, and so it displeases us. And when we're waltzed out to the long supper table at the head of the column & when men stand around in groups and stretch their ears to hear what we say, of course it's very unpleasant, & all that sort o' thing.

Nay, nay, wifie! Help me to remember that pleasing as all this is, it's not the *main thing*. No, no. I read the proof of my prisons article today. Ah! there's where I feel glad. I'm proud of that piece of work! And surely I am much mistaken if it don't make the land *ring* next February. And that's the comfort. When a man feels that his sword has cleft Appollyon till he roars again. That's better than "Rabbi, Rabbi."

Earlier, on November 8, he had written: "I don't fancy this reading business overmuch. It looks to[o] much [like] working merely to get money, & that hasn't been my way. I shouldn't feel so, I suppose, for I shall greatly increase the sale of my books, & I do think my books ought to do good." At another time he wrote, December 5: "Every dog has his day even the stump-tailed ones. This is mine. I'm the fashion of the moment. God help me to use it for the advancement of truth & righteousness & the blessed tidings of salvation."

The one outside his own family most likely to understand what the success would mean to him was Roswell Smith. To Louise he reported his parting with Smith on December 8:

He said, "Well, it has come at last. Remember, we prayed to the Lord for this & He has given it to us"—meaning the success which is now pouring in upon me like a flood. I told him yes, but that the thing to watch now is to see that success makes a better man of me—not a worse one. "I know it," he exclaimed as if speaking from his own experiences, "I know that is the thing to look out for."

We shook hands: "I shall not try to tell you," he said, "how much I think of you."

CHAPTER XI

A TIME OF DECISIONS

WHEN CABLE reached New Orleans on December 21, he could count the closing year successful—it had ended with a flourish of acclaim he had never dreamed of—and could look ahead with a still greater hope. True, his writing had lagged, but the Creole history and *Dr. Sevier* were completed, and he had begun working up the Acadian materials. To his local reform work, furthermore, he had added his attack on the convict lease system. The honorary degree of Master of Arts awarded him by Yale University on June 27 was a token of recognition in high quarters. But most important of all, he had discovered the source of income he must have to make possible his writing and his philanthropic work. One newspaper reporter had written that not even Edwin Booth or Henry Irving or Matthew Arnold, all of whom had appeared recently in Boston, had "been received with such exclusively distinguished attention"; and that his readings were "simply ovations."[1]

At Roswell Smith's suggestion he had engaged Major James B. Pond to manage his readings. Though the contract was not signed until the middle of December, after most programs had been filled for the season, Pond was able to make engagements beginning January 14 in the Eastern cities and as far west as Chicago and Ann Arbor later in the spring. The first two or three audiences in New York were slim, but soon the halls were full, as they had been in December. They went away delighted, especially with the Creole songs he sang at the end of each program. At New York on January 23 the audience called him back for an encore and stood while he sang "Aurore Pradère."

After a reading at Hartford on the twenty-sixth, Cable awoke at Mark Twain's house the next morning with what the doctor pronounced neuralgia in the lower jaw. More alarmed than anyone else, Mark kept Cable's friends posted and thought Louise should come from New Orleans, but was overruled. He or Olivia or one of the Warners wrote her daily. Pond came, and Dr. Francis Bacon from New Haven.

[1] Lilian Whiting, "Boston Letter," *Times-Democrat*, Dec. 16, 1883.

Roswell Smith wrote Louise to call on him for any money she might need and said he would himself bring her husband to New Orleans when he was well enough to travel. It was only after Cable had recovered and gone and the nurse, along with the Clemens children, had come down with the mumps that the diagnosis was corrected, to the great delight of all except the doctor. Cable then wrote to Mark, on February 21, "If I can pick up any other mild contagion about the country anywhere I'll bring it to your house. . . . If you ever get the whooping cough, come and see us down in New Orleans; Mrs. Cable will be delighted to see you."

After a week, when Cable was out of bed part of every day, the Clemenses' young daughters, Clara and Jean, would draw their chairs close on either side to hear him tell stories of New Orleans. At other times he would listen with Jean to the stories of tigers her father told her, or all would listen while Olivia read the tales of Robin Hood, which Mark enjoyed hugely. Cable and Mark would sit after breakfast opening their mail, in which there often were requests for autographs to set Mark off in a rage. Once they took down a volume of Audubon to identify a bird they had noticed through the window. Once Cable convulsed Mark by reading from a book Dr. Bacon had brought. Entitled *Love Triumphant, or the Enemy Conquered,* it was just the sort of absurd romance Mark hated. He borrowed it to read at the next meeting of the Saturday-Morning Club, and it was good for allusions in the letters he and Cable exchanged afterward, though it could not replace Bret Harte as a subject for his friends to use in taunting him.

Once the high talk which began at breakfast lasted all morning, and Mark was at the right pitch to concoct some new literary or publishing scheme. To carry out one of the schemes, they went together to New York when Cable was ready to leave on February 15. Mark Twain, Henry Ward Beecher, and Cable, with General Grant presiding, would appear at the Academy of Music to raise funds for flood sufferers along the Ohio River. But Grant was sick and Beecher had commitments he could not break. Cable went directly to Philadelphia to take up his platform engagements on February 19. From then until the end of March he averaged an appearance a day, giving enough matinee readings to offset the few days not filled. Pond traveled with him most of the time. They had grown fond of each other and had their greatest fun, often, when the encouragement was least. After the Milwaukee engagement on March 18 and 19, for example, the first place they had failed to make any money, they made merry in their hotel room, Cable "attitudinizing in the most laughable manner," he wrote Louise on

March 20, while Pond, six feet two inches tall, broad and heavy, danced about as they sang, "Hey, Yea, Roll a Man Down." As he turned back east on April 2, Cable wrote his wife, "The South makes me sick, the West makes me tired, the East makes me glad. It is the intellectual treasury of the United States. Here is cultivation, & refinement, & taste."

While Cable was sick at Hartford, he and Mark Twain had concocted a plan for five or six authors to write a story jointly. It held their attention several months but came to nothing. Cable told Roswell Smith and Gilder of the plan in April, and thereafter Gilder served as intermediary. Mark and Cable agreed in the first stages of the planning: all the authors would start with the same group of characters, perhaps members of one family; then each author would picture those characters in his own way as they met approximately the same experiences. The characters must have the same names in all versions; but variety might come, Cable suggested, from giving the characters different nationalities in the different versions and adjusting the names accordingly. But Mark had in mind a take-off on the old-fashioned novel; Cable was sure "the thing must be a square, honest hurdle-race, but not a mule-race." As he saw it, the best possibilities lay in letting each author in his own way show how in a special location and under particular circumstances a set of characters ceased to be European and became American. Further, he suggested a plot which would bring two unrelated children to America and then allow each writer to take them through a predetermined series of experiences, love and some sort of tragedy.[2]

By July Gilder had let Robert Underwood Johnson in on the secret and had invited Frances Hodgson Burnett to be one of the authors. He and Cable were in full agreement and on July 25 he outlined a framework into which the half a dozen stories might be embedded. A newspaper advertisement would ask for information on two children who had been orphaned during their voyage to America. The stories would be in answer, each telling of just such people the author had known— "they came to such and such a place & the results were so and so," as Cable had said earlier. But the plan went no farther. Mrs. Burnett had been ill, but, more important, Cable and Mark Twain had not come to any exact agreement. This was another of the many schemes bred in the Colonel Sellers side of Mark Twain's mind which looked less feasible on closer study.

[2] One of Cable's letters to Gilder commenting on proposals made by Mark Twain is printed in Harry R. Warfel, "George W. Cable Amends a Mark Twain Plot," *American Literature*, VI (Nov., 1934), 328-31.

The twinkle everyone saw in Cable's eyes betokened the strain of mirth and joviality his father had bequeathed him, and he believed it a part of one's obligation to be cheerful. Though he was unwilling to join Mark Twain in burlesquing the old-fashioned novel, he shared Mark's fondness for jokes. Within a week, in fact, after leaving the Clemens household in February he had made Joseph Pennell the butt of such a joke of his own by pretending to be sick when Pennell called at his room in Philadelphia. His most successful joke was at Mark Twain's expense. Remembering the tirades against autograph seekers he had heard at the Clemens breakfast table, he sent a mimeographed letter to 150 of Mark's friends asking them to write for his autograph, timing their letters to reach him on April first. No one should send stamp or envelope, and all should enlist others to join in, so long as no stranger to Mark should be included. Cable wrote on March 29, after speaking in mock-praise of Mark's works: "Let me assure you, however, that I do not say these things to play upon your vanity. I do not believe you have any. No man who has the least spark of vanity could write your books." Mark Twain gave the newspapers a report on the deluge of letters and telegrams, and said he planned to exhibit them in Barnum's show. While they were traveling together a few months later, autograph seekers remained a source of fun to Mark and Cable.

On May 15, 1884, three weeks after his spring tour had ended, Cable gave a reading at Grunewald Hall in New Orleans for the benefit of the Southern Art Union, of which he was an honorary member. He gave the kind of program that had been most successful in the East. He opened with a Creole-African song and next read a selection of Raoul Innerarity's speech from *The Grandissimes*. After a descriptive passage from the same novel, he read from advance sheets of *Dr. Sevier* Narcisse's obituary remarks on Lady Byron. This pleased his audience most, and "Posson Jone'," read almost in its entirety, pleased them least. He concluded with another Creole song.

The *Picayune* of the next day said the audience was perhaps the largest that had ever gathered in Grunewald Hall; the *Times-Democrat* called it "probably the most cultivated audience ever assembled in New Orleans." Yet the performance left something to be desired. Sensitive to the charges the Creoles had made against him, Cable had hoped *The Creoles of Louisiana* would convince everyone of his fairness and also his admiration for the Creoles. The local papers of recent months, especially the *Times-Democrat* through the efforts of Marion Baker and Lafcadio Hearn, had reported his movements almost daily and had quoted the praise he had received in the Eastern papers. Still, he knew that some of the Creoles were feeding their resentment with the thought that he pleased his audiences by holding them up for laughter. Now he hoped to convince them that the laughter at Raoul and Narcisse was at individual characters, not social groups, and that the final result was to impress on his listeners the admirable qualities of the Creoles. He hoped those in New Orleans would say, as his listeners elsewhere often said, that no people could be really as charming as his fictional Creoles.

But very few Creoles were present, and many of them would continue their protests, so it seemed, while saying in effect what one of them wrote in *L'Abeille* at the time, that he had not the pleasure of knowing Mr. Cable's works. The *Times-Democrat* said, "It seems unfortunate that so few Creoles were present to hear Mr. Cable's tribute to them and to the beautiful characters he has drawn and whom he loves." The local papers complimented the artistry of the writings but were cautious on the aspects of his reading that were the subjects of local controversy.

They mentioned the performance for some time afterward, "that ever remarkable and delightful reading." The *Critic* printed squibs about it, as on June 21, noting that it had set the Creoles buzzing more than ever. A letter from "A Creole Who Attended Cable's Reading," printed in the *Critic* of June 21 from the *Times-Democrat,* was one to please Cable, for while raising objections, it reflected a willingness to judge his writings on their merits. The Creole wrote:

I confess I was carried away by the great talent he displayed. His powers of observation and of delineation, his poetic appreciation and picturing of our Louisiana scenery, his striking representation of the characters he selected for the occasion from among the Americans and the Creoles that are made to live in his writings, charmed me exceedingly. He revealed himself in unexpected brilliancy, surpassing the most favorable estimate I had formed of him. . . . I had never read any of his works, I felt determined to soon make up my neglect. . . .

I acknowledge the truthfulness of the Creole characters as far as he depicts them. I concede that they are vivid, living; that I seem to recognize the individuals.

Still the writer had other feelings to confess: Cable had failed to write of the noble and heroic Creoles of history, had in fact given the impression that the Creoles were all of the type that peopled his stories.

This Creole was stating in unemotional terms what was apparently at the bottom of the objections of others who had read the stories and were not simply voicing an uninformed resentment. If Cable was going to write of the Creoles at all—and many of them doubted the propriety of that to begin with—then he must include their heroes and by all means must make it clear that among the descendants of the Latin colonials the European stratifications of caste were zealously guarded. Preferably he would have confined himself to the "chivalry and beauty" of the Creole population, as those two words were relished in the South at the time. If he included other classes, he should allow no confusion of the social elite with the others, to whom the word "Creole" could be applied only as it was applied in the phrase "Creole gumbo" or "Creole onions." Actually, the cause for much of the objection lay in the word "Creole," which remained troublesome in spite of Cable's attempts to define it exactly, for he was obliged to use it in its more inclusive sense, which would be understood locally but not necessarily by outsiders. Another difficulty arose from the traditional attitude toward fiction. The aristocrats were willing to see themselves delineated in fiction only as such medieval chivalric figures as they knew in Sir Walter Scott. Here Cable transgressed: in studying his characters as human beings, he pictured them either as unhampered by class restrictions, or, more often, as straining against those restrictions.

The reception of the reading at Grunewald Hall sums up in effect Cable's standing in New Orleans in May, 1884. He was recognized to be not only the most distinguished author the city had produced and one of the greatest novelists who had yet written in the South, but also one of the foremost novelists in America. His books had been commended in quarters undeniably to be respected. His artistry and his devotion to authorship were unquestioned. As a leader of conservative businessmen in social reform he had won the gratitude of all except such corruptionists as the public generally condemned. As with his fiction, his prison reform work had won national approval of which his fellow townsmen were proud. Local editors and critics had in effect pleaded for acceptance of his low characters, even the quadroons, by saying his books belonged to the new realism, and besides, the race question had been discussed increasingly more freely during the last ten years. Furthermore, the chief spokesmen for the Creoles, Père Rouquette and Placide Canonge of L'Abeille, had made such irrational charges as to throw doubt over their entire case, even in the minds of many Creoles, some of whom, G. H. Clements and Louis Lejeune among them, had openly defended Cable.

In May, 1884, to sum up, Cable was acclaimed on every hand in New Orleans except among part of the Creole population, and he had even Creole defenders in that quarter. Before the end of the summer, however, he had taken a position which lost him many supporters and gave the Creoles an opening for renewing their attack. At the same time he made a tentative move north with his family.

Before returning to New Orleans in April, he had decided to take his family to a cooler climate for the summer. But it would hardly make sense to bring his family back south in the autumn just when he would be opening the reading season in the North and East. By mid-June his friends in New York had rented a house for him at Simsbury, Connecticut. Pond wrote Cable on May 23 that earlier Roswell Smith had proposed that Mark Twain locate the Cables a house, perhaps in the vicinity of Hartford, and that several of them, including also Pond and Gilder, pay the rent; but Mark Twain and Olivia thought the offer would be resented as too much like passing the hat.

On July 1 Cable, his wife, and five small daughters sailed from New Orleans on the steamer *Hudson*. One event of the voyage showed him in a typical role, planning and staging an entertainment among the passengers and crew on the Fourth. One of the passengers reported it later and added, "None present on that occasion will ever forget the modest but earnest mild manner of George W. Cable."[3] What had first been planned as an escape from the New Orleans summer and the fear of yellow fever had become a move for at least a year, with the possibility that it would become a permanent move. The house at Simsbury was leased for a year, and Cable's home on Eighth Street was offered on a year's lease with an option for a second year provided it was for rent. To the speculations among his friends that he would stay north, his sister Mary Louise said she was sure he would return to the South and try to help "our people" to better things. Cable's home was leased by his friend Major E. A. Burke, formerly manager of the *Times-Democrat* and now director-general of the Cotton Exposition which was to open on December 16, and was occupied from October to January by Joaquin Miller, who came to report the Exposition for the national press. In his syndicated reports from New Orleans the poet of the Sierras told how delighted he was with the house and the flowers and the shrubs, as he was in fact with most of what he saw in New Orleans.[4]

At the time Cable was deciding to move north for a year, he was reaching another decision which was to have far greater consequence, the decision to campaign for Negro rights. It was a deliberate decision, perhaps an inevitable one in the evolution of his opinions and attitudes. The time seemed auspicious: there was encouragement in his success

---

[3] From a newspaper clipping among Cable's papers which I have not identified.

[4] See my article "Joaquin Miller in New Orleans," *Louisiana Historical Quarterly,* XXII (Jan., 1939), 216-25.

in prison reform; the income he could expect from the platform allowed him some feeling of security; and he had said more than once, with the sanction of his wife, that his other successes would be acceptable only if he could turn them to social and moral usefulness. He had been moving toward the decision during almost twenty years, and even now he weighed the considerations carefully before taking the first step, for he could foresee that once committed he would be unwilling or unable to draw back short of an extended campaign. In the years following the war he had been unable to reconcile the treatment of the Negroes with Christian principles. With shock and with no little bitterness he had recognized the fallacy, if indeed not the dishonesty, he thought, of the people and the institutions, including the churches, who had defended slavery. Reluctant to condemn individuals or his church, he yet could have only the deepest scorn for the faulty logic he encountered or the reluctance of his neighbors to face the issues. Writing the letters to the newspaper in 1875 revealed to him the magnitude and the difficulty of the problem. A speech he made on the Good Samaritan before the Sunday School Association on April 4, 1881, showed him aware that any assault on the accepted attitudes must be made cautiously and only when there could be some hope of success.[5]

Some of his early stories and *The Grandissimes* had broached the race question in a way to have obvious application to his own times. *The Creoles of Louisiana* and the two commencement addresses pointed unequivocally to effects of slavery on the ruling whites and on the Southern economy. The conviction and the feeling lying back of these comments would prompt him to go farther, it was clear, when he thought the time was fitting. The futile war on the lottery and the gratifying work for prison and asylum reform had taught him, as he interpreted them, that only from enlightening and arousing the public would results be achieved. And the conviction had grown on him that the greatest injustices of all centered on the Negroes, that in the whole social structure they most needed a champion. When he found in Southern penitentiary records what he thought proof that the Freedman was denied fundamental rights in the courts, he felt he must speak out.

Yet he was cautious, aware that the task was to remold the thinking of millions, not simply to lead public thought in channels the majority would readily accept, as was true of prison reform. He knew the fears and prejudices, the forces of tradition and established modes of thought, and the vested interests which focused on the Negro. He could be pa-

[5] The manuscript of this address is at Tulane University.

tient with temporizing if there was still some movement in the right direction; he could grant the plea that the Negro must prove himself worthy of the privileges of society, provided fundamental rights were not denied. He had known the Negro in his ignorance and superstition and childishness; he had seen the results when during Reconstruction unscrupulous whites had manipulated Negro legislators like pawns on a chessboard. But it was another matter for the Freedmen to be issued a special brand of justice in the law courts. He could not accept the argument of expediency here, that sentences should be pronounced not in strict justice but to set examples or to protect society from supposed dangers.

In preparing the address for Louisville, he introduced statistics which showed, he concluded, exorbitant sentences meted out to Negroes and disproportionate numbers of them among the convicts. His purpose was to suggest that as long as the lease system remained, judges and juries might be tempted to return the blacks to a type of slavery in the prisons and at the same time to secure public works that would not be possible otherwise. But he deleted the passage finally, not wishing to complicate his main thesis in the address. The Negro was excluded from the address also when it was printed in the *Century*. And he might never have taken the matter up again, he afterward wrote in "My Politics," except for an incident he witnessed on the train to Louisville. "I resolved then & there," he wrote, "to tell first the South & then the world what I had seen, and demand a trial, in the court of the world's conscience, of the Freedman's Case on its Equities."

His new resolve drew support from the applause that greeted his address in the hall at Louisville and in the Southern press. Further, the president of the American Social Science Association, after hearing the address, asked him to prepare for the next meeting of that organization a paper on the Negro in the courts; but he hesitated, for he was reluctant, he declared later, to discuss a Southern problem before an outside audience, at least before raising it in the South. Then came invitations to make commencement addresses on three Southern campuses: at Vanderbilt University, Emory College, and the University of Alabama. In February he declined all three, but later he accepted the invitation to the University of Alabama, where he spoke on June 18, sponsored by the Alabama Historical Society.[6] He went to the platform in Tuscaloosa, he explained afterward, emboldened to speak more candidly than ever before. The widely heralded material progress in Alabama

[6] See the Mobile *Daily Register*, June 18, 19, 1884.

had led him to suppose its citizens would be receptive to progressive social and political thought. And since no forces outside the South were then pressing for solution of the Negro problem and it was generally assumed to be one the South must solve alone, he thought no one could accuse him of catering to Northern prejudices.

But he found these assumptions were wrong. For weeks after the address the Alabama press rang with such phrases as "New England Puritan." The Mobile *Register* of July 6 carried a letter by Henry St. John, who had not heard the address but built a tirade of accusations against Cable's portrayal of the Creoles in his books. A similar but less frantic letter by an "Old Creole," quoted from a New Orleans paper in the *Critic* of July 5, concluded by saying that if Cable had any doubts as to the courage of the Creoles he had "a free field." Though the Alabama papers were uniformly abusive, the New Orleans editors made no issue of the Tuscaloosa address, and the *Picayune* of July 7 quoted an editorial from the Chattanooga *Times* which called the reaction in Alabama stupid and accounted for it by saying that "the great novelist and historian offended some of the Tuscaloosa bumpkins by some philosophical observations." "But for private expressions of approval and accord I had no lack," Cable wrote in "My Politics" afterward, "and I left Alabama more deeply impressed than ever before with the fact that behind all the fierce and resentful conservatism of the South there was a progressive though silent South which needed to be urged to speak and act. To this end somebody must speak first, and as I was now out in the storm, and as one may say, wet to the skin, why should it not be I?" He then accepted the renewed invitation to address the Social Science Association on the Freedmen.

CHAPTER XII

"DR. SEVIER"

IN SEPTEMBER, 1884, *Dr. Sevier* was issued by Osgood; it completed its run in the magazine the next month. In several ways the new novel broke from the pattern of Cable's earlier fiction. It is not primarily a Creole story and it touches but lightly on the Negro problem. The announcement of these facts in the New Orleans newspapers ahead of the first installment probably reflects a wish Cable shared with Marion Baker and Lafcadio Hearn to meet the charge that he was exploiting the Creoles and the race issue for his own aggrandizement. This was his first story, furthermore, to be set in his own lifetime.

The action takes place between 1856 and the end of the Civil War, with a concluding glimpse of the characters ten years later. With the focus held on three characters, the book has a singleness and directness that *The Grandissimes* lacks. The minor characters are fewer and remain auxiliaries while the main characters work out a philosophy of charity and philanthropy. The title character is the dispenser; John and Mary Richling are the recipients. One is tempted to say the Richlings are auxiliaries also, present only for the doctor's experimentation and edification, for they seem less individuals than types of humanity. Yet their surroundings are so real and the situations they confront so humanly actual that they take on a vitality from the scene about them. Dr. Sevier comes fully alive, though he is on stage much less than the Richlings. His austerity, his skepticism, and his analysis of his patients and associates alike, together with his informed concern for the social and political affairs around him, fit him admirably to be the author's spokesman. But he is a human being as well as a social critic.

The greatest success of the book is with the lesser characters, who taken together embrace the sweep of New Orleans society. There is only one quadroon of any prominence, Mme Zenobie, a *rentier,* renter of rooms, at the periphery of the story who is the embodiment of generosity and devotion and affection, but whose tragic status is no more than hinted. The only Creole included, the comical Narcisse, Dr. Sevier's bookkeeper, is a caricature of Creole manners and speech, but is also the type of Byronic youth, full of illusions and pretenses and yet capable of measureless bravery when he goes away, joyous and singing, to meet his death in battle. Through him the author pays tribute to the worth which lies below the surface of the Creole's character. Raphael Risto-falo, the Sicilian who bows to no adversity, is a foil to John Richling, and his wife, the Irish widow Kate Riley, supports him in proving that, as the book almost says, poverty is criminal—if it lasts.

This novel lacks the picturesqueness of *The Grandissimes.* It has no character with the bewitching charm of the Nancanou women, no episode so compellingly tragic as that of Bras Coupé, no such assemblage of strange persons, places, customs, and events. But it has also less confusion and indefiniteness to puzzle the reader. The mystery of the Rich-lings' past remains largely unresolved until the last chapter, but it remains plausibly so and as the hints appear, they are adequate for the reader's expectations.

The book plays down the exotic background. The rooms and furniture and dress have the naturalness of actuality. The author had read more of Turgenev and Howells. It is as if he had eschewed startling characters and had kept the action out of the romance-laden French Quarter, as if his purpose had been, like that of Howells, to show that ordinary people in an ordinary environment could have the kind of human experience fiction demands. The Civil War opens and New Orleans falls but the bearing on the characters is next to nothing. Mary's ride through the lines to reach her dying husband in New Orleans is a satisfying denouement, but it is hardly in the main thread of the story. The tragedy of the Richlings evolves in the quiet scenes in their meager apartment, in equally quiet conversations with Dr. Sevier, in their observation of Kate Riley or Raphael Ristofalo, in John's walking the streets in search of work, or, to mention the relatively momentous episodes in their existence, in Mary's illness and in John's stay in the Parish Prison.

Most of the social problems Cable saw in the New Orleans of his day are explored: corruption in public institutions, sanitation and disease, poverty and charity, the relations of officialdom, the churches, and individuals to all these problems. Joel Chandler Harris had sent word that he would like to see Cable write of his own time, and Allen C. Redwood and Joseph Pennell had argued that the New Orleans of the present was all any novelist could wish. Cable had subscribed to the same view when, it is reported, he said he had at his finger tips as good materials as Bret Harte had in the mining camps. Yet *Dr. Sevier* is not a local-color novel; instead of exploiting the local, it often passes over the peculiar and the odd for the common, the normal.

Though Cable first conceived of the story as an exposé of prison abuses and wrote it while he was steeped in prison reform work, the case against the prisons appears in only a few short chapters. Using language from his newspaper articles on the Parish Prison in 1881, these chapters dramatize through Richling's own experiences in arrest, trial, and incarceration, the charges Cable made elsewhere against the prison. Some of the incidents, furthermore, were drawn from what Cable had learned of the local prison. Ristofalo, to cite an instance, while under sentence for murder, visits his wife and others over the city in the company of a jailer, and afterward assists the drunken keeper back to the prison. On January 6, 1882, the *Times-Democrat* reported that a prisoner and a jailer went across town together, an occurrence not unusual; but this time the expedition turned into a drunken orgy, and they rifled a house and afterward shot and wounded a boy they met on the street. Lest anyone misunderstand, Cable remarked, the prison still stood at the same place, unchanged.

The yellow fever epidemic of 1858, the worst since 1853, touches all the characters, but it is Dr. Sevier who points up the real issues: The newspapers, in the interests of business, hush all reports until the epidemic can no longer be denied; care of the sick and the orphans is magnanimous; but all are criminally accountable, as with the prisons, because they have not taken steps to prevent such visitations. This matter belongs to the thesis of the entire story, which focuses on poverty and suffering and the role of charity. Dr. Sevier has held a stern theory that charity works evil unless it takes account of causes, unless it strengthens the recipient and helps him toward ultimate self-support. Promiscuous charity, that is to say, may be an evil. The case of the Richlings is the testing ground for his thoughts. They have a blind pride that lets them suffer while refusing aid, but they prove finally that pride need not be sacrificed, nor need it stand in the way; that charity can be noble without blindly preparing for greater destitution.

This is the position Cable took in helping organize a local conference of charities. He had in mind chiefly the needy who for several decades had unloaded at the New Orleans docks by thousands, especially the German and Irish immigrants. To Cable's mind the problem was intricate in ramifications and delicate in shadings, affecting the needy and the affluent both, for betterment would extend beyond food and clothing to all the activities and interests of a society. His manner is that of Howells—instead of dogmatizing he lets Dr. Sevier protest that poverty is criminal, and lets Richling voice the self-destructive pride of the needy in declining help. But ultimately the author's view comes fairly clear.

The one Creole in the book, Narcisse, is talkative, and the dialects of other groups are added, the Irish, the Italians, the Germans, and the backwoodsmen. In handling these dialects Cable employed an orthographic representation that is at times difficult simply because of his concern for accuracy. He felt he could not rely on the suggestion of occasional phrases and syntactical peculiarities which he had learned to make so effective in the Creole speech. Kate Riley's speech requires close attention, as does the Germanized language of the Reisens, whose name and speech likely came from the author's friend the Baron von Reizenstein. The language of the Mississippi backwoodsman, Mary's guide through the lines, is represented simply, and the result is effective realism with no sacrifice in ease of reading. Writing in a series on "The American Type" in the Chicago *Current,* Joel Chandler Harris called this guide "the most distinctive American type in recent fiction" he had encountered. "The character is a mere sketch," he said, "but not another line is necessary to make it complete. It is a figure that preserves its humor and its dignity—its honesty and its vitality."[1]

There is a ring of immediacy in *Dr. Sevier.* For almost every detail of the book Cable could supplement his customary research with his own observations. Prompted by his usual reverence for authenticity, he told soon after the book was in print how his family physician had told him the story, and added, "The characters, that is, the principal ones, and the main incidents of the work, are true."[2] When Cable was ready in 1881 to begin work on the novel in earnest, he asked his physician, Dr. D. Warren Brickell, for further details. Brickell cautioned changing the names of the Ritchies, Cable's Richlings, since the wife might be living, and paid especial tribute to the quadroon proprietress of the "Chambers à Louer," Mme Zenobie in the novel.[3] Brickell had told earlier of the brutal treatment a young man received in the Parish Prison, and Cable had visited the prison with his story as well as possible reform in mind at least as early as 1879. He told a reporter in St. Louis on January 11, 1885, "The assault upon John in the cell is word for word as I found it in an affidavit made by the young man who had suffered."[4]

[1] Quoted in the *Times-Democrat,* Dec. 16, 1884.
[2] An interview in the Milwaukee *Sentinel,* Jan. 30, 1885; reprinted in the *Critic,* March 28.
[3] Brickell's manuscript notes are at Tulane University.
[4] Reprinted in Fred W. Lorch, "Cable and His Reading Tour with Mark Twain in 1884-1885," *American Literature,* XXIII (Jan., 1952), 482.

Dr. Brickell became Dr. Sevier, as the author himself stated. He had come from South Carolina, Sevier from Virginia. Both had offices in Carondelet Street; both practiced in the Charity Hospital and held the chair of obstetrics at the New Orleans School of Medicine; both were active in civic affairs and often addressed political gatherings. The fictional doctor owed to his original also something of his brusqueness, independence of thought, and skepticism. Brickell took a leading part in the political struggles of the 1870's and when Cable wrote to attack the lottery company in 1872 was chairman of the board of managers of the company owning the *Picayune.*[5]

A story of Americans, not Creoles, *Dr. Sevier* takes place across Canal Street in the new city. The characters live where Cable himself had lived and had offices where he had worked. The building mentioned toward the end of the book as the one from which seventeen Confederate soldiers escaped during the Federal occupation was the office in which he kept books. John Richling was also a bookkeeper. Similarly much of the action derived from the author's direct knowledge. The rush of trade, the loading and unloading along Tchoupitoulas Street he had watched as a boy. Where Narcisse rowed his canoe on Prieur Street following a heavy rain, Cable himself once had rowed at flood time. What Richling saw as the Union fleet anchored to occupy the city was what Cable had seen and later described in the essay on "New Orleans Before the Capture." In her ride through the battle lines in Mississippi, Mary crossed terrain familiar to the author from his cavalry forays of the war. She waited for a schooner to take her across to the city at the spot where he and his sisters had landed when they were expelled from New Orleans and where his sister Mary Louise taught school after the war. He must have had his own parents in mind, furthermore, when he told of the Richlings' coming down the river to make their home, their hopes through their poverty, and the wife's going north to live with her mother in hard times. The Richlings use phrases, in fact, echoing those used often in the Cable family during the war and afterward, phrases of hope and assurance that soon, in better times, they would remember their days of trial. Cable surely thought of himself as one who, unlike Dr. Sevier, had known Want and had received of her "a liberal education."

Press comment on *Dr. Sevier* began before the first magazine installment. These notices and the reviews of the book when it was published trace out the turn Cable's reputation took in the South during

[5] See the obituary in the *Times-Democrat,* Dec. 12, 1881; also Edwin L. Jewell, ed., *Crescent City Illustrated* (New Orleans, 1873), p. 143.

that time. The turn was reflected most acutely in the *Times-Democrat,* which until mid-1884 might have been called a Cable organ, and in the attitude of Lafcadio Hearn, until then his steadiest supporter in print.

After hearing the new book read in manuscript, Hearn wrote Krehbiel that he expected it to surpass Cable's earlier work, and on September 9, 1883, still two months before the serial began, he previewed it for the *Times-Democrat.*[6] Here he wrote in unrestrained praise. Cable's books were as well received across the Atlantic as in America, he said; Mary Richling was superior to any of Cable's other women characters and more charming "than any recent conception of the New England school," but Ristofalo was the most remarkable in the rich variety of characters presented. No novel in England or America could compare with the novel; those of Daudet and the Goncourts were closest to it in the "combination of the minutest realism with the purest idealism." Its "audacious theme," something of a "new chapter in social philosophy," "not many would venture to use."

At about the same time Hearn had another occasion to compliment the work of his friend in an article for the November *Century* entitled "The Scenes of Cable's Romances," which was accompanied by five of the drawings Joseph Pennell had made of the houses appearing in Cable's stories. In locating the houses by street and number, Hearn extolled Cable's faithfulness to actuality and wrote fascinating descriptions of his own. Visitors to the Cotton Exposition in 1884 and 1885 used the article as a guide to the streets and houses Cable had described.

Other newspapers echoed Hearn's praise, and on the next February 17 the New Orleans *States* lamented that the city had not honored Cable properly. But before *Dr. Sevier* had finished in the magazine, Cable delivered the commencement address at Tuscaloosa, and a chill ran through the local press, affecting even the criticism of his fiction. The severity of the Alabama papers in discussing the speech brought rejoinders in a few Southern papers, and the New Orleans editors mainly avoided comment; but Marion Baker was barely able to dissuade his brother Page from throwing the *Times-Democrat* into an attack on what he called Cable's un-Southern views. As editor of the *Bulletin* in 1875 Page Baker had said Cable should be ashamed of the two letters he wrote defending the unsegregated high schools, and he was no less sensitive now to un-Southern views. In 1883 he had followed E. A. Burke as managing editor of the *Times-Democrat.*

---

[6] This review has not been attributed to Hearn, I believe, but I have no doubt it is from his pen.

On July 12 *L'Abeille* repeated with still greater vigor the thrusts it had made from time to time over several years. L. Placide Canonge, the editor, prompted by Cable's address at Tuscaloosa, turned a eulogy of Paul Morphy, a world-renowned Creole chess player, into a diatribe against Cable. Restating in sarcastic phrases the contention that Cable wrote of the low characters because he had never been accepted in the higher classes, he concluded that Morphy's fame as a chess player was adequate refutation of all Cable's characterizations.

The tone of this editorial was not new for *L'Abeille,* but the appearance of a similar tone and similar though milder charges in the English-language papers was new. A two-column editorial in the *Picayune* of July, 28, with its mixture of opinions, shows Cable's star in transition in the New Orleans press. After an initial gesture toward his reform work, which the editor found echoed in *Dr. Sevier,* he said he doubted that Narcisse was typical in his character or his speech of the educated Creoles, and he found the other dialects distorted for effect—"We would only warn him that he should not play too much to the galleries." Then the editor reached the point he had been approaching:

This brings us to say that Mr. Cable is an artist. In our judgment he is an artist rather than a philosopher. We know that he has many sound sentiments, and that he is a thinker; but it seems to us that he is sometimes too hasty in selecting his point of view, and that he has too much the courage of opinions that have been rashly reached. We have been occasionally somewhat amused, and, we confess, a little indignant, at reports that have reached us of some of Mr. Cable's deliverances at the seats of Southern learning where his reputation as a novelist has secured him audience. He seems to have been under the impression that it was his mission to preach progress to the most thoughtful and erudite men of this section, and he has done it, we understand, with wonderful *aplomb.*

Continuing, he noted Cable's belief "that Southern civilization has still further concessions to make, which it is as yet unwilling to make, to the negro race," and he cited also the words addressed in *Dr. Sevier* to the Union soldiers: "your cause is just." To these the editor must protest just as strongly as he would have done "when first the Lost Cause was shrouded in the bonnie blue flag of Dixie, and buried in its bloody grave."

This editorial charted the course of newspaper comment for the next several years. Cable's artistry was acknowledged, with some concession to the contention of the Creoles that they had been misrepresented; his prison reform work was recognized, but his stand on the Negro must be challenged. A review of *Dr. Sevier* in the *Picayune* of September 28 was favorable, except that the writer thought it implausible for Richling's father to have disinherited him for choosing a Northern wife much below his own status. A reviewer who objected to this implied criticism of the Southern aristocratic tradition might be expected, after further provocation of the sectional question, to find it still more difficult to see literary merits in such a book.

When Marion Baker clipped the review of *Dr. Sevier* from the *Times-Democrat* of October 5 and sent it to Cable three days later, he explained:

Page wanted to attack the work viciously, on account of its anti-Southern tone, but Hearn & I persuaded him out of it. Hearn wrote the notice, but does not care for you to know. He is hopelessly down upon you & there is no kind of use trying to argue him out of it. . . . He confessed to me that, but for Page's antagonism he would have said more in your praise, because he cannot but accord to you marvellous power. He told me, last night, that he was visiting some ladies, a short time since, & upon the table was a copy of the Century in which the scene of the steamer leaving for Mobile was given. In a conversation which ensued, the women made, or attempted to make, light of your abilities as a writer. Hearn defended you and turning to the table took up the Magazine & asked them to let him read aloud this particular Chapter. He says, before he had finished they were all in tears, & he quietly closed the book & walked out. Now, said Hearn, it is simply ridiculous to deny that Cable has wonderful power, when such a result is possible.

The unqualified praise Hearn had written on September 9 of the year before became in this review partial endorsement and almost quibbling at points. At one point he exclaimed, ". . . how fine the workmanship!" But he found the ornamentation burdensome, the dialect wearying, and the force insufficient to support the book to its full length. Cable's best work, therefore, would always be in the "short, bright, graceful stories," but he added, "we do not hesitate to class the beauties of 'Dr. Sevier' as matchless in their way, and the work generally as one of the most remarkable of recent American literary productions." These judgments are more fitting to the book than Hearn's glowing statements on it earlier, but they reflect his pique at the moment as well as a more careful evaluation. Another passage of the review owes more to Page Baker's opinions, surely, than to Hearn's own attitudes. The book would be judged by many of its readers

whom Mr. Cable has necessarily antagonized by the anti-Southern tone of his work, by side-thrusts at political and social ideas which he himself once fought in defense of. We do not wish, indeed, to discuss these points with Mr. Cable; but we may certainly take opportunity to observe in a friendly way that it is more than doubtful whether the pages in which these political touches appear really add dignity or value to his novel.

Outside of New Orleans *Dr. Sevier* was reviewed widely and in general very favorably. Most of the critics thought it the best of Cable's books; a good many called it one of the greatest American novels. The *Critic* was not sure Cable should not be called *the* American novelist of the time; the New York *Times* said he showed "more genius" and "more inborn talent than any other American romance writer"; the Chicago *Dial* said he was doing "perhaps the most valuable literary work done in this country at the present day." One reviewer saw *Dr. Sevier* as the desirable antithesis of Henry James's "silly twaddle"; another saw it as an antidote for the materialism of Howells's paint-maker trying to marry his daughter into society. Cable was most often likened to Dickens and was compared also to Hawthorne, Victor Hugo, and Daudet. Some of the reviewers were more reserved; a few were adverse. The *Critic* on November 8, 1884, commended the book's simplicity and exquisite detail but found it lacking in "the grand general plan." The reviewer thought Cable had excelled Dickens in making his readers know and feel real poverty, but he apparently shared the feeling of an anonymous letter writer who asked Cable please to put one of his characters "into a comfortable position for a little while." The Boston *Literary World* of October 18 thought the plot faulty but commended the author for seeing both the sad and the humorous in life.

The Louisville *Commercial* voiced an attitude that within a few months had spread through the Southern press. After remarking that Cable had been accepted by the "coterie of saints who stand around the throne of culture in Cambridge," the reviewer labeled *Dr. Sevier* "unspeakably 'preachy.'" He was thinking of the implied preaching on such matters as the planter aristocracy and the Southern scorn of physical labor. Those reviewers who found anti-Southern views in the book were likely to think it excessively didactic and of course wrong-headed in its views. Those who saw the didacticism as related only to poverty, unemployment, charity, and pride most often thought it not excessive.

The reviews all recognized the attention to actual detail and the focus on simple, day-to-day events in ordinary lives, but they did not agree in evaluating this quality. Some found the details tedious and seemed to want exciting scenes and commanding action. Others found the story powerful because it works out the fortunes of its characters in situations that millions encounter in one degree or another; they were happy not to find the melodrama and the sensationalism so common in the recent novel. One critic wondered whether this book did not predict the novel of the future, in which direct struggles among characters would give way to exploration of the intellectual and moral influences people exert on those around them, as in Dr. Sevier's relations with the Richlings. The reviewer in the *Nation* on November 20 was one of those least prepared to accept the realism of *Dr. Sevier*: "Mr. Cable can devote ten pages to an unsuccessful hunt for lodgings, and a whole paragraph to a gesture." This statement hints at the critical attitude which Howells and Henry James met in their attempt to establish the new realism.

The reviews which Douglas sent from the British press were highly complimentary. Most of the reviewers had missed *The Grandissimes* but had read Douglas's edition of *Old Creole Days* and found *Dr. Sevier* a worthy sequel to the earlier stories. The *Academy* of September 1 put Cable in the company of Hawthorne and a few other authors "striking out a vein of indigenous American fiction which is no mere provincial copying of English literature." The *Athenæum* of September 22 found Cable's mastery of pathos reminiscent of Daudet. The reviewer for the Nottingham *Journal* of October 30 recalled that he had written earlier of *Old Creole Days* that "here was a novelist who, for pathos and delicate character studies, was not to be matched on this side of the Atlantic," and added that *Dr. Sevier* surpassed any novel he had read from Howells.

The charge that *Dr. Sevier* was anti-Southern focused on one passage, the statement to the Union soldiers, ". . . your cause is just. Lo, now, since nigh twenty-five years have passed, we of the South can say it! / 'And yet—and yet, we cannot forget'—/ and we would not." In addition to demurrers in the Southern newspapers the October *Century* had a communication in which Malcolm McKay granted that Cable had a right to his sentiments but disclaimed them for most Southerners. Cable intended his reply, "We of the South" in the November issue, to make clear to the national audience that he was by both "rearing and affection" a Southerner, that he would not "yield to any one in pride in our struggle and in all the noble men and women who bore its burdens," but that he now considered the cause he had once opposed in battle to be just. He believed that the war was fought over slavery, but if he granted the sole issue was the constitutional right of secession, he would still call it an error, for he believed accomplished secession would have been ruinous. He continued:

Nay, sir, we thank no man for buffets; we make no pretense of humility; but before an issue where both sides could be brave and conscientious and yet each be wrong in many words and acts; but where, as to the ultimate question, both could not be right; with the verdict of the whole enlightened world against us, it is surely not too much to maintain that in the fullest stature of human dignity we can stand up and say to our brethren,—no longer our adversaries,—"Time has taught us you were right."

Cable's sister Mary Louise was delighted with his reply, for it would show everyone that his stand was honorable. The *Century* published two additional letters on the subject. "A Southern Democrat" in January said he thought Cable was stating "a bold and fresh interpretation of the attitude and expressions of thousands and thousands of Southern people." "The Blue and the Gray" by C. N. Jenkins in March said Cable spoke for most Southerners. "A Louisianian" writing in the New Orleans *Item* of March 22 defended Cable's right to his own opinions on the Southern cause and his right to speak them. Other statements in the Southern press were more likely to disagree with his views but to defend his right to have and to express them. But this discussion was of secession and slavery in historical perspective. Discussion of the Negro in the current South, Cable had discovered after his address at the University of Alabama and was to have still more forcefully driven home to him soon, would not draw such gentlemanly response.

CHAPTER XIII

"THE HIGHWAY ROBBERY BUSINESS"

IN THE SPRING of 1884 Cable had renewed his contract with Pond and soon afterward learned that Mark Twain had a scheme that would tickle him. It was a scheme for a joint reading tour. In 1877 Mark had proposed such a tour to Thomas Nast, then in full career as a political cartoonist, and in 1882 he had hoped to take a "menagerie" on the road, consisting of himself, Cable, Howells, Joel Chandler Harris, and Thomas Bailey Aldrich. In March, 1883, he wrote Cable, then lecturing at Johns Hopkins University, not to make any commitments for the platform until he reached Hartford. But nothing materialized until 1884. Mark would take the risk, pay Cable $350 a week and expenses for twenty weeks. Pond did not urge acceptance, and Cable hesitated; then Mark said he would rather pay Cable $450 a week than to have anyone else. On these terms the contract was drawn by July 15.[1] Pond, as traveling manager, was to receive from Mark 10 per cent of the net receipts, with his own railroad fare in addition, and he would have also his 25 per cent commission on Cable's portion. A new line appeared in the heading of Pond's circulars: "Samuel L. Clemens ('Mark Twain') and George W. Cable Reading from Their Own Works."

From beginning to end publicity kept far ahead of the tour. In July the rumor that the venture was in the making ran through the newspapers. The New Orleans papers picked up the report and one of them, the *Picayune* on July 28, touched it up in keeping with the cooling attitude toward Cable since his Alabama address a few days earlier: "Twain will be the comedian and do the funny business for the show, while Cable keeps up the prayer-meeting end and scoops in the churches." Pond's circular billed neither as the lead; they would divide the time, "so that the pathos of the one will alternate with the humor of the other, and the genius of both will be presented in a rapidly changing programme,"

[1] Mark Twain mistakenly remembered the figure in 1907 as six hundred dollars (*Mark Twain in Eruption*, ed. Bernard DeVoto, New York, [1940,] p. 216), perhaps following the error Pond made in his volume *Eccentricities of Genius* (New York, 1900), p. 231.

to which the Lounger column in the *Critic* remarked on August 9; "I am at a loss to see how Major Pond is going to divide Mr. Cable so as to cut the humor out of him. To do this he will certainly have to give him very different selections to read from those that delighted Chickering Hall audiences last winter."

The first appearance was in New Haven on November 5, the day following the national election. But before that time Cable had to settle his family at Simsbury, secure a piano for the children, and prepare for their first winter in the North. He was at home most of the summer, which was one of the happiest the family had ever spent. They enjoyed their neighbors and the comfort and beauty of the summer months in the mild climate. In September and October he took quarters in New York and resumed his voice training, first with Harold Henderson and later with his former teacher, Franklin Sargent. Besides working up his own repertoire and helping Mark Twain choose selections to read, he filled several reading engagements Pond had made for him in New Haven, New Britain, Germantown, and Doylestown. In the time left over he wrote at his desk in New York as he had done at times in the past, but now he could spend the week ends with his family. In September he went to Saratoga to address the American Social Science Association on the Freedman's status before the law. The step he took in delivering this address he knew to be momentous, but the full repercussion he could not know until the address was printed in the *Century* of January the next year.

In the letters Cable wrote Louise it is possible to follow the reading tour in minute detail. He wrote almost every day, often from the wings of the stage while his partner took his turn before the audience, at times from their hotel while Mark was walking the floor and singing or pronouncing judgment on things large and small. Thus the letters breathe the very air of the halls, the hotels, and the trains. They afford a fascinatingly intimate view of the tour from the first day to the last, and there was hardly a day without something well worth reporting.

Once the readings began, the schedule was full to the end of February, except for a Christmas holiday of ten days. Part of almost every day or night they spent traveling, doubling back and forth along the east coast from Washington north into Canada and as far west as Iowa. Bantering and joking and a happy congeniality made the exhausting schedule bearable. They often fell into clowning, Cable and Pond along with Mark Twain. The Cincinnati *Enquirer* of January 3 reported an interview in the hotel dining room after an evening's performance. Mark drank ale and Cable ate ice cream. Before the interview was over, Cable had threatened Mark with an empty ale bottle, and Mark had threatened Pond. Afterward the reporter's query to Cable as to how he liked Mark Twain was answered: "We fight all the time. I think that in four three minute rounds with soft gloves I could knock him out; he's not much on science." Pond told the reporter his two companions had made it up not to laugh at anything he said, especially his puns. They were registered at the hotel as "J. B. Pond and two servants."

There were occasional high spots to break the monotony of trains, hotels, lecture halls, and autograph seekers, as when President Arthur came to the dressing room after the readings in Washington and said, for one thing, that Cable's books were favorites of his, and when they met Grover Cleveland, governor of New York and president-elect. After this meeting Cable was sure the right man had been elected.

At many stops they were entertained by friends. In fact they often had to decline invitations in order to get what rest they could between the platforms and the trains. In New Haven there was tea at the home of Cable's friend Dr. Francis Bacon, with Mark included, and also Olivia Clemens, who was with them at the time. At Morristown, New Jersey, on Thanksgiving, they were the guests of Thomas Nast. Mark made the occasion memorable when, unable to sleep, he decided the clocks were responsible and must be removed. The drawing Nast made afterward showed Mark carrying the clocks outside and Cable holding a candle—both in nightshirts.[2] At another time they were in a bookstore at Rochester looking for something to read. Mark asked about one book that was a stranger to him; it was the *Morte d'Arthur,* which Cable recommended with the prediction, "You will never lay it down until you have read it from cover to cover." The prediction was borne out, and as Mark read in it during the next few days his companion noticed his mind was working with all its energy, and he was not surprised when the reading bore fruit later in *A Connecticut Yankee in King Arthur's Court.* As Cable told of the incident in the Mark Twain memorial program in 1910, he recalled also that while writing *A Connecticut Yankee* Mark had called him its godfather.[3]

Soon after Major Pond's brother Ozias had replaced him on January 1 as traveling manager of the tour, Mark gave Ozias a copy of Malory's work and named him Sir Sagramore. Then on February 3, when they

[2] See Paine, *Mark Twain,* II, 787; Mary Lawton, *A Lifetime with Mark Twain* (New York, [1925]), pp. 78-79.

[3] See *Proceedings* of the American Academy and National Institute (New York, [1911]), III, 21-24; and Paine, *Mark Twain,* II, 790.

had been forced to leave Ozias at Milwaukee sick, Cable and Mark Twain wired him from Chicago:

Now wit you well, Sir Sagramore, thou good knight and gentle, that there be two that right wonderly do love thee, grieving passing sore and making great dole at thy heavy travail. And we will well that thou prosper at the hand of the leach, and come lightly forth of thy hurts, and be as thou were tofore.

SIR MARK TWAIN
SIR GEO. W. CABLE

Cable made copies of the telegram for Olivia and Louise, and Ozias copied it into his diary. This diary, of which Major Pond gave Cable a copy in 1894, two years after Ozias's death, traces the doings of the "Twain," as he called his charges, through the month of January.[4] When Ozias took to his bed, he had the kindest treatment from both. Though Mark "dreads to look upon suffering," he wrote, "the close observer can always see the sadness in his eyes and his aching heart, when human suffering is brought within his sight." It was Cable who called the doctor, wired for Ozias's wife to come, and sat through the day reading to the patient and talking to him. Ozias wrote in his diary, "He is the most perfect man that it has ever been my good fortune to meet. He has the courage of his convictions and will make his influence felt in this land if his health is spared. . . . I have never known a kinder, nobler, manlier man."

In St. Louis Cable met Mark Twain's cousin James Lampton, the original of Colonel Sellers in *The Gilded Age*. From an adjoining room, with the door purposely left ajar, he overheard Lampton telling in true Sellers fashion of a fantastic venture he had undertaken with his son. He jotted down the conversation he overheard and later added what ensued after Mark had summoned him into the room.[5] At Toledo on December 16 Cable and Mark Twain had supper with David Ross Locke, who had become famous as Petroleum V. Nasby, "a big man," Cable wrote Louise, "with disheveled hair, knotted forehead, heavy middle and dowdy dress. An easy talker, a coarse man of the harder world, successful and unsatisfied. . . . How the fine lines—so often hid from view in Mark's face—did shine out as I compared the two men." Nasby told of his fearful work in quitting drink and of his own days on the platform. He had given one lecture 480 times, he said, often

[4] This copy is at Tulane University.
[5] This manuscript, at Tulane University, is printed in an article of mine, "James Lampton, Mark Twain's Original for Colonel Sellers," *Modern Language Notes*, LXX (Dec., 1955), 592-94.

when he was so drunk that the audience was *invisible*. This was not a conversation or a character to please Cable. "He is, maybe, less sordid than he pretends," he said, but later he added, "He's a bad dream." Henry Watterson similarly entertained Cable and Mark Twain at a supper after the program at Louisville on January 5, and he did not please Cable for similar reasons. "Talks shamelessly about getting drunk &c &c. Strange that such moral distortion can go with a certain large integrity & public honor but so it is at times."

These were comments to his wife and hence likely to turn on immediate impressions rather than larger matters of character and work. Actually, however, these remarks on Nasby and Watterson are as severe as any he wrote Louise about anyone he met on the tour—or at any other time, for that matter, with but few exceptions. It was his habit, even in writing her, to indicate no displeasure with his associates on matters small or large. When he first met R. H. Stoddard in New York, he remarked in a letter of June 4, 1881, on Stoddard's familiarity as lacking both appropriateness and genuineness, and then he added, "I wish I had not written this." In the hundred or more letters he wrote home while on the road with Mark Twain he never indicated the slightest irritation with Mark or their traveling manager, though Pond's letters to him and Mark's letters to Olivia indicate there was irritation, or room for irritation, all the way round.

Mark Twain, in contrast, was never slow to display irritation; explosive protest was a part of his lifelong manner. An entry in Ozias Pond's diary made at St. Louis on January 12 will illustrate. They were to take a train at 9:40 in the morning. "Mark got wrathy because he didn't feel like getting up so early and vented his anger by squaring off with the window shutter and knocking it completely out in one round. Cable and I looked on with bated breath, but didn't interfere." With similar lack of restraint and no doubt similar enjoyment he protested about local accommodations, about the management of Pond and his agents, and in letters to Olivia about his companions.

Their second excursion into Canada, in February, showed Cable a fairyland of wonders, as he was whisked here and there by sleigh, wrapped to the eyes in scarfs and robes. More than anywhere else he and Mark accepted invitations that drained energy they needed to conserve. At Helmuth Female College of London, Ontario, they found themselves on February 13 surrounded by the inevitable autograph albums and later in the midst of hilarious, giggly toboggan rides with the girls. At Montreal, following a reception at the Athenaeum Club in the afternoon and then the evening's reading, they rode in jingling sleighs over the snow under the stars to a meeting of the Toute Bleue Club, where they were initiated with the customary ceremony. They made short speeches and afterwards Cable sang "Pov' Piti' Momzelle Zizi," with the club members taking up the chorus. Cable also met Dr. Louis Frechette, the Canadian poet who had translated some of his stories into French.

The partners shared the stage equally. They were both endmen, one quipster said, and Pond was in the middle. Cable read first, was followed by Mark Twain, and then each had another turn. Or both might have the stage twice before a short intermission and twice afterward, as at Troy, New York, on December 2. As a rule they used no introducers and no formal introductions. Cable might walk to the center of the stage alone and say, "I'm not Mark Twain." Both might enter together, with Clemens walking slightly ahead. He would say, according to one reporter, "Lays sun gen'l'men, I intorduce to you Mr. Caaa-ble," and for Mark's first number Cable would introduce him in the same way. This method served a good purpose, Cable told his audience when he appeared alone during their Christmas vacation: "First he would introduce me, so that the audience would know which of us was which; and then I would introduce him—so that they would know which of us was the other."[6] After a week of this procedure Mark Twain astonished his partner at Buffalo on December 10 by launching into a burlesque introduction that set the house laughing. "But I was [in] luck nevertheless," Cable wrote, "for just at the end of his little speech he really without intention betrayed a little opening in his harness and in went my dagger and the laugh was turned upon him in a torrent." They preferred entering together in order to invite laughter simply from the physical contrast. They would walk to the front of the stage as if Cable were a boy following just behind his father. After hearing them in Boston, Hamlin Garland said that Mark Twain looked six feet tall beside Cable and that he had never seen "two more divergent types."[7]

The programs were advertised as readings from their own works, and for the most part they were. Cable had enough tried numbers for three programs, which were sometimes needed for consecutive readings in the same city. They often made matinee and evening appearances in the same auditorium and at Boston in November they filled Chickering Hall three times in twenty-four hours. Cable read most from *Dr. Sevier,*

[6] *Critic*, V (Dec. 27, 1884), 308.
[7] *Roadside Meetings* (New York, 1930), pp. 352-53.

released only in September. He often opened with Narcisse trying to borrow money from the Richlings, followed in his next turn with a scene including Kate Riley, Richling, and Ristofalo, and then Narcisse mourning for Lady Byron. His program concluded as a rule with Mary's ride through the battle lines in Mississippi and one or two Creole songs. The audiences were usually not satisfied if either of the last two numbers was omitted and often requested them if they were not on the printed program. At Washington on November 24 the manager had received a dozen requests in advance for him to sing "Zizi." It was encored and he read "Mary's Night Ride," and as a further encore he sang "Aurore Pradère." As alternative pieces from *Dr. Sevier* he might give Narcisse and the inundation, Narcisse's views on chirography, or the fall of New Orleans. His other programs were made up of selections tested the preceding season from *Old Creole Days* and *The Grandissimes*.

A typical program of Mark Twain's included "Huck Finn and Tom Sawyer's Brilliant Achievement" and "King Sollermun" from the advance sheets of *Huckleberry Finn,* "The Tragic Tale of the Fishwife," "A Trying Situation," and "A Ghost Story." Other choices were "A Desperate Encounter with an Interviewer," "Why I Lost the Editorship," "A Sure Cure," "Certain Personal Episodes," "Tom Bowlin's Encounter with the Governor of Massachusetts," "The Jumping Frog," and "The Stammerer," which was a favorite with his listeners. A few times he read from other authors—Joel Chandler Harris's Tar Baby story, for example, as well as Browning and Shakespeare. Like Cable he experimented constantly with his program, so that when he made up the repertoire for his tour around the world ten years later, he said he could pick from seventy-five pieces he had already tried out on the platform.

Clemens was new at this particular variation of what they called "the highway robbery business." He had heard Charles Dickens read at Steinway Hall fifteen years earlier and recalled the effects wrought by his combination of acting and reading. Such was Cable's method and the one Mark had in mind when he asked Cable to help him choose pieces to use. But as Mark remembered years afterward,[8] he soon learned that just reading was not enough, at least for him; the pieces must be "limbered up, broken up, colloquialized, and turned into the common forms of unpremeditated talk." After that, he said, with the parts

[8] See *Mark Twain in Eruption,* pp. 213-24.

memorized but not the words, he went to the stage without book or manuscript.

After allowance for Mark Twain's usual hyperbole in remembering his past experiences and his habit, as shown repeatedly in his *Autobiography,* of recalling things in a way to support his views at the moment, this account sounds plausible enough. His yarns depend so much on the oral quality and the illusion of spontaneity that understandably even his own reading would make them seem artificial, second-hand. He is always present on his pages, to be sure, but as a drolling storyteller, not an author. In Cable's stories, and most others as well, the incidents are narrated; in Mark Twain's they are acted, in that the author is more a participant than a narrator. Cable is always in his stories, but in a different way. He comments on his characters; he even looks over their shoulders, revealing all he can see, regretting that he can see no more; he overhears part of a conversation but tantalizingly misses part of it. The reader finds Mark Twain's personality in every phrase; Cable's reader forgets the author as he follows the story. And so on the stage Cable stood quite naturally with a book in his hand, reading of very real but remote people and happenings; Mark must stand and seem to extemporize, to spin his yarns *de novo* and to flavor them with his own personality, of which everyone in his presence was aware.

Those who heard Cable remembered that "his slimness and his high-keyed, soft-toned voice were proper to his material," in Hamlin Garland's words;[9] that he was masterful, as another said, in "working up to climaxes with refined passion and casting over his efforts a peculiarly fascinating glamour of quaintness."[10] One listener objected to "a touch here and there of amateurishness and a certain self-consciousness that rather interfered with the recital"; H. C. Bunner thought the reading was "clever, earnest, and utterly amateurish" but "simply nowhere" as a professional performance.[11] But others, including those who knew best the subtler qualities of the stories, put greatest value on the amateurishness of the reading and singing. Mark Twain was one; Charles Dudley Warner and Major Pond were others.

Pond and Mark Twain both said years afterward that Cable's voice training destroyed the best quality of his reading. They remembered his natural talent for reading which had been demonstrated in "the splendid days of his ignorance," as Mark put it; but the early readings

[9] *Roadside Meetings,* p. 352.

[10] *Picayune,* Nov. 28, 1884.

[11] Gerard E. Jensen, *The Life and Letters of Henry Cuyler Bunner* (Durham, N. C., 1939), p. 77.

they recalled were in drawing rooms or little halls. Furthermore, Mark's comments were made in the context of explaining the method he had evolved for himself without any professional training. No doubt Cable's later readings lacked the charm and the intimacy of the one, say, that he gave in the Warners' drawing room in April, 1883, but it is not easy to say how much of the artificiality, the professionalism was essential for reading to larger audiences—2200 in the Music Hall in Boston on November 14, 1884, and 3000 in Philadelphia the next February 26— or how much of it was the natural result of reading night after night, hundreds of times. "They were difficult audiences," Mark wrote afterward, "those untrained squads, and Cable and I had a hard time with them sometimes."[12] Actually, the audiences could have needed little training—the show was of a sort to carry itself unassisted from one number to another. Howells once wrote to Clemens: "You simply straddled down to the footlights and took that house up in the hollow of your hand and *tickled it*."[13] From the time he began, the laughter was all but continuous. Then, as someone turned the phrase, "Cable like a poultice came, to heal the blows of Twain." Cable afterward could recall only once in all their appearances when Clemens laughed with his audience.[14]

However unstudied the effects may have seemed to be, such was far from the case. Both were sensitive to the responses they drew, and when the audiences could not be lifted, as they put it, they puzzled to find the reason and worked hopefully for the next performance. Normally Cable's initial number went without an encore, but a few times he was called back even after it, as at Louisville on January 6, and then as a matter of course all the others would be encored. As a rule, though, the response was slower, as at Toledo on December 15, where the audience had to be waked "out of the depths of apathy." Cable explained as the program developed:

Our experience with such houses is that I lift them a little with my first number, then he lifts them from that stage a little higher, then with my 2/d number I lift them to a third elevation & with his 2/d no. (being the 4th) he gets them into a good strong glow. I am happy to see it is working just so now, after all. If he can get an encore from them on this we shall have them to the end without any trouble.

[12] *Mark Twain in Eruption*, p. 215.
[13] *Mark Twain's Letters*, II, 454. See also E. F. Pabody, "Mark Twain's Ghost Story," *Minnesota History: A Quarterly Magazine*, XVIII (March, 1937), 28-35.
[14] "Mark Twain's 70th Birthday," *Harper's Weekly*, XLIX (Dec. 23, 1905), 1889.

There! Mark gets the call back twice over. Now we're all right. It will be encores right through to the end.

It turns out as I said; each one called back at the end of each number.

At Burlington, Iowa, on January 15 Cable had to go on the stage alone. Mark Twain had stayed over with his mother in Keokuk and was delayed by a late train. "I had to lift a stone-dead audience out of the grave, as it were," Cable wrote, "and put life & mirth into them & keep their spirits rising for an hour & a half all alone. I did it, however, & when Clemens came into the house at 9/35 my work was much more than done & he had an enthusiasm to start on. I was proud of the job." At Chicago two days later he wrote, ". . . when I gave 'A Sound of Drums' I saw persons in tears all over the house. I was called back twice after my Creole songs and twice after Mary's Night Ride. Mark & I both seemed specially inspired tonight & to inspire each other." From Milwaukee on January 29 he wrote again as the readings progressed, beginning when Mark was on the stage for his first number:

I hear the ladies laughing at the tops of their voices, & whenever they do that the encore is certain to come....

Now here is the strangest thing! A house full of people, seemingly highly entertained but feeble in their final applauses. Mark was not called back & I, following, was so feebly encored that I did not feel justified in doing more than bowing. Fact is Mark is under a cloud tonight—feels it, confesses it, but cannot explain it. He doesn't take hold of his hearers & swing them as usual. . . .

Strongest, hardiest kind of a reception to "Mary's Ride." Now Mark is on to finish; but I know he is going to come off wringing his hands with vexation. Fact is our hard railroad travel is telling on us—has let out—slackened—our nerves. Queerly, but truly, we feel it most after a partial resting spell. I am not feeling it much tonight & I think it is because I have been so busy all day. Mark has done nothing and is knocked up....

Finis. Mark explains it all. He had a *warm bath* ½ an hour before the reading. He'll never take another.

At Rockford, Illinois, the next night he wrote again from the waiting room:

I am reminded by something Mark is saying, of what a fine instinctive art he has for the platform. He has worked & worked incessantly on these programmes until he has effected in all of them—there are 3—a gradual growth of both interest & humor so that the audience never has to find anything less, but always more, entertaining than what precedes it. He says "I don't want them to get tired out laughing before we get to the end." The result is we have always a steady crescendo ending in a double climax. My

insight into his careful, untiring, incessant labors are an education almost
as valuable as that got from Sargent & Henderson. There! It does me good
to hear them call him back at the place where the encores generally begin,
instead of letting him go as they did in Milwaukee last night. Goodbye.
I sang badly tonight. They encored me, but they hadn't ort to a-done it.

Again, at Chicago on February 3:

There is a vast audience in the house rising tier upon tier from pit to dome
to tell us good-bye. Mark's very first number was encored. I followed as
you will see (other side) with "A Sound of Drums." Every word of it came
from the bottom of my heart, I was in superb voice, and they called me back.
They wouldn't take a mere bow & I sang "Brave Boys" to loud applause.
Mark is telling one of his very best numbers & the old surf-roar is booming.
They will encore every number to the end.

Ah! what a noble applause calls Mark back. . . .

Funny thing just now. I had been out & sung two Creole songs & on
retiring the applause died down & Mark in his nervous way stepping out
on the platform a little too promptly was met by a pattering encore intended
for the singer. It was awkward for him, but he was equal to the emergency.
He stood still a moment, then said in the drollest way imaginable—"I'll go
back and get him"—At which there was a roar of laughter & applause in
the midst of which he came back to make his word good. Of course I would
not go, so he went back and raised another laugh, saying, "He's sung all
he knows"—and went on with "The Jumping Frog," which is getting a
superb reception.

Well, my work is done. Mary's Night Ride was encored all right & I
sang "Salangudou." Mark is finishing. What a fine night it has been.

Cable's report of the reading at Oberlin, Ohio, on February 12 is of
special interest because there the press was particularly severe on Mark
Twain.[15]

We reached Oberlin at a quarter to seven and were to go upon the platform
at *seven*. I did get on the platform at 7/20 & even then was inconvenienced
by the tardy incoming of a special train from another town, that brought
about a hundred auditors.

Strange to say I went to work fresh & bright & from the very start did,
by verdict of all, the finest evening's reading thus far in my experience.
The very first number, that generally goes to make me acquainted & set the

[15] In an article "Mark Twain in Oberlin," *Ohio State Archaeological and Historical
Quarterly*, XLVIII (Jan., 1938), 69-70, Russell B. Nye has presented the arguments that
Mark Twain intended to ridicule Oberlin in "The Man That Corrupted Hadleyburg." In
"Mark Twain's Hadleyburg," published in the same journal, LX (July, 1951), 257-64,
Guy A. Cardwell argues against this view.

people a-smiling, was met with almost boistrous delight from the very start.

Clemens, on the contrary, found himself as heavy as lead—I mean in his own consciousness, and although the audience showed some heartiness of appreciation while he was before them, yet he came off disheartened, vexed, & full of lamentations over his condition.

On my 2d number I instantly shot ahead of any rendering I have ever before made of it. I was full of new inspirations, was interrupted early with applause, and when I came to where Ristofalo puts his arm around Kate they would not let me go any farther but drowned in applause my repeated efforts to proceed & when I finally got the better of them & went on, it was, so to speak, through breakers of laughter and applause, to the end, which was, however, just at hand.

Clemens met me behind the door with pantomimic expressions of amazement & was about to go on for his turn, when a rush of applause called me back. I went, but excused myself in an impromptu remark or two, as I wanted Mark to get back & redeem himself without delay & knew he was nearly sick to do so. As I came off once more I saw intense gratification in his face. —"That was most gracefully said," he exclaimed, and went out on the platform.

But still he rolled in the trough of the sea. . . .

He felt his deficiency the more distressingly because the previous night he had been nearly as bad. However it was, he began at length to rally. In Mary's Night Ride I introduced some improvements that had occurred to me the night before. . . .

In the midst of the story a comical thing occurred. At the point where the negro guide speaks his loud whispered goodbye to Mary & the spy, saying "I feared you gwine fo'git it, boss," in the midst of the death-like stillness which always reigns throughout the house just then, a black man, sitting behind me in a sort of choir loft all alone & in sight of every one, recognizing the mimicked African enunciation and the old southern title of respect, let go a suppressed but loud titter of the purest Ethiopian character, and its character as well as its irrelevancy brought down the house. Yet it rather helped than hindered me, and when I came to the fierce thrilling end I knew by every symptom, both inward & outward that I had done the best bit of reading I had ever done in my life.

In response to the encore I excused myself—Mark *never* objects to my declining an encore—& read a little note that had come in while Mark was on the platform, asking him to read the story of the "Golden Arm." So then out he came and read it & did it well & was called back & did another thing and did it his very best & so the evening ended, and presently the retiring room was full of new friends.

In the efforts to lift their audiences they often found circumstances against them and at other times quite helpful. At Cincinnati on January 2, Cable's preliminary remarks being drowned out by the latecomers, he announced he would sit down until the aisles had emptied into the chairs. When two hundred had found seats, and the laughter had died down, he remarked that he had never before attempted to read to a procession; the laughter and applause began anew and his first number "went off with the happiest effect." Mary's Night Ride was assisted at Buffalo on December 10 when, at the point where Cable said, "And they made it," a man in the front row jumped and yelled "Good" so that he could be heard all over the house. But no assistance could be drawn in the four instances during the first two months of the tour when a lady had to be carried from the hall during his reading of the same piece. He and Mark Twain had grown so annoyed at persons leaving the hall during a number that they had agreed "to give any such person a shot across the bows." Then at Hamilton, Ohio, "a man with creaking shoes stalked out of the hall in the midst of one of Mark's numbers. . . . So Mark calls out in the most benevolent & persuasive tone, 'take your shoes off, please; take your shoes off'—to the great delight of the applauding audience."

There was much sameness but much variety from day to day and hall to hall. At Philadelphia Cable wrote on November 26: "Mark is on the stage reading (reciting) his 'Desperate Encounter with an Interviewer,' and the roars of laughter fall regularly as a surf. I think it's a great thing to be able to hold my own with so wonderful a platform figure." At Ann Arbor on December 13: "In the Kate Riley courtship scene I was at one point interrupted by applause so long that for the first time in my experience I had to abandon my impersonations of the character and stand & wait until they would let me resume. Mary's Night Ride received a double encore. We were kept 30 minutes longer on the platform than we had expected to be. It is astonishing how much like the steady tumble of the surf the laughter was when Mark was reading."

At Toronto December 8, Cable mentioned the Creole songs in writing Louise and added, "I always shrink from this, the only thing I do shrink from; though it's always encored." He had included the Creole songs in his earliest programs but had been troubled about them. His advisers did not agree. Pond and others more interested in his drawing power heartily approved, but those like Gilder who thought of him primarily as an author disapproved, and a decision was deferred. His songs were more popular than anything else he did except possibly Mary's Night Ride; newspaper reporters saved their warmest praise for them.

When H. C. Bunner heard him in January, 1884, he wrote his friend
Walter Learned he was only moderately impressed with the reading.

But the singing—that caught everybody. It was absolutely artless. He took
the key as a kind Providence gave it to him. If it didn't happen to be the
right one, he cheerfully announced the fact, and made a new guess for the
next verse. But the *go,* and the lilt, and the solid, keen enjoyment he took
in it! And the strong, pulsing wild melodies! Nigger from the ground
up, and full of life. The huge house woke up as if you had turned a dynamo
on it.[16]

Toward the end of their fourth month on the road they felt and
showed the effects of the grind. They could joke about the hardships, as
they did early in February when they left Chicago for the "dreary, dis-
mal taverns, and dingy, dirty platforms & auditoriums" of the small
Indiana towns, as Cable described them. Mark Twain said, "Once more
we resume a dog's life," to which Cable added, "Worse than that;—two
dogs' lives." Mark still walked in his room in his nightshirt and sang
"We Shall Walk Through the Valley," or the two sang together—but
less often than before. Much of the travel had been exhausting. Often
they had to catch trains after an evening's reading, or worse still, between
midnight and morning, and there were a few such experiences as the
trip from Rockford, Illinois, to Davenport, Iowa, at the end of January:

Took a passenger coach on the end of a freight train at eleven, (the train
kept back an *hour* & furnished with the coach, for our special convenience,
by the superintendent, who came to see us off) changed cars (trains) into
a sleeper at Davis Junction, at 12/15 A.M., changed again into another train
& sleeper at 3/45 at "Savanna," were wakened at 7 o'clock, took the sleigh
trip through the snow & across the Mississippi that I told you of, got breakfast here, wrote letters (Mark & Adams played billiards) received Miss San-
ders's call at 12/30 P.M., dined at 1/15, read till 2/30, went to bed, slept
until nearly 6, supped lightly & felt ready for anything. Found Clemens
heavy as lead—all unstrung. Advised a cup of black coffee. He took it,
braced up in a moment, & we had as nearly perfect an entertainment as
we have ever produced.

At Detroit on February 12, the night after Mark Twain was helplessly down at Oberlin, Cable wrote:

I've got to say it's my turn tonight. I'm going all to pieces. Have read
two numbers & don't get hold of the audience with any force at all. Dear,
dear! how dreadful the feeling is! especially when one knows, sees & feels
that the fault is not in the audience at all but in the utter looseness and soft-

[16] Jensen, *The Life and Letters of Henry Cuyler Bunner,* p. 77.

ness—flabbiness of all his energies. O me! I've got to go out there presently and sing.

At Philadelphia it was Mark's turn to be at a low ebb again, for no apparent reason except that he was tired out. The next night at Baltimore Mark was himself again, and Cable wrote Louise, "It's a great comfort."

They closed at Washington on February 28. Mark Twain turned north, after a few days, and Cable took the train for New Orleans. The tour had brought the two members of the team into a closer and more constant association than would have been likely in any other kind of undertaking. Though it was Mark Twain's habit to ride in the smoking car often and to sleep or read in bed while Cable attended church on Sunday, they were still together many hours of every day. With but one or two exceptions they traveled together; they normally had adjoining hotel rooms; whenever there was entertainment both were included. They made jokes at each other's expense; they sang together in their rooms, especially the Mississippi ditty "Jan and Dan," which they sang almost nightly.

Yet the differences between the two were great, no less in other respects than in physical appearance. "They were a curiously-assorted pair," wrote Albert Bigelow Paine, Mark Twain's friend and biographer: "Cable was of orthodox religion, exact as to habits, neat, prim, all that Clemens was not."[17] They were farthest from agreement in religious observances, and the subject remained, as it had been before the tour, the basis for many of Mark's jokes. When Pond informed him while the arrangements were first being discussed that Cable refused to travel on the Sabbath and that the itinerary must be made accordingly, Mark's reply was, "Well, I guess I shall meet him in Heaven, finally. I had some fears on the subject."[18] A time or two Mark Twain proceeded on Sunday to the next stop while Cable waited until Monday morning, but most often staying over Sunday after a Saturday night's reading was the plausible thing for Mark to do also.

Cable was not one to waver, now or at any other time, in what he considered his religious obligations. To travel on Sunday in order to work Monday was to his mind no different from working on the Sabbath. He liked for Sunday meals to be simple, for then he would not feel that their preparation had made the day into a working-day for anyone. Travel on the Sabbath would meet the same objection. Sun-

[17] *Mark Twain's Letters,* II, 447. See also Lawton, *A Lifetime with Mark Twain,* p. 78.
[18] Pond to Cable, June 18, 1884.

day should be not less but more pleasant than other days; and to him quiet visiting with friends, reading, or walking would provide the highest pleasure. The significance of the Sabbath to him is suggested in his words to Louise closing a long résumé of his day's activities in Grand Rapids on December 14: "This hasn't been one of my best Sundays. I do not feel that spiritual refreshment I want. But the next one, God willing, will be spent with you in our quiet valley home among our five darlings and our gentle, quiet friends."

He liked to set out from his hotel and attend whatever church he first came to. At Louisville on January 4 he stumbled upon an African-Methodist-Temperance Church, where he was the only white person in the house. In Davenport, Iowa, on February 1 he attended the Presbyterian Church in the morning and the Congregational Church in the evening. In Minneapolis he attended the Presbyterian Church, hoping not to be recognized, but was found out and as usual was persuaded to take a part in the service. At Grand Rapids he dropped in at a Baptist Sunday School, with the following result, as he wrote Louise on December 14:

The preacher came round. Asked me if I was a stranger. Yes. Where did I live. O, a great way off; just in town for a day; tho't I'd drop in, &c. But he would have my name & town. I gave it—joy! still unrecognized! Presently he came back. "Did you say you were from New Orleans?" "Yes." "Do you, or did you ever, know a gentleman there named Sevier?—Dr. Sevier?" "No, sir." He looked me in the eye. I did as much to him. Then he said, "Is Dr. Sevier dead?" "Yes, sir." I threw up the sponge. He got me upon the platform.

Some of Mark Twain's funniest jibes had their starting point in Cable's religiousness. Some of them are in his letters to Cable, others in his letters to Howells; others he spoke in the good fellowship of gatherings at Hartford and elsewhere. Delivered under such circumstances, they do not belong with his thrusts at Bret Harte, which stemmed from a genuine distaste,[19] but with his jibes at his friend Reverend Joseph Twichell. Howells knew how to read the letter he had from Mark at the close of the reading tour in which he wrote:

My four-months platform campaign . . . has been a curious experience. It has taught me that Cable's gifts of mind are greater and higher than I had suspected. But—
That "But" is pointing toward his religion. You will never, never know,

[19] For Mark Twain's appraisal of Bret Harte written in 1906 and 1907, see *Mark Twain in Eruption*, pp. 254-92.

never divine, guess, imagine, how loathsome a thing the Christian religion can be made until you come to know and study Cable daily and hourly. Mind you, I like him; he is pleasant company; I rage and swear at him sometimes, but we do not quarrel; we get along mighty happily together; but in him and his person I have learned to hate all religions. He has taught me to abhor and detest the Sabbath-day and hunt up new and troublesome ways to dishonor it.[20]

Similarly those attending the celebration on Mark's seventieth birthday in New York understood and enjoyed his passing use of the phrase "a sterile moralist" and then backing up to change it to *the* sterile moralist," with the remark that there was only one.[21] At his turn to speak on the same occasion Cable said: "We have heard that the friend whom we celebrate has said he likes Cable well except for his religion. Well, I am bound to declare the exception well taken. The longer I live the less I am satisfied with my religion myself. But for all that, I must say that from the depth of my religion—Heaven send long years yet, Mark Twain, because you keep yourself too busy with more important matters."

Albert Bigelow Paine is authority for the statement that at the opening of the tour Cable began reading the Bible to his companion in their hotel rooms and that Mark Twain stopped him.[22] Both parts of this statement are readily believable. To Cable daily Bible reading, with his family or with others, was routine; and Mark had rebelled against the practice in his own home. Cable of course regretted that his friend did not attend church. He wrote of Mark to Louise on December 7: "Oh! how I wish he were a man of prayer & worship. But he has more nobleness of nature & is more to be admired than I knew before now." At Indianapolis on February 8 he wrote her that he had returned to the hotel from Church and "entrapped Mark into a discussion on the duty of practicing religion—from his point of view—whipped him off the field & left him, he saying as I went he wished he had gone to church with me. Would to God I might prevail to take him there." Then on March 2, Sunday, two days after their last reading together, they stayed through the day together in Washington, chiefly with friends Cable had known earlier in New Orleans. Cable wrote Louise, "I got him out to church at last!"

These remarks suggest that Cable had pressed the subject at other times, but there are no further references in the letters to Louise. One

[20] *Mark Twain's Letters*, II, 450.
[21] "Mark Twain's 70th Birthday," *Harper's Weekly*, XLIX (Dec. 23, 1905), 1884-1914.
[22] Paine, *Mark Twain*, II, 786.

feels safe in taking Mark's saying in Indianapolis he wished he had gone to church with Cable to mean that if he had gone he would have escaped the discussion afterward. Yet Cable did not take the remark in that way. And there is the additional fact that they did attend church together in Washington. It seems that while Mark was learning from Cable's example to hate all religions, as he wrote Howells, he still respected his companion's sincerity. He made jibes at Cable's religious practices before, during, and after the tour, and the liberties he took in doing so may be the best evidence of the understanding that existed between the two men. Cable enjoyed the jokes too, as he showed more than once in repeating them in letters to Louise; and they were delightfully quotable among their friends. That Cable thought of Mark Twain in the same connection even afterward is shown in his remark to a newspaper reporter at Utica on May 6, 1889, after hearing a sermon he especially liked: "I wish that Twain had been here to-day. He is not much of a church-goer. But such a service as we have had would have taken hold upon him, and given him great pleasure. His sensibilities are quick and deep when rightly touched."

Well before the tour closed, Pond had proposed continuing through March. Cable was willing but Mark Twain was not. The venture had been a financial success. After all expenses it had paid Mark Twain, in round figures, $16,000, Cable $5,000, and Pond $3,000.[23] And it had been satisfying in other ways. They had seen old friends and made new ones; they had been entertained flatteringly, though to a superfluity; they had read to full houses of sympathetic listeners who were as a rule pleasingly responsive; the press had been almost invariably kind and usually extravagant in praise. Mark Twain had wanted Cable for his partner because he considered him both a good performer and an agreeable companion. He had himself lectured at intervals since his beginning at San Francisco in 1866, but he was an apprentice at public reading. Cable was the old hand, having packed halls in the larger cities during the season of 1883-1884 and cleared $1000 in one series of readings at Boston. Though it is true that Mark Twain made the better newspaper copy and attracted greater notice wherever they went, his partner was equally respected by both audiences and reviewers and many times received the better notices. It was not uncommon for a reporter to give more space to Mark Twain's doings and sayings but to reserve his chief accolade for the art of Cable's writings and his reading of them.[24] A reporter in

---

[23] The figure of $35,000 repeated in the newspapers as the net yield to Mark Twain would be close to the total receipts from ticket sales.

[24] Fred W. Lorch, in "Cable and His Reading Tour with Mark Twain in 1884-1885,"

the Boston *Journal* of March 31, 1885, remarked that if either Cable or Twain were to be lost in the other as a consequence of their close association he would prefer to bid farewell to Twain.

Three times after the tour closed, Cable paid public homage to Mark Twain as a great man and as an esteemed friend: in a sketch written for the *Letter* of the Home Culture Clubs on February 1, 1896; at the seventieth birthday party in 1905; and at the memorial service in 1910. In the *Letter* he called Mark Twain "beyond compare the greatest humorist in America, and one of the greatest in the world's literature," and continued: "A humor like his is never mere humor nor mere nature; it is wisdom and truth and art as well. . . . Few writers have ever disguised so much subtle art under such cunning ostentation of awkwardness." The thesis of his remarks at the memorial service was that "the rare beauty" of Mark Twain's mind was no less a part of him than "the vast grotesqueness of his wit and humor." He went on:

I mean a beauty such as the illimitable haphazard of Nature a few times in our planet's history has hit upon, where angels would seem to have builded in a moment of careless sport, as in the Grand Cañon of the Colorado, or some equal wonder of supernal color and titanic form in that great West which had so much to do with the shaping of his genius—in so far as his genius was ever really shaped.

The beauty of that mind was a beauty of form and color, so to speak, rather than of mechanism. The marvelous union of crudeness and grace in those vast natural formations in the West symbolizes well the energy of his purposes, as the marvelous variety and intensity of their colors do the many passions of his spirit.

Apparently in no utterance that has come down in any record did Cable disparage his friend in the slightest way.

Mark Twain was annoyed by Cable during their four months on the road. In his habitual manner he voiced his annoyance to Olivia and no doubt to others as well, usually avowing at the same time his affection and respect for his companion. As it became evident after the tour had closed, some of his adverse remarks were repeated outside the circle of his and Cable's friends to his own discomfort, apparently, as well as Cable's, for slanders were carried in the press which could have grown only from remarks of his. And much as he had been irked by Cable during their weeks together, he assuredly did not want to further such public accusations.

American Literature, XXIII (Jan., 1952), 471-86, and Guy A. Cardwell, in *Twins of Genius,* reach the same conclusions as these after consulting reports of the readings in the newspapers.

It seems to have been Mark Twain's habit to plant words or entire passages in manuscripts as he wrote them as a game with Olivia, inviting her protests. His charges against Cable may have been worded in part with the same purpose in mind, but he no doubt was genuinely irritated at times. He delivered himself most fully in the letters on Cable's "idiotic Sunday-superstition." Warming to this subject on February 5, he wrote Olivia how he had exploded in what amounted to an insult to Cable.[25] They were at a reception given them in Indianapolis by friends of James Guthrie, Cable's friend in New Orleans. Cable wrote Louise of the reception on February 8 but made no reference to the incident Mark reported to Olivia. Mark put into letters to Olivia equally fantastic charges that Cable was close in money matters: that he included in the general expense account laundry costs that he should have paid himself; that, on Pond's authority, he starved himself when paying his own expenses but had an insatiable appetite when someone else was paying; that he sponged hotel stationery for his writing. Olivia had written by February 13 that she was to transmit to Cable the request for a benefit reading before the Decorative Art Society of Hartford. Writing on that day, Mark charged her under no conditions to have anything to do with the request, adding that Cable "wouldn't read in Heaven for nothing." How much weight Olivia gave to the charge is attested by the fact that she sent Cable the request soon afterward, buttressed by her own plea.[26]

These accusations seem to be a mixture of fun and venom, but some of Mark's comments show a greater portion of venom. It was his habit to distrust his business associates and to believe they had swindled him. He had picked Cable for his partner because his ability had been proved, but he came to begrudge Cable's time on the stage, if not to resent his success. Mark wrote his brother Orion that he did not like to think of the Burlington performance, in which Cable had held the platform an hour and a half before he arrived. "I had to cut myself shorter than I wanted to," he added, "& I did not talk well, anyway, because I felt myself so heavily handicapped by the hellish circumstances."[27] It may not have been by accident that they began at once a new plan. "Cable

[25] Dixon Wecter, ed., *The Love Letters of Mark Twain* (New York, 1949), p. 234. Other references to Mark's letters to Olivia during the tour are to this volume, pp. 219-40. In annotating the letters, Mr. Wecter slips into the error made by others of Mark Twain's biographers of assuming that Cable was an inconsequential, envious appendage hindering Mark's efforts as he toured the country. Unhappily too he does not quote but summarizes some portions of what Mark wrote about Cable.

[26] Olivia Clemens to Cable, March 2, 1885.

[27] Samuel Charles Webster, *Mark Twain, Business Man* (Boston, 1946), pp. 292-93.

goes on at the very stroke of the hour," Mark wrote Olivia on January 17, "& talks fifteen minutes to an *assembling* house. . . . The good effect is beyond estimation. (And privately, *another* thing—only half the house hear C's first piece—so there isn't too much of C any more—whereas heretofore there has been a thundering sight too much of him.)" Cable wrote Louise that he liked the new plan. On February 10 Mark groaned to his wife that Cable kept his program strung out to an hour (about half their total time) in spite of all he could do: "That infernal Night Ride of Mary's," he wrote, "has grown from 6 minutes (in New Haven) to *fifteen*! And it is in *every* program." It was in almost every program, but it was Cable's most popular number, was surest of being encored, and was often requested when not included. Mark was thinking, he told Olivia, of cutting out another of Cable's numbers.

Mark Twain's letters to Olivia as they have been published contain no unfavorable references to Cable during their first two and a half months on the road, save for a remark early in January on Cable's laundry. The disparaging comments are bunched in the weeks after the reading at Burlington. Several reasons can be adduced for Mark's growing irritation, besides his weariness and his dissatisfaction with his own performances. For one thing, his multitudinous business concerns had become more distracting. He could not get from his partner Charles L. Webster as much information as he wanted on his complex interests. He questioned Pond's accounting of the returns for the readings; he bedeviled Pond so about the traveling managers that Major Pond asked Cable to intercede and get Mark to be reasonable.

For another thing, Mark apparently was not satisfied with the financial returns. On January 25 he wrote Webster he should have stayed at home and written another book—it would have paid him better. In the preceding weeks he had been screaming at Webster by letter and telegram about the publication of *Huckleberry Finn,* the negotiations for publishing General Grant's memoirs, a lawsuit he had begun and others he wanted to begin, and the several promotional schemes that were going to make him rich. It is no wonder, in fact, that money came too slowly from the tour and that his patience was short with the partner and the manager traveling with him. The wonder is rather that, a man of moods and in the mood he was in during the last few weeks, he exploded about Cable only a few times and then mainly to his wife.

It is worth noting also that Cable's prominence was greatly augmented after the middle of January. Both men were tired in the last weeks, but it was more often Mark who rolled in the trough of the sea and he fretted because he could not take hold on his audiences as he had formerly done. Furthermore, Cable had become a celebrated man with the publication in January of his essay on "The Freedman's Case in Equity." The nation's newspapers were full and many of them were loud with their comment on his analysis of the Southern race problem. Reporters flocked to him, and prominent people came often to discuss the subject with him. It may have been this situation which prompted Mark Twain to write Olivia on February 13, "He is one of the most spoiled men, by success in life, you ever saw," though he could not have expected her to take the remark seriously. Certainly in the last six weeks on the road Mark saw himself, not eclipsed, but nearly equaled in popularity both on and off the platform.

Mark Twain's comments to Olivia were of course unknown to Cable, as were also any similar remarks he may have made to Pond or others. The tour came to an end with ostensibly good feeling all the way round. Mary Twain said he would not return to the platform, but it could be only inference that the decision owed anything to the tour with Cable. Pond had complained to Cable often that he had never done so much work for so little pay—but he made the same complaint as long as he managed Cable's lectures, and his letters make it clear that Mark Twain was the one he thought unreasonable in his demands. When Mark Twain returned to the platform in the round-the-world tour, Pond was his manager; there was no cooling in Cable's and Pond's relations; and Cable kept his high regard for Mark, who in turn was without doubt speaking his mind honestly when he told Howells he had learned that Cable's gifts of mind were greater and higher than he had suspected and that they had got along "mighty happily together." A letter he wrote Cable after ten years, on June 25, 1895, seems an adequate summary of what he thought of his lecture companion, religion and all:

Yes, *sir!* I liked you in spite of your religion; & I always said to myself that a man that could be good & kindly with that kind of a load on him was entitled to homage—& I *paid* it. And I have always said, & still maintain, that as a railroad-comrade you were perfect—the only railroad-comrade in the world that a man of moods & frets & uncertainties of disposition could travel with, a third of a year, and never weary of his company. We always had good times in the cars, & never minded the length of the trips—& my, but they *were* sockdolagers for length![28]

[28] Three weeks later than this letter Mark Twain set out on his round-the-world reading tour, accompanied across the country by Major Pond as his manager. Pond kept a diary (later printed in part in his book *Eccentricities of Genius,* pp. 200-25)

Yet within a few weeks after the reading team had disbanded, the newspapers printed comments on the tour, critical particularly of Cable, some of which could have originated ultimately with no one but Mark Twain. These slanderous charges were written and published, however, after the way had been prepared by the stand Cable had taken on the race question and the newspapers had heaped abuse on him for that reason.

---

which he thought of making into an illustrated volume on the tour. He wrote Cable on Aug. 20 asking whether he would edit the book for him, saying he thought Mark and Olivia would approve him as editor. In the same letter Pond made a remark on Olivia's part in Mark's work which takes weight from the fact that he had traveled in their company more than a month: "Mrs. C. is the great editor of all Mark's writings & doings. Her conception of the idea of continuity of stories & introduction of pathos has made Mark Twain the greatest one-man attraction living."

CHAPTER XIV

THE FREEDMAN'S CASE

WHEN Cable published "The Freedman's Case in Equity," his relatives and friends realized, as he of course did, the consequences he might expect. Marion Baker was concerned; his sister Mary Louise asked him to be as lenient with the poor South as he could and hoped the ultimate result would be good; his mother-in-law wished he could find it in his conscience to leave the Negro question alone. He asked Roswell Smith's opinion and had unequivocal endorsement of his case. We who are educated, who understand the real import of the question, Smith continued, "must lay down broad principles—and stand by our profession of principles through whatever of obloquy or reproach." By August the national press reported the paper in preparation. Cable was proceeding carefully and thoughtfully. A New Orleans friend of his, R. C. Hitchcock, was in correspondence with people in the Louisiana parishes, colored as well as white, to collect facts for him.

"The Freedman's Case in Equity" had been taking shape for two years before its publication, and its seeds had been germinating at least ten years. Every page of the essay shows that he knew how touchy the subject was—he remarked that he was an ex-Confederate soldier, the son and grandson of slaveholders; he conceded what he could; and when he had rounded out the case, he asked, "Is it not well to have done so?" He had already made it clear he had no doubts about the justice of the charges or the propriety of making them.

Though his convictions and his feelings were nowhere obscured, he held himself to a calm statement, reminding the reader often that he was speaking from firsthand observation. Further, he founded his case on close logic and common sense, reverting constantly to morality and justice as touchstones against expediency and half-measures. He avoided quoting Negroes in their own behalf, and with a few exceptions he omitted examples, preferring to state the situation in general terms and escape the emotion such testimony and examples would incite. His hope was to raise the ethical question, to invite open discussion, and thus to support those in the South who, he said, "are beginning to see very

plainly that the whole community is sinned against in every act or attitude of oppression, however gross or however refined."

Opening with the assertion that "The greatest social problem before
the American people to-day is, as it has been for a hundred years, the
presence among us of the negro," he asserted that no section was without
blame in the establishment and perpetuation of slavery, and hence for
the consequent ills also. Recently, however, the Supreme Court ruling
that the Federal statutes to enforce civil rights were unconstitutional
had left the matter to the individual states. He raised no protest at
this decision but urged that the whole nation nevertheless had an interest
in the results.

He saw two roots of the problem: (1) the conception of the Negro
as an alien and the perpetuation of that stigma in the Southern mind as
a means whereby intelligent, upright people could justify slaveholding
in a country dedicated to liberty for all men; and (2) the belief that the
faults and vices natural to a people long in servitude were God-ordained
and that in consequence no acquirement of freedom or wealth or training or culture could remove the stigma. Legal guarantees of rights
would have slight effect if these two sentiments, unworthy of an intelligent people, should persist. Similarly "the question of instinct." Even
if valid, "it would not necessarily be a proper moral guide," and "it
stands to reason that just in degree as it is a real thing it will take care
of itself."

To argue that the Negro was suffering any real abridgment of rights,
he cited only a few generalized instances such as the exclusion from
juries. From the pages first written for the convict lease paper he took
statistics showing a preponderant number of Negroes in the state penitentiaries. In the light of the need of the South for material improvements which it was supposed the leases made possible, he said, "we
may almost assert beforehand that the popular mind will—not so ma-
liciously as unreflectingly—yield to the tremendous temptation to hustle
the misbehaving black man into the State prison under extravagant
sentence, and sell his labor to the highest bidder who will use him in
the construction of public works." He cited also the incident he had
witnessed in the railway cars to Louisville which he later said persuaded
him to take up the question of Negro rights—he had seen a clean,
neatly dressed Negro woman and her daughter forced to ride in a
crowded coach with nineteen chained, filthy convicts on their way to
the mines. If she had been traveling as the nurse of a white child, she
would have ridden in the nearly empty white coach.

He thought it "wise that all have agreed not to handicap education with the race question," but he added, recalling his observation as a reporter in 1872, that he had seen "the two races sitting in the same public high-school and grammar-school rooms, reciting in the same classes and taking recess on the same ground at the same time, without one particle of detriment that any one ever pretended to discover, although the fiercest enemies of the system swarmed about it on every side." And he questioned whether the insistence on separate schools could be justified at a time when funds for public education were so limited. In other areas of segregation and exclusion he found enough to indict the idea of "separate and equal" accommodations, and he observed, as he had done ten years earlier, that bloodshed would surely result if segregation were forced upon any racial or national group besides the ex-slaves. The last paragraph reads in part:

And the answer must—it shall—come from the South. And it shall be practical. It will not cost much. We have had a strange experience: the withholding of simple rights has cost much blood; such concessions of them as we have made have never yet cost a drop. The answer is coming. Is politics in the way? Then let it clear the track or get run over, just as it prefers. But, as I have said over and over to my brethren in the South, I take upon me to say again here, that there is a moral and intellectual intelligence there which is not going to be much longer beguiled out of its moral right of way by questions of political punctilio, but will seek that plane of universal justice and equity which it is every people's duty before God to seek.

"The Freedman's Case in Equity" is an impressive document, though it has not the indignation of the letters in 1875 on segregation in the schools, or the bill of particulars against the social structure recited at the University of Mississippi. The author hoped not to be misunderstood and not to antagonize when he hoped to convince. On the subject of the public schools, he wrote:

I know that just here looms up the huge bugbear of Social Equality. Our eyes are filled with absurd visions of all Shanty-town pouring its hordes of unwashed imps into the company and companionship of our own sunny-headed darlings. What utter nonsense! As if our public schools had no gauge of cleanliness, decorum, or moral character! Social Equality! What a godsend it would be if the advocates of the old Southern régime could only see that the color line points straight in the direction of social equality by tending toward the equalization of all whites on one side of the line and of all blacks on the other. We may reach the moon some day, but not social equality.

To the conservative, this was of course no answer, for to him the only answer lay in phrases such as "race superiority" and "white supremacy."

In other instances also Cable's way of seeing or saying a thing evoked the resentment he hoped to prevent. More than once he observed the irony of history or of the contemporary situation, as for example the fact that a government dedicated to liberty and inalienable rights had from its inception tolerated chattel slavery. Or the argument heard in his time that the Negro question was a small matter that would settle itself, when six million citizens were being denied rights guaranteed by the Constitution. Or the acceptance of Negroes in any public accommodations if they appeared as servants, but not if they appeared as free citizens. By pointing up such ironies and predicating "the habit of oppression" for the South and calling slavery an "extinct and now universally execrated institution" which was condemned by "the rest of the civilized world" before it was abolished in the South, he no doubt antagonized many. A generalized plea for the Negro would have been given lip endorsement and then ignored, but these phrases, the specific charges, and the overtones of moral condemnation could not be ignored or quickly forgotten. It may be that the irritating elements in the essay supplied its strength.

The opposition was not long in showing itself, and with a sweep and virulence that surpassed anything Cable had expected. By the middle of January the clamor was running throughout the South and was being reviewed in Northern papers. Southern editors either assumed or asserted that Cable advocated social equality. Those who had read his essay found affirmation in what he stated as denial; the others—apparently a majority—simply repeated the charge. The tone was often sarcastic. The *Times-Democrat* of February 2 quoted nine Southern newspapers attacking Cable: He was anti-Southern and a traitor to his section; his chief concern was to please Northern readers and to drum up audiences for his public readings; intermarriage, social ruin, and racial warfare would result if his views were followed. In the light of the new essay some editors now saw his earlier writing on the convict lease system as an appeal to Northern eagerness to condemn the South. The "your cause was just" passage in *Dr. Sevier* was revived for further comment, as was also the Creole issue, though rarely without some prompting from New Orleans, where the Creoles saw their charges voiced in the English-language papers with little more restraint than in *L'Abeille*.[1]

[1] J. L. Tucker, rector of St. Andrew's Episcopal Church of Jackson, Mississippi, reported in *The Relations of the Church to the Colored Race* (Jackson, 1882) an experience of his own with interesting parallels to Cable's. Addressing the Church Con-

Occasionally a less extravagant note was struck among the Southern editors. Some admitted Cable's artistry in his fiction but added that his "crime" was no less reprehensible on that account; some conceded that the Freedman should have better treatment—but that "would not do for Mr. Cable"; some argued that his fault was not malice but ignorance; others regretted that he had abandoned fiction and invited the scorn of those who would prefer to praise him. Such notes were usually minor, however, and as a rule were drowned out by the more raucous notes of ironic condescension.

An editorial in the *Times-Democrat* may have been literally accurate in saying that not a paper in the entire South had spoken up to defend Cable's views. Marion Baker wrote him on February 5 that the *Times-Democrat* was "heading the pack" in the newspaper abuse and added, "You can form no idea of how bitter the feeling is against you, as bitter as it used to be against Garrison & men of his way of thinking in ante-bellum times." Actually, the New Orleans papers had waited two or three weeks to take the lead. The editor of the *Picayune* said on January 6 that he feared intermarriage and believed the Negro incapable of civilized government, but he agreed that the Negro should have better treatment and that public status should not be on the basis of color. The same paper on January 11 ignored the new issues in a review of *The Creoles of Louisiana*. Similarly the *Times-Democrat* on January 18 passed over the current discussion when it introduced Cable into a review of the *Historical Sketch-Book and Guide to New Orleans*,[2] which had been compiled for sale during the Exposition by Marion Baker, with assistance from Hearn, Norman Walker, and Mrs. James Durno, and with a prefatory recommendation by Cable. The book quoted Cable's works extensively and printed Hearn's essay "The Scenes of Cable's Romances" from the *Century*. It identified many of the landmarks Cable had described and said of the French Quarter, "Try speaking English to any of the dwellers in this neighborhood, and one is answered in the caressing accents and delicious dialect that makes so large a part of the charm of Cable's books." Another guide-book for Exposition visitors,

---

gress at Richmond, he had proposed a series of steps the church might undertake to spread true Christianity among the Negroes. In a passing remark he condemned slavery as an evil. "I was not aware, before," he said in telling of the response his address received, "how much abuse could be heaped upon one man, not a politician or candidate for office, whose sole object was the good of others; nor was I aware how such abuse could hurt. I notice one conspicuous fact, that among all attacks and denials that have reached me, not one of my critics undertakes to furnish proof that I am wrong."

[2] New York, 1885.

New Orleans As It Is. With a Correct Guide to All Places of Interest,[3] displayed Cable and his books no less.

These books suggest how much New Orleanians had learned about their city from Cable and how prominently it seemed proper to display him to visitors. He was the main authority, furthermore, on which both books leaned. Ironically, thousands of visitors explored the city with these guidebooks or Cable's books themselves in their hands at a time when many residents and particularly the Creoles wished to mark him as a traitor unqualified to speak on any phase of Southern life.

On January 19—to note the chronology—a long article on "Cable and the Creoles" in the *Times-Democrat* conceded that he must necessarily sustain attacks for the heterodox views in "The Freedman's Case in Equity" but proceeded to defend his portrayal of the Creoles, saying that he had dispelled erroneous and unfavorable ideas of them held in the North, and telling of a distinguished Creole who had first damned Cable without reading him but now "declared he was never more charmed and delighted than with Cable and his delineation of the Creoles." This article was beyond all doubt by Marion Baker, the literary editor, who was doing all he could on the book page to support his friend. In this purpose he had the help of his assistant, Elizabeth Bisland, later the editor of Lafcadio Hearn's letters. But the editorial department of the *Times-Democrat* was a house divided. Page Baker was prepared to resent warmly "The Freedman's Case in Equity," and from January 22 on, his paper took undisputed lead in the assault on Cable, through editorials, some of them surely from his own pen, excerpts from other Southern papers, contributed articles, reports of public addresses, and miscellaneous comments. Thus the newspaper which four years before had adopted and supported with all its power Cable's program of social reform and since then had applauded his every success, through the writing of Marion Baker and Hearn, now turned on him with all the fury it could command.

Before its course was clearly charted, however, the *Times-Democrat* had the assistance of a zealous warrior against Cable, the Creole historian Charles Gayarré, who turned from the historical articles he had been writing occasionally for the Sunday papers to attacks on Cable in print and in public lectures. His sincerity could not be doubted, but the energy and the apparent pleasure with which he went about his self-imposed task seem hardly in keeping with either the position he had achieved as an author and public official or the relations that had existed between him and Cable in the immediate past.

[3] Cleveland, 1885.

When Cable published his first story, Gayarré was the most distinguished scholar and author in Louisiana. A Creole of proud ancestry, he had added to a notable public career the authorship of literary and historical works which had been praised by William Gilmore Simms, George Bancroft, and others. He and Cable were charter members of the Louisiana Historical Society when it was reorganized by an act of the state legislature in 1877, and the younger writer as a matter of course came to lean heavily on the other's published volumes in his own writing of local history. The letters from Gayarré which Cable preserved, some of them passed within the city, bear dates from 1879 to 1883, encompassing the years in which *Old Creole Days, The Grandissimes,* and *Madame Delphine* were published. They reflect cordiality and respect, a willingness to ask and grant favors, and as much social intercourse, surely, as could have been expected between two so widely separated in age and background.

On February 9, 1883, Gayarré wrote to accept an invitation to Cable's house to meet J. O. Davidson, the illustrator from the Harper's company whom Cable, after declining to write himself for the Harper's publications, was introducing to other writers, including Hearn and Gayarré. Earlier he had asked Cable for advice on writing and finding a publisher (October 27, 1880), had invited Cable to attend the lectures on the French Revolution he gave in his home (March 30, 1882), had tendered thanks for letters of introduction to Charles Scribner and James R. Osgood and lecture managers in the East, and had reported on his plans for writing and lecturing (August 6, 8, 1882). One long letter, dated October 27, 1880, just when *The Grandissimes* was finishing in *Scribner's Monthly,* discusses a series of articles Gayarré was writing on "The Blacks of Louisiana" and wanted Cable to read. "It will be a book, I think, highly interesting in the North and West, and particularly to the colored people," he wrote. "I should like to profit by your advice and experience." Expanded to include the Negroes of the entire South, the manuscript was submitted to Charles Scribner, along with Cable's recommendation of his friend as "a laborious, conscientious, accomplished historian," but it was rejected.[4]

Early in 1882 Cable found occasion in the local press to praise the historical research of Gayarré, then president of the Louisiana Historical

[4] Cable also recommended Gayarré to write the article on New Orleans for the *Encyclopaedia Britannica.* See Cable to Scribner, Feb. 11, Dec. 19, 24, 1881 (in the Scribner archives); Scribner to Cable, March 5, Dec. 10, 1881 (at Tulane University). An unpublished manuscript of Gayarré's, "The Quadroons of Louisiana," is in the archives at Louisiana State University.

Society.[5] Through the remainder of the year and into the next their relations were friendlier than ever before. The first hint of any cooling came, apparently, in the newspaper debate of May, 1883, between Cable and Gayarré on the one side and James Wilkinson on the other as to the guilt of General Wilkinson. Their friendship had not been shaken by *Old Creole Days* or *The Grandissimes* or *Madame Delphine,* but beginning with the debate on General Wilkinson Gayarré made several thrusts indicating that he resented Cable in his role as historian. In the *Times-Democrat* of June 24 he argued that a novelist cannot be taken seriously as a historian. Then on August 12 he published a three-column satire in the same paper, "The Nineteenth Century Interviewed in Louisiana," which did not name Cable but obviously aimed at him in the assertion of the Nineteenth Century that books would sell and would reward an author handsomely if they were derogatory of the South and used such materials as the Creole Negro patois and the Acadians. Gayarré protested, however, that the writer of such books would be a traitor to his region. He seems to have forgotten that he had hoped to publish a book on the Negroes, which would sell widely in the North and West and among the Negroes.

Here for the first time Gayarré echoed the feelings expressed earlier by the Abbé Rouquette and the editor of *L'Abeille.* It may be that his own depressed circumstances fed his resentment. Left without means at the end of the war, he had kept a law office through the 1870's and had held a minor public office part of that time; but after he had abandoned law in 1881, both appointive and elective offices eluded him, and he lived on the proceeds from lectures that often were in effect benefits sponsored by his friends, occasional pieces in the newspapers and magazines, and sales from his collection of books and paintings. It is understandable that he saw Cable's success in writing of the Creoles in both fiction and history in contrast to the results of his own efforts at the same time with the same materials. Two essays of his on "The Creoles of Louisiana," in the *Times-Democrat* of December 28, 1884, and the next January 4, were implicit rather than avowed rebuttals to Cable's history of the Creoles, but he needed only "The Freedman's Case in Equity" and the newspaper abuse that greeted it to prompt him to an open assault on his friend of a few months earlier.

His two articles on Cable's essay, in the Sunday issues of January 11 and 18, won him the title among his friends "Champion of the South."[6]

---

[5] See the *Times-Democrat,* Jan. 20, 22, 26, Feb. 12, 1882.
[6] See John Smith Kendall, "The Last Days of Charles Gayarré," *Louisiana Historical Quarterly,* XV (July, 1932), 367.

He advanced no new arguments but he set a tone which later writers were to imitate. Wishing to refrain from "expressing any opinion on the literary value of Mr. Cable's predatory incursions into the domain of fiction," he felt it his duty to say, however, that Cable was "completely ignorant of the elements that constitute the idiosyncrasy of that populace, among whom there are many who believe that his whole stock of knowledge as to the French language and the negro *patois* would not overload the back of a mouse." Of Cable's essay itself he said he feared he could not ascertain "the true quality and nature of the driftwood which he hurries on to market, and which floats indistinctly on a foggy stream of illogical reasonings and more than doubtful statements," and so he could not profit from "the discoveries of that learned professor of ethic and Darwinian evolver of new equities, on which a new order of society is to be established under his auspices." The contents of the essay he thought too grave to be treated with the "unpardonable flippancy of a sentimental aspirant to notoriety, the arrogant superciliousness of an improvised pedagogue, the exorbitant conceit of a self-worshiping censor of public and private morals, or with the raving imprecations, the howlings and the maniac gesticulations of an Orlando Furioso."

Thus Gayarré continued through the two long articles. He thought that for the protection of the Negro himself he must be kept subordinate. As a former slaveowner he had the "conscientious conviction that we were more tormented and oppressed by our slaves than they were by us." His attack was of a piece in its tone and its attitude but hardly consistent in its supporting views, except for its steady assumption of an inviolable aristocratic superiority. The presence of the blacks in the South, he said, had made aristocrats of all white men; yet, "So far as I am personally concerned, I have no hesitation in saying, so intense is my love of intellect, honesty, and high-mindedness, that I would rather breakfast, dine, and sup, and even sleep, with a noble-hearted, refined, and classically educated hybrid than with a dishonest, ignorant, and brutish white man."

The two articles form a crude, often cleverly turned philippic well calculated to delight all who had the same beliefs and feelings. By discussing miscegenation as if he were thus meeting Cable's arguments, by impugning his motives, even in the work for prison reform (which he had himself supported three years earlier), by refusing to recognize that any questions of public morality were involved, Gayarré failed to meet Cable on any common grounds for debate, and in fact removed the matter altogether from the level of useful discussion.

In the article of January 11 Gayarré said: "When the 'Grandissimes' appeared, we were requested by the editor of THE TIMES-DEMOCRAT to review the work. We refused from motives of delicacy. Mr. Cable having heard of it and having requested us to change our decision, we replied that we would, if he could name two Creole families with whom he was intimately acquainted. He could not." *The Grandissimes* was published in September, 1880, more than a year before the *Times-Democrat* was formed by the merging of the two earlier papers. Such a request may have come from E. A. Burke, editor of the *Democrat* in 1880 and of the *Times-Democrat* later, but this seems unlikely, for in October, a month after the book had been published, Gayarré wrote Cable on the friendliest terms asking advice on his own writing and publishing. It may be' that Cable had asked Gayarré to review *Old Creole Days* rather than *The Grandissimes*. Among Gayarré's letters to Cable is a note which reads, "I have reflected on the subject and have concluded to decline. Thanks for having thought of me." The note is not dated but is on the back of an envelope scrap, with the return-address of William C. Black, Cable's employer, and postmarked New Orleans, April 23. This date corresponds closely enough to the publication date of *Old Creole Days*, May 17, but not of *The Grandissimes*. Furthermore, the intercourse between the two men when the novel appeared and for the ensuing two years was so cordial that such an exchange as Gayarré later described would have been less than fitting.

Next Gayarré carried his campaign to the lecture platform. Speaking in French at the hall of the Union Française on January 25 and March 8 on the subject "La Race Latine en Louisiane," he brought Cable in for side thrusts.[7] In the same hall on March 22 he lectured on *"Les Grandissimes,"* under the sponsorship of eighteen ladies, who thought of the occasion as a benefit for the speaker comparable to others they had sponsored. The burden of his comment is suggested by his assertion that "Mr. Cable's aim is to degrade, lower in the public opinion the reputation of the population of Louisiana, Creole or not, to put it socially, civilly, and politically below the black race, which he considers superior to ours and destined to africanize the entire South"; and that "what I am indeed convinced of is that the author of the *Grandissimes* is as deprived of all moral sense as the crocodile."[8] Still another lecture, "The Creoles of History and the Creoles of Romance," delivered on April 25,

[7] The two lectures were later published as a pamphlet and in the 1885-1887 volume of the *Comptes rendus* of the Athénée.

[8] Gayarré published "Revue des Grandissimes" in *Le Propagateur Catholique,* Dec. 12, 1886, and Jan. 1, 1887.

was largely a compressed, English version of the two earlier addresses on the Latin race.[9]

Marion Baker wrote Cable on March 9 that Gayarré "charges you with making money by your pictures of the Creoles, & he goes whining around getting women to get up entertainments for him—Creole women, whom he poses before in the light of a knight who has slain the offender, Cable. I warned you against him long ago." Baker returned to the subject with equal feeling in other letters. Knowing the previous relations between Cable and Gayarré and seeing the betrayal of a friendship that others did not see, he was not inclined to credit Gayarré with speaking his own convictions and also those of many others in the South, among them his brother Page Baker. That Gayarré was restrained in his public utterances is shown by the contrast with his language in letters to Paul Hamilton Hayne in 1885.[10] Hayne found his friend's judgment of Cable acceptable and after echoing it in a letter to another correspondent he added, "Of his books I know nothing; nor do I ever expect to read them."[11] Like the Creoles, he did not hesitate to condemn the author of books he had not read.

But during these weeks the *Times-Democrat* did not rely solely on the redoubtable Gayarré for its war on Cable. An editorial on January 22 objected to Cable's calling himself a Southerner and asserted that since race prejudices exist around the world, he had in effect launched an attack on all mankind. Three days later appeared a satirical editorial entitled "Mr. Violet Cable," which suggests Hearn's touch but more probably came from the pen of Page Baker.[12] If Hearn was the author it is clear that he had passed entirely from the influence of Marion Baker into the orbit of Page Baker, who continued to be something of a protector of his as long as he stayed in New Orleans. Under the title "Fie! Fie! George" the editor of the *Picayune* took Cable to task on February 15, in haughty sarcasm, for a letter he had written to a Negro in Wisconsin. Ironically, in that letter, which had been printed along with the one it answered in the *Wisconsin State Journal* of January 28, the editor

[9] The address was printed as a pamphlet in 1885 and in the magazine *Dixie* at Atlanta in Dec., 1888.

[10] The Hayne-Gayarré letters are printed in Charles R. Anderson, "Charles Gayarré and Paul Hayne: The Last Literary Cavaliers," *American Studies in Honor of William Kenneth Boyd* (Durham, N. C., 1940), pp. 221-81.

[11] Hayne to Jeannie A. Jones, Aug. 21, 1885. See also his letter to Julia C. R. Dorr, Aug. 30, 1885 (both in the Duke University Library).

[12] Vera McWilliams (*Lafcadio Hearn*, p. 158) attributes this editorial to Hearn, but P. D. and Ione Perkins (*Lafcadio Hearn: A Bibliography of His Writings*, Boston, 1934) do not include it, nor does Albert Mordell in his volumes of Hearn's writings drawn from the New Orleans newspapers.

could have found refutation of the charge he and other Southern journalists made that Cable was working toward race warfare and Negro dominance in the South, for in it Cable had written, "Let colored men show such sagacious, active interest in the rights and interests of all men, that all men, shall gradually be won to regard them as valuable accessions to the community, and most valuable when most free."[13]

The phrases of *L'Abeille,* no longer very different from those of the other papers, were still likely to be sarcastically clever. In printing a translation of an editorial by Placide Canonge, the *Critic* of March 28 noted that it had been forwarded by a Creole with these remarks:

You will be glad to see that my compatriots—*genus irritabile*—are "up and at" poor George W. Cable again. May the goddess Minerva, who protected Æneas, defend him! A committee of Creole ladies—not one of whom, or whose husbands, I warrant you, ever read Cable except in Bentzon's translations in the *Revue des Deux Mondes*—have called upon Gayarré to lecture on "The Grandissimes"; and Canonge has written one or two columns on the subject in *L'Abeille*. If you read them, you will know that he told the truth, as I know he did, when he said, some time ago, that he had not the advantage of knowing Mr. Cable's works.

A letter in the New Orleans *Item* of March 22 broke the pattern of the usual press comment by declaring that Cable had the right to his own opinions and had done a service by opening the question for discussion, and there were other entries in the ledger to offset the hostile Southern press. The *Critic* of January 9 praised Cable's courage in the fight on sectionalism, and the February *Century* said editorially that such open discussion as his was destroying narrow sectionalism. A correspondent's letter in the next issue cited evidence that sectional rancor was declining. While on a trip through the South, Major Pond wrote from Birmingham on March 22 that he found "all the intelligent men ...friendly and rather proud of" Cable. Dozens of letters came to Cable from whites and Negroes, north and south, applauding the stand he had taken. The testimony of Negroes, not admissable in the public debate, was nevertheless gratifying.

A letter from Hot Springs, Arkansas, signed by five "late subjects of bondage and oppression" said he deserved "the highest and holiest appreciation and support of the lovers of true freedom of every clime and nation." Three Negroes in Kansas City wrote: "In our hearts you rank

[13] Both letters are reprinted in Fred W. Lorch, "Cable and His Reading Tour with Mark Twain in 1884-1885," *American Literature,* XXIII (Jan., 1952), 485-86.

with the great philanthropists who made humanity their business when American liberty was mocked by the clank of bondsmen's chains." At Chicago an aged couple, the wife a sister of the staunch abolitionists Owen and Elijah Lovejoy, came to him and the man began, as Cable wrote Louise on January 17, " 'Mr. Cable I came to thank you for your paper on the Freedmen'—and there choked, burst into tears and could not speak. His wife tried & made the same failure." While he was in Louisville on January 6 with Mark Twain the publishers of a Negro newspaper, the *Bulletin,* brought a group of Negroes to thank him for his support of their cause. "You would have not got off with dry eyes had you been there," he wrote Louise. After discussing the Negro question at a reception of the Louisville Press Club he wrote: "Freedom of speech has yet to come to us in the South. Yet how far we have progressed beyond our old ante-bellum position; for I spoke with perfect freedom and gave no offense & two or three men even went so far as to say 'We admit (&c) but how are you going'—&c?"

Interviewers flocked to Cable, and more than once he sat with two or three at once. From Chicago on January 17 he wrote Louise, "That paper is turning out to be the greatest thing I've ever done." Clippings from the Southern papers had only begun to reach him then, and in Louisville he found that everyone he met knew of his Freedman essay and yet it had "no effect against" him. He was invited to speak at both white and Negro high schools and Pond turned people away from the hall. Before the tour ended six weeks later, however, the outcry against him had reached a fierce peak.

Yet he had foreseen at the opening of the year that it held rough spots for him. In a sober letter to Louise from Dayton he had written on the night of December 31:

So we end another year. It has been full of bounty to us. How much happiness—how little trouble have fallen to us. It is right and best that the future should be kept from our knowledge so that we may walk by faith and not by sight.

It is not easy to do this when all is prosperous. . . . But we shall have opportunity enough the coming year.

. . . But you know we have agreed that I should (we should) never lay our plans in the mere light of pecuniary profits or selfish profits of any kind. We are just as completely dedicated to God's service as though we were Chinese missionaries. Am I not right? And so I shall do this year whatever seems to me—I hope I may say we shall do whatever seems to us— to be the best thing we can do for the greatest good of our fellow-creatures.

Later his wife mentioned the newspaper slanders against him. On January 31 he replied: "But don't forget that men who speak boldly for the truth must have slanderers no matter where they live, North, South, East, West." In a similar context three years later, March 4, 1888, he wrote her, "I remember my favorite text & it is a great consolation: 'Woe unto you when all men speak well of you.'"

CHAPTER XV

THE AFTERMATH OF THE STORM

WHEN Cable parted with Mark Twain in Washington on March 2, he took the train for New Orleans. "I trust God to direct my steps," he wrote Louise on February 27. "I have prayed for wisdom, & believe I am doing my simple duty to His blessed service. I go in love to Him & to my fellow citizens among whom I go. I believe I shall do good." He had been away from the South almost a year, and he needed a short run among the Acadians for the benefit of the stories he was writing. The Negro question demanded further attention, and the *Century* editors had assured him its pages were always open to him on that or any other subject. He had no doubt that the light he could throw on Southern problems would produce ultimate good. Such had been his thought when he proposed late in January to print the Freedman essay as a pamphlet and distribute it through the South. He had given up the idea on Roswell Smith's advice.

His greatest hurt yet came in New Orleans. Except for Marion Baker, James B. Guthrie, and a few others, including the pastor of his church, who was writing something in his defense, his associates of a year ago were uncomfortable at seeing him. The wives of his former friends E. A. Burke and Adolph Schreiber had been among the sponsors of Gayarré's lecture on *The Grandissimes*. His stay in the city was short. On March 9, after a visit to the western parishes, he passed back through New Orleans on his way home. Marion Baker wrote him on that day a pained letter. He thought Cable was to stay longer and so had missed the long talk he had expected. He was afraid he would appear to have turned his back on his friend. He had come "within an ace" of handing in his resignation when his paper began the attacks on Cable. "I am very sure you will down the whole crowd," he said, "but in the meantime you will have to grin & bear the ravings of the old-timers." If there was any strain on their friendship, it was only momentary, and until Baker's death twenty-one years later he remained one of Cable's most understanding and sympathetic friends. While the Southern controversy lasted, for another ten years, Baker was in effect an undercover agent in New Orleans, reporting on public feeling, giving advice, collecting information, putting as much for defense into the *Times-Democrat* as he dared.

Back at Simsbury on March 13, Cable was worn out himself and found his wife sick. Their son William Noble was born on May 11. He had instructed Pond to make no reading dates earlier than the one already arranged for Boston on March 27, and on his first day home he wrote Pond that the proposed benefit reading with Mark Twain for the Hartford Decorative Art Society was bothering him. He recognized the claims Hartford had on him, but the request came at an unlucky moment. "If I should subscribe $75 to their Art Society they would be astonished; and yet you know," he wrote Pond, "I have refused to read for that sum at a town actually on the road between here and Hartford." To Hartford he wrote that if Pond could make a date after March 27 suitable to Mark Twain he would "respond with the alacrity of one who knows when he is highly honored." A date was not arranged, and when Cable met Mark Twain at New Haven on March 30, they "fell atalking about the Hartford appointment," Cable wrote Louise. Mark said he "had scolded at the mistakes made" and had "smashed the whole affair out of all recoverable shape." Cable expected to hear nothing more about the request, but as it turned out he did.

The wild recriminations elicited by the Freedman article had been appearing in the press for two months, but Cable was yet to suffer abuse from other quarters and apparently on other scores, though perhaps ultimately the same.

In their eagerness for news about the reading tour the winter before, reporters had used personal notes often. Cable's Sabbatarian practices were mentioned often, as was his participation in church services wherever Sunday found him. At the middle of March a report entitled "A Triangular Row," originating with a New Jersey correspondent, said that Mark Twain, Cable, and Pond had broken up with a quarrel. Pond wrote Cable on March 19 that Mark said it was too trivial to think about and that he had himself demanded it be retracted. A far more gossipy report in the Boston *Herald* column "New York Literature" on May 7 was aimed solely at Cable. A special report appearing on May 10 in the *Herald,* the New Orleans *Times-Democrat,* and no doubt other papers gave assurances that there had been no fisticuffs, as at first rumored, "only a business disagreement so private and intangible that few particulars can be ascertained." After saying that the net returns from the joint readings had been shared equally by the principals and making other statements equally wide of the facts, the report continued:

Cable talked vaguely to his friends of hoggishness on the part of Twain in getting a disproportionate share of the glory, and Twain vowed in seeming acrimony that he would never, never go on the platform again; but Pond's plaint was less sentimental, for it related to the nature of the charges which his companions made as "traveling expenses." Cable was the chief offender in that way. His theory was that so highly luxurious a thing as champagne and so lowly a one as the blacking of his boots properly belonged to the partnership account, and Pond declares that the bills rendered by Cable are greater curiosities of literature than the best of his Creole dialect.

Advanced as this dispatch is in scandalmongering, it pales beside the one three days earlier in the *Herald*. When the column of May 7 came into Cable's hands, he wrote the editor on May 12, asking for an explanation, protesting that the "slanderous and libelous" statements made his friends, "by implication, party to slanders of which they are absolutely incapable." He telegraphed Mark Twain and then wrote him on May 16 the assurances he thought might be needed:

I add this to assure you that all statements that I have either openly or covertly intimated anything unpleasant about you to my friends or anybody else are false from beginning to end. If you care to know it, I esteem you more highly since our winter's experience than I ever did before & should deeply regret if scandal mongers were to make an estrangement between us.

Of course I do not believe that you have said ought against me that was not intended as a friend's fair criticism among friends. Nor do I think Pond has said a word that was meant in unkindness about either of us.

He had invited Mark Twain to say privately or publicly whatever he might like in refutation. The reply he had was that the "slander of a professional newspaper liar" had not disturbed Mark "for one single half of a half of a hundredth part of a second." But the charges were against Cable, and he had hoped for something more from his friend. His second letter to the editor of the *Herald* is printed here from a copy kept by Cable;[1] the original was presumably mailed. In taking up one after another the accusations that had been made, this letter makes clear what was included in the *Herald* column, except that it does not reflect the tone of such phrases in it as "something approaching meanness," "petty qualities," and "accounted a small man even by his friends." The managing editor, John H. Hohner, had replied to the earlier letter that he was asking an explanation from his New York correspondent.

[1] This copy is at Tulane University, as is also a copy of the letter of May 12 to Hohner. Both of these letters and the article in the *Herald* of May 7 are printed in my article "Mark Twain, Cable, and 'a Professional Newspaper Liar,' " *New England Quarterly*, XXVIII (March, 1955), 18-33.

SIMSBURY, CONN., May 14, 1885.

EDITOR HERALD;

DEAR SIR:

Yours of 13th rec'd. I thank you for its tone and hope you will receive my reply in the same reasonable spirit.

My protest must still stand. The matter against which I complain was not news, but gossip. It was an attack upon my private character. It neither contained nor was accompanied privately by any authority for its statements. If it had been true it would keep, for nothing in it required that it be hurried into print. If false it was an outrage against a gentleman, which no retraction could entirely undo.

Moreover it was on its face full of improbabilities. For it charges me with wanton, useless, *purblind* incivility to my most valued friends. And again, some of the statements concerning my behavior in a friend's house could be well authorized only when they had come first from that friend; but you know whose guest I was and that ought to have been at least cumulative proof to you that no such statement had been made; for that friend is not one who could so far forget himself as to make such complaints against a guest; and a man who could would not be good authority. And still again, it stands to reason that had I in his house last spring behaved with such meanness as is attributed to me in your paper, he could not a few months later have made an engagement with me that made us daily, nightly, constant and only companions for four months.

The name Coleman in your correspondent's letter is either a slip of the pen or a printer's error. While ill at my friend's house last spring (1884) I did not "for nearly 3 weeks almost live on champagne." For a few days while my stomach was in a very delicate condition my physician prescribed champagne with my food in such limited quantities as a medical man would, and I insisted on using it more sparingly than it was prescribed. I was in a house where champagne is not "ordered expressly" for any guest, but where an offer to pay for my champagne would have been about as proper as an offer to pay for my food and lodging. The day I left Hartford I paid for everything I could persuade anybody to let me know of; but had I let my friends have their way I could not have paid a farthing for anything. The statement that I "audited" any memorandum of outlays of any sort—unless to see if I could add some overlooked item—is utterly false. No church in Hartford has asked my aid in any shape. An Art School (as well as I remember) asked me through Hartford friends and acquaintances, to take part in a public reading, and, as my standing contract with my agent requires, I referred them to him, and he consented, but they could not accept the date he gave them. It is ungentlemanly to say of a person's private life "Rumor has it"—thus & so, making the issue turn upon the existence of the rumor instead of upon its truth. But it is preposterous that my companion and friend in our late reading tour should have been made uncomfortable by my "parsimony." All the outlays were made by the traveling manager, except when for the convenience of all concerned I sometimes made small expenditures that the manager would afterward pay back to me, and it was a standing jest between us that I generally had to prevent him cheating himself. The statement that I ordered $5 breakfasts and the like is all absolutely false. Our stay was almost invariably at hotels on the American plan, and as to apartments, I never saw mine until it had been engaged by the manager, and rarely was & never cared to be consulted about it. It is equally false that I rudely declined to join in the "Authors" Readings in New York. I declined, without rudeness, because it fell at a time when I had instructed my agent, on no account and for no pecuniary consideration to make any appointment that would carry me away from home for a single night, as my wife's health did not permit me to leave her side. It is false that I am not a loser by the lack of a just copyright law. I belong to both the English & American copyright leagues, and as far as I know I have contributed to every subscription made in America for their objects. It is false that I was expected in Hartford or elsewhere the Sunday I stopped over in Worcester or that I disappointed anybody. If ever anything was exclusively my private business, that was. It is true that by the letter of my contract I was, under no circumstances to be required to travel much or little or any part of Sunday. What I might have chosen to concede in case of emergency is also my own private affair. It is false that I ever declined to argue the moral propriety of writing novels. That I ever this last season disappointed an audience in the matter of time or attendance is false. It is true that I have been poor. It is false that I am unwilling to help others. It is even false that I "have resolved to make my future secure." How could you suppose your correspondent got that from good authority? It is true that I spend little on myself, and that I would rather not be so poor as I have been; but I give you my word for what it is worth, I would sooner starve than get my living—as your correspondent seems willing to get his—by slandering unoffending gentlemen.

I have written you thus mainly to facilitate you in exacting from him that full explanation and amends which you have so promptly promised. I shall await it with anxiety.

The motives of my public utterances have been impugned all over one half of this country; but the charges were the hot words of people who believed themselves aggrieved, and such as public men are generally subject to. They are false & injurious, yet they spring from a wounded pride in those who make them and I cannot find it in my heart to resent them or do anything but wait patiently for time to disprove them. But it has been reserved, my dear sir, for your correspondent to print in the Boston Herald the first careful slander upon my private character that I have ever known.

Be assured I shall be grateful for all the expedition you may be able to give this distressing affair. and that I hope to remain ever

Yours respectfully
G. W. CABLE.

The editor was as good as his word, and after hearing from his New York correspondent published a contrite editorial apology. Cable asked his friend Marion Baker to print a similar retraction in the *Times-Democrat* of the milder article it had published, but Marion either did not dare try or could not persuade his brother Page; and Cable had to draw what satisfaction he could from Marion's assurance that no one believed he had "done anything unbecoming." Marion asked why Mark Twain and Pond did not speak up to scotch all the rumors. But neither had a word to say publicly.

In a letter to Charles L. Webster of May 10 Mark Twain wrote: "...from this out, write nothing in any private letter to friend, relative, or *anybody,* which you do not want published. . . . *Nobody* is to be trusted. . . . I have been burnt so often, in my own experience that I feel like warning & saving you."[2] His immediate concern was for the intricate manipulations to secure publication rights to Grant's memoirs, but written three days after the first slanderous column appeared in the *Herald* and the same day that the second one appeared, this comes close to being a confession. He must have realized—and must have known that Cable realized—that the columnist's remarks on the champagne, the telegrams, the five-dollar breakfasts, the delayed arrival at Hartford, and the proposed reading for the Hartford Decorative Art Society could have come ultimately from no one but him or someone close to him. In fact the parallels between the newspaper notes and those in Mark's letters to Olivia are striking. That he regretted the public charges can be assumed, but his unwillingness to make what amends he could probably grew from a combination of his lifelong tendency to helpless self-blame and a residue of resentment against Cable. In letters to Howells on May 5 and June 5, 1885,[3] he left no doubt that he still harbored resentment over the reading tour.

Marion Baker understood what the situation was, that whatever the origin of the dispatches or the bases for them, they were being added to the journalistic sniping at Cable because of his Freedman essay. Marion was able to identify the writer of another personal attack which appeared in the Washington *Post* of July 14 and stated as a simple matter of fact that Cable had never been in the army and claimed to have been a soldier in order to help sell his books. The writer was Richard Weightman, Marion said, formerly on the *Times-Democrat* staff in New Orleans and then its Washington correspondent. A year later Weightman

[2] S. C. Webster, *Mark Twain, Business Man,* p. 322.

[3] Excerpts of these letters are printed in Guy A. Cardwell, *Twins of Genius,* pp. 65-66.

wrote again, as Marion identified him, in the New York *Star's* Washington column of May 30. By saying nothing of the race question, Marion remarked in a letter of June 10, 1886, Weightman could get his irresponsible articles printed and thus do damage no frontal attack could do.

The *Century* office had been deluged with letters on the Freedman essay. Before the end of January the decision had been made not to print any of them but to ask Henry W. Grady to write for the opposition in reply to Cable. As editor of the Atlanta *Constitution* since 1881 Grady had distinguished himself as a champion of rehabilitation and progress in the South. His essay in the April issue, "In Plain Black and White," became in effect the official answer of the South, for he submitted it to representative men, he said, for emendation. His article drew the discussion up to a plane far above the newspaper diatribes, so far in fact that both Charles Gayarré and Paul Hamilton Hayne were disgusted at its mildness.[4] Against Gilder's objection, Grady insisted on saying that Cable was of New England parentage and had never shown much understanding of Southern people or sympathy for their particular culture. "There may be here and there in the South," he added, "a dreaming theorist who subscribes to Mr. Cable's teachings. We have seen no signs of one." Aside from a few such remarks, however, Grady confronted the issues under discussion, assuming at the outset that his opponent was sincere but misguided. His own acceptance and Cable's rejection of race instinct Grady attributed to an honest difference of opinion, and he agreed that the Negroes should have equal rights and opportunities in education, in the courts, in public accommodations. But the races must remain separate and the supremacy of the whites must not be challenged because they possessed "intelligence, character, and property." How much he differed from Cable is suggested by his assertion, "Nowhere on earth is there kindlier feeling, closer sympathy, or less friction between two classes of society than between the whites and the blacks of the South to-day."

When put alongside Grady's subsequent statements, as in his address at Dallas two years later, October 26, 1887, "In Plain Black and White" is reserved. He granted that the Negro must have his rights guaranteed, but he held to the doctrine of white supremacy. He conceded that the Negro had been given the ballot to keep, though his belief in race superiority made him doubt the wisdom of it.

[4] See Charles R. Anderson, "Charles Gayarré and Paul Hayne: The Last Literary Cavaliers," *American Studies in Honor of William Kenneth Boyd*, pp. 221-81.

With time out for half a dozen platform readings, Cable completed his reply to Grady, not for simultaneous publication as his editors wished, but for the September issue. The original four magazine pages alloted him grew to seventeen. Gilder, Johnson, and Roswell Smith made extensive suggestions; they wanted him to avoid antagonizing phrases and to leave no room for rebuttal. "The Silent South" was Cable's rejoinder to Grady and also to the many other opponents who had gone into print since January. It did not name Grady and only a few times alluded to his article. The essay reveals the author's position more clearly than "The Freedman's Case in Equity," for the earlier article had opened the question in its broad aspects and had avoided the more controversial angles which had been introduced in the meanwhile. But the frightening thoughts of social intermingling and race amalgamation had been called up so often and such solemn doubts had been expressed as to whether the Negroes had any real grievances that point-by-point rebuttal was in order. The opportunity was welcome to Cable for it invited him to build up the total structure of his beliefs on the subject and to counter the specific arguments he had preferred not to acknowledge in advance.

In a degree possible to few men similarly provoked to self-justification, Cable chose to mention only those "calmer utterances" such as Grady's, which made the assumption, he said, "that recrimination and malignment of motive are the tactics of those who have no case; that the truth is worth more than any man's opinion; and that the domination of right is the end we are all bound to seek." What follows is Cable's most comprehensive statement on the Southern problem. By avowing his "faithful sonship to a Southern State," by allotting blame to the entire nation for slavery and its aftermath, by declaring that he had never imputed any wilful maliciousness in the Southern treatment of the Negro, and also by noting the civil rights statutes being enacted by Democratic state governments while "the Republican party has grown fat and lazy concerning civil rights," he set a conciliatory tone. But on the essential points he gave no ground. He pointed to the inconsistency of Grady's saying that Southerners would resolve the problem without emotion or prejudice, while saying also that if there were no such thing as race instinct, enough race feeling would be aroused in the South to produce the same result. He branded the states' rights argument as dishonest, saying that not the source but the substance of the Federal civil rights laws had been unacceptable. The political "Solid South" existed, he said, only because the Negroes would vote solid as long as their rights were withheld or threatened, and in turn the whites were forced into solidity. Attempts at unsegregated churches had failed because the church was erroneously considered an institution of social intercourse.

Grady had repeated the recurrent statement that the Negroes did not want the rights being demanded for them. Cable had doubts and could tell of one instance in which he had investigated such testimony. On February 2 the *Times-Democrat* had printed a letter from the *Times* of Selma, Alabama. Purporting to be written by Jack Brown, a Negro living in Columbia, South Carolina, the letter charged that such men as Cable championed the Negroes only for profit. The whites must stay at the top of the social structure, it continued, and the Negroes would fight anyone who attempted to disturb the existing peace. A letter of Cable's to Jack Brown on March 14 had come back unclaimed. Another inquiry sent to Columbia brought the reply, signed by the pastor of the A. M. E. Church and four others, including three post office employees, that the only Jack Brown, colored, known in or about Columbia was illiterate. Cable had sheafs of letters from Negroes stating views opposed to Jack Brown's. And even if one granted that the race as a whole was indifferent to its rights, to deny those rights to an individual seeking and deserving them would still be indefensible. To Grady's contention that the "right to rule" belongs to the whites because they possess "character, intelligence, and property," Cable protested that thus any white man, however illiterate and reprehensible morally, is given the right to rule the most intelligent and cultured Negro.

Only by illogical inference could Cable's earlier essay be read as a plea for social equality, in the current meaning of the term, but even Grady had so read it. This time Cable spelled out his meaning in a way to prevent any but wilful misinterpretation. "Social equality is a fool's dream," he said. Social intercourse, a matter of private choice always, not of rights or law, would surely be prevented by race instinct, if that were such a force as Grady believed; and yet, Cable noted the irony, the believers in race instinct were the ones most insistent on legal restrictions. After citing Oberlin, Ohio, and Berea, Kentucky, as places with least legal restriction and yet little social intermingling, Cable remarked, in a sentence which he kept subdued in order to avoid antagonizing, that "just in proportion to the rigor, the fierceness, and the injustice with which excommunication from the common rights of man has fallen upon the darker race, has amalgamation taken place."

Alluding to the readjustment of his own thinking in the preceding ten years, he took courage from the evolution of Southern thought. Progress was being made, "geologically speaking," but what was considered expediency was not expedient after all, since the needed immigration and capital were avoiding the South. And he refused to weigh expediency against morality and justice. The matter was the South's to solve he agreed with Grady, but the solution was overdue. Suffrage for the blacks he assumed to be permanently achieved, but "civil caste" would negate all other gains. "Let us, neighbor with neighbor, and friend with friend, speak of it, think of it, write of it, get rid of it."

Though this essay attempts to avoid the overtones of moral condemnation in "The Freedman's Case in Equity," it speaks repeatedly of class and caste. The idea of caste had shown through much of the opposition to the earlier essay. Against the assumption basic to Cable's thought that the welfare of all depended on raising the lower masses, he encountered the assumption, implied if not stated, that a peasantry must be maintained in place of slavery to support Southern culture. The concept was anathema to him, and from this point on he warred against caste with new vigor. Since the Negro was at the bottom of the scale, it was for the Negro that he bent his efforts.

When "The Silent South" appeared in September, Cable's friends were elated, feeling that it would lay the storm of abuse he had suffered. Gilder paid $500 for it instead of the $250 intended—an extraordinary rate of pay, he said, for an extraordinary article. The author's sister Mary Louise was delighted, for now, she wrote him on September 3, no one could doubt the honesty and the justice of his position. Charles Scribner, who planned to make a volume of this essay and its two predecessors, wrote Cable on September 5:

I can hardly express how greatly I was stirred by it. . . . I do not see how any reply *can* be even attempted; but it was not even that that moved me so much. There is something truly ennobling in your discussion of the subject; you lift the whole question into a higher moral plane. It is an article which must do great good and the constant tributes of gratitude which you will receive must make it one of the proudest achievements of your life. You know that I do not often overflow in this way but I really cannot help writing this to you.

"The Silent South" met these expectations in part, but only in part. Its positive statements on social equality and miscegenation denied to Cable's opponents some of the weapons they had used against him; and though the newspaper attacks continued with little change except for lessened frequency, there appeared now and then a calm statement like one written from Atlanta to the Boston *Daily Advertiser* of April 2, 1885, pointing out that whereas Grady assumed that Negroes in the South could attend musical and artistic performances provided they use separate entrances and sit apart, actually they could not attend such performances at all in Atlanta, Grady's home city. A long editorial in *The Southern Bivouac* of October, 1885, disagreed with Cable's conclusions, but it treated the matter as one on which there could be open discussion and honest differences of opinion.

Those willing to debate the subject in this spirit were still outnumbered, however, by those who preferred to say that Cable was a "negrophilist" and that his goal was miscegenation and black supremacy.[5] A superlative in comments of this kind was reached in the 1885 volume of the *Southern Historical Society Papers*,[6] in which R. L. Dabney repeated the refrain that Cable had turned traitor to his own people for profit and added that no one but "a predestined slave and born dolt" could believe as Cable did that slavery was the cause of the Civil War. The editor of the *Papers* introduced Dabney's article by saying, "Not a few of us have been heartily disgusted with the cringing, crawling, dirt-eating spirit shown by Mr. Cable and some of his satellites."

If Cable had not believed there was a Silent South with views widely different from Dabney's, he could have had little heart to continue the debate.

[5] See for example B—z, "Mr. Cable, the 'Negrophilist,' " in Thomas M'Caleb, ed., *The Louisiana Book: Selections from the Literature of the State* (New Orleans, 1894), pp. 203-5.

[6] XIII, 148-53.

CHAPTER XVI

REORIENTATION

AMONG Cable's Boston friends were Annie T. Fields, widow of James T. Fields, publisher and confidant of Nathaniel Hawthorne, and her companion, Sarah Orne Jewett. They sent gifts to his wife and children, and in their home he read from his manuscripts and heard Miss Jewett read from hers. On July 23, 1885, he wrote Mrs. Fields declining an invitation to Boston: ". . . my work keeps me. I do not think it ever before went so slow. Nor have I for years felt so like a broken vessel thrown aside as I do this summer. I must stay at my desk." The first half of the year had brought, if not discouragement, surely disturbance of a sort he had never before encountered, in the belligerent rejection of his views on Negro rights, the personal vilification, and the defection of associates in New Orleans. Yet the debate must be continued, and he was happy to go on with it, satisfied that open and full discussion provided the only hope for a solution. But the debate required time he could ill spare from remunerative work.

He could not abandon the platform as Mark Twain had done at the end of February, for it provided his chief income. He must give public readings to make up for the income he could gain only from steady writing for extended periods, but the readings left him no such periods. Late in March and through April he had read in New England halls, including Boston, where he was introduced on April 1 by Howells and was given a reception by former governor William C. Claflin. His pay was only from $100 to $135 plus local expenses, and the work was lonely and anticlimactic after the tour with Mark Twain.

It had become his habit to turn for help and advice to Roswell Smith, in whom he found more sympathetic understanding than in anyone else outside his immediate family, except perhaps his lifelong friends Marion Baker and James B. Guthrie. It was Roswell Smith who first interested him in Berea College, located in the foothills of the Cumberland Mountains, fifteen miles south of Richmond, Kentucky, and conducted for unsegregated instruction of both races, its enrollment of about 300 being half colored. In the spring of 1884 Smith suggested that Cable join him at the Berea commencement the following month; a year later he made the same proposal and this time arranged for Cable to address the graduating class of two on June 24. They made the trip together and were joined in Cincinnati by Dr. Robert West, editor of the *Advance,* published in Chicago.

"These people are very, very poor here," Cable wrote Louise on June 23, "and it touches me deeply to see virtue, worth, and cultivation have to struggle so for the ordinary comforts of poor men's lives." He met John Gregg Fee, the aged zealot who had come to the foot of the Cumberlands in slave days to establish a church and later a college for both black and white among the mountain folk, and at the close of the war had returned to see the college reopened. "It was grand to see & hear the old martyr," Cable wrote. "He is exactly what John Woolman might have been."

Cable's address was on "Christianity as a Business," rather than on the Negro question as had been expected. Dr. West published it in the *Advance* of July 30 with the title "Professional Christianity" and also distributed it as a pamphlet. It was in effect a sermon arguing an old thesis of Cable's, that Christianity ought to be taken over into all activities. Several others spoke at Berea, but the one who touched most directly on the questions posed by the existence of the college was Judge W. M. Beckner, who envisaged the two races living peacefully in the South, intermingling to their mutual benefit in all public activities.[1] After the address had been printed and applauded in the *Independent,* it received in the Southern press a milder form of the response Cable's essays had received, the Louisville *Courier-Journal,* for example, asserting that the college was a center from which the entire South would be infected and therefore had no claim to the support or countenance of the public. During the next three decades Cable visited Berea almost annually; he was consulted on matters of policy and on petty disagreements. To him Berea proved that equal privileges and opportunities were feasible, and as he wrote once in soliciting funds for its support, he thought its fortunes "peculiarly a matter of national concern."[2] Roswell Smith's gifts to the college exceeded $50,000.

In the first half of 1885 Cable had done next to nothing on his literary work. The Acadian stories, the only fiction he had undertaken since *Dr. Sevier,* had not been finished. The article "New Orleans before the Capture," a simple report published in April, 1885, in the *Century's* war series, had been written at a snail's pace. Another article in the same

---

[1] See the Louisville *Courier-Journal,* June 25, 1885.
[2] Cable to Thomas N. Hart, Dec. 26, 1889. Copy at Tulane University.

series, "Diary of the Siege of Vicksburg," was in the September issue. Some years back Cable had purchased from Dora Richards Miller the diary she had kept from the time she left New Orleans at the opening of the war to the fall of Vicksburg. He had bought the diary partly because of Mrs. Miller's need for money and had found no use to make of it until the editors proposed this use of the Vicksburg portion, with revisions and an introduction from his pen. Another piece written virtually at intervals between other engagements was the sketch "Margaret," in the *Christian Union* of January 1, 1885, which told of a simple, heroic woman in New Orleans who had made her way from menial tasks to the dispensing of large sums for charity.

These were only bits, but Cable had the satisfaction of seeing his Southern essays collected into a volume in November, *The Silent South*. He accepted Scribner's advice not to include Grady's article, but the second edition, 1889, contained two essays from the *Century* attacking his views, each followed by his reply, in keeping with his aim to encourage discussion by presenting different views of the problem. His friends at both Scribner's and the Century Company urged him gently away from the Southern controversy, though they all respected his devotion to the cause. They recognized his need to make his works yield him more. An accounting he drew up on May 31, 1885, showed that he owed $1600 he had borrowed on New Orleans Cotton Exchange stock that was worth at the moment but $1200, and $4000 against his New Orleans home on four notes maturing over the next ten months and not to be renewed, he had just been informed. The earnings on the tour with Mark Twain had gone to paying debts and to the expenses of his own home and the "other house" in New Orleans. At the publication of *Dr. Sevier* his account with his publishers had been overdrawn $1000. What he had expected to live on through the summer, furthermore, was tied up by the bankruptcy of J. R. Osgood, the publisher of *Dr. Sevier*. Scribner was ready to bring out new editions of his works whenever they seemed warranted, and he proposed to buy *Dr. Sevier* from Osgood and issue it uniformly with the other volumes. But terms could not be agreed on, even after Osgood's bankruptcy, and the book remained with the reorganized company until 1887. Scribner was less hopeful than Cable, but he tried to garner more from foreign publication. In April he sold sheets of *The Creoles of Louisiana* to Nimo for a British edition, from which the author would receive twenty-five cents a copy and Scribner the same amount. But David Douglas's experience with two of his books published at Edinburgh was not encouraging. He had taken *Dr. Sevier* on the basis of 10 per cent royalty and had *Old Creole Days* in his

American Authors Series. In October he was still £150 behind on the books, but he had faith enough to want to publish any new book Cable would write.

In the summer of 1885, furthermore, Cable had to decide where to live. The move to Simsbury had been tentative, but the possibility of a permanent move had been in his mind for several years. The New England climate had proved good for Louise, and the other reasons for the move a year earlier had even more weight now. New England had attracted him for some time. Invited to attend a celebration of Harriet Beecher Stowe's birthday in 1882, he wrote a letter, which was printed in the Boston *Evening Transcript* of June 15, to explain that he could not attend. In it he said: "To be in New England would be enough for me. I was there once—a year ago—and it seemed as though I had never been home till then." This was in part a manner of speaking, surely, but not altogether. On every hand generous friends urged him to settle in the East, and the treatment he had received in the South could not fail to have weight. On January 31, 1885, when the newspaper attacks on him on account of the Freedman essay had just begun, he wrote Louise, "I must admit I shall not from choice bring up my daughters in that state of society. The more carefully I study it the less I expect of it; and though there is no reason why I should indulge ungracious feelings toward it I cannot admire it or want my children to be brought up under its influence."

Still the thought of leaving the South brought pangs. For forty years his home had been "la belle New Orleans," and for almost two decades he had been a part of the struggle to rebuild and redeem her. During the last year, just as in his former absences, he had been consulted on the affairs of his church and its mission school; on June 3 he wrote a friend to subscribe to the church budget in his name a sum equal to half the total subscribed by the two highest subscribers. Accustomed to giving first importance to his work for public betterment and being most pleased when the South was the beneficiary, he could not escape a twinge when a fellow worker in the Prytania Street Church mission school said, as his sister Mary Louise wrote him on October 5, "You may find plenty to do but no where are you so much needed as here." A permanent move had to include, soon if not at once, his mother, past seventy years old, his two sisters, and the three children who made up the second household. Mary Louise still told friends he would of course come back, even when she no longer believed it herself. When he had decided not to return she announced herself reconciled and thankful that he had been spared for another years's work; but her sadness showed through the lines of every letter she wrote him.

Before the end of August Cable had chosen Northampton, Massachusetts, for his home. Its advantages were obvious. Smith College was no small attraction to a family of four girls, and living there would be cheaper than in a larger city. Accessible to both New York and Boston, it put him in easy reach of his publishers and the lecture circuit. He had considered other towns, but from his first visit to Northampton to read there on January 21, 1884, it had seemed ideal for his needs. With the eager help of S. E. Bridgeman, a publisher and bookstore owner, he located a house early in September, 1885, the Red House. His New Orleans home sold in November for $5500, leaving $1500 after the mortgage was paid off. The remainder of the $5000 purchase price he raised by drawing advances of $1000 each from Scribner and Roswell Smith, selling two shares of New Orleans Cotton Exchange stock, and mortgaging the new property.

Not long before selling the house in New Orleans, Cable had further evidence of the treatment he could expect there and no doubt further support for his decision to move away. The assessment on his property was raised $2500, including a new item of $1000 for statuary and paintings. James B. Guthrie thought the assessment an outrage and surmised that whoever revised the earlier figure "thought it was patriotic to do so." He filed suit at once in Cable's behalf and could report on February 6 that the appraiser for the court had assessed the movable property at $225 instead of the earlier $2500. On September 8, 1887, Guthrie was still more eager to champion his friend in the courts. Incensed by an article in the New Orleans *States* of the day before, he begged Cable to authorize him to enter a libel suit against the paper.

The move to the Red House was complete early in October, 1885. In the summer of 1886 the second household was moved to Northampton, and with his dependents all brought together again, Cable began a routine that was little changed for half a dozen years. On one front were lectures, essays, and an extensive correspondence on the Southern question; on another was his work in the church and civic organizations; on a third was his platform reading. Not much time was left over for writing fiction. For nearly another decade he kept platform readings at the center of his endeavors, fitting his other activities to them. Since he rarely felt he could afford to pass up an engagement, his readings were often so scattered on the calendar and on the map that he spent as much time traveling as if his schedule had been full. He read most in the seaboard states between Baltimore and Portland, Maine, with usually two or three excursions a year into the Midwest. His sponsors were Y.M.-C.A.'s, Sunday School associations, teachers associations, or individual theater managers. Often he appeared as one member of a course of lyceum performances. His pay was usually $100 plus local expenses; occasionally $75 and a few times as low as $50. Each year he looked for a fuller schedule, hoping to reduce his financial obligations and gain more time for his other work.

By the end of 1885 he was convinced he must achieve greater excellence to replace the novelty of the early readings. He rarely appeared now where he had not read before, and in the larger cities he had read many times. Even in Boston, his best city from the beginning, he no longer drew a full house. Early in 1886 he began voice training again, under Harold Henderson in New York; and later on he began playing the cornet to strengthen his lungs. He took his cornet on the road and surprised his neighbors in the hotels by practicing in his room. He must have new numbers too. In May, 1885, he planned a program to be formed around the Creole songs he had been assembling for publication. The framework would be a lecture on the background, nature, and origins of the songs and dances, with songs interpolated and also excerpts from his stories and novels. But this program was abandoned before the new season opened, for he had finally decided to sing no more on the stage. He was no doubt sensitive to the charge of his Southern detractors that he was a minstrel amusing Northern audiences with ridicule of his New Orleans neighbors, and Gilder's advice was that continuing to sing them would destroy his serious literary reputation.

As a substitute he tried "Grande Pointe," a story of the Acadians which he had promised to the *Century* late in 1884 but had held out of print for platform use. He first gave it as a two-part reading, appearing twice in the same auditorium, but it failed, as might have been predicted. Beginning in Boston on March 9, 1886, he cut the story to one reading, with better but not yet satisfactory results, partly because the plot was difficult to follow and had no such scenes or characters as had delighted the audiences of the earlier readings. After this reading he wrote Louise, "I must accept the fact that I am not 'the fashion' just now in Boston.... The hearing an author read his pages is no longer a novelty, and not being that, there's an end of it." Half a dozen readings at Wallack's Theatre in New York at the middle of March were disappointing, but he could still draw full houses in the small New England towns.

Though Cable had slipped into a routine which had little of the excitement of the tour with Mark Twain or the eager acceptance of his first readings alone, he still met pleasant and varied experiences. At Boston to read on March 9 and 10, 1886, for example, he was the guest of William C. Claflin, a former governor, when Whittier and Beecher were also guests. He had warm friendships with the families of James B. Weaver in Des Moines, Franklin H. Head in Chicago, Pitts Burt in Cincinnati, and others who delighted in his visits. He wrote or revised manuscripts between engagements along the way or hurried proof off to New York.

On November 28, 1887, Cable appeared with Mark Twain, James Whitcomb Riley, and others in New York in the annual reading sponsored by the International Copyright League. He had meant to read from the manuscript of a new Acadian story, "Au Large," but because of a recent illness was obliged to read a portion of "Grande Pointe." Pond had laid plans in 1885 for a group, including Cable and Mark Twain, to appear in the larger Eastern cities but had to give up the idea because, he said, the authors did not want to work. On April 6, 1888, he succeeded in staging a "Grand Reading Tournament," with Max O'Rell, Bill Nye, Edward Eggleston, Riley, and Cable as performers. The tournament was intended as a testimonial benefit for Pond but turned out to be a mixture of the comic and for Pond the tragic. A creditor of Pond's attached the receipts, but there were no receipts after the expenses had been paid. In March of the next year Cable, Riley, Nye, and Richard Malcolm Johnston appeared together in New York and Philadelphia to raise money for the Wellesley College Alumnae association.[3] In 1888 Cable made his first of three reading tours on the West Coast, beginning at the Dalles, Oregon, on September 10 and working south.

Pond remained Cable's manager through these years, and between them existed a warm friendship that was never seriously strained. A note of whining was usual with Pond in writing of business matters, but otherwise he was jovial and effusive and was never restrained in speaking to or about Cable. He wrote Cable's mother in 1884 that he was a better man for knowing her son. Another time, June 24, 1894, he wrote Cable, "I can never serve you enough to half—or a hundredth part I better say —to show my appreciation of you, my dearest friend." Again, June 30, 1895: "Such a letter as that now lying before me has made me more anxious than ever I have been to be worthy of so near a place in your great heart." At the death of his mother early in their acquaintance he asked Cable to write a memorial tribute, saying that he was more like

[3] For another attempt to include Cable in joint readings, see Harriet R. Holman, "A Letter from Henry W. Grady Regarding Southern Authors and the Piedmont Chautauqua," *Georgia Historical Quarterly*, XXX (Dec., 1946), 308-11.

Christ than any other man he had ever known, and he later asked him to write memorials to his father and to his brother Ozias. After Henry Ward Beecher's death in 1887, he called Cable his closest friend and said he was the only man he could talk with about religious problems. When confronted with writing to do, he went to Cable, asking him to revise a statement for the press or to write the prospectus for platform tours by Nye and Riley or Howells.

After managing a lecture tour of Beecher's in England in 1886, Pond planned a book on the tour and asked Cable to edit it. Later he thought of it as a full account of his association with Beecher, to be written by Cable rather than edited. Hearing of the proposal, Beecher remarked on the strangeness of having a Southerner write his life.[4] Cable apparently did not seriously consider writing the book on Beecher, and when it was published after Beecher's death, his part was a tribute which Pond used in the preface and the extensive additions he had made in revising Pond's manuscript.[5] He contributed also to a memorial volume compiled by Edward Bok.[6]

A strong bond of mutual respect had grown between Cable and Beecher, in spite of the caution which Cable brought with him from his Southern background. After Cable first heard Beecher in his Brooklyn church on January 13, 1884, they drew together quickly. He had dinner with the Beechers the same day, in the company of Major Pond, and afterward wrote Louise, "Well there is one table—in 8th Street, N. Orleans—where there is as much fun & hard joking as at Mr. Beecher's, but I don't know of any more." Two days later Beecher heard his reading in Brooklyn and they were jointly honored at dinner after another two days. Beecher recommended Cable's books and his readings to his congregation. He visited the Cables at the Red House and planted a tree in the garden, "the Beecher Elm." For one of the memorial volumes Cable wrote, "I can only testify that my contact with him . . . reshaped my life when I had reached years where not many lives are reshaped."[7] At every one of their meetings he had been impressed by Beecher's enveloping humanity, his fatherliness to all mankind.

[4] See Pond to Cable, Oct. 31, Nov. 4, 1886, and Jan. 24, 1887.

[5] *A Summer in England with Henry Ward Beecher* . . . , ed. James B. Pond (New York, 1887). Nothing is indicated as written by Cable.

[6] *Beecher Memorial: Contemporary Tributes to the Memory of Henry Ward Beecher* (Brooklyn, 1887), pp. 33-34.

[7] *Ibid.,* p. 130.

CHAPTER XVII

CREOLES AND ACADIANS

NO NEW FICTION from Cable's pen was printed in 1885 and 1886, his busiest years in the Southern controversy. He had published none in fact since *Dr. Sevier,* which began its serial run in November, 1883. His most important literary work of these years was two long articles in the *Century* of February and April, 1886, "The Dance in Place Congo" and "Creole Slave Songs."

He had wanted to insert some of the songs in his first two books but at the objection of his editors had omitted all but a few snippets. Meanwhile he had added to his collection of words and music and related information. In the summer of 1884 he and Henry Edward Krehbiel, music editor of the New York *Tribune,* began collaboration to work up the songs. The first plan was for him to construct a lecture employing a few of the songs for illustration, to publish one or two articles, and then to issue a thin volume jointly with Krehbiel. In August, 1884, a manuscript was in the hands of the *Century* editors, but they found it too long and too weighted with the "heavy artillery" of philology. After giving up the idea of a lecture he lightened the material of the original manuscript and cut it into the two essays as they appeared in the *Century,* illustrated by E. W. Kemble.

The subject had held Cable's interest for at least a decade. It took him back to his childhood on Annunciation Square, to an ancient black woman balancing on her head a basket of *calas,* rice croquettes, and singing snatches of an African dance song, the "Calinda." Her parents had sung the tune before her, fitted with words poking fun at Judge Préval or Attorney-General Mazureau or some other of the master class. It was always a song loaded with meaning half-concealed in the mystery of the language and the equivocal allusiveness so common among oppressed peoples, and yet it was tolerated by the whites or even repeated by those who enjoyed the subtle thrusts at the great or the pretentious. More than once Cable had heard some black boy play quills of his own making and sing new words to a tune with its roots in the African jungle; he had heard the slow, barbaric chant of the field hands; he had set down on a scrap of paper the tune a Negro boy played on his harmonica as he ambled along the street. Other songs he knew from manuscripts, some of which had lain near to a hundred years in an old trunk in Mme Sidonie de la Houssaye's attic at Franklin, Louisiana; some the Creole scholar Alexander Dimitry had written down in New Orleans and in the parishes. *Slave Songs of the United States* (1867), collected by Charles Pickard Ware and his associates, supplied others; the Creole composer Louis Gottschalk had reclaimed one, "Bamboula," and had given it a world-wide audience. In an appended note Cable acknowledged his debt to these and others, including Lafcadio Hearn, "that skillful French translator and natural adept in research." Krehbiel had withdrawn from the collaboration but only after he had supplied one song and instrumental accompaniments to others. The extent of Cable's original collecting, however, is attested in Krehbiel's heavy reliance on these two articles when he published his volume on *Afro-American Folksongs* in 1914, in which he printed several of Cable's songs, including original words, translations, and musical scores.

Always careful in research and inclined to overload his fiction with facts from the archives, Cable welcomed the liberty these essays gave him. He could avoid the technical information his editors feared and still analyze the Creole patois and set down for comparison, as he did in a few instances, the original version, an English translation, and a rendering in representative African-English. Printed books gave little help with the patois of Louisiana, though he knew Alfred Mercier's essay on the subject in the Athénée Louisianais publications[1] and another by James A. Harrison in the *American Journal of Philology*,[2] and in Ware's *Slave Songs of the United States* he found brief notes on the Creole patois, as well as scores and words for seven plantation songs collected in St. Charles Parish before the war. The language of the West Indies had been more fully studied and recorded. J. J. Thomas's little volume *The Theory and Practice of Creole Grammar*[3] was useful to him, as it was also to Lafcadio Hearn in preparing his own collection of Creole proverbs, *Gombo Zhebes*.[4] J. Turiault's "Étude sur le langage créole de la Martinique,"[5] which Hearn and Cable both valued, employs parallel versions of fables to compare the languages of Martinique, Guadaloupe, and Guiana. Such comparisons could not but fascinate Cable and Hearn

---

[1] "Etude sur la langue créole en Louisiane," *Comptes rendus de l'Athénée louisianais*, I (1880), 378-83.
[2] "The Creole Patois of Louisiana," III (1882), 285-96.
[3] Port of Spain, Trinidad, 1869.
[4] New York, 1885.
[5] In *Extrait du bulletin de la Société Académique* (Brest, 1869).

as they struggled in New Orleans with a language showing kinship to all those dialects and also modifications peculiarly its own. The richest information was in the books of Medéric Louis Elie Moreau de Saint-Méry, especially the two thick volumes of his *Description topographique, physique, civile, politique et historique de la partie française de l'Isle Saint Domingue,* which had been Cable's authority on the African tribes represented among the slaves in *The Grandissimes.* Moreau had published in 1796 two similar volumes on the Spanish part of the island, and in the small volume *De la danse*[6] he had described the music and the execution of different dances in an amount of detail to be most useful to Cable.

Cable's purpose in these two articles was to give the songs and dances a setting in the life of colonial New Orleans, and secondarily to trace the threads of history to his own day, noting the continuities and the contrasts that always impressed him in reading history. No spot in New Orleans could better than Congo Square suggest the history of the lower half of the population, and through contrasts the upper half as well. From Cable's boyhood the square had officially another name, but any child attending a circus there knew it was really Congo Square and that once the fabulous Cayetano's Circus from Havana had performed in it, and that in those dimly reported times the black folk, not long from Africa, had gathered there in the late Sunday afternoons to sing and dance, and in the hours before the curfew gun would send them back to their quarters, to recapture in memory and feeling their former home and freedom.

In Cable's imagination the turf of the old square had absorbed a history extending back to the time when Bienville had designated it, then outside the back palisade of the city, as a meeting place for the slaves. He saw it as the epitome of the sorrow and suffering, the joys and hopes, the longing and resignation of those who had frequented it through a century and a half. It had witnessed the barbaric dances born in the African jungles; it had seen murder and insurrection planned and undertaken; it had echoed to songs of lament and resignation, protest and hate. Looking at it as Nathaniel Hawthorne had looked at the old seven-gabled house in Salem or the main street or the town pump of a New England village, Cable saw a panorama of past generations, with their contrasts and ironies. As the essays appeared finally, the author's views on slavery and in turn on the condition of the ex-slaves in his own time have only such oblique statement as in references to the square and to the old Black Code. But in the first draft, written

[6] Parme, 1801.

in 1884 while he was at work also on "The Freedman's Case in Equity,"
he had been less willing to gloss over those crueler times, and after
summarizing the treatment of slaves legalized in the Black Code, he
added:

That was in the old times. Yes, but it was down within the recollection of
men not yet old that the Calaboose retained its horrid fame. Talk of the
Bastile? Here stood, yet, the old Calaboza just behind the Place d'Armes,
and the later Calaboose just behind the Place Congo—it was here, not in
the Bastile, that any wretch could send his slave, man or woman, aged or
young, innocent or guilty, and without one word of testimony, nay without
even a charge of wrong doing, with nothing but a written request fixing the
number of lashes, have the culprit stripped to the skin, laid prone, fastened
by hands and feet to four stakes, and whipped—raw. "In passing the prison
in the morning the cries of the poor creatures are dreadful," wrote an ear-
witness. God be praised, those cries are heard no more.[7]

The *Century* editors thought the passage rubbed "the vinegar of recollection into the wounds of defeat" needlessly, and it was struck out.
Cable had himself tasted the vinegar of recollection, for his parents and
grandparents had owned slaves and he had reached maturity without
ever questioning the "peculiar institution." But as he saw the continuity
of history, the recollection need not run so far back, for he thought the
relations and the attitudes between the Negroes and the master race had
not been changed except superficially in the twenty years since emancipation. The essays are studies of the heart and soul of the slave in
colonial New Orleans, but only slightly less of the Creole Negro in the
1880's. Cable was prompted equally by a desire to understand the spirit
of the race and a humanitarian urge to plead their cause before human
society.

For the dances he relied mainly on Moreau's account, feeling certain
that those common in San Domingo were performed also in Louisiana:
the frantic bamboula and the sorcerer's voodoo, the calinda and the
lascivious chico. The last two he mentioned only briefly, saying that
only their songs deserved to survive. Yet he was the sympathetic student
of a primitive culture, concerned not to condemn the crudities or inde-
cencies but rather to record the spirit of a child-like race. It was not
difficult to localize the dances in Louisiana, actually, for on the scraps
of paper which held his findings in Creole songs Cable had the words
and the tunes for the bamboula and the calinda and other dances which
he had heard on the streets. Furthermore, since the weekly gatherings at
Congo Square had continued into the 1840's, he could learn something

[7] This draft is at Tulane University.

from former participants; and the voodoo rites, long forbidden in the city, were still enacted along Bayou St. John.[8] He had once seen Marie Laveau herself, shortly before her death, in a cottage near Congo Square, but she was in no way the model for Palmyre in *The Grandissimes,* he said, as had been asserted in print.[9] He saw in the dances—as he heard in the songs—the vestiges of a primitive culture, rooted in ignorance, superstition, and barbarism, and only slightly modified by association with the white race.

The songs allowed a fuller study than could be made from the flimsy reconstruction of the dances, for Cable had many songs and their tunes and could translate the words. Some of the songs were still remembered in Creole families from some black mammy's singing to the white child in her arms. They were songs of love, jealousy, anger, toil, superstition. They had often a plaintive note, a faint and gentle melancholy, at times a stately lamentation, as in the "Dirge of St. Malo," which Alexander Dimitry gave Cable, at times a subdued protest at the fate of the free men and women of color, whose freedom was ironically meaningless. The jealousy poured into such a song as "Pov' Piti' Momzel Zizi," which Cable sang many times on the platform, was frequently that of one colored or mulatto mistress for favors bestowed on a rival—an embroidered petticoat and a Madras turban, in this instance. The song of the quadroon man watching the quadroon women going to the ball, from which he is of course excluded, echoes the protest mixed with self-pity expressed so often in the songs.

Except for the songs to accompany the wilder dances, they reflected the quieter elements of the Negro characters. They were likely to speak with a directness which Cable felt he could not record exactly. "Nigger Lover's Despair," for example, as it is preserved in his pencil notes, has lines hardly usable in the essay: "So dé tétons té rond zis comm boule" ("Her titties as round as a cannon ball," in his translation), and "Et quand li té marce, gogo tremblé" ("And when she walked, buttocks trembled"). The singer often took advantage of his special language and framed his song so deftly with confused or double meanings that he could sing it under the very nose of the one satirized. Cable found preserved among both whites and blacks satirical verses to the calinda tune aimed at public officials a century earlier.[10]

The author took occasion in "Creole Slave Songs" to characterize the

[8] See the *Times-Democrat,* June 24, 1884; also the *Picayune,* June 24, 25, 1873.
[9] Cable to Mary L. Bartlett, July 30, 1881.
[10] Most of the songs printed in Cable's article were rendered by a music society at the Nashville College for Young Ladies in a public program of May 21, 1886. See the Nashville *Daily American* of May 22.

patois of the songs and to explain something of its syntax and word formation. He could not translate some of the songs, he confessed, presumably songs mainly African in their language; and he added, "We are sappers and miners in this quest, not philologists." He explained the broad use of the word *Creole* to designate anything associated with the Creoles and explained also the relation between the Creoles of pure blood and the patois. The whites often employed the language in speaking to the slaves and occasionally among themselves, half-facetiously or familiarly, for they knew it from the household servants and the colored nurses. Remembering no doubt the charge made by Gayarré and others that he had given his Creole characters a Negro-patois speech, he made it clear that occasional use of the patois by educated Creoles cast no reflection on their correctness when they spoke French. The Creoles might still object that their English had less of the Gallicized phrasing and pronunciation than he gave them, but some of them testified that he had caught their speech exactly. They might object also to his asumption that many of them paid deference to the voodoo superstitions, but on this point and also on the Creole's use of the patois the writings of both Lafcadio Hearn and Alfred Mercier, a Creole scholar of the language and a novelist, bear him out.[11]

Cable interpolated in "The Dance in Place Congo" a final word in what two years earlier had been the lively but friendly "Banjo Controversy." Writing on "Plantation Music" in the *Critic* of December 15, 1883, Joel Chandler Harris had said that the fiddle was the Negro's most characteristic instrument, rather than the banjo as generally represented in books and on the stage. There followed a series of letters to magazines and newspapers, most of them citing localities in which the Negroes did play the banjo. Cable's statement that he had heard the banjo played in New Orleans, though the violin was a hundred to one commoner, was quoted in the *Critic* of June 28, 1884, and also in the London *Saturday Review,* the New York *Tribune,* and other newspapers. Harris answered in the *Critic* of July 19, continuing the good-natured argument and objecting that he should be "overthrown with a Creole dandy song." In a letter to Harris on July 28, 1884,[12] and later in "The Dance in Place

[11] On Jan. 3, 1883, so the *Times-Democrat* reported the next day, a Mr. P. Genega testified that a Mary Smith, whom he called a voodoo, and a bad one, had put coal oil on his doorstep at three o'clock in the morning. Mary Smith denied the charge, but Judge Ford gave her thirty days. See Hearn's numerous newspaper and magazine articles collected in Albert Mordell's *An American Miscellany* (New York, 1924), 2 vols., and in E. L. Tinker's *Lafcadio Hearn's American Days.* See also Alfred Mercier's *L'Habitation Saint-Ybars, ou maitres et esclaves en Louisiane. Recit social* (Nouvelle-Orléans, 1881).

[12] Printed in Biklé, p. 128.

Congo," Cable agreed with Harris that the chief instrument of the Negro was the fiddle, insisting only that the banjo was the favored accompaniment for the sensual African dance.

The interest Cable and Lafcadio Hearn shared in the slave songs was one of the strongest bonds between them and seems also to have been one cause if not the main cause of the coolness that later came between them. Cable had begun the collecting long before Hearn came to New Orleans and had planned to make literary use of the songs. Hearn was fascinated by the richly exotic materials Cable had assembled and began himself studying the language and songs and superstitions and epigrams of the French-speaking Negroes. In his first mention of Cable in writing his friend Krehbiel, in 1878, he said he had assisted in collecting the songs and that Cable was going to publish a study of them with examples accompanied by the musical scores.[13] Afterward he regretted that the songs had been excluded from Cable's first two books, and he undertook himself to send Krehbiel the words and music of the native songs. In "The Scenes of Cable's Romances" he wrote that when he first began collecting the songs and kindred lore Cable lent him his collection with permission to make selections for his own private use.

But Hearn met difficulties. Often the people who knew the songs were suspicious and would give him no help; he could not write down the music and had to rely on Cable, as he did once when he heard an aged black woman singing a voodoo song and repeated it later as best he could for Cable to transcribe. Through the year 1883 Hearn and Cable continued their collaboration in song collecting. Hearn visited on Eighth Street to talk literature or folklore or to read or hear read a new manuscript, or to meet a visitor to the city. He was Cable's greatest booster in the local newspapers, and Cable in turn found tangible ways of befriending him, as in proposing late in 1882 that Hearn be sent in his place with Joseph Pennell to the West Indies. Late in January, 1883, when J. O. Davidson came to New Orleans with the proposal that Cable write articles to accompany the drawings he would make for *Harper's Weekly,* Cable threw the work instead to Hearn. After this beginning Hearn wrote a dozen or more articles for the Harper publications, and still later he was commissioned by the company to go to the West Indies and afterward to Japan.

Yet in the years of their closest association Hearn voiced some reservations about Cable and his works in writing to Krehbiel, most of them

---

[13] Elizabeth Bisland, *The Life and Letters of Lafcadio Hearn* (Boston, [1906]), I, 175-76. Except as indicated, other letters of Hearn's to Krehbiel mentioned below are in these volumes.

bearing somehow on the Creole songs and suggesting that he was piqued because Cable could record the tunes and he could not. In 1881 he said he doubted that Cable was enough of a musician to record accurately the fractions of tones common to the Creole music, and after Krehbiel and Cable had met in 1883 he sent Krehbiel a song and asked him not to show it to Cable. Later in 1883 he wrote:

Don't try to conceive how I could sympathize with Cable! Because I never sympathized with him at all. His awful faith—which to me represents an undeveloped mental structure—gives a neutral tint to his whole life among us. There is a Sunday-school atmosphere. . . . But Cable is more liberal-minded than his creed; he has also rare analytical powers on a small scale.

These remarks suggest that Hearn and Cable were never intimate. It seems rather that they respected each other's scholarly and literary accomplishments, assisted each other whenever possible but recognized the wide differences in background, attitude, and outlook that existed between them. The seeds of their subsequent estrangement were already present in 1883. In that year and afterward Cable was in New Orleans only for short periods and so rarely saw Hearn. In February, 1884, when Hearn reviewed *Dr. Sevier,* he was hopelessly down on Cable, Marion Baker said, for no apparent reason. Separation may have been the main reason. Hearn's friendships rarely lasted long, and as a rule not long beyond separation. Marion Baker, a colleague on the *Times-Democrat,* wrote Cable on August 14, 1889, two years after Hearn's departure from New Orleans: "He used to visit us several times a week before he left, & stay until after midnight. . . . Since then we have never heard a word from him; & although he seemed devoted to Page, he always shuns him when they happen to be in New York at the same time."

Hearn's nature was to fear that his friends would betray him when he was out of their presence. There was ample room for him to resent Cable's taking his place in collaboration with Krehbiel on the Creole songs. He was surely not one to disapprove of Cable's views on slavery and Negro rights, but his frame of mind was such when he reviewed *Dr. Sevier* that he questioned those views as a staunch Southerner might have done. Still the fairness of the review is evidence enough that he had not the sort of venom he displayed toward others he became down on. He had been drawn toward Page Baker's way of looking at Cable's "anti-Southern" views, while keeping his high regard for Cable's art; and after "The Freedman's Case in Equity" had appeared, he apparently moved still farther into the orbit of Page. He did not join Marion Baker and Elizabeth Bisland in saying a good word for Cable on the literary page whenever they dared; and in writing Krehbiel in January, 1885,[14] when Cable and Krehbiel were working on the Creole songs, he showed how much he was down on Cable—and also how irrational he had become on the matter, reflecting, it seems, both the prompting of Page Baker and his own resentment. Hearn's severity toward those he thought had wronged or slighted him being as unreasoned as it was, the wonder is, perhaps, that his strictures on Cable were so reserved.

One of Hearn's few references to Cable in print in his last two years in New Orleans came on January 2, 1887, in a review for the *Times-Democrat* of a novel, *Towards the Gulf,* published anonymously by Alice Morris Buckner. His remarks leave no doubt that his animosity had grown intense enough to affect either the fairness or the acuteness of his judgment. He called the book the "most powerful story that any Southern writer, without exception, has yet produced," and added: "There are certainly pages which suggest Cable;—but if Cable had written it, he would have written something compared with which all his previous creations were feeble."[15] Soon afterward Hearn left New Orleans, snapping all his ties there just as three years later he would move on to Japan, cut short his relations with the Harper firm, and enter his Japanese phase, which lasted until his death. In publishing the articles on the songs and dances, Cable gave credit generously to Hearn, and on July 5, 1888, he recommended Hearn, then in the West Indies, to an editor who asked him to write something on the Creole-English speech he did not have time to write himself. If he felt any resentment toward Hearn, apparently no records of it have been preserved.

Cable's three stories of the Acadians finally appeared in the *Century* in 1887 and 1888. From his first visit among the Acadians they had interested him only slightly less than the New Orleans Creoles. The notebook he kept while in the parishes of southwestern Louisiana in 1881 assembling material for the census report shows that he was no more interested in statistical and historical facts appropriate to the census than in traditions, customs, speech, superstitions, and other lore usable in fiction. The census report on these parishes was not wanted after all, but late

---

[14] This letter, published in part in Bisland, *The Life and Letters of Lafcadio Hearn,* I, 337, is in the possession of George Matthew Adams of New York.

[15] J. B. Gilder of the *Critic* wrote Cable on June 17, 1886, "I once asked Lafcadio Hearn if he would write of you for us, with your consent; only to be overwhelmed with abuse. He must be a terribly terrible man! What ails him?" E. L. Tinker (*Lafcadio Hearn's American Days,* p. 185) says, apparently on the authority of oral tradition, that Cable resented Hearn's telling in *Chita* (1889) the story he had first heard from Cable about the flood at Last Island, off the Louisiana coast. Vera McWilliams (*Lafcadio Hearn,* p. 228) makes a similar assertion, but I have come across no record that Cable ever made any uncomplimentary remark about Hearn.

in 1883 a draft of an Acadian story went to the *Century* office. No more was done with it, however, until Cable had visited the Acadian parishes in March, 1885, at the close of his tour with Mark Twain. In June he sent Gilder one story, "Grande Pointe," and was at work on another, "Carancro." Though "Grande Pointe" did not please Gilder at once, after he had read a revised version more than a year later, he wrote on August 18, 1886: "Your fierce editor is very light on you this time, is he not? Well it is a beautiful story and will belong to literature. There is only one Cable." "Carancro" was in the *Century* of January and February, 1887, followed the next month by "Grande Pointe" and by "Au Large," which ran for five months beginning the next November. The magazine paid $2550 for the three stories, of which $250 was a bonus. In March, 1888, Scribner brought the stories together in a volume entitled *Bonaventure*.

In the plan of writing three separate stories that could stand together as a novel something was lost to the whole book and also to each part. The three parts are not drawn together by the action, for the three plots are distinct, or by the characters, for the focus shifts from one story to another. Rather the unifying thread is the region and the people. Except for two or three excursions outside, the action remains in the land of prairie and swamp and bayou where the French peasants expelled from Nova Scotia in 1755 had gathered in the following years and had kept alive their traditions and habits from the old country, as well as their language, though after a hundred years it showed the effects of the remoteness and the association with other peoples and languages. The Acadians had kept close to their church, their simple virtues, and their agricultural and pastoral ways.

As with his Creole stories, a primary aim of Cable's was to represent the Acadians truthfully. On his trips among them, he sought out what was commonplace in their communities and yet peculiar to them. In 1887 while he was writing "Au Large," he visited the southwestern parishes again and at Franklin went over the manuscripts with Mme de la Houssaye, who had long been his friend and his authority on the Acadians of the past and the present. The book has a simplicity in its action not found in either of Cable's earlier novels, a simplicity the reader feels is appropriate to the directness and outward naivete of the Acadians which conceal the intensity and the depth of their characters. The author's purpose is to hold close to the line dividing reality from absurdity; if he avoids falling into absurdity, as in the spelling bee on which hangs the future of Bonaventure and also the school he teaches at Grande Pointe, he is saved because his characters are of such directness and simplicity that the action of melodrama is natural to them. The three stories all bear out one theme—selfless devotion to others as the key to happiness. In "Carancro" Bonaventure finds himself through a search which obviously represents self-abnegation and self-discipline reached through the standing off of temptation. At Grande Pointe in the second story he wins out in his venture and wins personal happiness because he has held to the faith reached through the testing of the earlier story. In "Au Large" it is one of Bonaventure's pupils, Claude St. Pierre, who proves again that one's happiness is always in "some other one's hands" and that concern for others before self is requisite to true nobility.

Bonaventure has the charm of the Acadian villages. Elemental in their natures and devoid of intricacy or subtlety, the characters live a story similarly direct and uncomplex. The book has no characters and no scenes to stick in the reader's mind as do those of Cable's earlier books, but the total picture is impressive, the picture of a gentle people, delightful in their simplicity and heroic in their minor way.

The novel was received with enthusiasm by some reviewers and favorably by almost all of them, the few exceptions being those who wrote on the Southern controversy rather than the book, as did the *Missouri Republican* of March 17, 1888, in saying that Cable's purpose had been to argue for Federal intervention in the public schools. To some reviewers *Bonaventure* was a welcome fusion of realism and idealism; it proved the methods of realism could produce something besides unleavened photography of life. It displayed a richness of life, the Boston *Literary World* said, even in the most stringent poverty. The Boston *Evening Traveller* of April 16 praised the author's skill in producing the drama of everyday life in a romantic environment without losing the sense of actuality. The *Critic,* May 26, found in it "simplicity made noble, and gentleness made manly" and a "gradual evolution of character in each individual which can hardly be called incident but which certainly is life." Some credited Cable with success where he had failed in his earlier books: in the character of Bonaventure he had made the force of goodness strong and active and utterly believable. They found his usual charm and humor and the faithfulness they had come to expect of him in his laying with delightful exactness the background of terrain, customs, and speech.

In November, 1888, Cable began a series of pieces in the *Century* which ran for twelve months and then formed the volume *Strange True Stories of Louisiana.* The opportunity to retell true stories was welcome to him. He could include the factual documentation he was tempted to crowd into his fiction and yet could give it an imaginative interpretation unsuited to historical writing. The occasion invited him to demonstrate his belief that true stories, but slightly dressed up, often have the interest of fiction. Some of the stories had lain in his desk several years before he had the first of them ready to show his publishers in the fall of 1885. Gilder was eager to run them in the magazine, and Scribner proposed book publication, but more pressing demands intervened and they were not taken up again until two years later.

Cable introduced the stories in an essay called "How I Got Them," which Gilder thought "one of the most graphic and interesting things" he had done. In it he said he had translated, clarified, and cut down but had added nothing to what had come from old manuscripts, archival records, yellowing newspapers, or the recollections of witnesses still living. He could hardly expect to transmit, he said, even with the photographs he included, the interest he felt because he had handled an ancient manuscript or had lived neighbor to the chief character in one story, or had known the descendants of the characters in another, or had visited the scene of another, or had traced the details of another in the newspaper files or in court records.

He first began collecting the true stories in 1883, and by the end of that year had in his desk the chief manuscripts and other documents relating to five of the seven he published later. Three of the stories came from Mme Sidonie de la Houssaye, a widow bringing up her children at Franklin, a village in St. Mary, one of the Acadian parishes. With literary inclinations and a wealth of information on the history and traditions of French Louisiana, much of it coming to her from ancestors among the early settlers, she published several books, in French, and wrote others that did not find a publisher. She had also trunks full of manuscripts, some of them aged through the greater part of a century. In the spring of 1883 Cable bought one of the manuscripts which was in line for partial publication in *L'Abeille,* "The Adventures of Françoise and Suzanne," an account of a trip from New Orleans into the southwestern parishes in 1795. With Guthrie as his agent and convinced that the narrative was genuine, he made sure also that the seller was pleased with the sale, as she gave assurances she was—the pay was twice what *Scribner's* had paid for Cable's first story and more than the pay for his fifth. From the same source came the shorter manuscript of "Alix de Morainville" and "The Young Aunt with White Hair," as well as some of the Creole songs Cable published later and an immeasurable store of knowledge Mme de la Houssaye gave him in her long, effusive letters and on his visits to Franklin.

For his part he advised her on her own writing and interceded in her behalf with Charles Scribner and other publishers. She felt no resentment at his treatment of the Creoles or the Acadians in his books or at his stand on the Negro question. In fact, she made common cause with him against his slanderers. She needed money and proposed sundry ways in which he might use her materials. When he objected that it would not be honorable for him to translate her stories and publish them as his own, she countered that Dumas had employed other writers in his own work. In one of her last letters, April 22, 1889, she was voluble as ever, though nearing seventy: "Soyez convaincu que votre noble conduite à mon égard n'est pas adressée à une ingrate et que vous aurez toujours des amis dévotés dans mes enfants et dans moi."

Before acquiring the first manuscript from Mme de la Houssaye, Cable had been put on the track of another true story by his friend Dr. Francis Bacon in New Haven, the story of Salome Müller, who the Louisiana Supreme Court decided in 1844-45 was white, a German immigrant of 1818, who had somehow passed into slavery as a child. Explored in the newspapers and the court records, this story became "Salome Müller, the White Slave." The story "Attalie Brouillard" came orally from a judge of the author's acquaintance. It tells how a shrewd free man of color drew a will, in the role of a man just dead, for the benefit of a quadroon woman who had been something more to the deceased white man, apparently, than a landlady. Convinced after inquiry that this "tale was true so many more times than was necessary," Cable told it with the lightness and humor appropriate to relieve the grimness some of the other stories have.

"The 'Haunted House' in Royal Street" is the grimmest of the seven tales. The old house at Royal and Hospital streets had been notorious for fifty years, and today it is pointed out to visitors as the Haunted House or the "city's first skyscraper." Its history has been told over and over in print since Cable's time. His narrative contains two episodes, the second of which tells how in December, 1874, when the house was used for an unsegregated girls' high school, a mob expelled the pupils not of white blood. It was to protest against this act and the supporting editorials and mass meetings that Cable wrote two letters to the editor of the Bulletin. Later he read an account of the incident written by Dora Richards Miller, who had been a teacher in the school at the time. She had laid it aside because she would lose her place teaching in New Orleans if she published it.

The earlier and stranger episode, the one that gave the house its haunts, dated back to 1834, when Mme Lalaurie had entertained Creole society at sparkling dinner parties in part of the house while at the same time torturing nine of her slaves in other parts with a cruelty reminiscent of the Dark Ages. Cable began with Harriet Martineau's account as she learned it in New Orleans two years after the event and reported it in her *Retrospect of Western Travel*.[16] James B. Guthrie and Mrs. Miller searched newspapers and documents for him and interviewed people whose memories dated back to 1834. The materials Cable had in his hands when he wrote the narrative of the Haunted House are fascinating in themselves and testify as to the care with which he used his sources. Where the reports did not agree in details, he sifted them for the points of agreement and qualified his account where there was not agreement. It is true that the subject involved two touchy subjects, slavery and the Creoles, but he no doubt was following his customary method of historical research.

The last of the *Strange True Stories of Louisiana* came from a manuscript of Dora Richards Miller's. While he was first assembling the tales in 1883, she brought him a diary she had kept during the war. The Vicksburg portion Cable published in the *Century* war series, the remainder along with the other true stories, and the complete diary in the volume. A Union sympathizer during the war, Mrs. Miller had returned to teaching in New Orleans afterward and had to conceal her authorship. She was in constant fear, as it was, lest the school board learn of it; though the names were changed in the published diary, several families in New Orleans recognized it as hers. A widow with children to support, she was glad to sell the manuscript to Cable and to earn wages doing research for him.

Of all his many friends with literary ambitions, Mrs. Miller was the one he tried most assiduously to help, partly because her needs were greatest and she persisted longest. At intervals in the ten years after he bought the diary from her, he employed her in searching New Orleans records for him, recommended her to editors and lecture managers, and advised her in her own writing. A piece of hers he recommended to *Lippincott's Magazine* was accepted, and another, "The Census as She Is Took," he revised and published in the *Independent* of December 17, 1891, as by Dora Richards Miller and edited by him. In a prefatory note he stated that she was the author of the "Diary of a Union Woman" he had published earlier. Since she had already lost her teaching position in New Orleans, her authorship could be acknowledged. He sent

[16] An account of Mme Lalaurie had been included in E. Bunner's *History of Louisiana* (New York, 1842).

the payment to her and at other times lent her money, but she asked him to collaborate with her still more directly.

In 1884 Cable had suggested that she write up her experiences during the insurrection on the island of Santa Cruz in 1848. After she had written the account and had tried for a year to find a publisher, he bought it in 1887 and laid it aside. He published it in *Scribner's Magazine* (December, 1892) as "A West Indian Slave Insurrection." In introducing it in the magazine, he said it was taken exactly from the manuscript of a friend, the Dora of the narrative, and reiterated that it was hers, not his. Actually he overstated, as he had done in publishing the war diary, his closeness in following the manuscript. Mrs. Miller was disappointed, however, at having herself identified only as Dora. After the *Times-Democrat* of December 4, 1892, had cited a paragraph from the "Slave Insurrection" for commendation, she wrote a letter for the December 11 issue of the paper stating that she was the Dora of the story and citing Cable's printed denial that he had done more than minor revising. She had no doubt, she said, that Cable would want her to make this statement. An anonymous letter in the same issue, no doubt drawing information from her, converted the matter into a charge that Cable had engaged in sharp dealings. The same charge was expanded in other publications and in at least one anonymous letter to Cable's publishers. At the request of the editor of the *Critic* Cable wrote an explanation for the issue of February 4, 1893. Dictated in haste on the train, he said, it was a reply only to Mrs. Miller's letter in the *Times-Democrat,* but he was obviously thinking more of the abusive charges others in New Orleans had written. Consequently he refuted more firmly the implications of her letter than he would have done otherwise, indicating how extensive his revision had been in reality, and added that the implications that he had concealed her literary ability should take account of her failure to publish her writings independently. Still he insisted that she was the writer of the story and he only the editor.

She replied in the *Critic* two weeks later, repeating with some reservations the accusations others had made. Their relations had come to what was perhaps the inevitable conclusion. Prompted by kindness and friendship he had encouraged her, advised her, recommended her to his friends; he had given her employment, had lent her money, and had given her money. Buying the manuscripts which she could not publish herself gave him a means of helping her in a way to bring some return to him. But this procedure failed to gain the entrance to the magazines she wanted for her own writings. In her poverty and bitterness she then

supplied new matter to his detractors. In his dealings with her and
Mme de la Houssaye alike he was mixing friendship and generosity with
a shaky type of business transaction that invited misunderstanding and
ill feeling. The wonder is less that misunderstanding accrued in his
relations with Mrs. Miller than that his relations with Mme de la
Houssaye remained on the friendliest basis.

After the *True Stories* had been completed in the *Century,* Cable
printed two supplementary letters. One of them, published in September, 1889, was written in embarrassment to explain two anachronisms in
the story "Alix de Morainville" which had escaped his attention and
seemed to compromise the genuineness of the manuscript he had used.
The other letter answered objections that had been raised to the implications in the account of the Haunted House that the White League
was organized against the black race. During Reconstruction the White
League, a semimilitary, semisecret organization, had been the spearhead
of the efforts of white Democrats to wrest the government from the
carpetbaggers. Cable replied in the issue of April, 1890, that "there are
harms deeper and far more lasting than bodily injuries," and that every
man in the state, black or white, had suffered from the extralegal action
of the White League. He was still deeply involved in the Southern controversy, as he had been while collecting and publishing the true stories.
Four of the seven dealt with phases of the great sore question, and he
would not have gainsaid that the tales reflected his own coloring. He
might have argued that the strangest stories of Louisiana always touched
on the question somehow.

In the ten years after the publication of *Dr. Sevier,* Cable's only important addition to his literary work was *Bonaventure.* The *Strange
True Stories of Louisiana* and some of the lesser pieces, such as the articles on Creole songs and dance, had been well received; but they were
primarily historical and antiquarian. The fact is that Cable in those years
was a literary man only with his left hand, and a fiction writer hardly
at all. That fact he regretted, and he winced when it was said that he
had let his reform work draw off his energy from literature. Yet in so
far as that was true, to his mind it was putting first things first. He
hoped his creative work would not suffer, and he was reluctant to admit
that it did, but if such was the case, it simply had to be.

CHAPTER XVIII

THE SOUTHERN DEBATE

FOLLOWING his two essays in 1885 on the Negro question, Cable might have decided the course of wisdom was to leave the controversy. His literary career, as his publishers reminded him, needed all his energy. He might have argued too, on the evidence of the response the two essays received, that his efforts were accomplishing but little. His sister Mary Louise was one who raised this question in a letter of May 10, 1886: "I wondered if sometimes in our great anxiety to set things right we may not do more harm by the strife than we do good by the urging." Roswell Smith's support could be counted on at every turn, as for example in his reply to a letter he had received disparaging Cable: "He is probably one of those to whom monuments will be erected in the next generation not only in the south but throughout the English speaking world."[1] Still, Smith took Cable's move north to symbolize a progression from sectional to national problems and urged him not to tie himself to narrow causes. On March 31, 1886, he quoted Gilder as saying, "If Cable would write a novel the scene of which is laid at the North, it would make him the most popular novelist in America."

Cable was not deterred however, though he must have looked with some longing back to the days when he had nothing but praise from all quarters, except for a few spokesmen of the Creoles; and for another five years the controversy remained primary in his activities. Knowing that his move from the South would be taken as flight and abandonment of the cause, as indeed was said more than once in print, he reiterated that he had lost none of his interest in her welfare. He expected to profit, he said, from the perspective of distance and from observing the problems of class and caste in the society of the New England town, the antithesis of the Southern plantation society. At least the whole subject had been pushed forward for thought and discussion, and further good would surely come, he thought, after the initial flaring of Southern tempers, as more light was thrown on the subject and as saner judgment was applied. Marion Baker assured him that a new attitude was evolving in the

[1] Roswell Smith to Mrs. W. H. Ball, Jan. 28, 1886. Copy at Tulane University.

South, and a writer in the New Orleans *Christian Advocate,* a former slaveholder himself, predicted that those who had most impulsively condemned Cable's stand would "on the second and sober study of the issue materially qualify, if, indeed, they did not retract their criticism." Booker T. Washingson wrote to one who apparently had sent a gift to Tuskegee at Cable's soliciting: "There are many in the South who *think* as Mr. Cable does but have not the moral courage to express their sentiments."[2] And as months passed, opposing views were advanced in a way to make replying seem worthwhile.

Cable had already begun assembling information on churches, schools, the crop lien system, as well as politics in the South. Whenever he spoke or wrote on the subject, he was fortified with statistics and other facts to support the position he had already taken. But he had learned how easy it was to provoke opposition, and so strove more diligently than before to avoid debating particular charges and countercharges and to hold attention to the issues involved in conditions on which there could be little disagreement.

From 1885 to 1892 Cable delivered a dozen addresses and published almost as many essays on the Southern question, in what was in effect a single-handed crusade, for no one else North or South gave him more than occasional support. Booker T. Washington, devoting a heroic life at Tuskegee Institute to uplifting his race, supplied information but asked that his name not be associated with it, for he must keep the friendship of the Southern whites. Seth Low, concluding in 1886 his second term as mayor of Brooklyn, shared Cable's aims for the colored race but was inclined to think progress was being made as rapidly as could be expected. Many others favored the same goals as Cable but thought time would bring the solution and believed he wanted to force the evolution unnaturally. Only after 1890, when the Negro had lost the ballot throughout the South and was firmly in the grip of segregation and economic dependence, did they realize that expediency and gradualism were false hopes. Whether Cable saw in advance how completely these hopes would fail or was prompted only by a sense of justice and right, his arguments have a prophetic ring when they are read alongside the history of the half a century after he advanced them.

Cable realized that answering personal attacks would be fruitless if not impossible, but it is remarkable that in the many letters to his wife there are no statements of resentment against his detractors, only a few

[2] Washington to Frederick C. Jones, Dec. 21, 1885; printed in Philip Butcher, "George W. Cable and Booker T. Washington," *Journal of Negro Education,* XVII (Fall, 1948), 463.

references to apostate friends in New Orleans which reflect less resentment than hurt. In a few instances he corresponded with individuals who were willing to discuss the subject rationally. George C. Burnap of Marietta, Georgia, was such a person. He questioned the statement in "The Freedman's Case in Equity" that a Negro had been sentenced to twenty years in the Georgia penitentiary for hog-stealing. A solicitor-general of the state had cast doubt on Cable's whole position by denying this one fact, not on the authority of the records but because "no judge could permit such a sentence." After Cable had replied with citations from the penitentiary records on this and three other cases, including that of a man under sentence of forty years for simple larceny, Burnap acknowledged his agreement with Cable's stand. "I confess to some shrinking from the immediate consequences," he wrote. ". . . But such personal preferences or prejudices as I may feel become insignificant, when a call like yours is sounded." At another time he wrote: "I have had men admit that the convict lease system was an evil—and yet condemn your efforts to abolish it as an attack upon the section you once claimed as your own."[3]

Both correspondents thought of publishing their letters and Cable used portions of them without naming Burnap in a reply to ex-Senator John W. Johnston of Virginia. Johnston's letter "The True South *vs.* the Silent South," and Cable's rejoinder were printed in the same issue of the *Century,* May, 1886, and appeared together again in the 1889 edition of *The Silent South.* Johnston challenged the facts given in "The Freedman's Case in Equity," citing Southern statutes to prove that "no such penalties as these are allowed by law"; Cable replied with the names of convicts under such sentences from the printed penitentiary reports. Johnston quoted a penitentiary keeper on the death rates in the convict camps; Cable cited the death rates revealed in the penitentiary reports. And so the debate went point by point. In the *Century* of October, 1886, A. E. Orr of Atlanta argued that in proportion to total population more Negroes were sent to prison in the North than in the South. A reply by Cable was in the same issue, and again the differences lay in both the statistics and their interpretation. Surely comparisons of the North and South added nothing, Cable wrote, but "I find but half a million dark sufferers from this error in all the North. There are twelve times that number in the South. . . . I have never yet spoken first in this matter, save under the conviction that silence was treason to the South. It is treason."

[3] Burnap's letters and copies of Cable's written late in 1885 and 1886, are at Tulane University.

These two were Cable's last printed statements in direct answer to his adversaries, but he continued to correspond with individuals who like Burnap seemed to be earnestly seeking a solution. One of these was Mrs. W. H. Felton of Cartersville, Georgia, whose husband as state legislator and Congressman had entered the lists against the convict lease of the state. In a series of letters beginning on June 28, 1886, she described the lease system of Georgia, especially as it affected Negro criminals. With the lease held by the United States Senators and the governor, and with the newspapers "careful to keep out the light from our own people," she said, hope for alleviation was slight. She sent Cable an essay on the subject which he was able to place in the *Forum*.[4]

In an address at Madison, Wisconsin, on October 29, 1885, Cable discussed the Freedman's schools. Following that he spoke for the first time before a society dedicated to Negro rights. The Lincoln Club of Meriden, Connecticut, invited him to a banquet at which he would be honored. Among those who addressed the three hundred present were the governor and the treasurer of the state, a United States Senator, the editor of the New York *Globe,* and the mayor of Meriden. Aware of the occasion and the audience, Cable said little of the Negroes' grievances and dwelt most pointedly on their needs and their obligations. They must never themselves draw the color line; they must always work to benefit both races. Their hope lay in education, tolerance, and work; and they must develop leaders in their own race.[5] Whenever he spoke or wrote to Negroes in the future, he returned to this theme.

Previously Cable had spoken and written with Southern whites primarily in mind, and so had stated or assumed the Negro's grievances and had dwelt on what the whites must do to give the Negro his rightful place as a citizen. Addressing the audience at Meriden required a modified approach. Another audience he addressed soon afterward required a further adjustment. Roswell Smith invited him to introduce Judge William M. Beckner on January 18, 1886, at a meeting of the New York Congregational Club to discuss "National Aid to Education." Since their association at Berea the preceding summer, Smith, Beckner, and Cable had made common cause of Berea College and the larger problem of which it was a symbol. At one with Beckner in supporting national aid, Cable said: "The safety of society lies in the elevation of the masses. The South lacked the belief in this idea in the days of slavery. There are men among you, your neighbors around the corner, here in New York to-day, who lack this idea and who actually cherish

---

[4] "The Convict System of Georgia," *Forum*, II (Jan., 1887), 484-90.
[5] See the New Haven *Evening Register*, Nov. 5 and 6, 1885.

the opinion that safety lies in the subjugation of the masses. The negro must be educated as the South is reconstructed." In his refusal to place all the blame in one place, a habit of his which challenged smugness in any quarter, he remarked, "I believe the South has made as much progress in the understanding of the negro as a citizen in the twenty years since the war as the North did in the twenty years before the war."[6] When he addressed posts of the Grand Army of the Republic, as he did in Simsbury while he lived there and at Pittsfield[7] and Concord, Massachusetts, in 1886, he reminded the former Union soldiers of the responsibility the entire nation shared for slavery and the evils spawned by it. Speaking on June 22 to the Young Men's Republican Club of Paterson, New Jersey, through the arrangement of Nicholas Murray Butler, he again dwelt on the national aspects of the question and not the particular injustices in the South.

In an address of January 12, 1887, before the Sumner League in Unity Hall at Hartford, where four years earlier he had appeared for the test of his public readings, Cable took as his subject "The Progress of the Negro Race."[8] He restated much of what he had said to other audiences mainly Negro. But while apportioning blame to the North and giving the Negroes conciliatory advice, he gave no quarter to the defenders of race superiority. "The reconstruction Mr. Grady wants," he said, "is a crime against society." Assuming that all would know Grady's views and in particular his speech on the New South on December 21, 1886, before the New England Club of New York, in which he had asserted that the South had kept faith with the former slaves, Cable concluded with seven stanzas made for the occasion, four of which are given below:

> You've probably heard of one, Grady,
> A speech to New Englanders made he.
>> They thought it delightful
>> Becuz he wa'n't spiteful
> And they're what they call "tickled" with Grady.
>
> He was eloquent, also, was Grady;
> Patriotic! and bright as a lady.
>> But on MEN'S EQUAL RIGHTS
>> The darkest of nights
> Compared with him wouldn't seem shady.

[6] See the New York *Tribune*, Jan. 19, 1886.
[7] See the Pittsfield *Evening Journal*, May 29 and 31, 1886.
[8] Reported in the Hartford *Courant*, Jan. 12 and 13, 1887.

There wasn't a line, good sirs, bless ye,
Of all that he chose to address ye,
    That touched the one point
    Where *his* South's out of joint,
For it wasn't his wish to distress ye. . . .

There's a day coming fast to the light, man,
When the Law shall appraise each upright man
    Not by skin nor by birth
    Nor by custom, but *worth*
And assure him the rights of a white man.

Cable declined to accept honorary membership in the Sumner Union League, asking instead to be an active member, glad to be the first from the former slave states. Henceforth he would be color-blind, he said, and if any doubt arose as to his social standing, he would let the social standing go. In the months that followed, a statement of his was used in the membership campaign, the constitution was framed from his speech of January 12 and other suggestions he made, and he drafted resolutions which were adopted in the summer. The president of the League, William B. Edwards, wrote him, "We look upon you as another Sumner."

Except for the speech at Berea College in 1885, which was hardly a real exception, Cable had not addressed a Southern audience since "The Freedman's Case in Equity" appeared. The faculty of Vanderbilt University invited him to make the literary address of commencement on June 14, 1887. The invitation came through Professor William M. Baskervill, who had read and reread Cable's books, intending to write a critical study of them, had led two sessions of the Nashville literary society devoted to Cable's works,[9] and had required his graduate students in American literature to read them entire, along with Hawthorne's. In their correspondence on Southern topics during the preceding year he had assured Cable that he could speak his views freely in Nashville.

Before Cable appeared in Nashville, however, he had traveled through the South. Pond proposed to book a reading tour in Southern cities to include the Vanderbilt engagement. Cable had vetoed Pond's earlier proposals for such a tour and was not sanguine when he consented this time. Pond's announcement to local managers drew twenty replies, and on May 18 he sent telegrams offering dates. By May 20 acceptances had come from four towns. The telegram from the Library Association in Atlanta, which had first been eager to have Cable, may be taken to

[9] See the Nashville *American* and the Nashville *Union*, May 27, 1886.

speak for the others in the original twenty: "After canvassing cannot lecture him on any terms." The next day came telegrams canceling three of the four engagements that had been made. From Wilmington, North Carolina: "Press here very hostile to Cable / friends advise cancel / announcement of reading not yet made / will you cancel and release me / better for all concerned / answer quick." From Columbia, South Carolina: "I find to my surprise there is great feeling here against Cable / release me." In forwarding a sheaf of telegrams, Pond said, "I guess you are a *pretty bad* man. . . . Three days ago I said you were the greatest Southern attraction. To-day all, including ministers, are frightened!!" The next few days brought letters from other Southern managers. The librarian of the Macon Public Library and Historical Society said, "Now we are a little *surprised* that Mr Cable could suppose he would be acceptable as a Lecturer in the Old South, remembering so well the *tone of his later* articles." One speaking for the Atlanta Y.M.C.A. wrote that Cable would not be insulted or injured personally if he appeared there, and dozens had said they would go to hear him, but the Y.M.C.A. could not afford to sponsor him.

These responses could only reinforce Cable's belief that it was a mistake to take the small minority who had a voice, chiefly the journalists, as spokesmen for all Southerners. He made the journey through the South nevertheless and found added support for the belief. Almost everywhere he stopped, people gathered about him to discuss the race question, most of them willing to consider all sides rationally.

He left New York on May 25, taking with him a list of journalists and educators to visit, for his main purpose was to study conditions in the Southern states, talk with the people, and wherever possible stimulate thought. At Richmond, where he addressed the students at the Colored Normal School, he wrote Louise, "The gentle negatives are very obvious. . . . It is not I but their own courtesy they are trying to take care of." At Spartanburg, South Carolina, where he was received into the family of F. C. Woodward, a professor at Wofford College, he was asked to read "Grande Pointe" one evening and to meet a group the next day to talk over the Southern question. "I believe I am doing a wise and good thing in making this tour," he wrote. "The light is breaking." At Macon, Georgia, he visited the teachers at the Lewis Institute, a mission school, and met with a large private gathering to discuss the social aspect of the question. The views he met were less liberal than in Spartanburg, but the people "debated in a very commendable spirit." On Sunday he led a hastily collected Bible class of 250, part of whom came to his hotel afterward to discuss "the great sore question." "It is a noble sign," he wrote, "of the change that is beginning to work in the public mind."

Without other stops, he was in New Orleans on May 31 and went after a few days to the Acadian country for the benefit of the stories he was writing. At Franklin he visited again in the family of Mme de la Houssaye, and in going over his recently published story "Carancro" with his hostess, "had the benefit of her few & wise criticisms upon local matters, manners & customs & speech." Ready as he always was to join the social circle about him, he sang with her children and grandchildren around the plaintive pianoforte. At his tavern a guitar had been provided for him to entertain the guests. He talked with the Acadians in the fields, and at Lafayette, formerly Vermillionville, an acquaintance of an earlier visit, Judge John Clegg, drove him about to refresh his memory of the area. On Sunday he attended the service in the frail wooden building to which the Acadians had come on their ponies and in their buggies. After hearing a sermon delivered in rapid French and taking lemonade with the priest in his house, he wrote Louise, "He is my curé of Carancro if ever any one in real life was."

Missing a train connection back in New Orleans gave him an extra day there that was only partly welcome. He had already visited in the Eighth Street neighborhood, and after attending the Prytania Street Church had written, "They love me yet, there." He was sensitive to his reception everywhere, for he had not been to New Orleans since his hasty visit in March two years earlier, when the uproar stirred by "The Freedman's Case in Equity" was at its highest. One day he called his best in the city—"No cold looks, but much hearty greeting everywhere." But on another day, "I meet great personal kindness from old friends, with now & then, with sad frequency, indeed, cold and dark looks from those once cordial acquaintances." On the train leaving New Orleans, "Saw Adolph Schreiber who was courteous but hardly cordial, got away and came no more back though he rode clear to Biloxi. He remembers me as his clerk, and doesn't know he is Honoré Grandissime the *sang pur*." Later, in mentioning the warmth he had found generally among the Southern people, he added, "New Orleans gives me least consideration; my hold there is merely personal & upon my friends."

Going on to Tennessee, he stopped at Columbia on June 7, hoping not to be recognized while he prepared his Vanderbilt speech. His presence became known, however, and before he left on the tenth, a delegation of citizens came to pay their respects, and he was showered with friendliness. He visited the town's two female academies and attended the commencement exercises of the colored school, which prompted him to write on June 11, "These Tennesseeans would be more just if they could realize what millions of solid public wealth it is costing to suppress the self-regard & aspirations of one third of their whole population. And yet the Tennesseeans are ahead of the people of many southern States." On June 10 he read "Grande Pointe" at Fayetteville as scheduled and the following night upon request lectured on the Southern question from a point of view that suggested the title "The Faith of Our Fathers." It was his first lecture given from only a few pencil notes but his success was no less for this, he said, or for the wind's blowing out the kerosene lamp beside him. On Sunday he conducted a Bible class which had gathered to hear him, two hundred from a town of a thousand adults. The minister, he wrote Louise, "prayed for me in a way that I never expected to hear in the South. You may be sure I was touched."

At Chattanooga on June 12 he filled an engagement Pond had made for a reading. Early the next day he reached Nashville and put up as the guest of Chancellor Landon Cabell Garland.

The reception in Nashville was generous. The *Daily American* of June 14 carried a biographical sketch threaded with praise of his literary work. His accomplishment was as unique as Hawthorne's; he had written "infinitely finer and subtler lines" than Bret Harte; he knew the New Orleans people "to their heart's core." An interviewer quoted him as to why he was resented in the South: "I advocate things and changes people are afraid to make. . . . We simply see that whoever professes to disturb their status quo comes into conflict with public sentiment." The Creoles resented less his writing of them than the bearing his writings had on the status quo. "I have not been unfaithful in my delineation of the Creole people, and they all know it—those at least who have read what I have written about them."

The full house at his address on June 14 "was a most complimentary recognition of one of the greatest men of letters who lives in this country today," the *American* reporter said. He spoke more than two hours, walking about the platform, and as he had done at Fayetteville, told in an earnest, conversational way what he had observed on his trip through the South. The beauty and richness of the country appeared everywhere; there was growing prosperity and evidence of a broader patriotism, a devotion to the good of all. But he had seen some of the worst Bourbonism in cities with greatest prosperity and material development. The route to genuine progress lay through the elevation of the masses; all questions must be referred to the will of the majority, for there will be strife as long as the will of a few prevails. And as to the Negro, the course must be to give him, not a place, but a chance to earn a place through education

and an open way to have those privileges in public society he could or
would earn. Social equality is absurd. No two races have ever amal-
gamated except when one has been the oppressor. Benevolent contact
between the races would hurt no one. The Negro had only a small
place in the address. Cable had come to see the race problem as only
one manifestation of the larger problem of the masses and the ruling
minority. To him it was axiomatic that only through reliance on the
will of the majority could natural private inequality be kept from
growing into public inequality. Hence the title of the address, "The
Faith of Our Fathers."

The *American* of June 16 editorialized on "Mr. George W. Cable's
Great Error," endorsing most of his points but protesting that he was
impractically striving to reach at one bound the goal the South was
working toward slowly. "His great error is one of judgment, not of
heart." Then the editor dropped into phrasing that had become common
among even the least antagonistic Southern editors: Cable should leave
the South alone; he should report the progress already made and not
ask for a faster pace. On June 8 Cable had written Louise: "The South
may be a free country one of these days; it is not so now. God give me
wisdom to do my poor little part in making it so."

Back in Northampton he heard from Pond, who had followed him
through newspaper reports: "I think you have done the biggest three
weeks' work of your life." The papers had dramatized his trip so un-
realistically at times that he had felt the need to wire Louise once that
the newspaper reports of his being molested or threatened were totally
unfounded.

The tour had confirmed Cable's beliefs in the "Silent South." The
people he met had been first wary or unfriendly, as the journalists and
politicians had taught them to be. But when he sat down with them
they had found him sincere and reasonable at least in his ultimate goals.
If they could not accept his means or feared rapid changes they could
acknowledge that his opinions were honest. Thus his conviction was
strengthened that he should speak and write on the subject whenever
he could find occasion.

This conviction dictated a major part of his work in the next five
years. His files grew bulky with information on Southern topics: the
abridgement of civil rights, lynchings, the crop lien system, taxes, the
distribution of wealth, migration in and out of the area, education, state
constitutions and statutes. Buttressed with a fuller knowledge of the
subjects than anyone else writing or lecturing in his time, he normally
loaded his first drafts with facts and statistics which he had to prune

away to suit the requirements of the lecture platform or the magazines. To give his arguments as wide a circulation as possible, he converted several of his addresses into magazine articles, distributed some of them as pamphlets, and then collected them into a volume. He realized, however, that his main purpose, to foster thought and discussion in the South, was poorly served through these means. His climactic effort to find new means was in founding the Open Letter Club in 1888, but in the meantime he continued to lecture and write on the subject.

No one could honestly doubt that he was utterly sincere in what he said in the controversy during these years. Deep conviction shows through every sentence but only in the preliminary drafts does the full intensity of his feeling appear. On every occasion he made sure to allow what concessions he could, to say that the South sincerely sought a resolution of the difficulties and that his opponents were honest in their beliefs. He said over and over furthermore that the whole nation was responsible for slavery in the beginning, that the South had suffered colossal injustices when the ballot had been denied to its best citizens during Reconstruction, and that the Negro had much less than full rights in the North. Early in the controversy he had learned that citing instances was more likely to antagonize than to convince Southern readers and he tempered his arguments accordingly. He reiterated that discrimination against the Negroes was effective against many whites as well, especially in education; and he hoped to prompt good citizens everywhere against every injustice to minorities, white and black.

Whatever his specific topic might be, he held out the same goals and saw all sides and angles as belonging to one whole. Right and justice were his touchstones. Practicality would follow, for nothing could be practical that was not also right and just. Expediency and gradualism seemed no more practical than a decade earlier, but as he grew convinced that there had been progress only geologically speaking, as he said, and that further progress was being stopped by legal and private means, he then did propose trying half-measures simply to prove that the often-recited fears were unwarranted.

Since 1885 his opponents had voiced over and over two great fears: that granting civil equality would lead to social mixing and that allowing Negroes to vote would wreck the governments of the South. At the end of his Southern tour in 1887, he acknowledged at Fayetteville and Vanderbilt that those fears were powerful among many fair-minded people. Then when he developed the lecture into the essay "The Negro Question in the United States" for the London *Contemporary Review* of March, 1888, at the request of the editor, he undertook as much as anything else to dispel those fears. He hoped the prestige of English publications in the South would give the essay wider and more sympathetic reading there than it would have in an American journal, but he arranged through the McClure newspaper syndicate to publish it also in the New York *Tribune* and the Chicago *Inter-Ocean* on March 4. It was then issued as a pamphlet by the American Missionary Association and distributed widely in the South, chiefly to likely readers whose names Cable had assembled with the help of friends.

Against the fear of social equality and miscegenation he returned to the arguments of his early essays: Private social affairs will remain within the choice of individuals themselves; wherever there might be mixing in the public schools, the children would know, as they know now, that "the public school relation is not a private social relation," and that there would be no need of "submitting to any sort of offensive contact from a colored person, that it would be right to resent if he were white." If the threat of miscegenation had any bearing at all, it was an argument for, rather than against, the granting of civil equality, for history records, he said, that race mixing has occurred mainly when one race held an inferior position. The fear of governmental chaos Cable thought less a matter of emotions and so easier to overcome. Reconstruction by no means allowed a fair test of Negro enfranchisement, but it did prove that when Negroes cast a majority of the votes, they elected whites to all offices except a few minor ones. The illiterate, unqualified segment of any free electorate, he concluded, would always be represented by the qualified minority of their choosing. Accepting this assumption would be returning to the "faith of our fathers."

In a short essay entitled "A Simpler Southern Question," in the *Forum* of December, 1888, he returned to this thesis. The editor had asked him for an article, and he used the occasion to answer others who had entered the discussion with articles in the *Forum* during the past year, including Henry Watterson of the Louisville *Courier-Journal* and several men of prominence on the national political scene. He found it encouraging that they made so many concessions in the direction of his position, but they were discussing only peripheral manifestations, he said; the core problem was simply this: "Shall the Negro, individually, enjoy equally, and only equally, with the white man individually, that full measure of an American citizen's public rights, civil and political, decreed to him. . . ?" Again he argued that wherever extended rights had received a fair trial, the fears had proved unwarranted. A short article in the Chicago *America* of June 13 the next year entitled "What Makes the Color Line?" referred again to the election of whites by black majorities in Reconstruction times and contended that only the solid white vote of one party on Negro rights had driven a solid Negro vote into the party which had given or promised rights the other refused.

On November 12, 1888, Cable addressed the Yale Y.M.C.A. on "Some Very Old Politics," and in December he spoke twice on restrictions of the ballot: before the Chicago Union League Club on the fifteenth on the subject "Can the Nation Afford a Suppressed Vote?" and before the Congregational Club of Cleveland on the twenty-first on "Moral Elements in Politics."[10] He had encountered the proposal to use an educational qualification to withhold the ballot from unqualified Negroes and whites and thus presumably insure better government. Such an enactment would destroy one of the chief supports of public education, he thought, and would leave illiterate whites and blacks alike helpless in their efforts to qualify for the ballot. These speeches were not published separately but were largely incorporated in another address delivered before the Massachusetts Club in Boston on Washington's Birthday, 1890, which was printed in abridged form in newspapers and magazines;[11] later the club published it as a pamphlet entitled "The Southern Struggle for Pure Government" and distributed over eight thousand copies in the South.

This was Cable's fullest statement on the subject. As he saw it in 1890, the cause of equal civil rights had been all but lost, and now for the first time he asked for only half-measures, as a final plea, in a sense, to halt what had become a steady retrogression. For the first time too he called for Federal intervention unless the states themselves adopted new policies. He said next to nothing of the component issues and dealt more with governmental theory than ever before. The fruits of his years of study and debate were brought here into an analysis of developments since emancipation and a sober plea for a new course—the only course open, he thought, to a free democracy and the only course offering any hope of public well-being. He had first intended the paper for magazine publication, but when the Massachusetts Club invited him to reply to recent speeches of Henry W. Grady (who died before the paper was delivered) he welcomed the opportunity to address the nation, as he saw it, from that platform. His wife said when the invitation came that she was happy to see him lock horns with Grady.

[10] Reported in the Chicago *Herald*, Dec. 16, and the Cleveland *Plain Dealer*, Dec. 22.
[11] See the Boston *Evening Transcript*, Feb. 24, 1890; the New York *Tribune*, Feb. 23, 1890; *The American*, XIX (March 1, 1890), 396-98; *Our Day: A Record and Review of Current Reform*, V (April, 1890), 308-19. Quotations in this chapter from this essay and others which were later collected in *The Negro Question* (New York, 1890) follow the text of that volume.

Granting again the sincere intentions of Southerners—and of all peoples—in wanting pure government, he saw them pursuing a mistaken but understandable course since 1877, when the Democrats won back the governments from troop-supported carpetbagger administrations. Believing the evils of Reconstruction were due to Negro suffrage, they saw exclusive white control as the means to pure government. But their mistake, which he thought the succeeding twelve years had proved, was in assuming that pure government could be had without free government. His distinction between the two is as follows: "a pure government is especially one where all the people are wholly and equally protected from the possible corruptness of officials; while a free government is one in which all civil classes, in office or out of office, and all political parties, in power or out of power, are fully and equally protected from each other." But "a government not free nor trying to become free, must become corrupt" and those denied the self-government essential to free government will not assist in achieving pure government. "The class proposing to rule the South alone, is honest in purpose," he said, but "They have proved for all time and for all mankind that it can never be done."

He took short account of such proposals as establishing a Negro territory, deporting the Negroes to Africa, and restricting the ballot by educational qualifications, or repeal of the Fourteenth Amendment. The arguments against Negro suffrage were the same, he said, as had been advanced earlier and everywhere against manhood suffrage, and were no more valid. "I hold that to prove the moral wrong of a thing is to prove just so far its practical worthlessness." The practical worthlessness of the plan being followed was evident in the facts that provisions for education were grossly inadequate; the crop lien laws and "anaconda mortgages" had pushed the blacks and many whites with them into deeper poverty; the nefarious convict lease system in the hands of the "penitentiary rings" was still an agent of injustice to the Negroes and in only a lesser degree to the poor whites, for "the poor suffer many times more chances than the rich of being legally punished for criminal errors." From New Orleans and Atlanta newspapers he quoted statements testifying to the practical worthlessness of the policies being followed. He asked for immediate steps, so that at least the direction of the movement might become clear. Let us start by extending a few public rights, if we fear that granting full rights at once would not be safe or expedient. Why not equal rights on the railroads and in the public libraries for a beginning?

Here he proposed a compromise of the sort he had usually not counte-
nanced. But he was convinced that restrictions were being buttressed by
state laws and were becoming so fixed in the established order that concessions were daily less likely. Previously he had said the problem belonged to the states, and now he saw Federal intervention only as a
last resort. But he could not support states rights when those rights
were used to deny rights to minorities within the states. He asked that
if any state had not at least begun by 1892 to establish equal rights for
all its citizens, a President and a Congress be elected who would establish them "peacefully, promptly, and forever."

What might be called a postscript to this essay is "Centralization in
North Carolina." It is in effect a case study of an attempt to gain pure
government without free government, by means of ironclad centralization written into the state constitution of 1876. "The story is as old as
history," he wrote. "First a 'safe' government instead of a free one; that
is itself the first step in corruption; then, to keep it safe, a 'strong' government; then to keep it strong, the exaltation of the one-party idea, the
idea that only the one party has any moral right to dominate and that to
belong to any other is a misdemeanor if not a crime. This idea will
corrupt the purest government and the purest political party under
heaven." The aptness of this analysis to the growth of totalitarian from
democratic governments in twentieth-century Europe is remarkable.

Committed to maintain free governments in the states, the national
government was obliged to step into the states to protect minorities within
them, Cable believed, and delay could no longer be justified. It was
this belief that in 1888 led him closer than at any other time to taking a
hand in practical politics. For some time he had exchanged ideas with
Seth Low, who thought his article on "The Negro Question" in the
New York *Tribune* was "the most philosophical utterance on the subject"
he had read at any time. Low asked him to draft for the Republican convention a plank on the Southern problem that Southern whites could
support. While Cable was working on the draft before the convention
met in June, he agreed to make it concede that progress had been about
as great as could be expected and that some ballot restrictions would be
desirable until Negro illiteracy could be reduced. Nothing came of the
plank, however, for at the convention Low withdrew his support from
both the platform and the ticket on account of the tariff issue.

Condemnation of segregation in the Southern churches had been implicit in all Cable had written on the race problem, but he had hesitated
to raise the issue, for he knew that in other ways the cause of the Negro
was supported by many who would not accept fellowship of the two

races in the church. But in 1889 the subject came up within his own church when the white Congregational churches of Georgia refused to carry out fully a resolution passed by the national body encouraging the white and colored churches of the state to unite. The September 26 issue of the Boston *Congregationalist* was given over largely to the questions involved, and Cable contributed an article called "Congregational Unity in Georgia." Qualified fellowship could have no justification in principle, he argued, and church fellowship could in logic have no bearing on private social intercourse. The national church government, he argued further, had an obligation to intercede when its principles were violated in its smaller units.

Cable spoke again on the churches and the Southern question before the American Missionary Association in its annual meeting at Northampton, October 21 to 23, 1890. His address was built mainly from one entitled "The South's First Needs" he had delivered in the Congregational Church at Washington the previous May 16 under the auspices of Howard University.[12] The address was printed first in the *American Missionary* of the following January and then in a pamphlet issued at the Association's Bible House in New York. The pamphlet had the title "What the Negro Must Learn," but the title of the address at Howard University was more appropriate, for his main purpose was to ask support for the Southern missions. The Negro must be helped to economic, civic, and intellectual improvement as a prerequisite to spiritual improvement, he said, and must not be allowed to abandon the struggle for his rights. In phrases apparently alluding to the compromises Booker T. Washington had thought it wise to make, Cable wrote that if the Negroes would give up their claim to full citizenship, would "consent to be not Americans, but only Africans in America," would ask for education only to make themselves "better laborers and servants," their demands would be met. "But if ever the colored race in the South should become satisfied with a debased civil and political status exclusively their own, they would stand, one great, dark, melancholy proof that they never deserved to be anything but slaves."

In urging the Negroes in the 1890's to learn trades, become useful members of communities, and let civil and political rights wait, Washington took a turn entirely unacceptable to Cable. But apparently Cable made no more direct reference than in these statements to their differences. At intervals since 1885 they had corresponded, usually Washington answering questions or volunteering information for use in the

[12] See the Washington *Post*, May 17, 1890.

Southern controversy. After Cable had failed in 1890 to secure for Washington and other prominent educators of his race an invitation to attend the Lake Mohonk Negro Conference, Washington wrote him on April 7. "Were it possible for any action of yours to increase my respect and love for you your position in this matter would certainly do so many fold. . . . I do not think I can be called a sensitive man, but the disposition on the part of many of our friends to consult *about* the Negro instead of *with*—to work for him instead of *with* him is rather trying and perplexing at times." In 1894 and again in 1897 Washington asked Cable to speak at meetings held in Boston in the interest of Tuskegee.[13] The fact that Cable did not speak on either occasion may have had no explanation except the press of other engagements, for he had more such requests than he could honor; but there can be no doubt that he thought Washington was making compromises the Negro could not afford to make.

On April 13, 1888, Cable addressed a meeting of the National League of colored men at Boston and at the invitation of the editor of the *Forum* published the address in the August number with the title "What Shall the Negro Do?" After reminding his listeners that they already enjoyed "a larger share of private, public, religious and political liberty" than falls to the lot of any but a few people, he spoke most of duties and responsibilities. Noting that the numbers of Negroes voting in the South had steadily fallen off for several years, he told them that above all things else they must vote. "For in this free land the people that do not vote do not get and do not deserve their rights." They must claim and exercise their political rights within their own states and communities, for liberties are determined largely at the local level. But they must make it clear also that they did not ask for offices on a *pro rata* basis, or for social equality in the usual sense of that term, and that they would not vote solid or in gratitude for favors granted by one party. Though he had said repeatedly to white audiences that it was a solid white vote that called out a solid Negro vote, here he said only that the Negroes must vote on issues and never as a block.

In this essay Cable spoke of the New South, a phrase that had come into common use. He rejected the idea of a New South of materialism and abridged human rights; instead there must be a "new South of American ideas," in which material progress would come with the elevation of the masses, not the raising of the few on the backs of a dis-

[13] Washington's letters to Cable, at Tulane University, have been printed in Philip Butcher, "George W. Cable and Booker T. Washington," *Journal of Negro Education,* XVII (Fall, 1948), 462-68.

franchised peasantry, white and black. Without naming Henry W. Grady, he was in effect crossing swords with him and others whose hope for prosperity and progress in the South was predicated on white supremacy.

By 1890 Cable had seen Southern states enact laws which "so one-sidedly protect the landlord, creditor and mortgagee that they work intensely toward the perpetuation of the landlessness, penury, unthrift, supineness, and vice of the laboring masses," and he had seen the "greedy expansion of the mortgage system to movable property, standing crops, and even crops unplanted." This economic pattern, buttressed by the assumption that any Negro was inferior to any white man, and by restriction of the ballot, had become so pervasive that "the ex-slave was not a free man; he was only a free negro." As he read American history from colonial times, he saw two opposed views underlying the social structure: that of the New England town, symbolized by the school house, and that of the Southern plantation, symbolized by the slave pen. In this simplified view the first saw prosperity as dependent on the elevation of all strata through the education and well-being of the lowest; the second assumed that a society and its culture would flourish in proportion as the masses were kept productive to support the upper stratum. And as Cable interpreted the South of his time, this attitude toward the masses bore fruit among whites as well as blacks, and even the whites at the top of the pyramid suffered from the economic, social, and moral degradation of those below. This conviction about class and caste is echoed somehow in everything Cable wrote. Acknowledging that men fall into gradations in all aspects of their nature, he yet condemned every public restriction that would reinforce stratification.

Believing education the key to the problem and recognizing the dangers inherent in an unqualified electorate, and also disappointed in the provisions that had been made to educate the Freedmen, he came to say more and more about education. In the *Independent* of August 29, 1889, he published a short article entitled "A National Debt," which was reprinted in the *Northwestern Congregationalist* (Minneapolis) of September 6 and in his volume of the next year, *The Negro Question,* with the title "National Aid to Southern Schools." Directing his charge mainly to the North and West, he said only in passing that the Southern states were not doing all they could for education and argued chiefly that it was a national debt, for slavery had been "the Nation's crime," "a moral error as wide as the nation."

Continuing his study of education in the South, Cable wrote out a long manuscript on the subject. It supplied the matter for an address,

"Northern Wine in Southern Bottles," before the Union League Club of Chicago on January 9, 1892, and in the same year he published two essays from it, "Does the Negro Pay for His Education?" in the July *Forum* and "Education for the Common People in the South" in the *Cosmopolitan* of November. Its title notwithstanding, the first as well as the second is concerned with the whole subject of public education in the South. From the reports of state superintendents and national commissioners of education he drew an overwhelming array of facts and he compared the state constitutions written under the Reconstruction governments with those written later by the restored Democratic administrations. He made comparisons with states outside the South, but they interested him less than the retrenchments Southern states had made in educational provisions since Reconstruction. Some states had enacted statutory limitations on the taxes that could be levied for education at the state level or locally. Because the chief burden of the schools fell on the poll tax, the Negro was "far from being the educational pauper" he was commonly reputed to me. The greatest privation was naturally in the rural areas, where most of the Negroes lived, but the problem should be considered also in the light of what to him was an axiom: "It is black illiteracy that fosters white illiteracy." As provided by the legal enactments in the Southern states, "The policy becomes a devil-take-the-hindmost policy, and he takes the children of the poll-taxed Negro and white 'cracker' and mountaineer by the hundreds of thousands."

In the second article—the last he wrote directly on the Southern question—Cable advanced the particular thesis that the Southern states at the time gave from their meager school funds a disproportionate amount to their universities and colleges (restricted to whites, and in effect to the sons of gentlemen) and a similarly disproportionate amount to the cities and towns. He was citing particularly the Negro's hardships, he said, "not because he is the negro, but because, in such vast numbers, he is the South's poor man and underling; one of the *other men* under a gentlemen's government." In keeping with his interpretation of the total situation in the South, he read into the educational enactments a determination of the ruling class to reserve education to gentlemen and thus to nullify the Negroes' political emancipation. And the effects on the poor whites and the Negroes differed only in degree.

This essay was first entitled "A Gentleman's Government." When Cable sent it to *Scribner's Magazine* on July 11, 1891, he wrote to Edward Burlingame, the editor: "I don't know whether you care to print this kind of paper from anybody, but somebody's got to print it. . . . Whether you take it or not, if you see any phrase or word which I can make more kind without weakening the truth, please check it." In the preceding article he had written: "I believe I am here presenting indisputable facts; and not merely facts, but—what is of far more importance—the truth. Whatever the truth is, I believe it is best to know the truth, best for all, best that all know it, and that all of it is better than any part of it." After these articles he abandoned the Southern debate except for his fiction and occasional statements the rest of his life. But before leaving the controversy he had made a still more ambitious attempt in founding the Open Letter Club for discussing Southern topics—and had seen it fail.

CHAPTER XIX

THE OPEN LETTER CLUB

CABLE'S experiences writing and lecturing on the Southern question had persuaded him by 1888 that his voice alone was a voice in the wilderness. Many in the South he knew endorsed his views entirely and in the public debate some had accepted parts of his program while violently rejecting other parts. But most of the time his voice seemed drowned out by charges that he was an outsider or a traitor to his region. Addressing Northern audiences, publishing in national journals, even distributing his essays in the Southern states were all of doubtful efficacy.

Yet the Silent South was real, he believed, and others, like Woodward at Wofford College and Baskervill at Vanderbilt University, would be willing to lead and speak for that Silent South if they could see a way to do it. Others needed to be brought into the discussion whose loyalty would not be questioned and who would gain a hearing in the South he could no longer expect. He had distributed the essay "The Negro Question in the United States" in pamphlet form and had assembled hundreds of names of people who presumably would read such discussions with an open mind, and he had a list of men who might write on Southern topics.

During the summer of 1888 the plan took shape for a Southern correspondence club as a joint undertaking with William M. Baskervill, who had become one of Cable's most faithful supporters. Six weeks after Cable's lecture at Vanderbilt in June, 1887, he had returned to Tennessee, again under Baskervill's auspices, to lecture at the Monteagle Assembly on top of Cumberland Mountain. He had spoken on "Cobwebs in the Church," rather than the Southern question, and though the audience was not altogether friendly, Baskervill thought he had made friends through his appearance and only needed to be heard more to be appreciated more. Baskervill planned to write a magazine article: "I could, I think, by a calm, impartial study show that you are working for the best interests of the South (of Whites & Blacks)." But he added, "I might bring down on my . . . head the whole weight of our Juggernaut machine."

Thus in the spring of 1888 Baskervill was one who responded eagerly when Cable asked for names of people to receive his essay on the Negro question, and he quickly endorsed the plan for a club to exchange and publish views on the South. He had considered once starting a magazine to be called "The New South," but he could see that beginning with pamphlets was more feasible. The members of the club would write on appropriate topics, would exchange and criticize and revise their essays, and then would publish them in symposia. Cable would take the main responsibility for management and the routine work. To lessen the demands on the writers, he and his secretary would smooth out the preliminary drafts and make copies and summaries for the others, and would edit the final drafts for publication. The affiliation must be clearly Southern: the headquarters would be listed as Nashville and New York —not Northampton—and public statements would bear Baskervill's name. Outwardly Cable would appear simply as a member.

By the end of the year the initial membership had been lined up, and the Open Letter Club had been chosen as the name. The New South Club had been first proposed, but Cable and others thought that name had objectionable associations. The purpose, Cable wrote prospective members, was "to keep under public discussion every aspect of the great moral, political and industrial revolution going on in the South, and to disseminate in printed form among thousands of good citizens, especially, though not exclusively, in the South, the most valuable matter printed on every branch of this subject." The members were mainly Southern and made a distinguished list. There was a college president, J. D. Dreher of Roanoke College; university professors were Baskervill and Charles F. Smith of Vanderbilt, Robert T. Hill of the University of Texas, F. C. Woodward now of the University of South Carolina, and Richard T. Ely of Johns Hopkins University. The medical profession was represented by James H. Carlyle of South Carolina, James F. Latimer of Virginia, P. D. Sims of the Tennessee State Board of Health, and Joseph Holt, formerly president of the Board of Health in New Orleans; law and politics by Rufus B. Bullock, former Radical governor of Georgia, James B. Guthrie, Cable's friend in New Orleans, William M. Beckner of Kentucky, Judge John Clegg of Lafayette, Louisiana, and Seth Low, who in 1889 became president of Columbia College. Ministers were J. J. Tigert of Nashville, Atticus G. Haygood, president of Emory College and later bishop in the Methodist Church, John H. Boyd of Mississippi, and H. Price Collier of Brooklyn. Among the others were Edward Atkinson, R. T. Bingham, principal of the Bingham School, North Carolina, Richard F. Beirne, editor of *The State* in Richmond, the Negro author Charles W. Chesnutt, and Cable's Creole artist friend George H. Clements.

Senator J. B. Eustis of Louisiana had published an article on "Race Antagonism in the South" in the *Forum* of October, 1888, and Bishop Haygood had answered in the *Independent* of November 8. Cable had three thousand copies of Haygood's essay printed in Northampton and mailed them to the names on the list he had assembled. Here was a timely subject inviting debate. So he asked members of the club to write and exchange short essays which would then be published as a symposium. In mailing out seven hundred copies of his own article "The Negro Question" earlier he had included an announcement that later pamphlets would be furnished to all who sent their names to Baskervill. With six to ten names coming in a day Baskervill wrote Cable on February 26, 1889, "There is a chance now to awaken public interest and to touch the Southern conscience on this question, I verily believe."

On November 13, 1888, Cable asked Roswell Smith, Gilder, Lyman Abbott of the *Christian Union,* and Lorettus S. Metcalf of the *Forum* to meet with him and form a compact of editors to stand by each other in telling the truth and "shaming the devil," in Smith's phrase. Cable's aim was to get the editors to agree to print the symposia produced in the Open Letter Club and thus give them the circulation and the prestige of their magazines. Abbott said, as Cable summarized the meeting in his diary, "You have altered the attitude of the 'Christian Union' on this question." Metcalf could be counted on, and so could the *Independent.* But Smith and Gilder backed out. "I understand them," Cable wrote in a diary; "they don't want me to get off on a pamphleteering enterprise, they want me to write 'a great novel.' They're right; but I must do both."

The first symposium of comment on Haywood's essay appeared in the *Independent* for February 21, 1889, with the title "Shall the Negro Be Educated or Suppressed?" There were eight contributors, including Cable and Baskervill, and three others were included when the symposium was reprinted and distributed as a pamphlet, the fifty dollars paid by the magazine going for that purpose. Baskervill wrote a brief introduction, and Cable's name appeared only as one of the authors. The topic of another symposium presented itself in a letter of May 10, 1889, to Baskervill from Daniel H. Chamberlain, formerly governor of South Carolina and now a lawyer in New York, who volunteered views of his own. By January 1, 1890, six men were writing on the subject, which in fact continued the question of education or suppression of the Negro with particular reference to higher education. Two of them held differing views but failed to answer the same points even after they had exchanged manuscripts. "They pass by on the other side," Cable wrote Baskervill. "Now this a fatal weakness, & we want both sides in this debate as strong as they can possibly be, and then God save the Right! So hurry up your reinforcements; no matter which side you're on, gallop up, unlimber and begin firing! This is going to be a great paper."

Cable had thought of a means to draw a still larger number into the discussion: The six articles might be printed in summary and sent to twenty other members of the club, and also to three senators, three bishops, and three editors in the South, whose comments would be asked and published in the final symposium. He had in mind other subjects on which he had been collecting information and asking opinions: the centralization of governmental control in North Carolina, for one, the crop-lien laws, and the eight-box voting system established in South Carolina in 1882. He had enlisted Richard T. Ely, professor of economics at Johns Hopkins University, and Edward Atkinson, a New England capitalist who had written and spoken widely on Southern industry, to write along with others on "The Economics of the Southern Question." "Never mind their points of view," he said, "we want all points of view."

In the clerical work of the Open Letter Club he had the assistance of Adelene Moffat, who was associated with his endeavors of a similar nature for the next twenty years. She had heard his address at Monteagle in 1887, and in letters of the ensuing months she revealed herself to be an intelligent young school teacher who combined a sincere admiration for Cable with a desire to grasp the line to the outside world his acquaintance promised. Soon he offered her a way to enter that world and to fulfil her desire to study art. She came to Northampton in June, 1888, to work as his secretary during the summer and in the fall to attend the Art Institute in New York on money he would advance her. Living in the Cable home during the summer, she became devoted to the idea of the Open Letter Club, and in New York early in October she used odd hours from her art study to do reasearch for him and to advance the work of the club. Concluding her study in the spring of 1889, she returned to Northampton. Often in the ensuing years she remarked how grateful she was that Cable had given her a way to escape the surroundings of her early years.

Though the Open Letter Club began with fine prospects, it was abandoned before the papers for the second symposium were finished. Opinion in the South had grown steadily more conservative, Baskervill observed, and concurrently antagonism had increased toward Cable in quarters that earlier had been friendly. His Southern tour in 1887 had shown him spots where conditions had seemed to be improving, but it was still true that the spokesmen of the region, chiefly the newspapers, were either antagonistic or afraid to speak. The newspapers in Nashville, probably the most liberal city in the South, had shown less tolerance than he had expected in discussing his speech there.

Cable might have been content to slip into the background, as he had done in planning the Open Letter Club, or to drop out of the debate altogether, except that as he saw it, those in the South like Henry Watterson and Henry W. Grady and Booker T. Washington who were working to improve the Negro's lot were trying to do it while holding him in an inferior position defined by law. That purpose Cable thought both wrong and unworkable. He was convinced that the snail's progress of the past twenty years was being brought to a total stop by the state laws which both restricted the Negro's civil rights and fixed his economic status in the South. Yet he knew he could not get a fair hearing for his arguments, and it rankled with him that he had no means of combating the accusations, leveled at him. He proposed to write an apologia which would explain his views and tell how they had developed, as well as what he had done to carry them out. On the train home after his Forefathers' Day address in Cleveland in December, 1888, he began the draft of an essay which he continued at half a dozen intervals in a pocket diary. He had thought to publish it in the magazine and afterward as the preface to a new edition of *The Silent South*. But Gilder and Johnson were positive when they read it that it should not appear in either place but should be laid away for posthumous publication.

This essay has been preserved in both the first and the final drafts[1] but has not been published except for excerpts in Mrs. Biklé's volume. It is the most important autobiographical sketch Cable wrote, for its plan is to defend his views and his public activities by surveying the development of his thinking from childhood onward. More than anything else, he wanted to show that he had always considered himself a Southerner and had never ceased to work for the South first of all. To the charges that he had sold out his section for profit, he pointed out that his first essays had been delivered as addresses in the South, and that he had discussed Southern problems outside of the region afterward only when he was convinced the result would benefit the South. It was not difficult to argue further that the controversy had lost rather than gained readers for his books and hence had cost him money. For another thing, he wanted to say he had not gone into the Republican party, though he had voted the Republican ticket once or twice and one of those times in the worst Reconstruction days in New Orleans. Regardless

[1] Both are at Tulane University.

of party, he wrote in concluding the essay, in the words of the initial draft:

I dedicate my powers of public speech and my pen to the elucidation of that question—not of party exigency but of political ethics—on which I am best qualified to speak & write, to which as a native Louisianian & an 'ex-Confederate' I am duty bound, and which is still, I believe, the most serious & urgent question before the nation: a peaceable Renaissance of the Southern States upon the political foundations laid by the nation's fathers, northern & southern.

Late in 1889 Cable had an experience which laid him open to new and more pointed attacks. On his desk when he returned from a platform tour, he found three clippings from the *American* of Nashville, where he had been at the end of November, mainly to talk over with Baskervill the work of the Open Letter Club. While there he had addressed the students of Fisk University and had gone to the Cumberland Mountains to make notes for a novel he had begun to plan. The earliest clipping was an editorial of December 6:

Mr. George W. Cable, just before he took his departure for the East, was entertained by J. C. Napier, colored, where he spent a most agreeable evening in the society of our colored elite. Mr. Cable has often urged social equality of the races, and we are glad to see him following his own advice on the subject. In the South, however, a man must choose the race with which he associates and Mr. Cable having signified his preference for the negro race over his own should be left undisturbed to his choice. We do not mean to say that Cable lowered himself by accepting the hospitalities of Mr. Napier, colored; on the contrary we think he found his proper level. J. C. Napier is a respectable Negro, but, of course, with the prejudices of his race.... He probably did not reflect that Mr. Cable is a Southern man who has turned renegade with an eye to Yankee taste and Yankee money, and that it is money in his pocket to slander the people among whom he was born.

Another editorial of December 22, answering a letter the editor had received in defense of Cable, continued in the tone of the first, and on December 10 a columnist, "The Gossiper," said Cable had insulted his friends in Nashville, Baskervill among them.

Cable wrote a letter to the editor at once and two more later. Each was printed in the *American* (December 31, January 12, February 9), the last only at his insistence, and each was accompanied by an editorial rejoinder. The first letter asked the editor to print a statement of what specifically in his acts and writings deserved the public resentment the editor had asked for. The second letter was mainly a copy of one sent earlier to a Miss Ford. In it he recounted the incident in question, in summary as follows: In Nashville Cable made an appointment with a colored lawyer, J. C. Napier, to discuss with him and others of his race the program of the Open Letter Club. Since he knew that in a Southern hotel the Negroes would not be permitted to sit down in any public room, he met them in Napier's parlor and furthermore granted their request to have some of their wives and daughters join them and use a few minutes to thank him for his service to their race. "When all were gone," he wrote, "I, seeing that my host and hostess were in a dilemma between asking a white man to sit at their board and sending him away supperless, said bluntly I had not eaten. We broke bread together. Was I wrong in that? To anyone who answers yes, I can only reply, Shame on you! Shame on you!!" At Cleveland a month earlier he had taken tea with Charles W. Chesnutt and his family while he was in their home reading and revising a manuscript of Chesnutt's intended for the Open Letter Club symposium, but he did not volunteer that fact to the *American*.

The letter did more, however, than recount the incident; it included also Cable's reply to other charges: He had never uttered a word in favor of mixing the blood of the races, and he had never "in so much as a sentence, whether spoken or written, advocated any private commingling of the two races." The charges and the language of the *American* had stung Cable, as the tone of his replies showed. "One may often see gatherings of colored people where in three-fourths of their number the blood of the two races is already mingled. Who has mingled it? Let your Nashville American answer that. Probably not one in a thousand owes his or her mixture of blood to anyone suspected of advocating 'social equality.'" Farther on, "And first of all, please mark, I do not unsay nor call back one single word that I have ever written or spoken on any phase of the race problem." And at the end, "If the friendship of any friend of mine North or South, old or new, hangs on the condition that I must never do again what I did the other day in Nashville, I bid such a friendship a regretful goodbye. I will break bread with the murderer in his cell if I choose. I have no fear that I shall lose all my friends but I know that I shall keep my self-respect; and that the more friends I lose, the stronger will be my affection for those that remain to me."

The editor remarked in printing Cable's first letter that he could make excerpts from his writings that would support his broad condemnation. Cable asked him to do so and enclosed Scribner's written permission to print anything he chose. The reply was a sweeping reference to *The Silent South*. Cable wrote again: "I charge that if you could have found passages deserving popular resentment you would have quoted them, and that you do not quote them because you cannot find them."

With this and the accompanying rejoinder the newspaper exchange ended. It was the only one Cable pursued with such vigor, but whether he had gained anything in it is doubtful. The editor had printed his letters but had made no concessions, and many readers would remember only the extravagant charges. The paper continued to use such expressions as Cable's "latest bid for Northern popularity."[2]

Whatever else the Napier affair did, it made Cable as untouchable in Nashville as he had been elsewhere in the South and it doomed the Open Letter Club. Difficulties had already beset the club. For one thing, no way had been found to finance publication of the pamphlets. For another, two of the members who had written in the first symposium, President Dreher and Professor Hill, grew reluctant because of their positions in public institutions. In answering Dreher's demurrer, Cable suggested on November 12, 1889, that he write in the club as intended but remain anonymous. "Men of the South must speak out. How on earth is deliverance from error and misrule ever to come if the men who hold places of trust and influence cannot or do not give their counsel to the people?" Moreover, the second series of papers were progressing slowly, and hardly to Cable's satisfaction. Judge John Clegg, his friend in Acadian Louisiana, and Charles Waddell Chesnutt were at one extreme, along with Cable, arguing for greater education of the Negroes as essential to the welfare of both races. Chamberlain, who had been a carpetbagger governor of South Carolina, took the cautious, conservative position and was supported by Baskervill and John H. Boyd, a minister in Durant, Mississippi. While transmitting the essays among the contributors, Cable composed on December 30 a lengthy rejoinder to Boyd, in which he revealed to Boyd apparently for the first time that Chesnutt was colored.

Baskervill completed his paper for this symposium only after the Napier affair. Since his views were at variance with Cable's on this topic, he wrote on February 24, 1890, to explain his political stand. Brought up a rabid Southerner, he had become a liberal Republican. Then with the election of Cleveland he had returned to the Democratic

---

[2] The *Times-Democrat* of Aug. 3, 1891, reported the Creole historian Alcée Fortier as saying of Cable at Monteagle among other things: "He . . . has not one feeling of a Southern man. No true Southerner would have taken dinner with a negro as he did in Nashville last winter; no true Southerner would wish for the supremacy of an ignorant and inferior race." To Cable's request in the same newspaper on Aug. 22 that Fortier quote any paragraph from his writings he disagreed with, the reply two days later was further generalizations but no specific citations.

Courtesy of the Tulane University Library

GEORGE W. CABLE

party. In 1890 he hated the Republican party, favored local government and states rights, and feared Federal interference. Already, on January 8, he had written Cable his appraisal of the Napier incident. He had no respect for the editor of the *American,* but the damage to the cause he and Cable had championed jointly was irreparable. Before that, he said, "you could have come here & filled a house. Now your coming would be the signal for a personal attack on you in every newspaper in the city, and all manner of false representations and malicious and lying charges would be made against you." He had been threatened himself with physical violence if he invited Cable back to Nashville. Cable's reply to Baskervill on January 14 reflected the mood that was still on him:

I am heartily sorry that you had to suffer annoyance on my account. I thank you for telling me frankly what you think of the Napier matter. I have had now a good while to think about it and I think I can say, uninfluenced by any sentiment of defiance, that as far as my private acts are of interest to Southerners, I am glad they know just where I stand. I tell you, this soothing and pacifying and conciliating these people intoxicated with prejudice and political bigotry, is helping neither them nor any worthy interest. I am glad my record is made and that I stand before them as unclothed with any reservation as a swimmer.[3]

On March 5 Baskervill wrote, "The two sections are just now further apart than they have been since 1861," and his former tone of optimism had disappeared. On March 24 he shipped Cable the files of the Open Letter Club. There had been no personal estrangement between them, however, and a passage in one of his last letters on the business of the club, February 24, sums up his regard for his friend:

My liking for you is based upon a genuine respect & profound esteem. First as a man-of-letters you drew me to you; then when you were maligned and calumniated I took the position which every occurrence has strengthened in me that you were honest & true to the depths of your heart and I had only unmitigated contempt for those who spoke of you as a renegade &c. I saw that you were unswerving in your ideas of right & justice & tho your views in regard to some things were not mine I held that you had as much right, if not more, right to them & that you had a perfect right to express them.[4]

[3] Copies Cable kept of this and others of his letters cited in this chapter are at Tulane University, as are also his letters from Baskervill.

[4] In the *Chautauquan* of May, 1897 (XXV, 179-84), and in a volume entitled *Southern Writers* published at Nashville later in the same year (pp. 299-356) Baskervill testified to the value he placed on Cable's works. In 1897, however, he was prepared to champion the South of segregation and exclusive white suffrage which was firmly established then; and though he characterized Cable as a lover "of abstract truth and perfect ideals" who was "actuated by thoroughgoing logic," he could only regret the stated or

With the Open Letter Club Cable's work for reform in the South reached its climax—during its existence he delivered more addresses and published more essays on the Southern question than in any other equal period. After its demise he never again undertook a positive program for the same purpose. He saw through the press the two articles he was writing on Southern education, and he spoke on the South when occasions arose. After another four years he published the novel on Reconstruction he had already begun, *John March, Southerner*. But when he had closed out the club early in 1890, he turned his direct efforts for reform into other channels, in one of which he had already made a beginning, the Home Culture Clubs.

implied arguments for Negro rights in Cable's stories and novels, and in consequence he lavished his greatest praise on *Bonaventure*, which advanced no thesis on the race question.

CHAPTER XX

RELIGION AND CULTURE

BEFORE the Open Letter Club came into existence, Cable had begun two other activities which likewise drew time away from his literary work and added nothing or almost nothing to his income. In 1886 he founded the first of the Home Culture Clubs and thus launched a program of practical social improvement in which he worked for the next thirty-five years. Beginning in 1887 he did two years of religious writing and teaching on a scale he had never undertaken before.

Roswell Smith and others warned him against spending so much of his energy away from his fiction writing, but it had long been his habit to think his most important work was that aimed at the betterment of the community and society in which he lived. From boyhood he had worked faithfully in the programs of his church and had sought means of enforcing Christian principles outside the doors of the church. At about the time he was married, he was chosen superintendent of the Prytania Street Presbyterian Church's Mission Sunday School, which met on Third Street near Dryades, and it was specifically to this work that he and his bride had dedicated themselves. His was the white Sunday school, meeting at four-thirty in the afternoon, after the colored Mission Sunday School, with his friend Henry Ginder superintendent, had met at three in the same rooms. His devotion to the work and the pupils can be read in the letters he sent weekly to the Sunday school while he was absent from New Orleans in 1883. The *Times-Democrat* on August 6 of that year applauded the Mission School and singled out for special comment Cable's success in making it "both interesting and instructive."[1] It was probably at his instigation that an industrial department was opened in the Mission rooms for instruction in cleanliness, politeness, housekeeping, and sewing. Many of the pupils were from immigrant Italian families.

He became deacon in the Prytania Street Church in 1882. On one occasion he managed with such astonishing success a meeting at which over nine thousand dollars was subscribed to retire the church debt that

[1] See also the issues of May 8, 1882; Nov. 21, 1883; and the *Democrat,* Oct. 16, 1881.

the whole proceedings were reported in the newspaper the next day.[2] In the first year after his move north, his sister Mary Louise wrote him, November 28, 1885, that the church deficit had been oversubscribed and added, "I believe every body feels this action to be the result of your influence in the past."

At Simsbury he attended the Congregational Church, taught a Sunday school class, and again took a hand in the raising of funds, with the result that soon the church was free of debt "for the first time in many years."[3] At Northampton he and his family entered the Edwards Congregational Church, and soon he was enlisted to teach an adult class. His preference was to teach non-church-goers and non-church-members. When his class had grown to nearly a hundred, he began Sunday afternoon meetings at the Opera House, which was soon filled to overflowing. Invitations were mailed weekly, chiefly to those who did not attend church, and he made sure there was good music. He invited questions and statements of doubts and beliefs from the class members and often surprised them with unconventional views. He succeeded in interesting those he most wanted to teach, the skeptics. A member of the class once said to a prominent Sunday school worker of the city: "Mr. Cable never abuses us or treats us as unworthy of any respect, as you fellows do. He calls us no names, but deals with us as honest thinkers and doubters."[4]

In 1887 Cable was chosen to conduct the Bible study class of the Boston Sunday School Teachers' Union on Saturday afternoon at Tremont Temple. This class was especially gratifying, for it reached an attendance of two thousand and thus gave him a means of lay teaching on a scale he had never found possible before. He was paid thirty-five dollars a week. Yet the demands for commuting weekly and adjusting his writing and his platform appearances to be in Boston every Saturday were too heavy to continue indefinitely. He resigned at the end of November, 1888.

He had kept the class at Northampton and now, in the same month he gave up the Boston class, he called a meeting of the town pastors to propose starting a Bible class in the City Hall. "No enthusiasm," he wrote in his diary on November 9; "some of them would just as lief I wouldn't start it." One of the pastors "wouldn't even attend the meeting called. He thinks I am 'no good,' as the feller says. So do I. I am. And yet I am not satisfied. . . . I am unreasonable—expecting men to be saints

[2] *Times-Democrat,* Feb. 19, 1883; reprinted in Biklé, pp. 198-99.
[3] Biklé, p. 199.
[4] Quoted in [Lyman Abbott], "Mr. Cable and His Church Work," *Christian Union,* XXXVI (Oct. 27, 1887), 428.

before their time. Still, I hope to start the class. My church class numbered 133 last Sunday. That means 500 in the town hall, fully."[5] On the first day in the City Hall the attendance was 400; it later reached 700. But the next spring he abandoned the class, the last he taught regularly.

Cable's term of lecturing to the Tremont Temple class paralleled roughly a year of writing for the *Sunday School Times,* a weekly published primarily for the aid of teachers. For several years there had been requests to write for various church publications, but he had written only two short articles. The editor of the *Sunday School Times* asked him for something on Bible teaching or a similar topic, and late in 1886 he made a tentative promise, but it was December 10 of the next year, after he had begun the class in Boston, that his first article appeared. It was entitled "The Busy Man's Bible" and was followed the next week by the first in a series called "A Layman's Hints," which ran weekly until December 15, 1888. "The Busy Man's Bible," as an introduction to the series, began with the assumption that his readers were busy and in consequence must be shown how to gain both nourishment and pleasure from short periods of Bible study. He proposed a quarter of an hour's study daily and an hour on Sunday, most of the time to be spent in thoughtful reading of the text rather than commentaries.

Meanwhile he pushed his layman's religious teaching into still another channel. Invited to address the Monteagle Assembly on July 30, 1887, he wrote a speech he called "Cobwebs in the Church." He tried it out two days earlier on an audience of the Chautauqua Association at Lakeside, Ohio, and read it again on October 27 before the New York Congregational Club, of which Roswell Smith was then president. He added it to his platform repertoire, and during the next two or three years he read it occasionally, often proposing it as a substitute when he was invited to read from his books. On March 6 and 7, 1890, he lectured before the students of the Yale Divinity School on "How to Study the Bible" and on "How to Teach the Bible."[6] The first of these addresses was printed in the *Sunday School Times* (November 15, 29, December 6, 1890) and the second in the *Ladies' Home Journal* (February, March, April, 1891), and then they were combined in a thin volume published by the Chautauqua Press, with the earlier essay "The Busy Man's Bible" incorporated and furnishing the title.[7]

This volume ended Cable's avowed religious teaching and writing. Much of it had been against the advice of his publisher friends. Smith

[5] Partly quoted in Biklé, pp. 201-2. This diary is in the possession of Mrs. Biklé.
[6] See the New Haven *Register* March 7 and 8, 1890.
[7] Meadville, Pa., 1891. Published in 1896 by the Sunday School Union in England.

had proposed more than once that he write an essay or a story or a novel aimed at moral and social improvement, but just as he had advised against sectional and party alignments, he advised also against sectarian and theological affiliations. Gilder's advice was to write for religious organs only what grew from his teaching. And so when Cable gave up his Bible classes and church writing, his editors were delighted, hoping more fiction would be forthcoming, and Pond was happy not to have to fix all reading dates around Saturday afternoon in Boston.

Such considerations, including his resolve in 1889 to press on with a new novel, would probably not have swayed Cable had not doubts arisen in his mind as to what he was accomplishing. When he had wondered in the past whether he did good in his teaching, he usually dismissed the question with some such remark as one he wrote Louise on October 1, 1888, after he had addressed a church group, "One can't stop blowing the organ bellows just to see if it is he making the music." But he had reached a stage in his thinking at which he found the framework of the church unsuitable to the teaching he wanted to do. He had told the council of the Boston class he wanted to give it up as soon as someone else could be found in his place. But he did not resign until he learned that a large minority on the council opposed him and the majority was growing tired of holding out against the constant urging. He was happy to be free of the class, but in his diary he wrote: "It is a triumph of ignorant bigotry and love of partizan doctrine over that simpler gospel which is so fast coming back to us." After he had concluded his last class on November 24, he wrote in his diary: "Never in life have I had such a farewell. . . . Hill choked and filled when he said—'Mr. Cable, one thing I must say, since I have sat under your teaching, I have got a higher conception than ever I had before, of what a christian gentleman can be.' I think that is the finest word I have ever had spoken to me."

The evolution of Cable's religious views had been gradual and deliberate but nonetheless considerable. From his youth onward, as a matter of fact, he had broadened steadily, crossing one restricting barrier after another, but never without thoughtful weighing of all arguments. In a home where the strictest tenets of the Presbyterian Church were held, his mind stayed open to liberalizing ideas. Convinced that novels might have good as well as bad effects, he became a reader and then a writer of fiction. Convinced later also that the theater might be an ennobling force, he was willing to have his books dramatized and to undertake dramatizations himself—only ten years after he had refused to attend theatrical productions on a newspaper reporter's assignments. He admitted the theater to respectability only when he was sure he was not compromising with his conscience but was simply correcting a misapprehension—he was on his guard for fear his success had dulled his moral sense.

Loosening the bonds of strictness appealed to Cable, however, only when the motives and the gains were worthy. He relaxed very little in his observance of the Sabbath, for as he saw it the result would have been pecuniary gain, as in traveling between platform engagements, or personal pleasure. The first time in his life he traveled on Sunday was on September 30, 1888, while on a reading tour in the West. Through his manager's mistake in scheduling, he must ride on Sunday or break an engagement on Monday. The observance of the Sabbath was in fact a source of great satisfaction to him. Away from home his Sundays were times of meditation and rededication. Attending church services was a part of each Sunday, wherever he might be and however unsatisfying the sermon might be, and as he often wrote home, the day might be a good one or a bad one, depending less on externals than on his feelings within.

Actually his strictness was chiefly in self-discipline. Even in his earliest writings, published works or letters, there is little intolerance of other beliefs or other forms. In his attitude toward the Catholics of New Orleans, to choose perhaps the most salient example, there was little if any condemnation at all of their beliefs or behavior that differed from his, so long as their goals were commendable. While traveling, he attended services in various Protestant churches and the Catholic church as well, and the letters to his wife show, if any differences at all, greater eagerness to commend sincerity and enlightenment in other churches than his own. Such was especially true of his remarks on the Acadian Catholic priest he heard in the summer of 1887. To cite another example, he regretted that Mark Twain was impatient with the churches and did not attend their services, but he saw that actually his friend was one of the most religious men he had ever known. As he saw it, Mark ought to have given the churches the assistance his humanitarianism would have lent.

There had been no time, apparently, when Cable's religion was not primarily humanitarian and only secondarily a matter of dogma. In addressing the Sunday School Association in New Orleans on April 4, 1881, he spoke on the parable of the good Samaritan, with a directness of application to the social milieu that was rare in the churches of the time.[8] The work of the Mission School on Third Street interested him

[8] The manuscript of this address is at Tulane University.

because it was a workshop for practical Christianity; theological problems he was content to leave to others. In 1887 a newspaper in Northampton reported that his Bible class had been discontinued because his teaching had become "too liberalizing."[9] He denied the assertion, but it was true nevertheless that the local ministers were not pleased by his ignoring creeds in his teaching. A member of the Tremont Temple class wrote of him: "He sets traditions at naught; he tramples on conventionality. He sees with his own eyes, thinks with his own mind and decides with his own judgment."[10] At the Yale Divinity School he asserted that we go to the Bible for principles, not rules; that teaching the Bible should be a process of showing an individual what he can believe rather than trying to force him to believe what he cannot.[11]

Further evidence of Cable's liberalized views—and his concern for having things put right—appeared in his request to the Edwards Church on June 22, 1889, when his daughters Margaret and Lucy were ready to become members, that they be received simply on their acceptance of the Covenant, omitting the Confession of Faith, which they might not fully accept when they were older. At about the same time he published in the *Christian Union*, July 25, 1889, "A Word About Dr. Holland." It was a tribute to the founder of *Scribner's Monthly*, but its real purpose was to commend Holland's stand for ecclesiastical liberty, his teaching, in Cable's phrasing, "that what churches call Confessions of Faith are largely made up of the conclusions of human scholarship upon which men of true faith can widely differ and men without true faith can closely agree."

Thus by 1890 Cable had liberated himself, slowly and thoughtfully, to be sure, from his earlier narrowness, had in fact passed beyond orthodox dogma and creeds to a conception of life in which "truth, right, and liberty" are, as he said in writing of Dr. Holland, "the three and only three inexorable demands of divine government." Over several years, furthermore, he had grown more and more impatient with the churches and conventional religion. The defense of slavery and later of segregation by the Southern churches had pained him since his first shock at having the Biblical defense of slavery exploded. Rarely now did he hear a sermon that pleased him. In writing Louise of the preachers he heard, as he did almost every Sunday he was away from home, he spoke often of conspicuous insincerity and formalism, narrowness and bombast. From

[9] *Hampshire County Journal*, Nov. 2, 1887.
[10] Quoted in Biklé, p. 201.
[11] See the New Haven *Register*, March 7 and 8, 1890.

Nashville on July 31, 1887, he wrote after attending church, "Oh! the stuff the people are fed with!" He had sat in an adult Bible class:

It had some bright minds in it; but how rife they are with conventional superstitions & conventional morals. . . . the trouble is that where one gets his morals conventionally he will be sure to get the conventional vices with them. The trouble is, conventional morals are not real *virtues*. . . . And Christians don't know what a grand battle—with what mighty chances of loss and gain—there is in life until they have got their moral questions separated from conventional considerations. . . . Conventionality keeps the poor little life-barks of the average men & women ballasted down as a leaden keel does a toy boat or a yacht. Conventionality rises like great hills around a land-locked harbor & there they ride in their cockleshells and talk about the open sea!

All his mature life he had been attacking one manner of conventionality or another. In "Cobwebs in the Church" he protested that undue veneration was demanded and given to everything associated with the church, so much at times as to obscure the truths of religion. He protested against the scholastic approach to matters of religious belief, and also against the commercialism of rented pews and the atmosphere of exclusiveness which in effect barred strangers as well as lower social classes. The churches had ceased to be public institutions, he said, and had become agencies for "private hospitality" and "clique benevolence." After hearing him read this paper before the New York Congregational Club, a later speaker remarked, "I do pity the cobwebs when Mr. Cable gets after them."[12] After teaching one of his last classes in Boston, he wrote in his diary: "They were much pleased with the lesson. I was not. They have an average religion that is water-logged with last century bilgewater." A dozen years later, February 11, 1901, he wrote Louise, again after attending church: "O how the people need to be taught what has been so criminally neglected through all these centuries of religious teaching—not dogmas or views, but right methods of thought and inquiry; intellectual humility and integrity."

The evolution of his own personal creed did not stop with his last Bible class, and his subsequent writings have much to say about beauty and joy, love and unselfishness, brotherhood and humanity as the essentials of life.

Cable's humanitarianism had led him into a series of efforts for mass improvement: prison and asylum reform, Negro rights, public education, the conference of charities and the mission school in New Orleans.

[12] "Mr. Cable at the Congregational Club," *Christian Union*, XXXVI (Oct. 20, 1887), 394.

And it had been forced home to him that no agency supplied the educational wants of adults. He had been himself a member of a debating society; he had joined in group study and group discussion in the years following the war; and in his family it had always been the habit to read aloud and discuss the Bible, literary masterpieces, and current books and magazines. Concerned since childhood, literally, with self-education and conscious self-development, he realized that few could be expected to practice drawing or work mathematics problems between cavalry forays, as he had done, or read history at night after a day's work.

In the Drop Shot column he spoke many times of the cultural lacks of his community, and so it is not surprising that he included the word *culture* in his first plan for an adult program. In 1881, he met Miss Ticknor, head of the Women's Society for the Promotion of Culture at Home. Such organizations were often described in print; the *Century* of January, 1885, carried accounts of three similar schemes for group study. Cable had copiously annotated a copy of the printed annual report for 1886 of the Society to Encourage Studies at Home. His beginnings at Northampton were modest. The first Home Culture Club—of four factory girls—was organized on October 4, 1886; by the end of the year there were four clubs; and on February 9 of the next year there was a meeting at Philharmonic Hall, at which a musical program was the main fare and Cable reported on the clubs and explained their purpose and plan. There were then six clubs, with twenty-five members, representing twenty homes. Of the club leaders, whom Cable named, half were men. The newspaper report of the meeting remarked that "the success of the undertaking is already assured."[13] The New York *Tribune* of February 20 printed a detailed report, stressing as Cable had done the purpose of benefiting all rather than reforming or improving any one segment of the community.

In the spring of 1888 the clubs numbered twenty, a year later thirty. Inquiries from elsewhere came frequently, and at the third annual meeting in June, 1889, Cable announced that the formation of clubs in other communities would be encouraged.[14] Within a year there were clubs in Philadelphia, Baltimore, Chicago, Parkville, Missouri, and Orange, Massachusetts. In 1891 there were forty clubs; in 1894, there were fifty-four, thirty-five of them in Northampton, ten elsewhere in Massachusetts, nine outside the state, spread from Montreal to Tennessee, Alabama, and Nebraska. Of the total members, 46 per cent worked in stores or mills.

[13] The Northampton *Daily Herald*, Feb. 10, 1887. See also the *Hampshire Gazette* and the Northampton *Courier* of Feb. 15.

[14] See the Northampton *Daily Herald*, June 24, 1889.

All clubs reported their activities to the parent office weekly, and a composite report was printed and distributed.

In founding the Home Culture Clubs Cable was approaching a less immediate and less urgent problem than any he had dealt with before. His aim was to establish a procedure, an organization, and an attitude which would have limitless possibilities. Society and the individual would both profit, but there must be no confusion with settlement work or the usual uplift schemes, for in this plan one from the highest station might profit no less than one from the lowest. Still, such a program would aim most directly at those under greatest handicaps and with greatest needs. Cable had concluded, as he explained in writing on the clubs for the *Century* of August, 1888, that the normal methods of "elevating the masses" could hope for but little permanent effect, and yet "new influences from without may produce new inner powers and merits," and "To leave the unfortunate to fight ill-fortune with only their handicapped merit is to leave them to an unintelligent and merciless natural selection to which we would think it inhuman to leave ship-wrecked voyagers, and stupid to leave our cattle."

Remedy could not be expected from the state or commerce or the churches, for they could claim no right to meddle with what is largely a personal, individual matter. The need could be met best and perhaps only through private relationships. Otherwise, the one to be benefited would protest against interference or would resent charity. But an offer of friendship across social or economic barriers more often than not results in greater harm than good. Cable concluded, therefore, that the scheme must operate somewhere between charity and friendship, "between mass treatment and personal treatment." The aim must be to give "profit yielding pleasure," without levying any appreciable debt such as follows charity. Thus the scheme—reading and studying and discussing in one's home or his neighbor's. It must be in the home, for "the easiest, best, quickest way to lift almost any one is to lift him, house, and all." In an interview by Clifton Johnson printed in the *Outlook* of June 8, 1895, he said further: "Too many of our attempts at uplifting begin by extracting the individual from his home. When you do that you are in danger of fighting that person's own best interests."

Until his death almost forty years afterward Cable saw the work continue for "elevating the masses." Since relations in the clubs were not primarily social, class barriers need not become an issue. Cable remembered, of course, the strength of those barriers in New Orleans, and he realized that in Northampton also they would resist direct assault. Furthermore, he had said for years that social relations must be left to private choice; social agencies might work toward lessening them, but only through suasion. He said to the *Outlook* interviewer:

We want some way of making the different classes acquainted with each other. There's a marked stratification in society at present that puts us under temptation to forget one another's rights, interests, merits. It is astonishing how blind the fortunate are to the good points of those less well-to-do, how little understanding there is between the upholders of one political party and those of another, and even the lack of interest and sympathy with others that is possible simply because people live in different parts of the same town.... We are not democratic at all, and haven't been in all the century past.... In the home culture idea the question of social affinity is not touched on in the least. There has to be affinity of some sort in order to make things work smoothly and successfully; but it is affinity of mind and aspiration, not likeness in wealth and rank.

First of all the club members must consider themselves friendly equals in quest of culture. Instead of a teacher, a leader from their own number would read aloud and then preside over their questioning and discussion. If homes of widely divergent economic or cultural levels were represented in the same club, so much the better, but that should occur only if it came naturally and without embarrassment to anyone. In answering a query from another state, Cable summed up the idea thus:

It seems to us that what we pursue will do both us and others a deeper, finer benefit if pursued in concert, and actual contact, with minds and lives more or less different, sometimes even very different, from our own; share it with homes either much more, or much less, fortunate than ours.... This is Home Extension. Without any disturbance of necessary social distinctions and divergencies, (and many are highly necessary,) we seek to establish between homes of contrary fortunes—and between homes and the homeless—relations which *something* must establish before either church, courthouse or school can give us very much better results.[15]

The rule was for utter freedom of activity. Groups would organize themselves, in numbers from two to twenty or thirty, preferably below ten, and would meet weekly from September to June. Reading outside the meetings was encouraged but not expected, for it would have been impossible to many and taxing to others. Each club chose its own study topic. One read *Robert Elsmere,* another Bryant's poetry; others read American history or Shakespeare or current periodicals. One studied algebra; one was a debating society.

It was apparent early that the approach through the home was not

[15] This letter was printed in the *Letter,* Sept. 1, 1895.

always possible. In visiting the clubs, occasionally to read to them from his own works, Cable realized that many potential members thought their homes unsuitable for meetings or lived in boarding houses or college dormitories. Consequently, on May 1, 1888, when the first club was a year and a half old, reading rooms were leased at 152 Main Street. They were open from six to ten nightly, from the end of work hours, as Cable put it, until people should be in bed. The aim was to keep the rooms attractive, informal, and free of bothersome regulations. After six months there were four hundred volumes on the shelves, as well as newspapers and magazines, and there were six hundred readers a month. One room was reserved for ladies. In the season of 1888-1889 a music club gave thirteen chamber music concerts in the rooms to a total attendance of a thousand.

The initial plan supposed no money would be needed, though it was suggested that each member pay two cents at each meeting; but the reading rooms cost over four hundred dollars the first year. Cable held to his first plan, that dues not be collected and the clubs not be supported by charity. Instead he asked support from local citizens able to give it. To his mind these were not so much gifts to charity as investments to be returned through the dividends of public well-being. It was on the same basis later that he asked Andrew Carnegie for a gift—a gift to all the people of the city, not charity to one part alone.

From the outset the composite weekly report to the clubs was intended to bind them together by informing each of what the others were doing and to give them encouragement and direction. In 1892 the report became a larger publication, the *Letter,* issued monthly from September to June. It was prepared mainly by the secretary, Adelene Moffat, who had given full time to the clubs since the death of the Open Letter Club. As a rule each issue outlined some reading program that had proved successful in one club, announced classes being given at the reading rooms, and printed a paper by some member, "The Home Culture Club As Seen by a College Girl," for example. In 1892 eighteen of the clubs had Smith College students for leaders, usually serving in pairs. In 1894 the *Smith College Monthly* said: "To no other interest outside of the college have the students of Smith devoted so much time and energy as to the Home Culture Clubs."[16] The *Letter* once printed a sheaf of statements by the members of a club studying Shakespeare. They were all girls employed at the Nonotuck Silk Mill. There were announcements regularly: of the decision, for example, to lend books to clubs located in towns where

[16] Quoted in the *Letter* for Jan., 1894.

none were available, or of the plan in 1895 to open a basement club room "for young boys the barrenness of whose homes prompts them to find their evening diversion in the street," or of a lecture James B. Pond gave on June 4, 1894, for the benefit of the clubs. Cable wrote a sketch of Pond for the *Letter*.

Cable was quoted often in the publication, particularly his speeches at the meetings opening the clubs in September, closing the year late in December, and closing the season in May. Edward Atkinson in 1894 and Felix Adler the next year spoke at the May meetings, and their speeches were printed in the *Letter*. There were frequently such statements as the following of November, 1895:

To carry from one house into another, however like or unlike, whatever of a transferable sort is good in one and wanting in the other; to communicate from house to house the arts of true home-making and good neighborliness; to make the richly supplied and poorly supplied home—even the most richly and most poorly—acquainted through definite offices of mutually profitable, unburdensome entertainment; to "extend" the home as some with noble self-consecration are extending the college and university—this must always be our main business.

The growth of the Home Culture Clubs was uninterrupted. Cable was unsparing in his efforts, and Adelene Moffat was no less faithful in planning and working for the plans. The clubs became in fact her career. By 1890, when the hopes for the Open Letter Club had collapsed and little encouragement could be found in the campaign for Negro rights, the Home Culture Clubs were so well established and so well supported that Cable found in them gratification his other reform work had not yielded. He could not fail to note the contrast—his efforts in the Southern controversy had won him vilification and personal abuse even in New Orleans; his work in Northampton, begun when he had lived there only a year, had won hearty endorsement locally and nationality as well. With such encouragement he was ready to plan and push through a still more ambitious program. In 1890—and during the next thirty years of work he gave to the Home Culture Clubs and the related programs—he could not avoid a tinge of regret that he could find no effective way to work for the South in what he saw to be her great need. In his next book he was to try again, through the medium of fiction.

CHAPTER XXI

THE END OF A CRUSADE

WITHOUT the Open Letter Club and the Bible classes and the weekly Sunday school articles, Cable was now under less strain than at the height of the Southern debate, but he still found little more time or equanimity for his literary work. He had something to say on the Southern question when occasions arose, and that complex question was the subject of the novel he wrote between 1890 and 1894. Platform readings and lectures still furnished his main income.

His two households required more attention as the children grew up. His own children numbered seven since the birth of Dorothea in 1889, and his oldest, Louise, was married in 1894. On April 22, 1889, he wrote his wife, "I know no man who gives more attention to his children than I do." No one would have disputed that statement in his family or in the other house, where his mother and Mary Louise and Nettie and Nettie's children lived. His letters home while he was on the road conveyed love to all, often by name; he remembered all birthdays, usually with special letters; and he was always solicitous for the welfare of everyone in both houses.

As a rule he took pride in the children's doings and attempted to share the responsibility the large family loaded on his wife, but unavoidably his own obligations overflowed to her. Even with Adelene Moffat looking after the Open Letter Club and the Home Culture Clubs, any one of his letters home when he was away might set out half a dozen things for his wife to do. She lamented that her letters—and her days—had to be so filled with small affairs that she had no chance to be cheerful and affectionate. Over and over she had to spread the money he sent home over local bills they would not meet. On November 26, 1889, when he was deepest in the Southern controversy, she wrote. "How can you reason that it is right to give away so much of your time, when we owe so many bills, is quite beyond me. I am ashamed to go into the stores to order anything, we already owe so much, & entirely too much mortified to go near Dr. Cooper; and I thought November was to see us quite paid up." They depended on the reading season to pay them up.

The wonder is that in her faithfulness to her manifold duties she did not grow exasperated often. She endorsed his purposes with complete devotion and found time somehow, while managing the household and often while in poor health, to take part in the Home Culture Clubs, to give an address on lotteries, for example, in 1892 when the subject was of national interest, and to write for the *Letter;* and she seems to have won invariably the respect and affection of the scores of public and literary people who came into their home.

Cable's letters to her were an unrestrained outpouring of his affection and his plans and aspirations and worries. In a letter of November 1, 1889, he wrote: "Thinking, in my moments of solitude, of home, children, wife, I think what a hungry lover you have always been; of your absolute purity, steadfastness, and unflinching fidelity to whatever you clearly see to be your duty. Not many men can say all this of their wives after 20 years marriage, & those that can mustn't fail to do it." She permitted herself little display of emotion in her letters, and she lamented her inability to speak or write her feelings. She feared he did not understand this reserve in her nature. Yet the intimate record in their letters leaves no doubt that theirs was a remarkably understanding relationship.

Financial needs were invariably pressing in some degree. Cable's accounts with his publishers were normally overdrawn. In May, 1892, his debit at the Century Company was over four thousand dollars. And there seems not to have been a time in the years between 1876 and 1920 when there was not a mortgage against the house he lived in. His contributions to religious and charitable causes were generous, in money as well as work, and the people to whom he gave or lent money extended far beyond his and Louise's relatives. He had left New Orleans with a friend owing him five hundred dollars, lent without security and never paid; he advanced Adelene Moffat six hundred dollars to study art in 1888; he furnished about five hundred dollars a year to the second household, what was needed beyond his two sisters' earnings teaching and keeping boarders. He financed the art study of Nettie's son, Walter Cox, who gained a place in 1893 on the staff of the New York *Tribune.* At Northampton he financed a studio for Adelene Moffat and his daughter Louise, and later sent Louise to study art in New York.

In 1892, after seven years in the Red House, he moved his family to a new house at the edge of Paradise Woods, on a street he named Dryads' Green, for a street in New Orleans. He named the new home Tarryawhile, and from the beginning it was a source of deep satisfaction to him. Even before the house was finished, he began moving rocks and cedars and wild laurel to the ravine leading down at the back to Mill Creek, and in the summer he brought his friend George E. Waring from Newport to landscape the grounds. He now had scope for interests that had been his since boyhood. Besides what he brought in from the surrounding country, he got plants and fish from the government bureaus in Washington; he laid out gentle walkways in the deep woods toward the back of his property. The Beecher Elm was moved from the Red House and in the coming years other guests performed the symbolic act of planting a tree.

On July 31, 1890, Rebecca Cable died, nearing her seventy-seventh birthday. The hope George had stated in almost every letter to her during the Civil War and the disturbed years following, that they would find better days and would be together again, had been amply realized. It was more than an idle remark when he said once that all he was he owed to her. She was buried in the Bridge Street Cemetery at Northampton. Her tombstone bears the line "Her children rise up and call her blessed."

In 1892 Cable made his second tour on the West Coast, and he returned the next year, rounding out ten years on the reading circuit. Against Pond's urging, he now did much of his booking himself and at times dealt with other managers. He wrote letters and read proof on the train; in the hotel rooms or in the railway stations he wrote on his novel; in the cars he wrote in his pocket diary the speech of the other passengers or described the scene passing the window. His day on April 25, 1889, was not unusual: a tea party, his reading, a reception afterward, and a train at 1:20 A.M. for a twelve-hour ride to his next engagement. Missing a train connection in Ohio on January 20, 1896, he hired an engine and a special car to take him the last forty-five miles to meet his audience.

In almost every town he now had acquaintances to welcome him back. On every visit to Des Moines he visited in the family of James B. Weaver, a lawyer who was later in the state legislature. The Weavers talked Creole and called him Pas Trop Bon. He read from the stories he was writing, sang ballads, and played his cornet; they all made limericks and bantered and joked. One invitation for him to stop with them concluded: "And you shall have your big cup of hot water & sugar, with the spoonful of brandy, every evening,—and your five o'clock tea—and a rocking chair—in fact we'll try not to forget anything." Years later, December 11, 1903, Weaver reinforced his invitation with verse, of which this is one stanza:

We will doff our staid demeanor
And for days we'll revel free
With our pockets full of limericks
While our hearts are full of glee,
And we'll live the good days over
For no care did ever frown
In that mighty pleasant season
When—George Cable comes to town.

On November 25, 1908, Weaver published in the Des Moines *Capital* an article on "The Art and Personality of George W. Cable." Much later still, January 30, 1920, when his wife was dead and his children married, he recalled in a letter to Cable the happy times his visits had been, and "most of all the astonishingly alive individual who brought so much joy to two corn-fed Iowans in the olden days."

It was much the same with the Franklin H. Head family in Chicago. Besides sponsoring Cable in public circles, as in the Union League Club when he was its president, Head arranged gatherings in his own home such as that on January 15, 1892, which included Joseph Jefferson, Sol Smith Russell, and Eugene Field. At San Francisco Cable was taken into the family of John Vance Cheney, librarian of the Free Public Library.

Since the tour with Mark Twain, Cable had taken part in occasional joint readings. One variant of such readings was sponsored by Frank Lincoln, who headed an organization called the "Society of Uncut Leaves." At Chicago on January 9, 1893, Cable read a portion of his new novel in one of these programs which included also Hamlin Garland, Harriet Monroe, Richard Malcolm Johnston, and Francis Hopkinson Smith. On February 23 of the next year he read at New York under the same auspices. In 1890 Pond proposed that Cable join James Whitcomb Riley and Bill Nye, whom he was managing in readings together, and later that he join one or the other of them for a tour. Cable was reluctant to join either of them, fearing they would make little show of "fine work" and would likely turn the performance into "something akin to a circus." He added in a letter to Louise on April 1, 1888, "I fear I am getting too dignified for it." He appeared with Riley at Chicago, however, on January 12, 1892, at the Central Music Hall. The opening was delayed twenty minutes for the overflow crowd to be seated. Each took the stage four times, Cable reading twice from *Bonaventure* and twice from *Dr. Sevier*. Riley recited such favorite poems as "That Old Sweetheart of Mine" and "I Want to Hear the Band Play." Both were encored and the press treated the reading as a major attraction. Riley asked afterward whether they could not appear together regularly, and five years later he wrote Cable: "Surely your good work goes on, and with an ever broadening world of grateful beings I am lustily chiming in your sound praise and applause." Cable published a memorial to Riley in the *Writer* of October, 1915.

Cable and Eugene Field had a longer reading partnership. They were together in the Eastern cities late in 1892 and in the Midwest the next January. Employed on the Chicago *News Record,* Field had appeared with Nye and Riley, but his health would not permit the traveling that was regular fare with Cable. He was a delight to his audiences and his platform companions, though his happy eccentricity unfitted him for the demands of extended platform commitments.[1] Cable was one to enjoy Field's "irresponsible boyishness," as he termed it. In fact, there was much of the same ingredient in his own makeup. "In all the world's best meaning he was a boy," he wrote afterward in an introduction to *The Eugene Field Book* published by Scribner,[2] and all men and women were his boy and girl friends and playmates." This tour had much in common with the earlier Twain-Cable tour. Field committed a poem to memory for his program and in advance "tried it upon the dogs with gratifying results," he said. He inscribed one of his books to his "beloved and wicked partner, George W. Cable."[3] On the platform he made purposeful use of his naturally awkward gestures and his bass voice. The unpredictable might come any minute, whether some antic on the platform or an elaborate practical joke.

Wherever they went the situation was much as it was in Chicago: Cable was well known to the audiences and was always welcome, a newspaper reporter said; Field had not appeared before. Especially at Chicago was the attention on Field, for he was a local celebrity seen for the first time in this role. The audience overflowed into the aisles in Central Music Hall, and he was called back for half a dozen encores. The applause was so great as to embarrass him, the Chicago *Herald* said, but Cable remarked in *The Eugene Field Book* that Field could accept with equal aplomb such applause as this and the situation in another hall where a total of thirteen persons came to hear them.[4] At some

[1] See Francis Wilson, *The Eugene Field I Knew* (New York, 1898), p. 30.
[2] Ed. by Mary E. Burt and Mary B. Cable, 1898, p. xv.
[3] Wilson, *The Eugene Field I Knew,* p. 28.
[4] While in Chicago, Cable was honored by Melville E. Stone at a luncheon at the Union League Club when other guests were Hamlin Garland, Eugene Field, Richard Malcolm Johnston, and Sol Smith Russell. See the Chicago *Inter-Ocean,* Jan. 11, 1893.

places, as at Holyoke, Massachusetts, on November 30, Field did not meet the expectations of his audience, mainly because of his lack of experience on the platform. Cable, the reporters remarked more than once, maintained his usual high level and proved himself master of his material and his audience as well. First in the Home Culture Club *Letter,* April 1, 1896, and later in *The Eugene Field Book* Cable drew an affectionate portrait of Field as he had known him in their season together.

While his new novel was in progress, Cable published several small pieces, besides Dora Miller's "A West Indian Slave Insurrection," which he edited for the *Century* and twenty-five years later incorporated in the volume *The Flower of the Chapdelaines.* In 1892 he prepared *A Memory of Roswell Smith*[5] at the request of Smith's widow and colleagues at the Century Company. He quoted freely from others but wrote most of the volume himself, happy to pay his own tribute to one of his most devoted and most respected friends. "The Gentler Side of Two Great Southerners," in the *Century* of December, 1893, recounted episodes in the lives of Robert E. Lee and Stonewall Jackson. For the children's magazine *St. Nicholas* he wrote a two-part article on New Orleans which appeared in November and December, 1893. With but light intrusions of historical and descriptive facts, he pictured the world of New Orleans as a child would know it, or rather as a boy would, for he colored the picture with the luxuriance and the glamour in which half a lifetime had clothed his boyhood home.

At the editor's request Cable contributed "The Taxidermist" to *Scribner's Magazine* for May, 1893, his first piece of fiction since "Au Large" had concluded in the *Century* five years earlier. This story was combined with two others written later and published in 1899 in the volume *Strong Hearts.* These three stories and one novel were the only additions to his fiction in the twelve years before 1900. The novel had a longer and even more painful history than any of his earlier books before it was published in 1894. Its beginning was in 1889. Toward the end of a lecture tour he wrote Louise on May 5: "I am writing in good earnest, writing a story. It is very sermony & pamphlety as yet, but I shall lick it into shape by & by. I almost believe I have begun my novel." Soon he had settled on a plan, and when he returned to the platform at the middle of October the first chapter was written. At home in the summer he had gone into the country to take notes of "the landscape & season" for the novel. At Nashville in November he searched out books on the region, made notes as Baskervill drove him over the town, and then

---

[5] Privately printed, [New York, 1892].

took the train for Monteagle, accompanied by a guide he had engaged to answer questions while he made notes. On Cumberland Mountain he went to a former acquaintance, Mrs. Weir, talked with her, and left a list of questions for her to answer and send to him.

The novel was to be set in a region where in the postwar period outside capital came in for the development of mines and mills and factories. At first he had in mind Tennessee, but in the spring of 1890, when the plot was full blown in his mind, he decided to move the setting farther south; and so, taking advantage of a lecture engagement at Howard University, he swung down into Georgia. At Marietta he left the train, for there he had decided would be the center of his fictional state of Dixie. At Cartersville a day later, May 20, he found just the region he was looking for, and in a notebook he jotted down details to go directly into his novel; the Etowah River, the saltpeter cave, the cliffs, the abandoned furnaces, the piles of manganese ore, the streets and sidewalks, the railway station, the men in shirt sleeves in chairs tilted against the wall at the livery stable, and the phrases he heard on the street.[6] As he had done at Monteagle and earlier in the Acadian country, he left with his guide questions to be answered, especially on the boom days that followed the war. At home he reread the letters his mother and others had written him after the close of the war. His materials were in hand, and he settled down at home to write through the summer.

With enough written by July for two magazine installments and with hopes of selling the serial rights and drawing advances, he approached Gilder—but with greater deference than ever before, for Gilder had gone largely over to the view that peace and prosperity would be best served in the South by withholding civil rights from the Negroes, and had grown more and more frigid in rejecting the controversial essays Cable had submitted to him one after another before giving them to other editors. "I could weep for disappointment," Gilder wrote on August 29, after reading the manuscript. "Instead of a return *to* literature, an attempt to fetch everything into literature save & except literature itself. . . . Shades of Tourgee!" Then he added, *"Beware of the Fate of Tolstoi.* A greater user of language—and a more conscientious man never lived." Having no reply by October 20, he wrote again, "My letter about the book must have disappointed you. I trust it did not hurt you. I wrote in great disappointment myself, for I had great hopes of the next book to follow Bonaventure the Beautiful."

---

[6] This notebook is at Tulane University.

These letters all but closed the intimacy as author and editor that had begun twenty years earlier. In the remaining eighteen years of Gilder's life their relations were restrained and formal, reflecting still their mutual respect but also the divergence that came naturally when they no longer saw alike the matters of business they had to deal with. Yet Cable singled Gilder out as the second of four, following Mark Twain, on whom he wrote sketches two years later in the *Letter,* March 1, 1896. As he set about revising the manuscript, Marion Baker, visiting him in Northampton, urged him not to be bulldozed into emasculating the book to please Gilder.[7] When three chapters of revised manuscript reached the Century office in May, 1891, it was Johnson who undertook to read them. But soon he passed them on to Buel, saying he could not read Cable's handwriting and that earlier manuscripts of his had forced Gilder to wear glasses. The decision was that on the basis of these chapters the book would not do. The pique was considerable on both sides. There was a complication in that Cable's account with the Century Company was four thousand dollars overdrawn. Even so, the officers of the company assured him he was at liberty to place the novel elsewhere, and they could do business on his later work. At Roswell Smith's death early in 1892 F. H. Scott became president, Charles F. Chichester treasurer, and William Webster Ellsworth secretary. They had all been Cable's friends for a decade or more, but none of them approached the generous sympathy of Smith.

The manuscript went back to the Century offices a third time, when it was complete, in the summer of 1893. Cable had pushed the writing forward at every spare moment on his tour of the reading season. "And oh! how slowly I write! Still the end must come some day and I drudge on," he wrote Louise from St. Paul on April 9. "When I am not too weary I love the work." At another time he said his novel moved "with all the majestic acclivity of an old house on rollers impelled by an aged mule at a capstan." In June Gilder rejected the novel a third time. "There is an innate disagreeableness that seems to pertain largely to the conditions described," he said, and much to displease Southerners. "There is an apparent effort to conceal salutary purpose in the book—but it is there, all the same,—running along in a sort of irritating way." Gilder hoped Cable would after this turn his hand to "work in the old spirit of Beauty and Art."[8]

Within a few weeks the novel had been accepted by Scribner and Burlingame for *Scribner's Magazine,* January to December, 1894, and

[7] See Marion Baker to Cable, Sept. 6, 1890, Jan. 4, 1891.
[8] Gilder to Cable, June 23, 26, July 5, 1893.

later publication as a book. The original title, *Johnny Reb,* was first changed to *Widewood* and finally to *John March, Southerner* before the first installment went to press. To finish the last chapters Cable went in August, 1893, to a quiet village, Malone, in upper New York. There he wrote four pages a day, twice what he usually did at home. He arranged for a concert guitar and in the evening, he wrote Louise, would sing quietly to himself and make new accompaniments to old songs. The novel grew in length with the rewriting during serialization, and still more before it appeared as a book on February 11, 1895 (dated 1894 but delayed for Cable's revisions). Sampson, Low & Co. issued a London edition.

The theme of the book and the materials came naturally to Cable as he conceived and planned it in 1889 and 1890, when he was engrossed in the Southern debate. As he saw it, the hope of the South lay in the leadership of perceptive men who could rise, through mastery of themselves and their surroundings, to the demands made on them. *John March, Southerner* is a novel set in Suez, in the state of Dixie, in the troubled years after the Civil War. The theme is the struggle of the title character to master himself, to transcend the limitations bequeathed to him by his parents and the society of which he is a part.

Nurtured in the light of his father's idealism and his mother's simple but sincere poetic sentiment, he has the vision and the courage to win out, though slowly, over his adolescent love for Fannie Halliday, his hatred for Cornelius Leggett, his quick temper, and a series of defeating impulses. This struggle for self-mastery results as it did with Bonaventure of the earlier story in an unwavering devotion to the welfare of those around him. Others of Cable's characters besides Bonaventure, in fact, had passed through the same struggle to the same final nobility; Frowenfeld in *The Grandissimes,* for one, and Vignevielle in *Madame Delphine.* But they had lacked something of convincing humanity. Frowenfeld showed too little of human frailty; Vignevielle's transformation from pirate to public benefactor needed clearer motivation; Bonaventure's purification was more symbolic than real. John March is believably human. His foibles and weaknesses are overcome only through slow and painful self-searching and many bruises from without. Finally he wins Barbara Garnet and he sees his course plainly before him, but he must start from the trough of failure, which has resulted partly from his own blindness and partly from the dishonesty of others victimizing the public.

Cable's women characters stand apart from the women who populated most fiction of his time. They are real and distinguishable. Fanny Halliday, the object of John's young love, and Barbara Garnet, winner of his mature affection, lack the charm of the Creole mother and daughter of *The Grandissimes,* but they have wills of their own and distinct personalities. In Brother Garnet, Cable attempted, he said, his first full-scale villain. Garnet's evil is of a deep cast. Under the guise of religion and benevolence he betrays the public, his associates, and the widow of his former friend. Cornelius Leggett, the accomplice of Garnet's schemes, is not a successful character, for he has two incompatible roles. In one he is the conniving Negro politician drunk with the power circumstances have laid in his hands; and in the other he is the much-married buffoon who talks in the comic illiteracies common to the stage darkies of the time. Ravenel, the newspaper editor, assumes no clearly consistent character, perhaps reflecting the author's view of Southern journalists as at best sincere men wanting the good of the region but led to defeat their own purposes through lack of understanding.

As in most of Cable's books, the action grows complex, less from intricacy of plot than from the succession of crowded scenes that are presented through a hint here or a snatch of conversation there, with the result that the reader feels at times he cannot bring the background into focus. Into the background are woven all the vexing problems of the postwar South: public education, segregation in public activities, including the churches, Negro suffrage, mob violence, corruption in government and the embezzlement of public funds, immigration, outside capital, natural resources. Gilder's judgment quoted above is misleading, for the book does not argue these questions directly or dogmatically, and no specific solutions are offered. In fact no one character speaks for the author; rather his views come across, as they do in Howells's novels, as the residue from the conversations and actions of all the characters. At the conclusion the problem is still complex, bewilderingly complex, and the grounds for hope are that John March sees the direction in which to seek the solution and recognizes the by-passes lining the way. Outside capital is needed to develop the resources of an impoverished state, but sound investors like Henry Fair and his father are repelled by flaws in local government and local management; unscrupulous investors team with local corruptionists such as Garnet and Leggett to swindle the public. Prejudices and wrong-headed attitudes and gullibility are rife. Judge March and Brother Tombs hold noble ideals but are ineffectual. Leggett embodies all the evils a vengeful and unprincipled leader might perpetrate on the illiterate colored electorate which maintains him in power. These characters and these actions Cable could have documented over and over in the South of the 1880's.

At the point when John March is at his lowest, when the people about him have been "betrayed as foully in their fortunes as in their souls" and he can see only failure in his own affairs, he is invited to come north with his friend Henry Fair and join in a promising business venture. He answers: "I know that even without your offer there's a better chance for me North than here. But—O! it's no use, Fair, I just can't go! I mustn't! . . . You know, this Suez soil isn't something I can shake off my shoes as you might. George! I'm part of it! . . . I've got to stay here." His intensity rises as he explains his decision until finally he is trembling with emotion. Among other things he says: ". . . when our value is not mere wages, it isn't every man who's got the unqualified right to pick up and put out just whenever he gets ready . . . . right down there in those streets truth and justice are lying wounded and half-dead, and the public conscience is being drugged! . . . My place is here!"

Though Cable often thought of himself as beset by temptations and hampered by weaknesses such as John March had to conquer and of course saw his role in the Southern controversy as similar in may ways to that of March, he can in no strict sense be identified with his character. Yet in leaving March with an unshakable determination to stay in the South, he surely had in mind the decision he had faced in 1884 and 1885. Looking back now on the Southern controversy, in which his Northern residence may have appeared to be a defeating handicap, he seems to be saying that John March's decision was the right one. Or he may have seen it that in deciding ten years ago to stay in the controversy he had in effect chosen the course John chose.

The reviewer of *John March* in the *Atlantic* of June, 1895, was disappointed because the setting was not in Creole New Orleans, and he missed the earlier "optimism and hilarity." His was the same difficulty Gilder had found in reading the manscript. He liked the portrait of John March's father, a character who would have been at home in Thomas Nelson Page's South "befo' de war," but he spoke of the other characters as if he could scarcely bring himself to read about them. He objected to the dialect, as did the reviewer for the *Nation* on March 14, who supposed the author had a didactic purpose but could see no good to be accomplished. In contrast to these two reviewers, the one writing in the *Outlook,* March 2, was sympathetic with Cable's social views and so found this book "the most careful and thoroughgoing study of the reconstruction period in the South which has yet been offered the world in the form of fiction."

The editors and reviewers, many of them, had not been converted by the realists and like Gilder were swinging along with, if not leading a public which, as Boyesen said in the *Cosmopolitan* of October, 1895, knew the names of Howells and Cable but read the novels of Rider Haggard and other fashionable imported romances. *John March* was not a book for editors and critics who asked first of all for picturesqueness and condemned all unpleasantness and all social comment that might displease any group of readers. It was a book portraying a region with all the faithfulness made possible by the author's long acquaintance with it and his recent study of its problems. To gain accuracy in that portrayal and to give actuality to John March's struggle, he employed a realism offensive to many of his contemporaries.

Whether he had succeeded in his intention, he did not know, Cable wrote in "After-Thoughts of a Story-Teller," as he finished *John March*. He had wanted it to be a "pleasing story of the heroic in imagined lives; truth of the passions and affections, not advocated but portrayed; . . . a book able to keep you—not me, merely—always emotionally interested, and leave you profited; a story written for all readers, to all, and at none." Then he added, "I should call that a good novel, but alas!" He had succeeded, as a matter of fact, beyond what he seems to have thought, certainly beyond what Gilder and Johnson thought. He had given fictional reality to the postwar South, had brought into sharp focus in one book the major problems that had been left after the Civil War. That had been done at the same time that John March had been portrayed in an inner struggle with significance reaching well beyond the immediate issues. Readers in 1894 failed to be moved by John March's struggle because they had lost interest in the social maze through which he had to find his way. As a practical matter the station of the Negro in American society seemed to be fixed, and to puzzle over the justice or the larger implications of it, as John March did, could not seem real or vital. Over half a century afterward, when the role of the Negro in the American scene came up again for reassessment, the struggle delineated in *John March* regained some of the vitality it had for Cable in 1894.

CHAPTER XXII

EDITOR AND THEORIST

IN ITS FIRST three years the *Letter* was strictly an organ of the Home Culture Clubs prepared by Adelene Moffat. In 1895 Cable took it over to give it a more literary slant. He began a section of excerpts sent in by members, "Out of Great Books," and multiplied the editorial writing, going from discussion of club reading to biographical and critical sketches of contemporary authors. A new cover was designed by his daughter Mary, and it usually carried the photograph of a literary figure. Cable's wife wrote practical home articles, "Little Chapters on the Kitchen"; his nephew, Walter B. Cox, then employed by the New York *Tribune,* sent occasional illustrations; and his daughter Lucy contributed a story. Contributors of poems, stories, and critical articles during the club year 1895-1896 included Anna H. Branch, Viola Roseboro', Ruth McEnery Stuart, James Whitcomb Riley, Paul Laurence Dunbar, Mary E. Burt, Hamlin Garland, Albert Bigelow Paine, Eugene Field, and Paul van Dyke. Several of these Cable had advised previously in their attempts to publish their writings. From his own pen came sketches of Mark Twain, Field, Mrs. Stuart, who had been his neighbor and fellow worker in the mission school in New Orleans, Frank Stockton, Ian Maclaren, and Richard Watson Gilder. In the last two issues he had a department of literary discussion, "Thoughts and Views."

The *Letter* had become a literary magazine by the end of the year and was clearly being directed toward an independent existence. But as a forestudy of full-scale magazine publication it was misleading, for both advertisers and subscribers were attracted because of its connection with the clubs, and Cable could solicit unpaid contributions from friends.

The issue for May, 1896, was the last. In October appeared *The Symposium.* The earlier publication had changed "name, shape, bulk, type, and cover-design," Cable explained in the first number, but had not "changed hands, nor its purposes, nor its standards." The letter had grown into a bunch of letters, a symposium which would aim "to be entertaining to the untrained without being rude or illiterate, and interesting to the learned without being academical, . . . to make reading for entertainment as profitable, and reading for profit as entertaining, as they may be."

Adelene Moffat conducted a department "Home and Neighbor," taking as a particular thesis the necessity for the wealthy and the educated to accept responsibilities among their neighbors. Anna Gertrude Brewster outlined in her department, "In the Reading World," programs for the clubs. Cable, announced on the cover as editor and publisher, continued the editorial section "Thoughts and Views" from the *Letter* and had also a piece of some length in each issue: in October "The Brown Ghost," an anecdote told at second hand; in November the essay "To See Our Life as Romance Sees It"; and in December "A Visit from Barrie," an account of the three days in October James M. Barrie and his wife and Dr. W. Robertson Nicoll had spent as his guests at Northampton. The *Symposium* used both drawings and photographs. Among the illustrators were Nettie's daughter, Helen M. Cox, and Cable's friend from his New Orleans days, George Henry Clements. The first number was in a sense a Sidney Lanier number, having his photograph as frontispiece, an essay "The Genius of Sidney Lanier" by Mary E. Burt, and one by Mary Day Lanier, the poet's widow.

After the December number the magazine was absorbed by *The Book-Buyer,* published by the Scribner firm. Cable had accepted the editorship of *Current Literature* and in February, 1897, at the close of his reading engagements, went to New York on a six-months' contract at a low salary but with assurance that permanent arrangements could be made. He may have remembered that years earlier Roswell Smith had told him an author must have a steady income from some source such as editorial work. He was hopeful for the new venture, and during the first months was happy with the prospects and with his daily schedule. He did his imaginative writing in the forenoon and the editorial work in the afternoon.

The aim of the magazine, as he said in his first editorial, in the April number, was to answer the "dramatic, myriad-voiced" request, "Tell us what to read." Thus he could advance in its pages the purpose of the expanded *Letter* and the *Symposium*. Its nature was accurately suggested in its masthead quotation from Montaigne: "I have gathered me a posie of other men's flowers, and nothing but the thread that binds them is mine own"; and the thread had all but disappeared from the issues immediately before Cable took over.

His hand shows unmistakably in his issues, April to September. He secured a greater proportion of original contributions, included more critical and biographical pieces, employed by-lines for both contributors and compilers, and relied less on the scissors and paste pot. His own interests were reflected in the increasing space given to flowers, gardens, animals, and birds. He began a section on "Best Current Educational Matter" and a series of articles entitled "Some Editors of Great Magazines," which in July had as subjects Gilder, Johnson, Holland, Buel, and Scribner. The "Editor's Symposium" had a subtitle unmistakably his own: "An open tabletalk round the literary board, whereat any may speak whose art is not too awkward to unite truth and brevity with courtesy and wit." Here he interwove with his own comment short articles and letters solicited from others. It was in this department that he told in August of the incident when as a clerk under General Bedford Forrest late in the Civil War he had written out manumission papers for Forrest's slaves.

His editorials were as a rule more literary than this, however, though his subjects were often only at the fringes of literature. Strictly literary topics he broached were credibility and probability in fiction, prompted by comment on Henry James's novels; naturalism and morality in art, apropos of Zola; art for art's sake; and the function of dialect in literature. These excursions into criticism are in a sense disappointing, for they remain on a general plane when one would like to have him come to grips with such a subject, say, as the narrative method of Henry James, or the critical judgments of Howells—both of which are subjects he mentions but says he will not discuss at the time. Directly or indirectly, however, his issues of the magazine reveal the literary views he had already developed at length in a series of lectures and essays.

In July one of the proprietors said the current number was the best yet published, and Cable apparently was happy as editor except for his usual financial worries. During the summer he cut further into his writing time to fill what platform engagements he could make. Twice he borrowed money from his sister Mary Louise. On May 24 he wrote his wife: "One of my sources of dejection is my burden of toil and debt. It seems as though I should sink under it. I don't want to be a rich man or a man at ease, but oh! I long to be a good man and a man who can look his town in the face and say the only debt between him & it is to him." As the end of his contract approached, the publishers were not certain what they could do, and he was less sure he had found the way to a better future; but to his wife he wrote on August 1: "Let us keep it in view. If we doubt, if we disbelieve it, what does doubt or disbelief gain— what can they gain for us?"

Permanent arrangements did not materialize, and he returned home at the end of August. He was past fifty and still had not settled on a satisfactory means of supporting himself and his family. There was no choice but to depend on lectures and readings. All summer, furthermore, he had been torn in his mind as he looked to the future. On March 14 he wrote Louise: "I have merely learned a lesson—not to tie myself up with matters that interfere with my more legitimate work & office. I don't know that I have really learned the lesson, either, for I have sinned this way all my days." At a time when the editor's post looked more promising, he wrote on June 6, "There is little doubt left with me that my detachment from other men's activities was somehow destroying my powers." On August 4, shortly before leaving the magazine, he wrote on the matter again:

On one point I am determined; not to go back to a life of imaginative writing alone; it wears me out and keeps me worn out. I shall try my best to find something . . . which will keep me in the current of affairs. I must do it; the recluse's life has been the biggest mistake I have ever made and it is the inevitable rebound from it that has carried me off to bible-class teaching, Home-Culture Clubs and all that. With these I am done and I am going to use my wisest judgment to allot my hours and activities henceforth so as to make my life—our life—still as fruitful as it possibly may be.

When he took up his imaginative work again at the end of the summer, he was freer from conflicting interests than ever before. Since his long struggles to make his latest novel acceptable to himself and his publishers, he had spoken and written considerably on the art of fiction. In December, 1893, when *John March* was all but finished, a request came from the *North American Review* for an account of his method of composition. He welcomed the request and in two weeks wrote what he told the editor was "something like an alternation between the discussion of critical principles and the illuminating confessions of an author's experiences with his growing manuscript." It appeared in the January number as "After-Thoughts of a Story-Teller." Before the Nineteenth Century Club of New York on March 13, 1894, he joined Hamilton Mabie and Hamlin Garland in a discussion of "Realism and Romanticism."[1] On August 16 of the same year he was one of those who spoke at Cummington in an anniversary celebration honoring William Cullen Bryant.[2] The next year he gave the opening lecture in a series at Dwight Hall in New Haven, speaking on "The Newspaper and the

[1] Reported in the New York *Times,* March 14, 1894.
[2] Reported in the Boston *Evening Transcript,* Aug. 16, 1894.

Fireside."[3] He was invited to give a series of lectures at the Lowell Institute in Boston and from February 10 to 27, 1896, delivered six lectures on "The Story-Teller and His Art," one of which he had tried out on an audience in Arlington, Massachusetts, on January 21. It was from these lectures that he mined editorial matter in 1896 and 1897 and also five magazine essays: "Speculations of a Story-Teller" (*Atlantic,* July, 1896), "Extracts from a Story-Teller's Dictionary" (*Chap-Book,* September 15, 1896), "To See Our Life as Romance Sees It"[4] (*Symposium,* November, 1896), "At the Edge of the Woods" (*Bradley: His Book,* November, 1896), "Art and Morals in Books" (*Independent,* December 16, 1897).

These addresses and essays, supported by oddments in his editorials, broach the literary topics most discussed at the time: realism and romance, art for art's sake, didacticism, morality in literature, the legitimate materials of fiction, imagination and emotion in art. In one way and in one degree or another he touched on the authors most in the public mind—Henry James, Howells, Barrie, Kipling, Zola—but his chief interest was in the more philosophical concepts of fiction, and he enunciated a theory of fiction consistent within itself and with the practical moral philosophy he had already evolved.

He spoke as a fiction writer, not a critic. Still, the art is the artist, he said, and every artist is eager to reveal his art; hence these attempts. In the first of the essays, "After-Thoughts of a Story-Teller," his intention was to tell how he had written *John March,* and he did that, but he told also how in his earlier books he had drawn this or that character from a model, had joined fact with fiction, had woven in information from his notebooks, had incorporated the independent story of Bras Coupé in *The Grandissimes,* and had combined three separate stories in *Bonaventure.* He confessed he had what might be called inspiration to write but never inspiration to write a particular thing. His books came from "hard hammering of the brain," and oh, how slowly! Many of his characters were drawn consciously from one person or a combination of persons; others were based unawares on people who had dropped from his consciousness years before; still others were identical with people he did not meet until years afterward. But reporting what an author has learned through observation and research is not enough. He must apprehend everything that goes into his book and must feel most of it. His characters, therefore, come from within him, are in a real sense himself;

---

[3] See *ibid.,* Nov. 19, 1895.

[4] He gave a lecture with this title before the Chicago Twentieth Century Club on Feb. 12, 1898.

otherwise they will be photographs rather than portraits. So even his only villain, Garnet in *John March,* was molded from traits potentially within himself real enough for him to feel them.

In this essay he opened also the general subjects he was to develop in the later essays. "The field of romance is wherever man is," he said; a novelist's materials are underfoot; they are made art by his genius, his spirit. Thus he was at one with Howells in denying the necessity or even the wisdom of going to remote places or great moments in history for the materials of fiction. In letters to Boyesen almost twenty years earlier, while writing his first novel, he had wanted most to say that fiction must reflect real life and must carry its didacticism lightly and unobtrusively. But now, with the tenets of realism more generally established and with Zola on the scene, he felt the need to stress the role of selection in true realism.

"Extracts from a Story-Teller's Dictionary" is concerned chiefly to define fiction. It is constructed from "extracts of life"; it is "but a refinement of truth harmoniously concentrated and foreshortened." Fiction must feed on facts; otherwise it lies. In *Dr. Sevier,* he said, his purpose was to combine fact with fiction in a way he had not attempted again. In *Bonaventure* he had worked from a notebook with a faithfulness he had decided was a mistake; keeping a notebook is a good practice, he said, but its contents should go into a novel only as the author cannot forget them. For the whole truth, he wrote in the essay "To See Our Life as Romance Sees It," means selected, appropriate facts as they remain in the memory, not as they are recorded by a camera or in an observer's notebook. Facts and the supposable must be kept reconciled. The idiosyncratic, even what is only supposable, is often most useful to the novelist, for people are revealed better, the universal in them is more apparent, when thus "the great and the beautiful rise from their concealment amid the dwindling commonplace."

"Romancist and realist in one," he concluded, "that is what every story-teller should be, and in fact cannot escape being, however he may theorize." The novelist will substitute "in place of the actual the harmoniously supposable, whether probable, or only possible, or wholly fantastical; yet only in so far as the actual is less effective to his ends." He need not demand that his reader believe, only that he suppose. He editorialized in the *Symposium* for May, "an author shall *secondarily* be true to nature but *primarily* true to art." His imagination will feed on facts, but as the gateway "to the temple of emotions," the imagination fits the right emotions to facts and thus selects facts appropriate to the proper directing of the emotions. There can be no art for art's sake, Cable said, for there can be nothing for its own sake. There is an enveloping "law of spiritual gravitation," he wrote in the *Symposium* for September; "everything by its normal condition and attitude tends to fall into the service of something else, and can perfectly serve itself only by this indirection." Our emotions, our feelings are our ultimate wealth. Through art our emotions are "aroused, nourished, purified, enriched by a pleasingly ordered contemplation of an experience potentially real."

It is of some significance, surely, that these essays and editorials contain references to Emerson, Thoreau, Whitman, and Carlyle. He read Carlyle extensively in these years (*Sartor Resartus, Past and Present, Heroes and Hero Worship*), quoted him in the *Letter* and the *Symposium,* and wrote once when he had been reading Carlyle on the train, ". . . what a companion! I dread the hour when I shall come to the end of the volume." His "law of spiritual gravitation" and his insistence that the artist minister to the emotions, to the spirit, no doubt owe something to these authors. The artist aims at delight, for delight is "the finishing touch of all goodness and so of all existence." After quoting lines from Whitman saying that "the whole earth and all the stars in the sky are for religion's sake," he added, "in their best meanings, religion and romance come to the same thing . . . . every one of us has it in his power to make his own daily life a good story." Art and morals are coequal. Religion is man's making every day "into as thrilling and noble a story as he knows how"; like the novelist he can distill away the dross and cherish the great and the beautiful.

Four of these essays take the form of a dialogue in which the author talks with his neighbors in a town easily recognizable as Northampton. In person or through his ideas reported at second-hand, there is also the author's imagined friend Smith of New Orleans, a fiction writer to be loosely identified with the author. In writing "Art and Morals in Books" Cable based his comment on the analogy of tree-pruning which went on as he and his neighbors talked on the ground below. The pruning was "turning fact into fiction, by simply stripping away the falsehoods and cutting out the irrelevancies and trivialities." It was "Art investing Nature with the Magic veil of poetry without taking away her robe of truth." After the operation, no observer should be aware that the tree had been pruned. Twisted limbs need not be cut away, for "to make Nature, or any pretended portrait of her, faultless is to set aside a profound truth for whose displacement, unless it be merely playful and momentary, no charm of art is a sufficient recompense even to our art sense; to our disciplined imaginations and emotions, that is."

Hence a novelist need not avoid the sordid or degraded or immoral, he wrote in *Current Literature* for June. "A picture of blood or mud need not be bloody or muddy. Whether or not it really is so depends simply upon whether or not it bloodies or muddies the mind of the reader." The only law is that the effect on our minds and feelings must be "the constant increase and unfailing ennoblement of our spiritual experiences." He could not suppose good art could exist in any work without good morals any more than he could accept bad art on the sole recommendation of good morals. Yet the great storytellers, the author and his friend Smith agree in "Speculations of a Story-Teller," are not simply drillmasters conducting "spiritual skirmish drills and sham battles." They are instead "sappers and miners, scouts, skirmishers, spies . . . ; always out on the farthest line of debated ground . . . ; all of them doing gay, rough service, and hardly so much to be blamed as some other sorts of folk if they do not show up regularly at dress parade."

A few lines below these, Smith remarks: "I once said to my wife I wished I were a man of such strong living that my very sins might always be so big they would have to be left behind whenever I broke camp, and my warfare so active I should have to break camp every day; but she sighed something about 'doing more harm than good,' and I gave up the idea." Here Smith is speaking for Cable, whose inclinations had been to plunge ahead time after time when his wife, but more often others in reality, had cautioned more reserved steps. Such had been true of his moves in the Southern controversy; his religious teaching had made his church uncomfortable; and his editors had begged him from the beginning to stay more within the conservative literary tradition. Now he could not help feeling he had been through the wars; as a reformer and as a novelist he was assessing the gains and losses and charting his course for the future. For a quarter of a century he had waged an unceasing fight for the illiterate and dispossessed of his region, or for the sufferers from feudal injustice in the courts and prisons and asylums, or for the victims of legally and publicly sanctioned segregation and discrimination. He had abandoned those causes now and had kept only the Culture Clubs, to which he would soon add garden clubs. He was ready to turn from the "strong living," the strong writing of *The Grandissimes, Dr. Sevier,* and *John March,* to stories that would not run the risk of great sins but might still "make you feel to-day that you are entertained, and find to-morrow that you are profited."

CHAPTER XXIII

A HOLIDAY ABROAD

JAMES M. BARRIE landed in New York on October 3, 1896, accompanied by his wife and Dr. W. Robertson Nicoll of the London *British Weekly*. The next day Barrie wrote Cable that his first letter on American soil must be to accept his invitation to Northampton. The visitors were at Tarryawhile from October 9 to 12, and in that time Cable and Barrie developed a warm affection for each other. The Barries planted an elm between a hemlock spruce planted earlier by Felix Adler and a maple planted by A. Conan Doyle. Tricked into speaking in the Smith College chapel, Barrie said, for one thing, "no American novelist merits a higher rank than Mr. George W. Cable."[1]

There was a reception in the Cable home which Nicoll said "nearly all the town attended." The last evening of the visit was such as was common in the household. Cable sang Creole songs, and Barrie imitated Henry Irving. The two men found they had more in common than shortness of stature. They delighted equally in the October coloring as they drove through the Old Hadley meadows and along the Connecticut River. In an article on Barrie's visit published in the December *Symposium,* Cable remarked on two other elements in his friend's character that had their counterpart in his own: "I am of the notion that human sympathy is so strong in him as to be a burden, a freight too heavy for a light heart, or at least for a light-hearted habit." And "His slow smile is never far off, and, when surprised by some sudden call for a pointed utterance the flash of his wit is as bright as it is kind."

Under the spell of his host, Barrie decided suddenly to cancel the intended trip into Canada and go instead to New Orleans. Howells, Garland, William James, and Charles Scribner were among those Barrie had met in America. "The literary men were good fellows," he wrote

---

[1] E. F. Harkins, *Little Pilgrimages among the Men Who Have Written Famous Books* (Boston, 1901), p. 75; *Daily Hampshire Gazette,* Oct. 13; *Boston Transcript,* Oct. 14, 1896. For Barrie's and Nicoll's comments on their acquaintance with Cable see Barrie's *Letters,* ed. Viola Meynell (New York, 1947), pp. 10 ff.; Denis Mackail, *Barrie: The Story of J. M. B.* (New York, 1941), pp. 246 ff.; John A. Hammerton, *Barrie: The Story of a Genius* (New York, 1929), pp. 274-75.

Arthur Quiller-Couch. "Cable is the prince among them. The quaintest and most lovable of human beings. We were some days with him and they are my best memory of America."[2] Cable wrote on *Margaret Ogilvy,* a new volume of Barrie's on his mother, in the February *Book-Buyer* and in *Current Literature* of the following April. It was just the sort of book to please him in its portrayal of nobility in a simple life, and he found in it an echo of his own feeling that his mother, like Barrie's, was "the true source of all his powers of achievement."

Before Barrie and Nicoll sailed, they had the understanding that Cable would return their visit. As plans evolved, he would come in June and give several readings to meet his expenses. In the meantime Barrie wrote in delighted enthusiasm that he was counting the months. After ending his reading season and visiting a week in New Orleans at the middle of February, Cable sailed from New York on April 20, 1898, on the White Star Line's *Majestic.* By train from Liverpool he reached London on the twenty-seventh, just in time to be hurried away to the dinner of the Omar Khayyam Club, where his response to a toast brought hearty applause and laughter and he began meeting the literary celebrities of England. Thus his first hours in London set a pace that was to hold up with little slackening until he left for home two and a half months later. He was constantly in distinguished company; hospitality was extended in profusion; and the press treated him generously.

There were three drawing-room readings in London, the first at Barrie's house on May 17, the next at Nicoll's on the twenty-first, and the third in the rooms of Sir George and Lady Lewis on the twenty-sixth. He gave the first program entirely to *Dr. Sevier,* the second to "Posson Jone'," and the third to "Grande Pointe"; and each time he included a Creole song. The rooms were lent for the purpose, the announcements said, and the admission charge was ten shillings or ten and six. The audiences ran from seventy to a hundred and included what was to Cable an awesome proportion of notables. Of the reading at the Lewises' Cable wrote in his diary-letter: "Sir Henry Irving was in the chair. . . . And sometimes as I thought what I was doing—reading in the capital of the world before its lords and ladies and authors and critics and the greatest theatrical manager and English-speaking actor living, I wondered why the floor didn't open under my feet. Instead of that, it was my crowning success." Before these small audiences he could achieve such naturalness and intimacy as had not been possible in the usual halls. The London *Times* said of the reading at Barrie's: "He

[2] Barrie's *Letters,* pp. 10-11.

JAMES M. BARRIE AND GEORGE W. CABLE

GEORGE W. CABLE IN HIS STUDY AT TARRYAWHILE

seemed to bring into a London drawing-room the languorous, scent-laden air of a Southern state, to make his hearers see the brilliant color-ing and rich profusion of a summer in the south, to leave a clear impres-sion in every passage of the scene as well as of the characters who figured in it."[3] The *Academy* said that it was not a reading but a "dramatic reci-tation" and that the character of Narcisse was "comedy at its best."

The only appearance before a larger audience was in Memorial Hall on June 3, when he read "Posson Jone'" before five hundred Congrega-tional ministers and their wives. On June 6 he read at Liverpool under the able and generous management of Dr. John Watson, the clergyman who wrote as Ian Maclaren, and on the ninth at Edinburgh in the charge of Professor Alexander Russell Simpson. Barrie and Nicoll had planned to introduce him only to small audiences such as they or a few of their friends could assemble; the English would not patronize strictly public readings at any time, and this was not the best season. But these audi-ences were flattering, and often where Cable was a guest he was asked to read or sing.

Cable thought he could not justify a long stay unless he could con-tinue work on the novel he had begun, and his English hosts made a point of giving him quarters and conditions suitable for work. But it was too pleasant and too valuable a holiday to cut short or to spend at a desk. As a matter of course, he studied everything around him and made jottings in a notebook. He also sent home in installments a long diary-letter describing people and places and recording conversations.

During his five weeks in London Barrie's home was his headquarters and there were far more invitations than he could accept. He attended a meeting of the Society of Authors; he responded to a toast at the Anglo-American dinner; he had dinner with Andrew Carnegie, whom he had met earlier in America, with Charles McArthur, a whip in the House of Commons, and with others. Nicoll took him for long walks and pointed out literary landmarks. "What an ecstasy there is," he wrote once, "in plucking, by wood and field, flowers that smell of dead poets' thoughts." He met George Meredith, George Gissing, Walter Besant, Leslie Stephen, Andrew Lang, Sidney Lee, and a score of others promi-nent on the literary and artistic scene. He had also many hours visiting and playing chess with his host, who wrote of him in a letter to Quiller-Couch on May 1: "He arrived on Wednesday and is delicious, goes into fits over the most unexpected things. The lamp posts in particular are a roaring delight to him and when he sees a pile of stones he asks if

[3] May 18; quoted in the *Critic*, June 11.

they are oyster shells. I have also to tell him how we build our houses and line them and keep out the damp and he takes my answers down in a note book. . . . The sweetness, the dignity of him are things to revel in."[4]

High points of these weeks, on the testimony of the diary-letter, were his visits with Conan Doyle, Edward Clodd, Rudyard Kipling, and Henry James.

On May 24 he took the train for Haslemere to spend two days with Conan Doyle in his sumptuous new home "Undershaw," renewing an acquaintance begun when Doyle visited Tarryawhile four years earlier. He had been told by all means to bring along his guitar and in the evening sang to his own accompaniment. Doyle sang also, and in the morning they took "a long walk over the great, barren, rolling land." Over the next week-end he was one of a distinguished party at the country home of Edward Clodd, a London banker. From the time he took the train on Friday until he returned to the city on Monday, he was on the peaks of enjoyment, and his report of the visit in his diary is punctuated with exclamations. They were at Aldeburgh, on the North Sea. One day they rowed along the coast for a picnic lunch in the ruins of Orford Castle, and on Sunday they visited the ruins of Framlingham Castle. Such use of the Sabbath did not fit Cable's normal practice, but he decided that in this way he would give himself a day that would "always remain a Sabbath" in his remembrance.

He went next to an experience even more charming. He visited Rudyard Kipling at Rotterdean, near Brighton, again picking up an acquaintance he had made earlier in America, at the Scribner office in New York. With only one other guest present, he had two days in the company of Kipling and his wife and three children. A guitar was borrowed across the street, and Cable sang Creole songs at his host's request. He was unstintingly fond of Kipling. He wrote in his diary:

At "The Elms" "Ruddy" came bounding out of the house like a school boy, bare-headed—very bare-headed—and all arms! I thought he would have hugged me. . . . He is of course, a glad, ardent, overflowing spirit, telling his likes and dislikes without pause, and taking a personal interest every moment in every part of the world. . . . A very free and hearty soul is Kipling's. He is wholly unspoiled by either fame or fortune. . . . Kipling is simply a strong, pure, bracing sea-breeze. . . . I suggested he write a Hymn to Alliance. He said, "I'd give five years of my life to do it!" He recited to me some verses full of his own saucy, soldierly humor and political insight,

---

[4] Barrie's *Letters*, p. 15.

which he has not printed; but they are not at all what the hour calls for and he knows it at least as well as I do.

Back in London on June 1, Cable went the next day to tea at Henry James's rooms in DeVere Gardens. James's invitation had read, "I want extremely to see you for a little interchange of soul—& to tell you how much I was struck & interested by your wonderful dramatic revelation of the other afternoon." Again it was a renewal of acquaintance, for he had met James at New York in 1883. In *Current Literature* of May, 1897, he had written: "We can say in sincerest homage to Mr. James's genius that no one need get into any kind of hurry about any new book of his; it is in no hurry itself; it has come to stay," and nothing he ever does can be denied the rank of high art. Now Cable had a closer look at James himself and summed up his impressions afterward in his diary:

But James was attractive beyond all my expectations and beyond all account I have ever had of him. To me he was positively affectionate. I am glad Barrie likes him so thoroughly. . . . His manner of speech is very amusing and strongly indicative of the studious finish of his writings. He will say— "Hm-m—I walked—eh—I walked to the—hm-m—the eh—hm-m-m—the what shall I say?—the corner! and took a—hm-m-m—a—I suppose I may call it—hm-m—a hansom—a hansom-cab!" But all the time the man impresses you as bringing honor to the name of gentleman; a clean, true man who always feels more than he says.

Before Cable sailed for America, James was at Lamb House at Rye on the Channel coast, and when he learned that Cable could not come down for a visit, he wrote, "I wanted to see you more—to talk with you *most;* to talk with you endlessly, . . . & your room will always be ready." The two men met again in 1906, when James had two days at Northampton.

After his reading in Liverpool, Cable was at Edinburgh on June 8 and began four weeks in Scotland that brought him great satisfaction. His first stop was in the home of Alexander Russell Simpson, a noted physician at the University of Edinburgh, who with his wife and his son James gave him the benefit of their love for the Scottish countryside and their great knowledge of its history. They showed him Edinburgh and then took him into the Trossachs, where he found a strange familiarity, so well did he remember *The Lady of the Lake* from his mother's reading in his childhood. In his diary-letter he quoted line after line of the poem from memory as he bubbled over with enjoyment at actually seeing Loch Lomond, Loch Katrine, Ben Venue, and Ellen's Isle. After three days at Fincastle, deep in the Highlands, and a night

at Inverness, he went yet farther north to Skibo Castle, Andrew Carnegie's twenty-thousand acre estate in Sutherland.

His week as guest of the Carnegies was in several ways the apex
of his holiday. Certainly he had never been so sumptuously entertained
before. On his second day at Skibo he wrote in his diary:

I really don't think I can stand being driven, in future, by ununiformed men
—it's been so long since I've had to put up with such disreputable nonsense.
However, we can discuss that on my return. I shall probably require also
that Lottie be dressed in male attire, blue, buff and brass, with knee-breeches
and pigeon-tails and that she lay out my clothes twice a day and take them
away to brush them every time I take them off. I must also have a bell to
my study—same as I have here, it's quite good enough,—and another to my
bedroom. Certain other things here I count almost as luxuries. For instance,
I must go in a few minutes to dress for dinner; that's a necessity; but then at
the sound of the sackbut—no, no! the bag-pipes! I must go down stairs into
the great hall (windows above windows and the ceiling 20 feet away) and
from every direction the household and guests will come pouring in as I do—
I shall pour in, you understand,—and Mr. Carnegie will give his arm to Mrs.
Rintoul, and there will be couples & couples and Mrs. C and I will bring
up the rear, and we'll all be hungry as bears and merry as larks, and the piper,
all tartan and windbag and pipes and silver clasps & buckles and streamers,
will meantime be strutting round and round the long board in the dining-
room, and as he comes by the door Mr. Carnegie (who always wants to
dance) will catch on behind and away will go after the piper each couple
dropping out at their seats and the piper vanishing in the hall but keeping
up the tune. Yesterday the tune was "All the blue bonnets over the border"
—*imagine it!*

One or two days at Skibo Cable wrote steadily on his novel; others
he worked in the morning and went with Carnegie in the afternoon
trout fishing in one of the lochs. He learned to fish with fly and reel.
He had come to like Carnegie much—for his merriment and wit, his
ready speech, his "candor that tempts the wariest out of himself and a
vivacity that only never becomes antic." One evening Cable sang to the
Carnegies and their dozen guests, and on his last night, when all the
servants attended also, he read "Posson Jone'." As an encore he read
some verse he had composed for the occasion:

> The great man is rewarded
> By being great. He loses
> The lesser joys, regarded
> By lesser minds. There's Moses:

Great Moses viewed from Nebo
The Promised Land afar;
But when *we* get to *Skibo*
We're in it! There we are!

In a copy of *Old Creole Days* he found on the drawing-room table he
wrote:

Don't put on airs, Old Creole Days;
If I'm a guest, you're but a vassal.
Did you bring me—or I bring you—
Or luck bring both—to Skibo Castle?

When it was time to take his leave on June 24, the coach and four
were readied for the first time of the season, and with the eight persons
who were to see him to the train at Bonar Bridge, he galloped away
behind Douglas and Marmion, Ivanhoe and Prince Charlie. At the
station Carnegie's aged uncle George Lauder said, "I feel just as though
I were bidding good-bye to my sweethear-r-r-rt!" Carnegie registered his
impression in writing to a friend:

We pronounce Mr. Cable the most delightful of visitors. Every day some new
charm is found in him. He glides into the bosom of the family before we are
aware, without effort, and becomes one of us. He carries an atmosphere with
him which gently and insensibly envelopes the household.

But the greatest charm of all was revealed when he gave Skibo Castle in-
mates a reading, for which the large hall was admirably adapted. Altogether
fine as the performance was, the most striking feature was this slender little
delicate writer of books, revealing himself as an actor of great dramatic
force. For an hour he held us spellbound.

There is, however, one serious fault with this wonderful man, his visits
are too short; although this has another side. He could not stay very long
before we should become so dependent upon his presence as to feel his absence
too severely. Better not get too well acquainted with him.[5]

Back in Edinburgh Cable was taken over by the Simpsons again
and David Douglas, the first publisher of his books in Great Britain,
now past eighty but a perfect guide to Abbotsford and Melrose Abbey,
where he took his guest on the twenty-seventh and gave him a glimpse
into the world of Scott second only to that Washington Irving had got
years before from the Wizard of the North himself. Another day the
distinguished scholar David Masson, then retired, was his guide at the
University of Edinburgh, Holyrood Palace, and the Castle. Leaving

[5] Quoted in *The Cable Story Book*, p. 174.

Edinburgh on June 30, he had three days on the Firth of Clyde with Douglas and his wife, and on July 4 he was taken through the Burns Country by Neil Munro, a young novelist, and W. Craibe Angus, a dealer in paintings and a friend of Robert Louis Stevenson's he had met at Skibo. As they went from one of Burns's "howfs" to another, he recalled the poems and the incidents of the poet's life, and at the Burns cottage he "stood silent with reverence & deeply touched before the humble, most *humble* little bed in the wall, wherein Robert Burns was born." He wrote a quatrain in the visitor's book:

> Of heavenly stature, but most human smile,
>   Gyved with our faults, he stands,
> Truth's white and Love's red roses offering us,
>   Whose thorns are in his hands.

Angus wrote him afterward, "we Scotch are very proud of" these lines. They had been printed in the daily and weekly newspapers.

Back in London Cable paid parting calls and for three days did nothing but write letters and inscribe copies to his friends of *The Grandissimes* which Stodder and Houghton had just issued with an introduction by Barrie. In several of them he wrote verses, of which this is one:

> I hear Queen London's Sabbath bells
>   Chime, "Get ye gone, gay rover";
> And in my heart the echo swells—
>   "At least, I was your lover."

On the ship *Friedrich der Grosse* three days out from Southampton, he concluded his diary on July 14: "I sit with my pencil poised. Have I really finished? I believe I have. How can I hope for heaven when I feel that this world, just as it is, is far too good for me. I never have lived up to it, I don't see that I ever shall. Still, I'm willing to try."

CHAPTER XXIV

TURNING WITH THE CENTURY

IN OCTOBER, 1898, Scribner brought out Cable's five volumes of fiction in a uniform binding, the Tarryawhile Edition. Cable liked the name, he wrote Scribner on October 12, because "It marks the present stage in the history of my literary production and career." His work had come to a pause several years back. At about 1890 he had left off religious writing and Bible teaching and had withdrawn from the open arena of the Southern controversy; in *John March, Southerner* he had given a fictional summing up of contemporary Southern problems. As magazine editor and theorizer on literature he had systematized his views on fiction. Except for *John March* and two stories, he had published no fiction in the last ten years. The sojourn in England had come just when he was ready to resume writing, like a holiday crowded in before a stretch of work.

The novel he had begun before going to England occupied him for two years after his return, but in the meantime there were three stories already written which could be made into a volume. "The Taxidermist" had been published in 1893, "Gregory's Island" in 1896, and after "The Entomologist" had appeared in three installments of *Scribner's Magazine* at the opening of 1899, the three stories were published together as *Strong Hearts*. This volume was a product of the author's needs, as *Bonaventure* had been, but was less satisfactory than the earlier book. The stories in it are unrelated except that they have the same narrator, Richard Thorndyke Smith, who is the author thinly disguised. A unifying purpose in the stories, Cable wrote Scribner on December 20, 1901, was to make each a "character portrayal through the medium of romantic and dramatic incidents." The first would be short and the succeeding stories progressively longer.

"The Taxidermist" is Richard Thorndyke Smith's account of a "romantic and dramatic" episode reflecting the character of P. T. B. Manouvrier, a taxidermist who was a perfectionist unwilling to sell inferior work and never content unless he had succeeded in restoring, or at least suggesting, the soul in the object of his work. After he had won $75,000 in Charlie Howard's lottery and for want of other uses for the money had built a house, a mansion in fact, he and his wife loved the new house but felt no inclination to move from their cramped home and workship on St. Peter Street. The cottage occupied by a poor orphanage burned down, and Manouvrier gave the new mansion to replace it. After that, he and his wife still walked in the late afternoon from their nook in St. Peter Street to gaze with happy affection on the new house. In this simple story of a man simple in his mixture of pride and humility in his work and in the quiet nobility of his life, Cable returned to the theme of selflessness and self-abnegation that had inspired *Bonaventure*. The story was planned as an exemplum, and it may be that the purpose shows through too clearly, but the naturalness of both the story and its telling and the unaffectedness of the characters serve to obscure the contrivance of the incidents. Manouvrier's initials stand for "Pas Trop Bon," the only given name he acknowledges having. It symbolizes his humility in both the artistic and the moral worlds. After they had read the story, Cable's friends the Weavers in Des Moines called him Pas Trop Bon.

"Gregory's Island," called "The Solitary" in the book, is Smith's story of his wartime comrade who was the victim of hopeless weakness of character except when he spurred himself to spasms of courage and virtue, as in chopping up his boat on a remote island and thus conquering his thirst for drink. The story is discursive and is perhaps the flimsiest of all Cable wrote. The facet of human character portrayed in Gregory is but vaguely defined and in consequence neither the character nor the situation assumes reality.

"The Entomologist" is of novelette length and has a full-drawn plot. Smith is again the narrator, but he is also a character in the story, such a manipulator of the action as Henry James liked to employ. He learns that the wife of a Creole neighbor and the Entomologist have become infatuated with each other, and he meddles and manages in the manner of the Jamesian auxiliary characters to keep them from hurting themselves and their spouses. The affair goes no farther than talk and worry, and the resolution comes only when both die of yellow fever. The story is told coldly, as Smith remarks toward the end, but there is a jarring incongruity in what amounts to puppy-love between two middle-aged characters in the shadow of an epidemic. The fever is simply a device of the plot. Its role is far different from that in Cable's early narratives, such as *Dr. Sevier*, in which the sense of actuality and the impressiveness grew from the author's recollection of its inroads in his own family and his desire to cry out against a society which through lethargy or ignorance or prejudice in effect invited the fever back year after year. Cable's purpose was to study moral uncleanness, and in the Entomologist he created a full-bodied character appropriate to the study, but in developing the story he refined the interrelations of the characters and restricted their actions and their show of feelings so much that their struggle seems much ado about little.

These three stories are set in and around New Orleans. Manouvrier in "The Taxidermist" and Fontenette in "The Entomologist" are Creoles and speak the same Gallicized English as Cable's earlier Creoles, though it is somewhat less literal and hence easier to read. They show few of the characteristics Cable had earlier attributed peculiarly to the Creoles; it is as if he remembered the Creoles' resentment of his earlier characters. Smith remarks in introducing the stories that they came out of his own experiences, and actually much in the stories came from Cable's experiences. Smith first met Gregory of "The Solitary" in the Confederate cavalry while he was recovering from a wound such as Cable received. They met next in New Orleans and in sailing to his island among the Chandeleurs Gregory followed the course Cable and Joseph Pennell took in 1882. In "The Taxidermist" Smith gives his birth date as December 9, 1844, missing Cable's by exactly two months; he takes his family north for the summer as the author did in 1881; his stuffed hummingbird and the incident of the ruby throat entrapped in the house had their originals in the Cable household. Smith speaks of the lottery in language quite similar to that Cable used in his editorials for the *Picayune* in 1872. The third story drew even more from Cable's own experiences. The Entomologist, a baron himself, was clearly modeled on the Baron Reizenstein, who in 1881 named the moth of his own discovery after Cable. As the story was planned in 1896, it had the title "The Old Baron Rodenberg." The Spanish moss hanging in Smith's hallway, the specimen cases bought from the Entomologist, the son and the servant dying of yellow fever are all autobiographical details.

The first story Cable conceived in 1893 for the sequence which later became the *Strong Hearts* volume threatened to be too long and was laid aside. He gave it some attention in 1896 and again the next year but did little with it until he went to New Orleans early in 1898 to collect material. He planned for it to equal in length the three previous stories and to follow them in a second volume. It would be in the same key, would have the same thesis, the same tone, the same idea, and would be told by the same narrator. It was this manuscript, *The Cavalier,* that he took with him to England. Then in May, 1899, he returned south to refresh his memory of the terrain he had chosen to use. After a stop-

over at Berea College, he reached Hazlehurst, Mississippi, on May 27 to
visit his messmate of the war, J. A. Covington. From there he rode
horseback to Gallatin, where he had first joined his company, and to
Franklin and Fayette and the other scenes he had known as a recruit
in Wirt Adams's cavalry. In midsummer he began trying to sell the
serial rights, hoping to get $7500. Scribner had made advances against
book royalties but did not want it for the magazine. Gilder declined it
for the *Century,* as did half a dozen other magazine editors, all of whom
wanted short stories or serials with simpler plots than his. Published
directly in book form on October 5, its sales immediately outstripped
anything Cable had known before. It was in its eighty-fifth thousand
by the middle of December and had reached a hundred thousand before Christmas.

Cable had long wanted to write about the Confederate cavalry in the
region where he had himself served in the war, and he was pleased as
The Cavalier took shape. On July 17, 1899, he wrote Scribner that there
were pages and chapters in *The Grandissimes* "which sink to a standard
of literary workmanship to which I do not believe one page of 'The
Cavalier' descends. I never before knew nearly so well just what I want
to write or how to write it. I have reached in it the point where my
doubts of success are all gone." As he finished the initial draft early the
next year, he wrote Louise, February 25: "I think I have done a beautiful thing. Certainly it is far better than John March." He enjoyed the
writing more than usual, in part because he was not working under
the insistent pressure Gilder and Johnson had exerted on his earlier books
from the time they read partial drafts until the final batch of page proof
was returned. When the manuscript of *The Cavalier* was complete,
Cable wrote again, April 8, 1900, "I never finished a novel in such good
shape, physically, before."

The book is a war romance. As the author looked back thirty-five
years to his cavalry experiences, a softening glamour obscured the dirt
and blood, the fatigue and pain of the war. The cavalrymen saddle their
horses at the end of a pleasant walk or an evening of dancing to gallop
away for a skirmish with the blue-coats, and ride back afterwards to
the arms and tears of the ladies. Wounds and death are blurred in the
heroic view, except for occasional touches such as the odor of the narrator's healing wound and the tatters of the Louisiana infantry. The characters are faced with the Elizabethan conflict between love and duty
and reach a satisfying reconciliation by subordinating their private wars
to the public one. The dashing Ned Ferry and the equally daring and
mysterious Charlotte Oliver dominate the story, surrounded by auxili-

aries, including the narrator, Richard Thorndyke Smith, who people the stage for their drama of love and war. Oliver, Charlotte's husband, is kept at the fringe of the story and remains a sort of Gothic villain adapted to the time and circumstances. Gholson, an obvious foil, stands for the narrow religiousness which is refuted through Smith himself and Ferry and Charlotte, who see beauty and joy as the substance of religion, and happiness as dependent on others. To them heroism, selflessness, and nobility toward others are the essentials of true religion. The author afterward summed up Ferry's creed in the statement that "the perfect Soldier is the perfect Gentleman."

The Cavalier lacks the realism that sinews Cable's first two novels; it was not inspired by the kind of urgent human problems that inspired those books. The issues back of the war are not mentioned; there is no more direct social criticism than the condemnation of bigoted religiousness. There is no episode that haunts the memory as does the story of Bras Coupé in *The Grandissimes* or John Richling's term in the parish prison in *Dr. Sevier*. It is the kind of book the author intended to write, and it is a good one. He caught the spirit of the cavalry forays he had known himself. Like Smith and Ferry in the novel he "denounced that dullness which fails to see the poetry of daily experience, and goes wandering after the mirages of fiction!" From his recollections he extracted what would reflect the poetry he had seen or his imagination had interpolated in the history of the war.

After *The Cavalier* had been published, Cable wrote, "My old messmates will be looking for history in my pages, from which I have carefully excluded the letter of history and wrought to preserve only its spirit."[1] Actually his messmates, among them J. A. Covington in Hazlehurst and William Henry Pascoe, a New Orleans lawyer, found in the book considerable history as they remembered it. Cable once said that the materials for the book had been in his mind half his life,[2] and he wrote this inscription in a presentation copy, "The author did not have to read up to write this story." Writing the book was a reliving of his war experiences. Smith is a native of New Orleans, nineteen years old but so slight of build that he is taken for sixteen; he is wounded twice and recovers in just such a plantation home as the Montgomerys' of Cable's experience; he serves once as a quartermaster's clerk. The action of the story stays within the area Cable had crossed and recrossed in Wirt Adams's brigade. The cat-and-mouse skirmishing is of the sort he had known, and the secret mission of sending gold across the river to pay

[1] Cable to [?] Garner, Nov. 7, 1901; copy at Tulane University.
[2] An interview in the *Times-Democrat*, March 3, 1903.

the Trans-Mississippi troops was the same mission that fell to Wirt Adams during Cable's first months in his command. *The Cavalier* drew more extensively on the author's personal experiences than any other of his books.

The reviews were mainly favorable, though most of them assigned the book a place below *The Grandissimes*. The reviewers began with the assumption that Cable was one of the best novelists of the time and compared the new work with what he had already done. The *Atlantic* reviewer said in December, 1901: "I think of no one fitter to stand— *quocumque intervallo*—in the place next to Hawthorne's than the author of Posson Jone' and The Grandissimes." He and most of the other reviewers noted that this was a new type of book for Cable—its characters are highly idealized types, and it displays the "fine old military virtues" in a way that would have been out of place in his earlier books. C. A. Pratt, writing in the *Critic* of January, 1902, thought the new style avoided the mannerisms and the overintricate plots but kept the charm of the first books. The *Nation* of December 12, 1901, said the author "appears to have yielded to the pressure of a fashion, and not to the urgency of an inward voice bidding him write." The *Tribune* and the *Post* in New York also charged that the book had been written to catch the market for romance. They noted that Cable's was a glamourized version of the war, undisturbed by the realities that had given *The Grandissimes* and *Dr. Sevier* their strength. Cable's reply to this comment, in a letter to Scribner on December 20, 1901, was that the story which finally became *The Cavalier* had been in his mind at least eight years and the writing had occupied him four years, that he wrote too slowly ever to succeed in catching a particular market.

These things were true, and Cable was apparently unaware that his new book had been shaped by any pressures outside himself. But pressures had made themselves felt. For twenty years he had received powerful urging toward such books as *The Cavalier*—that is, a pleasant romance of love and adventure set in the nostalgic, picturesque old days of heroism and beauty. Editors had asked repeatedly for more picturesqueness; Gilder and Johnson had held up pleasantness as essential. Editors of a family magazine which they wanted to make acceptable to everyone everywhere, they preferred only such social criticism as could be leveled out into inoffensive moral precepts. In his stories and novels through *John March* his reforming zeal had led him to weave urgent social questions into his plots. In the Acadian stories of *Bonaventure* the setting was so remote and so restricted, and the social comment so generalized that Gilder raised no objections, but he found *John March* altogether unacceptable. In the literary speculation Cable did in the half dozen years after he finished that book, he saw fiction more and more as the vehicle of broad moral concepts. It should first of all entertain and should leave the reader ennobled unawares; it should preach the gospel of joy and beauty. In such a story there would be no place for the grim actuality of a Bras Coupé or the horrors of a parish prison. Cable had reluctantly abandoned the causes he had championed in his fiction as well as his essays and lectures, and his aims for his novels had changed accordingly. Whether he was aware of the forces pushing him toward a new type of fiction, he realized it was a new type for him, and he had evolved a theoretical justification for it.

In the second half of 1900, when *The Cavalier* was finished except for revision, Cable wrote a novelette, *Bylow Hill,* which was serialized in the *Atlantic Monthly* in March, April, and May, 1902, and was between boards in May. The plot for the story had come from the professional experiences of Dr. S. Weir Mitchell, who told it briefly while visiting at Tarryawhile in 1896. He had no interest in using it himself and had "presumed the tale would scare the boldest novelist." The story Mitchell told was about a New England minister of distinguished but neurotic stock who grew insanely jealous of his wife and his close friend, with no basis in fact, and under the promptings of dreams and his distraught imagination became convinced that he had killed his wife and sunk her body in the mill pond. For the main elements of the situation Cable took just what he found in the original account, but he modified the conclusion. In the actual case the minister had been confined in an asylum, and before his release after several years his wife and child were killed in a train wreck. In *Bylow Hill* the minister, Arthur Winslow, dies after a fall on the stairs. He had won his wife, formerly Isabel Morris, after she had quarreled with her fiancé and his friend, Leonard Byington. Hence Arthur's jealousy gains in plausibility, and the way is prepared for Isabel and Leonard to marry at the conclusion of the story.

The first of Cable's stories laid outside the South, *Bylow Hill* is set in a New England town such as Northampton and on a street that might well be Dryads' Green. Isabel Morris and her mother have come from the South and have a delicious Southern speech, we are told, but it is not represented. Arthur is held at a distance, and hence his disintegration is shown from some remove, as in a clinical study. Instead of analysis there is a direct recounting of externals. The focus on the central problem, with the paring of everything else to a bare minimum, suggests Henry James; the revelation of psychological deterioration through

external manifestations suggests Hawthorne. The book reads like a
scenario, in fact, needing to be filled in to make a complete novel. And
in thus extracting the characters from place and time, the novelist elimi-
nated the elements in which his greatest strength lay: the portrayal of
real scenes, which in his earlier books had pulsed with a life he felt
himself intensely, and the interweaving of personal and public affairs,
which in books like *The Grandissimes* and *Dr. Sevier* had given weight
to both the individual and the social problems explored. *Bylow Hill* was
in this as well as other respects an experiment, and it is the only piece
of fiction Cable wrote, except for two or three brief narratives, which
did not draw on his personal knowledge of characters and events. Yet
Arthur Winslow is a convincing character, no less terrifyingly real to the
reader than to those about him who watch helplessly as he moves to
his destruction.

Most reviewers found the book undistinguished, though some spoke
of the power and the artistic passages in it.[3] One historian of American
fiction thinks it superior to *The Cavalier* and Cable's next book, *Kincaid's Battery*.[4]

The market for serial novels was all but closed to Cable. The *Century*
editors had rejected his last three novels but had asked for stories.
In August, 1901, they published "Père Raphaël," a companion story
to "Posson Jone'," which they had requested for what the magazine
would call its "Year of Romance." Johnson had said they wanted it
to have "the old charm" and wished it could bring in Aurore and
Clotilde from *The Grandissimes*. Before the story was published changes
were made in the interest of clarity—at Gilder's request, as had been
done again and again with the early stories and novels. In 1909 this
story and "Posson Jone' " were issued in a volume with an introduction
by the author in which he insisted in the playful manner so natural to
him that the two stories are one and the same, for all their differences.

One of the several editors who had rejected "Posson Jone'," Cable
remarked in introducing the volume, had done so because it was not a
love story. He would remedy that fault by giving Jules St. Ange, in
the new story, a delightful young Creole lover and would give double
measure by adding another pair of lovers. The time lapse is the same
as that of the early story, the intricacies of the two love threads being
tied at every point to the affairs of Jules and Posson Jone', Baptiste and
Colossus as narrated earlier. The easily duped, kindly Creole judge,
Jules's father, the understanding priest who is fond of gambling at

---

[3] See Francis W. Halsey in the *Book-Buyer*, XXIV (July, 1902), 469-70.
[4] A. H. Quinn, *American Fiction* (New York, [1936]), p. 349.

cards, the clever Florestine, who takes the disguise of Père Raphaël to advance her own romance and a friend's also, the ubiquitous colored maid, Caroline, who has her own affair with Baptiste to advance—these are the new characters. They have the Creole speech and the traits which had made Jules and Narcisse and Aurore and Clotilde favorites in Cable's early books. A young man receives the highest recommendation when it is said that he has "all the bad 'abit' nécessaire to a parfec' Creole gen'leman" and that "rather than change his ril-igion he sooner go to hell." The Creoles are drawn with obvious affection. Back of the kindly mendacity of Florestine and the profligacy of Jules and the parental stubbornness of Judge St. Ange lie a generosity and an unassailable honesty familiar to readers of *Old Creole Days* and *The Grandissimes*.

The *Youth's Companion* of September 5, 1901, contained "Some of My Pets," Cable's reminiscences of his boyhood in New Orleans. The editor at different times had asked for a manuscript and early in 1900 Cable had suggested an article of recollections. At the request of the same editor he wrote "The Clock in the Sky," but when the editor saw it he was afraid it would be resented in the South. It is a story of run-away slaves but treats the matter as simply a portion of a remote history. It was sold to *Scribner's Magazine* and appeared in September, 1901. A second story, "The Angel of the Lord," was completed in the fall at the request of Small, Maynard and Company of Boston for inclusion in a volume entitled *A House Party*. The twelve stories in the book were anonymous, the scheme being to let the readers, for a contest prize of $1000, identify the authors from a list of the twenty-five who had been asked to contribute. Cable's story, like "The Clock in the Sky," told of runaway slaves, and with the other story became a part of the volume *The Flower of the Chapdelaines,* published in 1918.

It was a matter of long habit with Cable to keep his hand in a multitude of things at the same time. He once wrote in his diary, November 11, 1888, "If I didn't keep going, going, I should go to pieces. I am like a top that will fall if it stops spinning." He now had no commitments outside his writing of fiction except the Home Culture Clubs and occasional lecturing and platform reading. He had to keep busy but could profitably spend no more than four or five hours a day at imaginative work. Not since his poetizing for the Drop Shot column had he written poetry seriously, but he always liked to compose verse for one occasion or another, to inscribe a book or to accompany a gift or to commemorate a friend's birthday. He had long been fond also of improvising verses and music, for a Sunday school class, say, a children's party, or some function at Smith College. *The Ladies' Home Journal* for December, 1899, printed "Children of Jesus: A Christmas Carol," previously rejected by the *Century,* with words and melody by Cable, harmonized by Harvey Rose Shelley. Another song, "The Lad with Ringlets," was sent to the same magazine but was declined. In 1900 he wrote the article on William Cullen Bryant for the new edition of *The Encyclopaedia Britannica* and also brought up to date the article on New Orleans he had supplied for the earlier edition.

Royalty payments on his books held up well. Sales were better in 1899 than for several years back, and payments from England—$175 from the new edition of *The Grandissimes* and $100 advance on *Strong Hearts*—were still small but larger than he had ever had at one time. On March 1, 1900, he told Scribner he was better off financially than in the three years past, but that statement must be taken alongside the fact that for nearly two years he had been drawing advances on *The Cavalier* and was almost monthly faced with paying off old debts and renewing notes at the bank. He never doubted that his books were being made to yield as much as possible. Scribner kept them in print, adding illustrations, changing bindings, or making new plates when they were needed, and worked constantly for more profitable arrangements abroad. In 1883 *Old Creole Days* had been put into two paper volumes at thirty cents each and at the same time into two deluxe volumes also. It was issued in 1897 with illustrations by Herter and again in two deluxe volumes. *Madame Delphine* appeared in a new binding with a preface added in 1896. *The Grandissimes* was issued in paper backs in 1890, again in 1899, with Herter's drawings and a new cover, only a year after it had appeared in the Tarryawhile edition. Laurence & Bullen took sheets for 250 copies of the illustrated *Old Creole Days* for the English market, and Hodder & Stoughton bought 100 copies of the illustrated *The Grandissimes* in sheets.

In 1899 *The Cable Story Book, Selections for School Reading* was added to the list of similar books published by Scribner for school use. The editors were Cable's daughter Lucy and Mary E. Burt, a public-school teacher and editor of several in the series, who became after this collaboration a warm friend of the Cable family. She later shared the cost of building a study at the rear of the Cables' house, one floor of which she would occupy during vacations. The *Story Book* included a sketch of the author's life and sample letters written to his children in the past. Two uncollected pieces were included, "The Children's New Orleans" and "New Orleans before the Capture," along with the story of Bras Coupé, "Jean-ah Poquelin," and "Gregory's Island." Cable had a hand in making the selections and in simplifying the dialect for school children.

At the end of 1901 financial matters stood better for Cable than ever before. In December, when *The Cavalier* had sold a hundred thousand copies, he could tell Scribner to send the odd dollars to him and leave ten thousand to his credit. The sale of *Bylow Hill* the next year was moderate but exceeded the immediate sale of any of his books before *The Cavalier*. Even so, his expenses were large and his income from other sources was almost nothing. The result was that before he had progressed far on another book he was again drawing advances from his publisher.

CHAPTER XXV

A TOWN FOR A GARDEN

A YEAR after *The Cavalier* was published, it was a play on the New York stage, and with this encouragement Cable worked more on dramatizations during the next two years than on the writing of fiction. For twenty years he had hoped to see his stories in the theater. Even before his decision in the summer of 1883 that the theater might be employed for moral purposes, proposals had come to him for adapting his writings for the stage. But not until 1889 did he undertake to write a stage play. Jamison Ball, formerly associated with the magazine *Judge,* had proposed to put "Grande Pointe" on the stage.[1] Cable confessed "a long-cherished intention to dramatize" the Bonaventure stories and so set to work with the assistance of the actor Frank Carlyle. But fearing that Ball was more daring than dependable, he declined to give him an option to buy the play outright. Joseph Jefferson read the book along with the acts Cable had written and joined Gilder, Mme Modjeska, and her husband, Charles Bozenta, in the opinion that further work on the play would be a waste of time.

The play was dropped, and no serious attempt was made for another ten years. In 1897 Lee Bernheim began a stage adaptation of *The Grandissimes,* and the next year Jeanette L. Gilder, of the *Critic,* Daniel Frohman, and Bronson Howard talked to Cable about theatrical possibilities, but nothing of his appeared on the stage except *Madame Delphine,* which had an experimental production in London.[2]

In the summer of 1901 Cable was wholly in theater business. He was himself writing a stage version of "Posson Jone'" and "Père Raphaël," in which both Daniel Frohman and Franklin Sargent showed some interest, and Minnie Maddern Fiske was considering *Madame Delphine.* But the liveliest concern was for *The Cavalier.* Julia Marlowe, encouraged by Robert Bridges of the Scribner house, read advance proof-sheets

---

[1] Ball proposed also to serialize *Bonaventure* and the stories of *Old Creole Days* through a newspaper syndicate, but Scribner did not encourage Cable to go into the venture.

[2] Bessie O'Connor had adapted and produced a one-act play of *Madame Delphine,* as she reported to Cable in letters of Aug. 4 and 8, 1900.

and by July had decided to accept the story. As the contract was drawn in November, the author and the dramatist, sharing equally, would receive $1000 in advance, 5 per cent royalty on the first $5000 a week, seven on the next $3000, and 10 per cent on all over $8000. At the opening of the new year, Paul Kester was at work on the dramatization, with assistance from Cable and another dramatist, George Middleton, and continued until the middle of November, when rehearsals began. On December 4 the play opened for two nights at the Hyperion in New Haven. Cable was present the first night and wired his wife, "The Cavalier is a great success. . . ." When Miss Marlowe had taken a series of curtain calls and the author was called, he went to the stage and said: "Ladies and Gentlemen—I cannot think of anything to say that would be entertaining—and true, and I cannot think of anything true that would be entertaining. For the first time in my life I am too inebriated to talk."[3]

Newspaper reports were favorable but reserved: the flavor of the novel and the characters had been kept and the role of Charlotte fitted Miss Marlowe better than any she had played for years, but there was too much talk and too little action. After an appearance at Troy on December 6, the play was at the Criterion in New York the following Monday, December 8. Seats were sold four weeks in advance, according to the notices. But it was apparent at once that all was not well. The *Tribune* reviewer wrote on December 9: "There are seventeen persons in the cast, and they are concerned in a military rigmarole that nobody can follow, unless, perhaps, by reading Mr. Cable's book. . . . The play is dreary." Improvements came in revisions made in the following weeks, as in the dropping of Charlotte's singing "The Star-Spangled Banner" at the deathbed of the Union captain. In the words of *Muncey's Magazine* in March, 1903, the play had in it "the elements that make for popular favor," and it drew a full house as a rule, but Jeanette L. Gilder wrote Cable late in the season,"it is generally known in the profession that it has not been a success, I mean not a success from the Marlowe point of view." The play was rented to Wallace Munro for road production the coming season, and in 1904-1905 it was on the road again for a short time.[4]

Following up his earlier attempt to make a play from "Posson Jone'," and "Père Raphaël," Cable struggled through much of the year 1902 with the scenario for a play from *Old Creole Days*. He finished a dramatization of *Madame Delphine* in the same year but failed to interest a producer. Varying his assault on the theater, he undertook next to pre-

[3] See the New Haven *Register*, Dec. 5, 1902.
[4] Dillingham to Cable, May 4, Oct. 21, 1905.

pare a new story directly for the stage. At the completion of *Bylow Hill* he turned at once to planning a new story, and by the end of 1902 was well into the book that would appear five years later as *Kincaid's Battery*. At this point he laid the novel aside and wrote a play using the same story. Augustus Thomas considered it late in 1903 but saw little hope for it. At the opening of 1904 Cable abandoned his dramatic undertakings and returned to the novel.

Louise Bartlett Cable died on February 27, 1904. Except for the death of Rebecca Cable in 1890, this was the first death in the large family since 1878, when the yellow fever had taken the child George Cable and Nettie Cox's husband. Before Louise's death there were fourteen in the family, counting those at the "other house," and she had been its hub and its anchor. At her death the family unity was shattered; without her standing firmly at the center, those on the fringes began to lose touch. And to Cable the loss disturbed every thread of his existence, for during their thirty-five years together they had shared their thoughts and aspirations with an uncommon completeness.

In 1904 the youngest child, Dorothea, was fifteen years old. She, Isabel, Margaret, and William were still at home, and the three oldest daughters were hardly less intimately in the family for having left the parental roof. The oldest daughter, Louise, had pursued her interest in art and in 1892 had kept a studio and taken pupils in Northampton. Late in that year she went to study in New York, where she had the advice of her father's friend, the Creole artist George Henry Clements. She was married to James Alfred Chard on December 7, 1894, choosing the seventh because it was a day of special significance in her family. Her parents had been married on the seventh, and they never failed to mention it in any of their letters written on that day. Mary, the second daughter, followed Louise to New York to do settlement work and in 1899—on June 7—was married to Alfred L. P. Dennis. Before leaving home she had been something of a secretary to her father and in New York she had joined Mary E. Burt in editing for Scribner's school series *The Eugene Field Book,* for which her father wrote an introduction.

The third daughter, Lucy, graduated from Smith College with literary honors in 1898 and soon had begun a career of her own. She edited with Mary E. Burt *The Cable Story Book* and *Don Quixote* and she served on the staff of the *Ladies' Home Journal*. William, who was nineteen in 1904, was a favorite of his father's. Because of a heart ailment he had required special attention as he grew up, and his father made occasion now and then to go with him into the woods or on a fishing trip. In August, 1903, the two of them had a two-weeks' vacation in New York.

In writing Alfred Chard of the projected trip on July 22, Cable fell into the playful note so much his habit in letters to members of his family and his friends: "We want to bum around on the water in any abandoned way, sailing, fishing and otherwise misbehaving, but keeping out of the lockup, and sleeping in bed under a roof."

W. Robertson Nicoll, after visiting at Northampton in 1896, wrote that Cable had "a beautiful wife with white hair, about fifty, tall and dark-eyed."[5] She had clear-cut features, softened by slightly full cheeks; intelligence, dignity, and kindliness blended in her eyes. The focal center of the multitudinous interests and activities of the Cable household, she yet managed to engage in remarkably varied activities. In addition to bearing eight children and managing the household while seven of them grew up, often with her husband away from home, she strove through reading and study of her own to keep pace with her husband and the associates that were theirs. Hardly one of her hundreds of letters to her husband failed to touch on household or financial matters. It happened often that she had to make decisions in his absence without the information she needed, perhaps because he had attempted to save her by turning the business of the Open Letter Club, say, or the Home Culture Clubs over to his assistants. Her nature was to take such matters seriously, as it was her husband's nature to discourage her doubts, to speak with assurance of the ultimate goal and to refer lightly or even flippantly to the intervening difficulties. Her temperament was a valuable foil and balance for his. Her letters written during a third of a century were as a rule matter-of-fact and restrained. Through hints rather than statements she said how much his letters meant to her—of one she said, "I read it over and put it under my pillow at night." At another time she wrote: "Such loving, sweet and tender letters as I used to get, before you allowed work to so thoroughly engross your thoughts, would go a very long way with me and largely satisfy my hunger."

At times Louise's health had been a matter for concern, especially in the 1870's, when five of her children were born. After the move north she had no serious complaints for two decades, though no doubt she stayed close to exhaustion much of the time. Vacations from the household were planned for her often, but whether she visited her daughters or her kinspeople or friends in New York or Boston, or went to seashore or mountain resorts, the family responsibilities were never long out of her mind. In June, 1901, she sailed for England with Mary E. Burt. Like her husband three years earlier, she sent home a diary-letter, and when

[5] John A. Hammerton, *Barrie*, pp. 274-75.

she landed at Portland, Maine, on September 16, she concluded what she called the vacation of her life. In December she was seriously ill, suffering from gallstones, but recovered and had long visits in New York and Boston in the spring. At the first of March, 1903, she went to New Orleans for her second visit since moving north. The first had been in 1888. Cable joined her for part of her visit and then continued his platform tour.[6]

Early in January, 1904, Louise was in New York, suffering from gallstones again. She had an operation late in the month and without leaving the hospital she died on February 27. The funeral was held at Tarryawhile the following Monday, and she was buried in Bridge Street Cemetery, where Rebecca had been buried fourteen years earlier. Henry van Dyke wrote Cable on March 2: "It always seemed to me as if she came out of the New Testament, as if she must have been one of those who saw Jesus and ministered to him." On March 5, a week after her death, Cable answered van Dyke:

My beloved one rejoiced for me in your affection for me, and now I bless you for your sweet words of her. I want to speak for a moment of her to you, to say no more than two or three reasons why her loss grows on me from hour to hour. One of these reasons was her beauty. . . .

I name these things because they are those which, more than some others, make sorrow so much sweeter than forgetting. And a second of them is her worship of me. It was glorious to see—it is glorious to remember—how in the days of her last illness, when she began to see her mortal peril, her love to her friends, her children and, most of all to me—who know as no one else ever may know how poorly merited it was—set in like a great storm and raged through all her being.

And the third of these reasons is her dependence on me. She never breathed of happiness, of any gladness, while believing that I was unhappy. She was not of nearly so joyous a nature as many friends believed her. I had always to keep her glad. This is why her pictures show that the longer she lived the more serenity and pleasantness was in her heart and mind. The latest of them all, post-dating fourteen years of her ailment, beams with the sweetest and most abundant light. I did not know how dear this task was to me until all at once it was taken away forever.

I will write no more. I have had a great share of happiness, more than my share, and even my bereavement is gilded with so many and such sweet extenuations that I am moved to seek others less comforted, less compensated, and take their sorrows into mine.

[6] See the *Times-Democrat*, March 8, 15, 1903.

The death of Louise of course broke the pattern of life at Tarry-awhile. Cable chose to stay close at home through the summer, except for a few short trips. Margaret, Isabel, Dorothea, and William had long visits with their married sisters and in summer camps. Lucy returned to New York and became a reader in the *Collier's* office. Cable had too many philosophical, rational resources to fall back on for his sorrow to weigh him down for long. The obligation to be cheerful was a cardinal belief of his, and prolonged mourning had seemed to him a violation of man's better nature. It was only natural for him to say to his children, as he wrote Alfred and Louise Chard on August 26: "God help us to live nobly in memory of her. Let us make courage and cheer our tribute to her and our oblation to Him." His own way to fill the vacancy left by his wife was to keep at his writing. *Kincaid's Battery* had been in writing already two years and it must continue growing to justify the advances he needed from Scribner.

On June 23 he received the Doctorate of Letters from Bowdoin College, which was honoring its alumnus Nathaniel Hawthorne on the hundredth anniversary of his birth. Yale University had conferred the same degree on him on October 23, 1901, when Mark Twain, Howells, Gilder, Thomas Nelson Page, Woodrow Wilson, and Theodore Roosevelt were among those similarly honored.[7]

The Home Culture Clubs marked on April 12, 1905, a new stage in their history. From the beginning Cable's plan had been to keep costs to members of the clubs to practically nothing and to meet expenses through special subscriptions. Contributions from Northampton citizens had been generous, but costs of the classes and the reading rooms grew year by year, and the greatest need was for better quarters. It was to meet this need that Cable approached his friend Andrew Carnegie. In February, 1903, Carnegie agreed to give fifty thousand dollars for buildings on the condition that five thousand dollars a year be guaranteed locally for five years. The condition was met, and in the spring of 1905 Carnegie Hall was completed.

April 12 was set for the dedication ceremonies. Original drawings used to illustrate Cable's books were borrowed from Scribner and the Century Company and hung in the rooms; the program was planned in great detail, and the parts were rehearsed. Carnegie and his wife came, making their first visit to Northampton. At the inspection of Carnegie Hall in the afternoon Mayor Connor and seven former mayors were present. Cable presented Mrs. Carnegie the key to the building, in a

[7] See Brander Matthews, *The Tocsin of Revolt* (New York, 1922), pp. 289-90.

jeweled box made of wood, satin, and metals from local factories. After a dinner party at Cable's house came the main ceremony at Carnegie Hall, attended by thirteen hundred. On the stage were the chorus of the clubs, the architect and the contractor, public-school teachers, the presidents and faculty members of Smith College, Amherst College, and Williston Seminary. In the audience officers and teachers of the clubs sat together, as did the women of the Old Members' Association, and a group of twenty-five Scotchmen honoring Carnegie. Mayor Connor said that in the clubs Cable had inaugurated a new experiment in education; Cable summarized the history and the aims of the clubs; Carnegie called Cable "our valued friend and model worker for the good of others."[8]

The Home Culture Clubs were eighteen years old when Carnegie Hall was dedicated. In those years the growth had been steady and great, and their nature and their methods had changed, though the goal was the same. The clubs still had as a motto "The private home is the public hope"; they were still preaching the doctrine of "culture in the home, . . . culture of the home, and of the individual for the home."[9] But experience in organizing the clubs had revealed that many of those in greatest need of what the clubs might supply either had no homes on which to build or had no interest in the weekly meetings. It would be a mistake, the conclusion was, not to exploit for the ultimate purpose of the clubs the desire that already existed for social amusement and for instruction in special subjects. In answer to these needs the functions of the clubs were transferred, at first slowly and then completely, to the headquarters.

The first step toward this end had been the reading rooms, from which the "Stranger's Rest" in Carnegie Hall was a development. Another need recognized early was presented by the boys whom barren homes or other causes forced to seek amusement and companionship on the streets. In answer the programs for young people were started. It was an innovation in the staid New England town for a public organization to teach social dancing and to open pool rooms to boys and men for the fee of only one and a half cents a cue. But in Cable's practical view these programs would meet the demands of young people that otherwise would be met by commercial enterprises in which public welfare would receive small consideration.

From the earliest home clubs, the desire for information, for instruction, had been apparent. Once Adelene Moffat learned that a club she

[8] See the Northampton *Daily Herald*, April 12, 13, 1905.
[9] Cable, "The Home-Culture Clubs," *World's Work*, XII (Oct., 1906), 8110-14.

had organized died after the first meeting because no one of the group was willing to read aloud to the others. Success in such a club would require leadership its own members could not supply. The solution lay in pulling the clubs into the clubhouse, where leaders, tutors, or instructors could be supplied to larger groups and hence more economically. Thus began the program of instruction which had expanded so much by 1905 that Cable could speak of "our People's College." Volunteer tutoring was done by 175 Smith College students and two dozen others. There were classes in almost any subjects that could be named. A priest taught English, for example, to a class of Polish migrants.

There were over five hundred clubhouse members, who paid one dollar initiation fee and another dollar a year dues, for which they received access to the buildings and as much tutoring as they wanted. The game rooms and reading rooms were open and free to anyone who might drop in. Special classes in gymnastics, dancing, singing, cooking, embroidery, gardening, and other such subjects were held by experts who were paid from the special dues collected. In addition there were free lectures, often series of lectures on a topic such as gardening. There were clubs within the larger organization which met in its rooms. One was the Social and Literary Club, which began shortly before the Home Culture Clubs were organized and continued more than thirty years. Another was the Economics Club, in which Cable was active, as was also Calvin Coolidge. The most active of the subgroups was the Women's Council, which occupied its own building, the Harriet James House, and concerned itself chiefly with household matters. It kept a file of literature on domestic subjects, and another file on gardening; it arranged art displays and the lending of prints; it managed an exchange of household goods, plants, and shrubs. It sponsored classes and lectures and through study and consultation attempted to foster better relations between household servants and their employers.

In 1906 the Home Culture Clubs had nine salaried workers and five working part time. The total "workers and beneficiaries" exceeded fifteen hundred. The yearly expenditures had passed seven thousand dollars.

On September 2, 1905, Cable wrote his sister Nettie: "I never expected to have a whole town for my garden, but that's how 'tis." A program he had begun six years earlier as a supplement to the main purpose of the Home Culture Clubs had enlisted hundreds of householders in a flower garden competition and was literally changing the face of Northampton. In starting the garden program, Cable was following one of his old loves. Growing up and living forty years in what was known as the garden district of New Orleans, which he called the garden city, and prompted by his mother's interest in flowers, he had loved flowers from boyhood. As he recalled New Orleans in writing about it years afterward, he told of the flowers, shrubs, trees, and birds in a way to leave no doubt of that love. To Northampton he transferred his interest in gardening and at the Red House he began the practice of having friends plant trees on his grounds. Henry Ward Beecher planted the first in 1889, the Beecher Elm, which was moved three years later to Tarryawhile and was joined afterwards by trees planted by James M. Barrie, Max O'Rell, Felix Adler, Henry van Dyke, Sol Smith Russell, Hamilton Wright Mabie, Arthur Conan Doyle, Sidney Lee, Minnie Maddern Fiske, and others. When Cable moved to the new home in 1892, he set about improving his own grounds and the street as well. His own three acres, in the edge of what had long been called Paradise Woods, dropped sharply at the back down to Mill River, affording a perfect setting for contour walks among the trees and for the three fish pools he built. Early in his gardening at Tarryawhile he had the advice and plans of his friend George E. Waring, and for thirty years afterward the garden was relaxation and pleasure to him. In a long essay published in 1914, "My Own Acre," he gave a description and a history of his garden, using it to illustrate his views on gardening and leaving no doubt of the joy he found in it.

This essay was one of six which were brought in 1914 into the volume *The Amateur Garden*. The other essays had appeared in magazines during the preceding ten years. In these essays Cable set forth the philosophy of gardening he had evolved over many years; all of them have their chief point of reference in the citywide garden program he had instituted in Northampton. During his visit to Scotland in 1898 he had learned of the garden competition Andrew Carnegie sponsored and financed along with other programs at Dunfermline, his birthplace. Cable brought the plan home with him, along with Carnegie's promise of money for prizes. Sixty gardens were entered the first season, 235 the fourth year, and more than 1000 in 1913, representing about a fourth of the houses in the town. At first Cable enrolled, visited, and judged the gardens largely by himself, but soon the Women's Council of the Home Culture Clubs took over much of the responsibility. In 1911 the gardeners were organized into neighborhood clubs of about 7 members each. The procedure in 1913 was for the Women's Council members to enroll the competitors, visit, and advise them through the season. The secretary then selected the best 150 gardens; after that Cable picked the gardens to receive the lesser of the 21 prizes and the 4 to be judged for the highest honors. Finally Cable with a professional gardener and another amateur judged these four.

As Cable conceived the American garden it should be democratic in all its aspects, and the competition was conducted accordingly. The work must be done by the competitor without hired help and with only such advice as could be had from books or neighbors or officers of the organization. The whole yard must be entered and must contain at least fifty square yards. Improvement from year to year, not simply the final result, was considered in the judging. The town was divided into seven areas, each of which would receive three awards, and no two of the three top awards could go to one area—thus the poorer sections were assured a share of the honors. The judging was on four points: layout, harmony, condition, and duration. To support the program, the Women's Council provided literature, lectures, and courses. The aim was as nearly as possible to prevent expense from being a barrier to anyone. Later a prize was added for gardens worked by hired help.

The Carnegie Garden Competition, as it was called, was proper to the broader activities of the Home Culture Clubs, and Cable's desire to promote it had the same logic as his desire to found the parent organization. Convinced that "beautiful things light up the affections," he wanted every house to wear the smile of a pleasant garden, to have the appropriate garments of trees, shrubs, flowers, and lawn. Every householder would have the benefit of his own garden, and besides would be drawn outside, and everyone would share the beauty of every garden. It was natural to Cable, further, to preach this particular gospel abroad, as he had done with other schemes for social betterment. He lectured on the subject in other towns and before the organizational meeting of the National Federation of Art at Washington, May 13, 1909, where he read the paper "The Northampton Prize Flower Garden Competition."[10] The Northampton example was followed elsewhere, at Springfield, Massachusetts, for example, where a local newspaper, the *Daily Republican,* and the Amateur Horticultural Society sponsored a similar program. Cable spoke in support of the effort on March 12, 1909, showing stereopticon views of gardens made before and after the owners had entered the competition.[11] At home Cable lent support to the gardening at Smith College and at the Williston Seminary in Easthampton.[12]

He remained president of the Carnegie Garden Competition, and until 1922 he was never absent from the annual program at which

[10] See the Washington *Post,* May 12, 1909.

[11] See the Springfield *Daily Republican,* March 13, 1909.

[12] See the *Daily Hampshire Gazette,* Oct. 5, 1904. Cable described the procedure and the results at Williston in the essay "Where to Plant What." See also Rose Bartlett, "How One Man Made His Town Bloom," *Ladies' Home Journal,* XXVII (March, 1910), 36, 80, 82.

awards were made. It was an activity he enjoyed greatly—for the conspicuous good results it achieved and for the delight he had in visiting the gardens. It was lovely, he wrote Nettie on September 2, 1905, "to see women's faces and men's too, light up with pleasure when I say I've come to see the garden."

In visiting the gardens as well as in writing on the subject, he expounded a few principles: soften angles, corners, fences, and walls by appropriate planting; avoid chopping up a yard into bits; adapt the shrubs and flowers, beds and walks to the house, and lead into a semblance of undisturbed nature at the farthest points from the house; keep the garden individual by imitating principles, not details; avoid formal gardens, as appropriate less to residences than to parks and cemeteries; cultivate a careful irregularity; employ "the roaming line," the free line bold in its curves; ornamentation must honestly be such and must lay no false claim to utility; a garden should reach its climax toward the back, not on the front; make the garden show that man is at the same time the child and the master of nature.

From the Carnegies' visit at the dedication of the new Home Culture Club building came an invitation for Cable to visit them again at Skibo. With Lucy he sailed on the *Cymric* on May 12 and was in London on the twentieth. After two weeks there, which included a run up to Oxford for two days, they went to Dunfermline, then to Edinburgh, and on to Skibo for a week at the middle of June. Returning to Liverpool, they sailed for home June 23 on the *Republic*. Much of the way Cable was retracing his steps of seven years earlier and seeing old friends: Barrie and Robertson Nicoll in London, Douglas, Simpson, and White in Edinburgh, and Carnegie at Skibo. From these men and their families he and Lucy had the warmest welcome, but they were committed to no public appearances and were happy to put up at hotels and do their own sightseeing. The manuscript of *Kincaid's Battery* had been left at home. This was a vacation, for rest and for relief from the lonely life at Tarryawhile. It was a pleasant task for him to sit with Lucy in Hyde Park and at Lincoln's Inn Fields to make notes for use in the garden program at home. It was especially pleasant to go for the first time to Dunfermline, the ancient capital of Scotland, where Carnegie had set up a fund of half a million pounds to maintain the park, the public bath, and the garden competition. In London he and Lucy visited the historic shrines and the galleries as well as the parks. At Skibo the welcome was even warmer than before; he and Carnegie felt closer now, since they had become virtually partners in the Home Culture Clubs.

Home early in July, Cable went back to the manuscript of *Kincaid's Battery*. Late in the year he had a serious illness and a minor operation from which he was slowly recovering through December. These were lonely days at Tarryawhile. To Alfred Chard he wrote on September 2: "August has been a lonesome month in spite of all I could do to fill it with work and play. I tell you so confidentially; I don't tell myself so, because that sort of thing spoils myself." Early in December he attended the banquet honoring Mark Twain, though the travel to New York taxed him heavily. In the speech there he kept pace with the hilarity and good fellowship of the occasion, recalling incidents of the reading tour twenty-one years earlier.[13] On December 8 he wrote Alfred and Louise Chard:

It was not practicable for me to celebrate the 7th as I should have done if I had been strong enough to go across town. The bleakness of the burial place at this time of year gives me not a little pain at heart.

But my dears, this is not the way to write to you for whom I should study every cheerful word and exhort against all fretting, chafing and re-pining. Oh, my bonnie little Louise, be bright. A courageous blitheness is . . . a get-rich-quick scheme without a tinge of fraud or error in it.

His housekeeper at Tarryawhile was Dorothea, who was sixteen years old and still in school. Isabel was in New York much of the time; Margaret had married recently and moved away. In writing to her husband, Harold Brewster, on December 12, he slipped into the cheerful banter which was habitual with him:

To begin to reply to your letter of yesterday at its latter end, I don't like my son to call himself my son-in-law; it may be close to the facts, but it's mighty poor poetry.

Secondly I am glad to hear that Margaret's happiness is confined within the bounds of reasonableness, ("reasonably happy" you pronounce her). When anyone can send oceans of love and still keep within rational bounds there is little more to be desired except continuance. . . .
P. S. Someone cut us off. I was going to say, deluges of love to you and Bunnie.

His nickname for Margaret had long been Bunnie. Isabel was married in May and after that Dorothea went to live with the Dennises at the University of Wisconsin. Tarryawhile was rented again in the summer. Cable and William lived in the study and took their meals with Mary Louise, as they had done the two preceding summers.

On November 24, 1906, Cable was married to Eva C. Stevenson, a native of Versailles, Kentucky. The letter he had written informing

[13] See *Harper's Weekly*, XLIX (Dec. 23, 1905), 1883-1914.

the Carnegies had prompted Carnegie to reply on November 2, "You have written us a beautiful letter. We think it the best ever written surely by man under similar conditions." He had written on October 31:

In addressing the lady who has honored me I gave her clearly to understand that I offered a heart which held and must ever hold the memory of a lost mate in tenderest love and devotion. But Miss Stevenson is one who can see as plainly as I that love never emptied a true heart or made its fountain run slack, and she knows that a cherished and sacred past no more diminishes the soul's capacity for a new love than does the love of my living children.

Miss Eva Colegate Stevenson is a woman of forty-eight, of charming social accomplishments, a beautiful musician, large in mind and heart, of a mirthful temper and ardent affections. My children seem as glad as I over my good fortune and I trust my dear friends may find cause to rejoice with me as well.

The newspaper story that Miss Stevenson is a woman of large fortune is —I am sorry for her sake to say—quite wide of the truth. She has merely enough income to assure her that our marriage adds nothing to my burdens.

Dear friends, I pray you rejoice with me! I will not say this matter makes me happy, for I was happy, and know that happiness comes only from within. But I know you will understand that this makes it easier to be happy and gives me more of myself to devote to the happiness of others. We marry sometime in the latter part of November as quietly as we can.

Cable had first met Eva with her mother at her home in Lexington, Kentucky, and had seen her on subsequent trips south. After seeing her once in Cincinnati, he wrote his wife, December 15, 1901: ". . . a gray haired spinster, she is, but a woman of fine quality, refined and accomplished." They were married among relatives of hers in Philadelphia and went directly to Tarryawhile, to fill the emptiness that had come almost two years earlier and had been intensified as Lucy, Margaret, and Isabel had moved away.

CHAPTER XXVI

NOVELS OF THE WAR AND THE RIVER

KINCAID'S BATTERY was published on November 14, 1908, after six years in its composition. Royalties on Cable's books had fallen away since the peak reached with *The Cavalier,* and in the interim his pen had added only bits to his income. The two garden articles in 1904 and the third in 1906, along with an article on "The Home-Culture Clubs" in the *World's Work* of October, 1906, were his only publications between *Bylow Hill* and *Kincaid's Battery*. He still lectured and read, but only occasionally. Before the new book was published Cable had drawn advances of $7500 on it, and had asked for a further advance which Scribner had refused. Scribner realized that Cable was spending more than his books were yielding, and it seemed unlikely that *Kincaid's Battery* would do more than repay the advances. Efforts to sell the serial rights were unsuccessful.

On October 25 Cable printed in the New York *Herald* a short article on the writing of the book. Already he had told Scribner he enjoyed writing *Kincaid's Battery* even more than *The Cavalier,* and now he said he thought the method he had followed the best he had ever employed. He began with the intention of "presenting a phase of life unfamiliar both to general experience and to literature," yet one with which he had exceptional familiarity. The story would be "a strong combination of character portrayal with plot, with . . . a conflict of passions, wills, schemes and adventurous and tragic fates," all harmonized with historic events. First he made a scenario, which he studied and revised for months before writing a page of narrative, so that he had every character so clearly and so fully in mind that in the composition no one of them ever balked. Though a story of the war, it was primarily a love story. In a letter to his publisher on September 24, as he finished the book, he said his intention had been to make neither the love interest nor the historical interest incidental to the other, but to make them "component parts of a thoroughly homogeneous whole."

"I believe I am blameless in this story," he wrote in the *Herald,* "of trying to prove anything or preach anything. . . . I hope it may preach

as character and conduct always will and must whenever they are, as
the critics say, convincing." There is never a glimpse in the novel of
the issues of the war or of the suffering. It is glamourized war in which
the bravery, the intrigue, and the pain are beautiful, or perhaps better,
pretty and pleasant. There has been bravery on both sides, as one would
remark of an athletic match, and when all is over, members of the
battery return home to resume their lives, proud of their heroism, and
with no particular regrets at their defeat. All controversy and unpleasantness is expunged from the war of the story. Even Beast Butler's rule in
New Orleans stands unjudged except for a few passing remarks by residents of the city.

Even so, the military incidents are the best in the book, for in them
the reader is caught up in the rush and excitement the author habitually
put into such scenes. The other scenes, mainly in boudoirs and parlors,
employ hinting and allusiveness, but the reader may not find enough
weight in them to justify the attention required to follow the development. The only issues in these scenes are the love entanglements. Cable
had remarked to his wife ten years earlier that his fiction had suffered
because he had withdrawn from the problems of the world around him.
Kincaid's Battery calls this remark to mind. It seems appropriately the
work of a man with half a dozen daughters who touches the world
chiefly through the Home Culture Clubs and the Garden Clubs—not a
man fighting the battles of right and justice against both his neighbors
and the institutions of his time, as Cable had done during the first twenty
years of his literary work.

Cable thought of *Kincaid's Battery* as a counterpart to *The Cavalier,*
telling of the artillerymen in the Civil War as the earlier book told of
the cavalrymen.[1] *The Cavalier* had followed his own tracks through
the fighting in Mississippi; the new book used his observations at the
fall of New Orleans and through the Federal occupation, and also the
siege of Vicksburg as he had it in the diary of Dora Miller he had published. The convincing portions of the book are those built closely on
his own experience; the rush of the youths into the Confederate army,
the blessing of the units and the presenting of their flags, the tension in
New Orleans before, during, and after the fall to Farragut's gunboats,
the banishment from the city and the escape to the Confederate line, the
moves about Mississippi, including Madison County and most of the
towns Cable knew as a soldier, the return of Albert Sidney Johnston's
body from Shiloh. The abolition school mistress of the story was based

[1] See an interview in the *Times-Democrat,* May 3, 1903.

on Mrs. Dora Miller. In *Kincaid's Battery* Cable continued a practice he had followed in earlier stories of alluding to characters and incidents of his other books. Dr. Sevier, Ned Ferry and Charlotte Durand, Richard Thorndyke Smith, Jules St. Ange, and various members of the Grandissime clan are mentioned.

Before *Kincaid's Battery* was finished, Cable had forgotten that he had once said it would be his last,[2] and he had begun repeating the cycle he had followed in each of his later novels. He had decided on the general material for his next book and before the end of 1908 had begun framing and filling in the plan, while at the same time assembling information before beginning to write. Like the preceding book the new one, *Gideon's Band,* occupied him six years. It was published in 1914, when he was seventy years old.

In the spring of 1907 had occurred an episode which worked itself out painfully for Cable, members of his family, some of his friends, and the future of the Home Culture Clubs. On March 8 he informed Adelene Moffat that the clubs could afford to employ only one full-time secretary and that the changed nature of the organization required that officer to be a man. He could not continue to fill himself the place of bookkeeper and cashier, as he had recently done in the interest of economy. Miss Moffat had been secretary of the clubs for eighteen years, and during that time had made them her career. Cable was aware of these facts when he wrote her in 1907: "In plain words, then, the work which we have so long pursued together offers you that release which I have longed to see it offer me these ten years and which I would joyfully accept in your place if I could." But this assertion left much unsaid, and in the ensuing weeks other reasons for her dismissal became known at least to those directly concerned. There were charges that she had grown neglectful of her work and in the past two years had attempted to alienate the other staff members from Cable. The vote of the board on March 18 was unanimous to ask for her resignation, but one member was absent, Frank Lyman, the son of E. H. R. Lyman, who had given the first building and had been the greatest single benefactor of the clubs before Carnegie's gifts. Since Lyman's death, his son and daughter had continued to contribute twelve hundred dollars a year. They had become close friends of Miss Moffat's and now abruptly discontinued their contribution. Furthermore, the Woman's Council asked the board to reconsider its action. Thus the organization was threatened with a drastic reduction in its income and a split within itself. It was a year before the clubs were in smooth water again.

[2] Cable to Louise Bartlett Cable, May 9, 1902.

In that year the books were audited by a firm of accountants and the financial affairs were studied by a local board. The two reports, presented publicly in January, 1908, commended the management of the club affairs, financial and otherwise. They threw more light on the whole program, and the more light, said the *Daily Hampshire Gazette* on January 24, "the better the whole admirable public benefaction." Lyman was replaced on the board, which already had as members the president of Williston Seminary, the president of Smith College, and among the others a Northampton lawyer, Calvin Coolidge, who had become a member of the board in 1904 and secretary in 1906. Carnegie came forward with $1500 a year to meet the current expenses, and Cable inaugurated a campaign to raise a permanent fund, against another such emergency. He contributed himself $1000 and later added $250 more. The goal of $30,000 was reached ten years later. Before the end of 1909 the clubs had been renamed The People's Institute, in recognition of the redefined purpose and activities, and the entire program moved forward with greater security and greater public support than ever before.

"Stoop low, lift gently, raise high, that is our rule," Cable once said of the Home Culture Clubs. The same rule had prompted his interest in Okolona Industrial College (more appropriately named School instead of College after 1911). In 1903 he sent a contribution to the lowly school which had been founded a few months earlier at the town of Okolona in northeastern Mississippi. Its founder and president was Wallace A. Battle, a negro graduate of Berea College. While in the East raising money the next year, Battle visited in Cable's home. In 1905 Cable became a trustee of Okolona; the next year he arranged for Battle to speak in a church at Northampton, and in 1907 he spoke himself in behalf of the school in Springfield, Massachusetts. In the years following, he visited Okolona on his trips south; he stood surety for part of the school indebtedness; and he was quoted in the press on the needs of the school for money.[3] As a trustee in the twenty years before his death he gave the school his support and the benefit of his long experience in similar endeavors.

Cable's son, William Noble, died on June 2, 1908. Virtually invalided by a faulty heart, he had grown even closer to his father because of his restricted activities. To Scribner Cable wrote on July 7: "My boy was my bosom friend and as perfect a gentleman and irreproachable as ever I knew."

Beginning with the winter of 1908-1909, Cable followed much the

[3] See the Boston *Evening Transcript*, April 16, 1912.

same yearly routine the rest of his life: wintering in Atlantic City, Bermuda, New Orleans, or Florida in his last two years, and spending the rest of each year at Northampton. New Orleans was especially attractive, for on the way down or back he could stop off at Okolona and Berea and Versailles, Kentucky, Eva's home; he could renew acquaintances in Louisiana and could refresh his memory or hunt out materials for his writing. He must have given some thought to the plea Robert Underwood Johnson repeated often, that he steep himself again in New Orleans and write more stories of the old Creole days.

On January 4, 1909, he and Eva reached New Orleans on the steamer *Antilles,* for her first visit to the city and his first since 1903. Walking the streets reminded him of his age and of the twenty-five years since he had moved north. He need look only at the graybeards, for he could know only them. Marion Baker had died recently, as had also Mollie E. Moore Davis, a fiction writer he had known thirty years ago. His brother James came over from his home at Long Beach on the Mississippi Gulf coast. His reception in the city was more satisfying than ever before. The *Picayune* and the *Times-Democrat* each carried a photograph and a more than friendly interview on January 5—he was a returned celebrity, worth quoting in whatever he had to say. He was invited to read before the girls of the New Orleans Institute. It warmed his heart to find the new friendliness and to have the numerous offers of assistance which followed the newspaper statements that he was collecting material for a novel.

Before returning north late in February, he had written three short pieces. For the *Book-News Monthly* of Philadelphia, which was to devote its April issue to him, he wrote "New Orleans Revisited."[4] He wrote also an introduction for the volume Scribner was to make of "Posson Jone'" and "Père Raphaël," illustrated by Stanley M. Arthurs, and an essay on the New Orleans gardens, the fourth of the essays later collected in *The Amateur Garden.* The next winter there was no trip south, and Cable suffered an attack of pneumonia which left him incapacitated for work until summer. Again the next year he was sick and stayed at Tarryawhile, but in the winter of 1911-1912 he and Eva returned to New Orleans. Again he was generously received. He addressed the Forum meeting in the Colonial Theater on February 4, 1912, on the subject "Civic Conscience and Civic Pride." The newspapers applauded his address, but the audience was disappointed, the *Picayune* reporter said, because he "neglected to tell stories and anecdotes, an art

[4] In the same issue Viola Roseboro' had an article on Cable, pp. 566-68.

in which he excels."[5] The next year he and Eva wintered at Paget, Bermuda, and on November 19, 1913, he had a cataract removed that had made one of his eyes useless for three years. He went to his friend S. Weir Mitchell in Philadelphia, who recommended a surgeon and looked after the arrangements. While his eye was regaining its strength, he began using a dictating machine, which he adopted enthusiastically.

During these years death was thinning Cable's friends among his contemporaries. Richard Watson Gilder died in November, 1909, and when Cable wrote a tribute to appear with others in the *Century* the next February, he stated without reservation his esteem for his former editor. In recent years they had grown close together again, though there was little business between them. Each had displayed frankness and mellowness enough to bridge the coolness stretching back almost twenty years to the time when they were enthusiastic editor and striving author. In 1910 Page Baker died in New Orleans. Mark Twain died in the same year, and Cable spoke at the memorial ceremonies in Carnegie Hall on November 30.

As his friends fell out, Cable was drawn closer to those who remained. His friendship with Charles Scribner had strengthened through its forty years' duration. Robert Underwood Johnson, successor in Gilder's editorial chair, restored much of the cordiality between Cable and the Century Company that had existed before 1890. Johnson was permanent secretary of the American Academy and in that office relied heavily on Cable as his confidential adviser. Already a member of the Institute, Cable was elected to the Academy in 1908. Johnson pleaded for stories just as he and Gilder had done nearly forty years earlier, and for the same kind of stories. Once he wrote, October 3, 1911: "If you could only be induced to write for the *Century* some new 'Old Creole Days' stories you could have shekels for them! . . . Some time I am going to take you out behind the barn and talk to you like a Dutch uncle about your neglect of that early field." But Cable got nothing ready to meet Johnson's special request for the fortieth anniversary number and he did not appear again in the *Century*. When Johnson resigned the editorship on May 31, 1913, Cable's ties with the magazine were severed finally.

Franklin Head came occasionally to Tarryawhile on his trips east from Chicago, as did William Beer, who was Cable's closest friend in New Orleans after Marion Baker's death. In April, 1907, he attended ceremonies at Pittsburgh honoring Andrew Carnegie, and a year later he went to New York for the dedication of the New York University

[5] Feb. 5. See also the *Picayune* of Feb. 3 and the *States* of Feb. 5.

buildings, but only because he felt an "imperative call" to go. He had slipped quietly into the routine of age, calmer but hardly less busy than formerly. From nine to one every day he wrote on his novel, considering one manuscript page a fair morning's work. In the afternoon he read proof, wrote letters, visited gardens, or supervised work in his own garden. In 1911 he stayed at his desk and for the first time in twelve years allowed a deputy to judge the garden competition in his place. More and more he acknowledged the need for recreation, which he found increasingly in his garden. On May 14, 1913, he wrote Eva: "What recreation—re-creation—the garden is to me! When I left the study at 4:30 I felt like a lost thing in a desert; now I am ready for to-morrow's work." Sometimes he walked to his sister Mary Louise's for tea, and perhaps played checkers with her.

Faithful to what had become a cardinal principal with him, he sought joy in every day, and usually found it. "It is not easy to keep one's due sense of appreciation up to all that is lovely in this life of ours," he wrote Eva on June 21, 1907, while she was away a few days. Exhaustion had forced him to take a nap during his working hours. But he wrote in the same letter: "The world is so beautiful to look upon to-day, so sweet to smell and hear; so full of peace, safety and abundance, so ready for almost any two human creatures to exchange kindness and joys." And farther on, "If you'll keep bright you may rely on me to do so." The tone of banter and quipping had not disappeared from the letters to his daughters but it was less common than it had once been. More characteristic now was the tone of a letter to Louise Chard written on December 7, 1908:

Though the day is darkening to its close and I ought to be out in the fresh air after hours at the desk, I must first write to my dear children in remembrance of this anniversary, the thirty-ninth of my first wedding day. I want to recall with her sweet, dear children and mine your mother's love, her beauty, her virtues, and her unselfish ambitions for all of us. It makes my loving memory of her grow the more glowing when I remind myself of all the goodness, intelligence and nobility of you, my sweet daughters, in whose characters, and in whose husbands and children I do so deeply rejoice. God bless and keep you all.

On September 14, 1910, his daughter Lucy was married to Henry Wolf Biklé, a lawyer for the Pennsylvania Railroad in Philadelphia. Only one daughter, Dorothea, was now unmarried.

Cable was elected in December, 1909, to the advisory council of the Simplified Spelling Board, and thus joined Mark Twain, Carnegie, Gilder, Brander Matthews, Theodore Roosevelt, William James, and others in arguing for more rational spelling; in 1913 he was elected a member of the Board.

For the *Book-News Monthly* of November, 1909, Cable wrote a short sketch, "Thomas Nelson Page: A Study in Reminiscence and Appreciation." He recalled that twenty-two years earlier Page had introduced himself as they stood waiting for a train in Washington and they had ridden to Richmond together. That had been in May, 1887, when the South was ringing with denunciation of Cable's stand on the Negro question. In the sketch of Page he restated what he had said many times in the early controversy, that the Southern system was "frankly and conscientiously designed to promote the elevation of one part of that community by purposely massing another part beneath it and by reserving the very name of public society, as well as of private, to the upper element alone"—in contrast to the New England system, which was "designed for the larger task of uplifting and advancing its entire people as one politically undivided mass." But he mentioned also "the crassness of the practical results" in both sections and he passed over, furthermore, the fact that Page's stand in his published writings was opposed to his own concerning the role of the Negro since emancipation. His purpose was merely to note the differences of opinion and to present Page as a noble representative of the upper element in Southern society, as "a striking instance of the things he so lovingly tells about," as "the story teller and novelist who stands unsurpassed as an interpreter of the highest social life in the choicest South of yesterday and to-day." His own views had not changed, but he no longer wished to debate the issues.

Except for two gardening articles, already mentioned, and the article on William Cullen Bryant for the eleventh edition of the *Encyclopaedia Britannica* in 1911, Cable published only one more short piece of any consequence. That was an essay entitled "My Philosophy," in *Good Housekeeping,* June, 1915, which he had read before the American Academy of Arts and Letters on November 19 of the previous year.[6] In this essay he said: "This world seems to me as definitely for joy as for use or discipline; not a world with which we should have as little to do as we may, but as much as we can. Both its joy and our own are one of the

[6] The address was printed in the *Proceedings* of the Academy the next year, after its magazine publication.

debts we daily owe it." The "graces of character" are courage, fidelity, and affection, and the products are beauty and joy. In words quoted here from Charlotte Oliver in *The Cavalier,* he concluded, "As to resurrection, punishment, and reward, I can't see what my noblest choice has to do with them; they seem to be God's part of the matter; mine is to love perfect beauty and perfect joy, both in and infinitely beyond myself."

The publication of *Kincaid's Battery* revived after four years the possibilities of getting a play on the stage. In 1909 Cable returned to the earlier dramatization of the novel and working with Albert Howard Hasbrook completed a new version by November 15. Half a dozen theater people showed an interest in this play or other possibilities in his books, but no play reached the stage. In 1914 there was a flurry involving a new stage version of *Madame Delphine* and a four-act play entitled *Old Creole Days* and employing characters from several of his books. In 1912 had come the first nibble in regard to movie production, and in 1914 a contract was drawn with the Vitagraph Company for the movie rights of *Madame Delphine.* The down payment of $250 was all Cable realized, however. These failures were the more disappointing because Cable needed money. In 1912 he had drawn the full $7500 Scribner had agreed to advance on the novel he was writing, and efforts to sell the serial rights were again disappointing. Late in 1911 Andrew Carnegie remarked that if Cable ever needed a pension, it would be forthcoming "mitey quick," and after a few weeks Cable inquired about borrowing $5000. Carnegie preferred instead to send $1000 a year until the new book would be finished. Thus it was that Carnegie began the assistance which Cable said saved his home and his eye, through the operation he had late in 1913.

The new novel, called *The Commodore* through the six years of its composition, was renamed *Gideon's Band* before publication on September 19, 1914. Cable had planned it to deal with the "wealth-makers" on the Mississippi who had built their own fortunes and the early commerce of the river simultaneously. It would take account of the fabulous immigration of the 1840's and 1850's and would touch his father's career at many points.[7] At the New Orleans archives in 1909 and again three years later he collected facts and refreshed the memories of his own boyhood experiences and the experiences of his parents that had stayed alive in the family. Of those experiences he used his mother's nursing cholera victims on the boat she had taken to Indiana. The goldminer

---

[7] See an interview in the *Picayune,* Jan. 5, 1909.

of the story probably owes something to the author's cousin James E. Cable, who went to the goldfields of California in 1849. The owning of a series of steamboats by one family suggests the family of T. P. Leathers, who had owned and operated the proud line of seven packets all named *Natchez*. The manuscript grew with painful slowness, as Cable's accounting to Scribner reveals. After seeing about half of it, Scribner wrote on July 31, 1912, "The work is of course done with the greatest care and technical excellence but I still cannot understand how it could have taken you so long."

Gideon's Band is a romance, as the author himself called it. The plot is contrived so as to concentrate all the action on a steamboat traveling up the river from New Orleans. The book contains more about Southern problems than either *Kincaid's Battery* or *The Cavalier*. The story of Phyllis touches the race question at the point where greatest tragedy lies just below the surface. She is almost white, is intelligent and accomplished, and is associated with her white kin. As her tragedy unfolds, flight from the South is clearly not a solution, nor is a white marriage, for the races must be kept pure, one character says, as the best way to improve both. Though this is not a Creole story, Phyllis has literary antecedents in Palmyre of *The Grandissimes* and Madame Delphine's daughter Olive. Hers is the same hard fate as theirs, and the author says in effect that the solution Olive found in marriage to a white man was no solution after all.

Through the Hayle twins, Cable returns to another subject he had explored in both his early fiction and his Southern essays. They are sons of Gideon Hayle and are passengers on a boat owned and captained by their father's arch rival on the river, John Courtney. Their mother and sister are aboard also, making up with them "Gideon's band." The love story involves the sister, Ramsey Hayle, and Hugh Courtney, who is understudying his father. The situation is one to provoke the twins to display the flaws of their upbringing, as they return insults for offers of kindness and demand satisfaction for imagined wrongs. In them the virtues of family pride, honor, courage, and punctilious courtesy have been nourished into vices.

On board is a back-country exhorter who calls himself John the Baptist and talks in a dialect akin to that of Posson Jone'. His narrowness and bigotry and his belligerent prejudices against the immigrants dying of cholera on the lower decks, supported by the conniving of another character, the senator, constitute a telling argument for breadth and tolerance. The moral obligation to help others in distress is barely greater, in the context of the book, than the obligation to remain cheerful in the face of adversity. Hence the episode in which Ramsey goes through with the dramatic skit which has been planned to bolster morale among the passengers, even while her brother is dying of the cholera. The episode is typical of Cable's method of dramatizing an idea, and it contains the kind of ironic contrast he liked to use.

A reviewer in the *Nation* of December 3, 1914, remarked on the complexities and obscurities which "the author does no more than his part in clearing up." The best of the book, as most of the reviewers noted,[8] is in the passages which the author could base most solidly on his own personal knowledge, as in the description of the New Orleans levee when the packets churned out into the current to head up the river. A reviewer in the *Catholic World* wrote in February, 1915: "No living American writer knows more about the South in the days before the war, or is more accurate and exact in the portrayal of types and his descriptions of scenery." The historian John Spencer Bassett wrote Cable on October 4, 1914, after reading *Gideon's Band,* "The younger generation should read it & understand a vanished phase of our mid-century life. . . . You have made the steamboating as attractive as the love-making." From one who introduced himself as an old steamboatman came a letter saying he wished more of the old river pilots were alive to read the book. "My hat off to you sir," he added. "But I am puzzled to know where you ever gained such familiarity with lower river steam boating."[9]

Gideon's Band sold twelve thousand copies in the first two and a half months, but those sales repaid less than half the advance Scribner had made. Only a few months back, six years after its publication, had *Kincaid's Battery* paid off the advance on it. Even so, a contract was drawn at once to cover another novel, with Scribner insisting that the advance this time could not exceed five thousand dollars. An author past his seventieth birthday could not quarrel with these terms.

[8] See the *Independent,* LXXIX (Sept. 28, 1914), 450; the *Nation,* XCIX (Oct. 1, 1914), 409; the *Outlook,* CVIII (Dec. 9, 1914), 844-45.

[9] W. A. Blair to Cable, March 9, 1915.

Chapter XXVII

THE PEN SLOWS TO A HALT

A MONTH after *Gideon's Band* was off the press, Cable had begun another novel, *Lovers of Louisiana,* which would have a contemporary setting, mainly in New Orleans, and would employ Creole characters. It was partly for this reason that he spent three of the next four winters in New Orleans. The other, 1916-1917, he spent in Bermuda. Reaching New Orleans early in 1915, he took lodging on Esplanade Avenue, in the district where Creole families had lived elegantly in the last century and where he would find the characters for his novel. He wrote Scribner on March 23, "I am most happily disappointed in my experiences with the Creole people themselves. It would be but little exaggeration for me to say that they are receiving me with open arms. Also I am living in a Creole household of the highest social standing."

On March 17 he received a token that the people of New Orleans had forgiven him, the Creoles not excepted. He had been invited to read before the Louisiana Historical Society. The Supreme Court room of the Cabildo was filled as long as there was standing room, thickly sprinkled with Creoles. The *Times-Picayune* said the next day, "The attendance was the largest the society has enjoyed at a regular meeting in several years." "I had never had such a procession of handshakers in my life," Cable wrote Eva after the reading. "There must have been fifty. A vote of thanks to me was past [Cable's simplified spelling] and as the gathering began prematurely to rise and a swarm of hands was offered me the society voted me an honorary member and bolted for better air, while I stood utterly taken aback and unable to respond because there was no longer anyone seated to respond to. . . . What an hour it was to me!" He was apparently mistaken in the matter of the honorary membership, for the printed minutes of the meeting made no mention of it.[1]

In the language of those minutes, Cable was introduced by the presiding officer "in most complimentary terms" and began with "a few remarks replete with expressions of affection and sentimental attachment

[1] *Publications* of the Louisiana Historical Society, VIII (1914-15), 23-26.

to his native city, which he said had been his home during the precious years of childhood and youth, in whose public schools he had received his education, and among whose men and women he had gained his first friends and where he had also sought and found inspiration for his work." He then read "The Maple Leaf: A Strange True Story of Louisiana and the War—1863." Written the preceding summer, it had been rejected by *Scribner's* and other magazines and was never published. To an editor's remark that its fault was diffuseness, he had said to Scribner on September 11, 1914, that the cause was "pure fatigue." It told how a band of Confederate prisoners, including several from New Orleans, escaped from the ship *Maple Leaf* and made their way to their own lines.[2] The minutes of the meeting conclude: "It was listened to with breathless interest and at the conclusion received enthusiastic applause. In acknowledgment of this, Mr. Cable gave one of his characteristic recitals, such as has made him famous on the lecture platform throughout the country. It was a unique and brilliant example of his genius, which also evoked enthusiastic plaudits."

Cable had waited thirty years to be forgiven in New Orleans, and his pleasure was accordingly great. From the time of his visit in 1898, and especially when he came in January, 1909, he had found evidence that the old rancor had lessened. Newspaper interviewers had spoken of his literary achievement and had ignored his divergence from Southern opinion—from the opinion that was vocal, he insisted still, but not the opinion of the great "silent South." Feelings had cooled in New Orleans and elsewhere in the South in the thirty-five years since *The Grandissimes* and the thirty years since "The Freedman's Case in Equity." The question of Negro rights had been settled with such apparent finality that his crusade of the 1880's had little more than a historical interest. Few of those who could not remember back past 1890 even knew of it. Yet he could know that his campaign had not been entirely futile. His appeal had been to right and justice and humanity. The question would come up again, he had no doubt, and the seeds he had planted in the public conscience would be harvested in a generation little aware of his efforts in the cause.

By 1915 the Creoles had found themselves portrayed in other novels and stories than his. More of them had moved uptown in New Orleans; they had intermarried with the Americans and had seen their proud exclusiveness lessen with each generation; they could view their ancestors

---

[2] The *Times-Democrat* of June 16, 1883, had printed an account of the escape from the *Maple Leaf*. Cable had learned the story while he was writing *The Cavalier* and had laid it away for fifteen years.

in history and in Cable's books with a perspective not possible earlier. In 1881 they had condemned one of their own people, Alfred Mercier, when he put them as characters into fiction. Since then, another among them had written Creole stories and had been honored for it. Grace King's literary path had intersected Cable's in a way to furnish significant comment on the subject of Cable and the Creoles.

It was Cable who caused her to begin writing, she reported afterward. Of distinguished Creole descent and a devoted friend of Charles Gayarré, she resented Cable's portrayal of the Creoles. Once she told Richard Watson Gilder of her resentment and he challenged her to write better stories of New Orleans herself. The response in her mind was, "I'll show him," and in the years that followed she published five volumes of fiction and several historical and biographical works. In *Monsieur Motte* (1888), *Tales of a Time and Place* (1892), and *Balcony Stories* (1893) she followed Cable's lead in telling stories of the old days in Creole New Orleans. In materials and in general treatment her stories differ little from his. Her best stories, like his, are built of the contrasts between whites and blacks, and between Creoles and *Américains;* the most memorable ones are stories of mixed blood. In 1915 Miss King, as secretary of the Louisiana Historical Society, wrote the minutes of the meeting at which Cable read "The Maple Leaf." Eight years later she spoke of him to a newspaper interviewer and recalled his reading before the Historical Society:

I understand him now. I would say he wrote too well about the Creoles. . . . He captured the audience. Everyone rushed up and shook hands with him. Many of us never dreamed the day would come when we would shake hands with Cable. . . . The hall was packed. When he finished everybody stood up, and I never heard such applause. I am so glad that at last he got this compliment from New Orleans. He deserved it, not only as a tribute to his genius, but as compensation for the way we had treated him. I am glad. He is an old man, very picturesque, very sad, with beautiful manners.[3]

In 1917 Cable wrote to congratulate Miss King on a recent book of hers. She replied on October 14, "Praise from you is indeed praise from 'Sir Walter,' " and she added, "I hope that you are still as ever sturdily em-

<hr />

[3] Boston *Evening Transcript,* Sept. 29, 1923. That the phrasing of this interview had Miss King's approval is to be assumed because it was printed in the *Louisiana Historical Quarterly* of July, 1923 (VI, 365-74), in connection with the report on a meeting of the Historical Society held in her honor. She was secretary of the Society and an advisory editor of the *Quarterly.* Seven years after Cable's death, however, she returned in her *Memories of a Southern Woman of Letters* (New York, 1932, p. 60), to the earlier charge that in his early books Cable "stabbed New Orleans in the back."

ployed—giving us the stories, that only you in all this great world can write."

Yet Cable knew that the forgiveness was not complete. In 1920 he referred to "the only diligent detractors I have left in the world—the newspaper men of that (my native) city. They nibble at me still, like little fishes at a post under water."[4] A year later corroborative testimony came from Joseph Pennell, who was then in New Orleans, recalling their association almost half a century earlier and writing reminiscences for the *Century* which would be issued later as a volume, *Adventures of an Illustrator*. "I realized yesterday," Pennell wrote on December 8, 1921, "how fine and true your work was—and how well remembered—and that you were remembered from the old days and not forgotten—or forgiven—but I *saw* endless more stories so pathetic and sad—and you did it so well."

While at New Orleans in 1915, Cable went to the newspaper files of the preceding two years for notes on local happenings to use in his novel. With William Beer he went to second-hand book shops in the French Quarter to learn details of a Negro book dealer of a few years back who would appear in the novel as Ovide Landry. At police headquarters he found the chief and others, including a secretary who had been an acquaintance of his thirty-five years earlier, eager to give him tales of clairvoyants the police force had dealt with. He attended the Easter service at the cathedral and visited some of "those closely shut-in courtyards of the old Spanish type which is now almost extinct in New Orleans."[5] Writing in Northampton during the summer and in his rooms on Esplanade Avenue again in the winter, he completed *Lovers of Louisiana* in 1916. After more than a year had been used up in attempts to sell the serial rights, it appeared in book form late in 1918.

Meanwhile Cable's finances had reached a crisis. At one time some of his children began sending small amounts to help out. The trip to Bermuda at the end of 1916 had exhausted the five thousand dollars Scribner had agreed to advance on the novel. Early the next year Scribner advanced two hundred dollars on an article entitled "The Garden and the Street," which was never published. Then a new scheme presented itself: Three uncollected stories, "A West Indian Slave Insurrection," "The Clock in the Sky," and "The Angel of the Lord," would be linked together to make a book, on which Scribner could make further advances. Though Scribner had told Cable more than once that he must have some income beyond what his writing produced and had argued that the ad-

[4] Cable to Benjamin B. Hampton, [Dec., 1920]; copy at Tulane University.
[5] To Eva, April 4, 1915; in Biklé, p. 294.

vances must be held down, he never actually denied Cable's requests. A letter of November 20, 1917, states his attitude. "It is very distressing to me to be obliged to stop these payments or even to limit them too strictly but the conditions will not permit any other course. . . . I find that we have advanced $10,000 which is more than we can hope to recover. I said something about consulting Arthur and my associates, for you know this is now a stock company, but I really cannot do that to advantage. Our relations extend over many years and I cannot and do not wish to escape any personal responsibility."

In putting the three stories together to make *The Flower of the Chapdelaines,* which appeared on March 30, 1918, Cable constructed a framework almost as long as the stories. The characters in the enveloping story, which is a separate love story, live in the French Quarter; part of them are Creole, using the speech the author had recently studied anew on Esplanade Avenue. There are allusions to several incidents and characters in Cable's earlier books, and there are the autobiographical references usual with him. The father of one of the characters, for example, lost his fortune and took work in the customhouse, as Cable's father had done. Since the stories all three deal with slave times, many of the comments echo views the author had advanced in the Southern debate thirty years earlier: "I suppose no one knows better than the practical statesman how disastrous measures are apt to be when designed for the *gradual* righting of a public evil," and "I believe the most blundering effort for the prompt undoing of a grievous wrong is safer than the shrewdest or strongest effort for its continuance." Reviewers found *The Flower of the Chapdelaines* a pleasant reminder of the excellences they had known in Cable's weightier early books.

In his last book, *Lovers of Louisiana,* Cable returned to the matter of his early books: the Creoles and the race problem. It is a summing up of his views a third of a century after the climax in the Southern debate in 1885. First place is given to the subject of Creole-American relations as dramatized in the relations in 1914 between the Durel and the Castleton families, who are mainly sensible people, able to discuss the matter rationally. Zéphire Durel embodies in hyberbole the Creole traits of pride, impetuosity, prejudiced isolation, and sensitivity to criticism, but he stands finally repudiated by the head of the Durel family. Rosalie Durel has the intelligence, beauty, and charm of Cable's earlier Creole women. Opposite her in the American family is Philip Castleton, who speaks for the author, and in winning her hand, with the sanction of her father, points the way to the future of both families, and of New Orleans and the South as well. The best of the old in both civilizations will be cherished, but it will be modified to profit from improvements that can be learned locally and from the outside. In the persons of Rosalie and Philip the old and the new of the two cultures are married. The sentiment is no less genuine and no less valid in its reflection of the intangibles involved for the fact that it respects good social theory and good sense.

Philip Castleton speaks for the author on the race question, and in that respect his career parallels the author's noticeably. He has had his eyes opened by a grand jury term, he has done research in the local archives and he has lectured to Negro audiences. Like Cable, he learns the personal cost of breaking from public opinion in his section. Like John March of the earlier novel, he refuses to leave the South. Through him and John March Cable seems to be saying that he had lessened his own usefulness to the South when he moved away. Philip believes full public rights are essential in a democracy, and he sees in Ovide Landry's relations with the Durels an object lesson in the mutually profitable cooperation between the races. A sentence in the notes Cable made while he was planning this book states his prophecy for the future of the Negro race: "The time will come when the negro will have risen by selection until his story shall be the great romance of American history."

Lovers of Louisiana is shorter than any of Cable's novels except *Bylow Hill,* and the plot is one of the simplest he employed. The story is worked out mainly in dialogue rather than action, as had been true of the four other novels he had published since 1900, but in this one the topics discussed are of moment enough to give weight which is lacking in *The Cavalier, Kincaid's Battery,* and *Gideon's Band.* Cable had returned to the social criticism which had been such an important element in his first books.

The World War left Cable by no means untouched. His oldest grandchild, George Cable Chard, was killed in the autumn of 1917. In the New York *Times* of December 24, 1916, he published "A Prayer for Peace." For the Vigilantes, of which he was a member, he wrote in behalf of the Liberty Loan drive. A song of his entitled "A Song for France," to the tune of "The Campbells Are Coming," was printed in *Life,* May 24, 1917; and a short article, "The Tocsin," appeared in the *Outlook* of June 12, 1918, and later in a pamphlet of comments on the war by members of the American Academy.[6] Earlier he had become a member of the League to Enforce Peace and had made speeches under its sponsorship. He became an advocate of the League of Nations, which

[6] *The World War: Utterances Concerning Its Issues and Conduct by Members of the American Academy of Arts and Letters* (New York, 1919), p. 15.

he termed in a letter to Henry van Dyke "the only thing that will allow us to look God in the face as we put away the sword."

The two books published in 1918 drew out a series of proposals for stage and movie adaptations, and Cable was heartened by the Metropolitan Opera Company's production in the spring of 1918 of a symphonic composition by Henry F. B. Gilbert based on "The Dance in Place Congo."[7] Other prospects were greater but produced nothing. In 1917 there was hope that Eddie Cantor would sing in the Ziegfeld Follies one of Cable's songs, "The Ladies' Man," which had first appeared, with the musical score, in *Kincaid's Battery*. Two of his books, *Posson Jone' and Père Raphaël* and *The Grandissimes,* were considered for stage production, and the hopes for movie production were still brighter for a time. In the summer of 1919 Cable entered into a contract with Benjamin B. Hampton, who had organized Great Authors Pictures, Inc., for the announced purpose of producing faithful movies from the books of such authors as Winston Churchill, Thomas Nelson Page, Edith Wharton, and Cable. The contract was generous, and testified to great optimism. It listed sixteen of Cable's books; one a year would be filmed, beginning no later than nine months after the date of the contract. Hampton had in mind, furthermore, making short films of the stories to follow the novels. He chose *Madame Delphine* for the first movie and was ready to start production. But no movies were made. The distributors would not agree to take the picture because of the racial issue inherent in it. The contract was renewed once, but the question of distribution could not be solved, Hampton wrote Cable, and in the fall of 1921, the contract lapsed.[8] There was another nibble two years later, on *Strange True Stories of Louisiana,* but only a nibble. Thus another was added to the "many and varied disappointments" Cable had experienced in trying to usher his stories into the theater.

By May, 1918, when *The Flower of the Chapdelaines* was just off the press and *Lovers of Louisiana* was in proof, Cable had written sixty pages on a new novel. On December 20, 1919, he wrote Scribner the manuscript was half finished and on the strength of that fact asked for and received an advance of two hundred and fifty dollars to tide him over until February, when he would draw his first annuity from the

[7] See letters from Gilbert to Cable, May 13, 22, 30, July 22, 1917; also the New York *Times,* March 3, 1917, and April 18, 1918. In the spring of 1920 the "symphonic poem" was given by the Boston Symphony Orchestra "with notable success," Gilbert wrote Cable on March 9, and in 1927 it was performed at Frankfurt-am-Main in the festival of the International Society for Contemporaneous Music.

[8] Letters from Hampton, copies of Cable's replies, and a copy of the contract are at Tulane University.

Carnegie estate. Carnegie, at his death in 1919, had left him a bequest of five thousand dollars a year for life, to be continued for Eva if she should survive him. In the autumn of 1920 Cable's doctor forbade him to work, and he admitted that his efforts during the last year had been useless. "I don't believe I am done for," he wrote Scribner on September 15, "I shall write again, I trust; but *when* is more than I can promise now." In the winter he and Eva visited New Orleans and then settled until May at Pass Christian, a village on the Gulf coast familiar to him half a century earlier. The next winter they returned to Bermuda.

The manuscript of the unfinished novel is among Cable's papers. It is in a typed copy of three hundred pages with very wide margins left for revisions, and so would not print more than a hundred pages. The story opens in New Orleans on New Year's Day, 1918. A young Creole soldier, home temporarily from France, epitomizes the highest idealism and heroism of the war. Around him are two young Creole women and several men who view the war as a business undertaking and are not displeased if it turns profitable business their way. Comedy is supplied by an aged Creole couple who quarrel endlessly at their card game and by a chauffeur who says he guesses he'd be a Creole too if he weren't a nigger. The story is carefully written, as far as it goes, and some of the dialogue has the life and naturalness usual in Cable's books, but the fragment is too short to permit speculation as to what the complete book would have been. Early in 1921 Cable began collecting information about the Livaudais mansion which in his boyhood he had known as the haunted house of Washington Street. It seems likely that he hoped to produce a story, perhaps a strange true story, after he had ceased to make any progress on his novel. In 1907 he had written but had not found a publisher for such a story, "Triomphe de Villandry," which is in manuscript among his papers. It is a strange true story, he says in the first paragraph, not of Louisiana, but of France, for the action is set in France, and both French and American characters appear.

There had been reminders that he was old. While in the South in 1915, he attended the funeral of his brother James, two years younger than he. On June 18, 1918, he had buried his sister Mary Louise, who at the age of seventy-eight had ended a quietly heroic life that had been incomparable satisfaction to the brother she idolized. In November, 1920, his daughter Margaret died in California. Eva's father died on July 22, 1922. Howells died in 1920; E. L. Burlingame, his lifetime friend at the Scribner house, in 1922. Writing a letter had become a task, but in 1923 he exchanged letters with Charles Scribner, Robert Underwood Johnson, Henry van Dyke, and George Henry Clements, among his friends of long standing, in addition to his daughters and grandchildren and his sister Nettie. His letters had lost the sparkle of his earlier days, just as age had lessened the resiliency of his spirit; but he was as intolerant of a sad face as he had ever been. On May 21, 1921, he answered a letter from Nettie: "You must not talk so about our never meeting again on earth. People, especially old people, should not talk themselves old."

One by one he gave up his public affiliations, keeping only those to which the prestige of his name rather than direct assistance was valuable, such as the Simplified Spelling Board. From 1919 he was an elector of the Hall of Fame at New York University. On September 15, 1920, he resigned the presidency of the People's Institute because he was away from Northampton every winter, the busy season of the Institute. He did nothing, he wrote his sister Nettie the following August 4, except keep up his place and visit the gardens in the competition. "I am not sturdy nor yet tough," he continued. "Where should we be but for Mr. Carnegie's heavenly goodness." He remembered the years when he drove his pen to meet his financial needs. In 1922 illness kept him away from the ceremony for awarding prizes in the garden competition, the first he had missed in twenty-three years.

At his seventy-eighth birthday, October 12, 1922, Cable told an interviewer in Northampton that his attempts to write during the past year had been to no avail but that he hoped to write again. He was still a wonderful conversationalist, the reporter said.[9] Through the autumn his health forced him to stay close, but in the winter he and Eva went again to Atlantic City. The following June 7 Eva died, after four months of confinement to her bed with arthritis; and after the funeral at Versailles, Kentucky, he returned to Paradise Road, where Dorothea, now Mrs. Charles Boardman Hawes, came to live with her husband and two children. In October he visited Louise and Alfred Chard at Montclair, New Jersey. On December 16 he was married to Mrs. Hanna Cowing, who had been a neighbor at Northampton. From Atlanta, on the way to St. Petersburg, Florida, he wrote Scribner on December 26: "You will be surprised to have me tell you that instead of dying I have married for the third time. . . . This hurried union only six months after my bereavement calls for an explanation. Mrs. Cable has been an intimate friend & neighbor of all my family for 35 years & has enjoyed their confidence and [they] have grown into each others lives completely."

[9] *Daily Hampshire Gazette,* Oct. 13, 1922.

The next summer he returned to Northampton and the following winter was at St. Petersburg again. He died there on January 31, 1925.

At Northampton the buildings of the People's Institute were draped in mourning. Cable's body arrived just before midnight Friday, February 6. His wife remained at St. Petersburg in the care of a doctor. All activities at the Institute were suspended for two days, while the body lay in state in Carnegie Hall from noon Saturday until the funeral Sunday afternoon, guarded by Boy Scouts and officials of the Institute. The funeral was held at Edwards Church, where the Reverend Kenneth B. Wells read the Episcopal service and President William Allan Neilson of Smith College read a tribute. Burial was in the family lot at the Bridge Street Cemetery, beside his first wife, his mother, his older sister, and his son.

The resolution passed by the board of the Institute and released to the press on February 13 said among other things that the Institute "was the child of his brain and his heart, and in fostering care and self-sacrificing devotion he gave it of his best." In the foyer of Carnegie Hall his picture hangs today facing that of Abraham Lincoln. That would have pleased him. It would have pleased him also to know that Wallace A. Battle, president of Okolona Industrial School, wrote to inquire about his death and added, "Here at this school we have learned to love him and regard him as one of the great souls of America."

BIBLIOGRAPHY

I. CABLE'S WRITINGS

A. BOOKS

(Chronologically arranged; published by Scribner except as indicated)

Old Creole Days, 1879
The Grandissimes, 1880 (revised in 1883)
Madame Delphine, 1881
The Creoles of Louisiana, 1884
Dr. Sevier, 1884 (Boston: J. R. Osgood and Company; Scribner after 1887)
The Silent South, 1885 (expanded edition, 1889)
Bonaventure, 1888
Strange True Stories of Louisiana, 1889
The Negro Question, 1890
The Busy Man's Bible, 1891 (Meadville, Pa.: Chautauqua-Century Press)
A Memory of Roswell Smith, [1892] (privately printed)
John March, Southerner, 1894 (published Feb. 11, 1895)
Strong Hearts, 1899
The Cable Story Book, Selections for School Reading, ed. Mary E. Burt and
     Lucy L. Cable, 1899 (revisions made by Cable for young readers)
The Cavalier, 1901
Bylow Hill, 1902
Kincaid's Battery, 1908
Posson Jone' and Père Raphaël, 1909
Gideon's Band, 1914
The Amateur Garden, 1914
The Flower of the Chapdelaines, 1918
Lovers of Louisiana, 1918

B. IN NEWSPAPERS, MAGAZINES, PAMPHLETS, AND MISCELLANEOUS VOLUMES

(Chronologically arranged)

For any piece that Cable published afterward in a different medium reference is made also to the later publication. A number of book reviews and letters to newspapers are listed, but no attempt has been made to include all such writings. Reports of lectures appear only if Cable's manuscript was printed complete or almost complete.

"Drop Shot," column of prose and verse in the New Orleans *Picayune,* February 27, 1870—July 9, 1871 (daily February 21—March 19, 1871; at other times Sundays only), also August 20, 1871, and February 11, 18, 25, 1872.

"Mistick Krewe of Comus" (prose and verse), *Picayune,* February 22, 1871; reprinted February 26.

"Dante Gabriel Rossetti (His English Poems)," *Present Age* (New Orleans), I, No. 2 (February, 1871), 25-27. (Signed "Drop Shot.")

"With Our Clothes Off," *Present Age* (New Orleans), I, No. 4 (October, 1871), 1-4. (Signed "Drop Shot.")

"Churches and Charities of New Orleans," *Picayune,* February 14, 18, 25, March 3, 10, 17, 1872.

Review of Henry Abbey, *Ballads of Good Deeds, Picayune,* July 14, 1872.

Review of G. H. Calvert, *Goethe: His Life and Works, Picayune,* July 14, 1872.

"The Louisiana State Lottery Company," *Picayune,* August 11, 1872.

"The Louisiana State Lottery Company," *Picayune,* August 25, 1872.

"Closing-Out Sale" (verse), *Picayune,* September 8, 1872.

" 'Sieur George," *Scribner's Monthly,* VI (October, 1873), 739-45. (In *Old Creole Days.*)

"The Rhyming Spider: Felix Lazarus to the Children," New Orleans *Morning Star and Catholic Messenger,* January 11, 1874.

"Belles Demoiselles Plantation," *Scribner's Monthly,* VII (April, 1874), 739-47. (In *Old Creole Days.*)

"The Locomotive" (verse), New Orleans *Sunday Times,* May 10, 1874.

" 'Tite Poulette," *Scribner's Monthly,* VIII (October, 1874), 674-84. (In *Old Creole Days.*)

"Jean-ah Poquelin," *Scribner's Monthly,* X (May, 1875), 91-100. (In *Old Creole Days.*)

"Madame Délicieuse," *Scribner's Monthly,* X (August, 1875), 498-508. (In *Old Creole Days.*)

"Don Joaquin." *Harper's Magazine,* LII (January, 1876), 281-89.

"Café des Exilés," *Scribner's Monthly,* XI (March, 1876), 727-36. (In *Old Creole Days.*)

"Posson Jone'," *Appletons' Journal,* XV (April 1, 1876), 422-26. (In *Old Creole Days.*)

The Grandissimes, Scribner's Monthly, XIX, XX (November, 1879—October, 1880), 97-110, 251-65, 369-83, 582-92, 690-703, 841-59; 24-34, 194-204, 380-91, 527-35, 696-704, 812-24.

Madame Delphine, Scribner's Monthly, XXII (May-July, 1881), 22-31, 191-99, 436-43. (In *Old Creole Days,* 1883 and afterward.)

Grand Jury Report, New Orleans *Democrat,* June 30, 1881.

"A Prisons and Asylums Aid Association," New Orleans *Times-Democrat,* December 25, 1881.

"Our Vice Mills and Jails for the Aged and Insane," *Times-Democrat*, December 25, 1881.

"Historical Sketch" of New Orleans, in *History and Present Condition of New Orleans, Louisiana, and Report on the City of Austin, Texas,* Social Statistics of Cities, Washington: Government Printing Office, 1881 (issued in 1882). (Included in the *Tenth Census, Report on the Social Statistics of Cities,* compiled by George E. Waring, Jr., 1887, XIX, Part II, 213-95.)

"Prison Reform," *Times-Democrat*, January 8, 1882.

"A Rogue's Congress," *Times-Democrat*, January 22, 1882.

"Our Mad-House Death-Rate Explained," *Times-Democrat*, February 5, 1882.

"How to Inspect a Prison," *Times-Democrat*, February 19, 1882.

"Prison and Asylum Reform," *Times-Democrat*, March 12, 1882.

Letter on Harriet Beecher Stowe's Seventieth Birthday, Boston *Evening Transcript*, June 15, 1882.

"A University Town," *Times-Democrat*, July 2, 1882; reprinted December 2, 1883.

"Who Are the Creoles?" *Century Magazine*, XXV (January, 1883), 384-98. (In *The Creoles of Louisiana*.)

"The Creoles in the American Revolution," *Century Magazine*, XXV (February, 1883), 538-51. (In *The Creoles of Louisiana*.)

"The End of Foreign Dominion in Louisiana," *Century Magazine*, XXV (March, 1883), 643-54. (In *The Creoles of Louisiana*.)

"Plotters and Pirates of Louisiana," *Century Magazine*, XXV (April, 1883), 852-67. (In *The Creoles of Louisiana*.)

"General Wilkinson's Treason," *Times-Democrat*, May 13, 1883.

"The Great South Gate," *Century Magazine*, XXVI (June, 1883), 218-32. (In *The Creoles of Louisiana*.)

An Address Delivered by George W. Cable, at the Commencement Exercises of the Academical Department, of the University of Louisiana, June 15th, 1883, New Orleans: Printed by the Board of Administrators, [1883].

"Flood and Plague in New Orleans," *Century Magazine*, XXVI (July, 1883), 419-31. (In *The Creoles of Louisiana*.)

Letter on Waldemir Kowaledsky's "My Acquaintance with Cable," *Critic*, III (August 25, 1883), 348.

Dr. Sevier, Century Magazine, XXVII, XXVIII (November, 1883—October, 1884), 54-68, 237-51, 422-30, 529-42, 753-65, 873-86; 70-81, 257-70, 418-26, 596-608, 698-711, 820-32.

"The Art of Novel Writing," Boston *Evening Transcript*, December 7, 1883. (Address before the Nineteenth Century Club, New York, December 6.)

"To 'Fatima' " (verse), *Times-Democrat*, December 25, 1883.

"The Convict Lease System in the Southern States," *Century Magazine*, XXVII (February, 1884), 582-99. (In *The Silent South*.)

"We of the South," *Century Magazine*, XXIX (November, 1884), 151-52.

Letter on Louis Gottschalk, *Times-Democrat*, November 9, 1884.

Letter on Women's Clubs, *Times-Democrat,* November 9, 1884.

"New Orleans," *Encyclopaedia Britannica,* ninth edition, 1884. (Revised for the tenth edition, 1902, and the eleventh edition, 1911.)

"Margaret," *Christian Union,* XXXI (January 1, 1885), 7. (Abridged in the New Orleans *Times-Democrat,* February 18, 1885.)

"The Freedman's Case in Equity," *Century Magazine,* XXIX (January, 1885), 409-18. (In *The Silent South.*)

"New Orleans before the Capture," *Century Magazine,* XXIX (April, 1885), 918-22. (In *Battles and Leaders of the Civil War,* New York, [1887,] II, 14-21.)

"Professional Christianity," *Advance* (Chicago), II (July 30, 1885), 1-2. (Issued as a pamphlet, Chicago, 1885.)

"A Woman's Diary of the Siege of Vicksburg," *Century Magazine,* XXX (September, 1885), 767-75. (In *Strange True Stories of Louisiana* and in *Famous Adventures and Prison Escapes of the Civil War,* New York, 1893, pp. 1-82.)

"The Silent South," *Century Magazine,* XXX (September, 1885), 674-91. (In *The Silent South.*)

Preface to William Head Coleman, compiler, *Historical Sketch Book and Guide to New Orleans and Environs,* New York, 1885.

"International Copyright," *Century Magazine,* XXXI (February, 1886), 628-29.

"The Dance in Place Congo," *Century Magazine,* XXXI (February, 1886), 517-32.

"Creole Slave Songs," *Century Magazine,* XXXI (April, 1886), 807-28.

"A Reply" to John W. Johnston's "The True South *vs.* the Silent South," *Century Magazine,* XXXII (May, 1886), 166-70. (In *The Silent South,* 1889 edition.)

"A Reply" to A. E. Orr's "Is It Sectional or National?" *Century Magazine,* XXXII (October, 1886), 962-63. (In *The Silent South,* 1889 edition.)

Address before the Sumner Union League, January 12, 1887, Hartford *Courant,* January 13, 1887.

"Carancro," *Century Magazine,* XXXIII (January-February, 1887), 355-65, 545-57. (In *Bonaventure.*)

"Grande Pointe," *Century Magazine,* XXXIII (March, 1887), 659-84. (In *Bonaventure.*)

Proposals for the Constitution of the Sumner Union League, Hartford *Courant,* April 13, 1887.

"Au Large," *Century Magazine,* XXXV (November, 1887–March, 1888), 89-99, 213-26, 344-56, 548-55, 732-40. (In *Bonaventure.*)

"The Busy Man's Bible," *Sunday School Times,* XXIX (December 10, 1887), 787. (Incorporated in *The Busy Man's Bible.*)

Tribute to John Greenleaf Whittier, Boston *Daily Advertiser,* December 17, 1887.

"A Layman's Hints," *Sunday School Times,* XXIX and XXX (December 17, 1887—December 15, 1888), each week's issue.

Review of Mary E. Baldwin, *Gurnet's Garden, Sunday School Times,* XXIX (December 24, 1887), 827.

Tribute to Henry Ward Beecher, in Edward William Bok, compiler, *Beecher Memorial: Contemporaneous Tributes to the Memory of Henry Ward Beecher,* Brooklyn, 1887, pp. 33-34.

"The Negro Question in the United States," *Contemporary Review,* LIII (March, 1888), 443-68. (In the Chicago *Inter-Ocean* and the New York *Tribune,* March 4, 1888; issued as a pamphlet, *The Negro Question,* New York: American Missionary Association, 1888; in *The Negro Question.*)

"On the Writing of Novels," *Critic,* XII (March 24, 1888), 136.

"What Shall the Negro Do?" *Forum,* V (August, 1888), 627-39. (In *The Negro Question.*)

"Home Culture Clubs," *Century Magazine,* XXXVI (August, 1888), 497-507.

"A Worthy Daughter of Her Race," *American Hebrew,* XXXVI (October 5, 1888), 130-31.

"Strange True Stories of Louisiana: How I Got Them," *Century Magazine,* XXXVII (November, 1888), 110-14. (In *Strange True Stories of Louisiana.*)

"The Young Aunt with White Hair," *Century Magazine,* XXXVII (November, 1888), 114-16. (In *Strange True Stories of Louisiana.*)

"A Simpler Southern Question," *Forum,* VI (December, 1888), 392-403. (In *The Negro Question.*)

"Françoise in Louisiana," *Century Magazine,* XXXVII (December, 1888–February, 1889), 254-60, 358-67, 512-20. (In *Strange True Stories of Louisiana.*)

"Shall the Negro Be Educated or Suppressed?" (in a symposium), *Independent,* XLI (February 21, 1889), 225-227. (Issued as a pamphlet, Nashville and New York: The Open Letter Club, 1889.)

Tribute to James Russell Lowell, *Critic,* XIV (February 23, 1889), 94.

"The History of Alix de Morainville," *Century Magazine,* XXXVII (March, 1889), 742-48. (In *Strange True Stories of Louisiana.*)

"Salome Müller," *Century Magazine,* XXXVIII (May, 1889), 56-69. (In *Strange True Stories of Louisiana.*)

"What Makes the Color Line?" Chicago *America,* II (June 13, 1889), 325-26. (In *The Negro Question.*)

"A Word About Dr. Holland," *Christian Union,* XL (July 25, 1889), 100.

"The Haunted House in Royal Street," *Century Magazine,* XXXVIII (August, 1889), 590-601. (In *Strange True Stories of Louisiana.*)

"The Nation and the Illiteracy of the South," *Independent,* XLI (August 29, 1889), 1106-7. (Expanded as "A National Debt," below.)

"Attalie Brouillard," *Century Magazine,* XXXVIII (September, 1889), 749-57. (In *Strange True Stories of Louisiana.*)

Letter, "Strange True Stories of Louisiana," *Century Magazine,* XXXVIII (September, 1889), 798-99.

"A National Debt," *Northwestern Congregationalist* (Minneapolis), I (September 6, 1889), 2-3. (In *The Negro Question* as "National Aid to Southern Schools.")

"Congregational Unity in Georgia," *Congregationalist* (Boston), LXXIV (September 26, 1889), 317.

"War Diary of a Union Woman in the South," *Century Magazine,* XXXVIII (October, 1889), 931-46. (In *Strange True Stories of Louisiana* and in *Famous Adventures and Prison Escapes of the Civil War,* New York, 1893, pp. 1-82.)

Letters on the Race Question, Nashville *Daily American,* December 31, 1889, January 12, February 9, 1890.

The Southern Struggle for Pure Government, Boston, 1890. (Distributed by the Massachusetts Club. Published in abridged form: "Equal Rights in the South," New York *Tribune,* February 23, 1890; "Pure Government: Free Government," *American,* XIX (March 1, 1890), 396-98; "Solutions for Southern Problems," *Our Day: A Record and Review of Current Reform,* V (April, 1890), 308-19. (Included in *The Negro Question.*)

"The White League in New Orleans," *Century Magazine,* XXXIX (April, 1890), 958-59.

"How to Study the Bible," *Sunday School Times,* XXXII (November 15, 29, December 6, 1890), 722-23, 754-55, 771-72. (Incorporated in *The Busy Man's Bible.*)

"Address . . . at the Annual Meeting Held at Northampton, October 22, 1890," *American Missionary,* XLV (January, 1891), 8-13. (Issued as a pamphlet, *What the Negro Must Learn,* New York: American Missionary Association, [1891?].)

"How to Teach the Bible," *Ladies' Home Journal,* VIII (February-April, 1891), 4, 6, 8 respectively. (Incorporated in *The Busy Man's Bible.*)

Introduction to Dora Richards Miller, "The Census As She Was Took," *Independent,* XLIII (December 17, 1891), 1865-66.

"Does the Negro Pay for His Education?" *Forum,* XIII (July, 1892), 640-49.

Miscellaneous writings in the *Letter* of the Home Culture Clubs, 1892—1896.

"Education for the Common People in the South," *Cosmopolitan,* XIV (November, 1892), 63-68.

"A West Indian Slave Insurrection," *Scribner's Magazine,* XII (December, 1892), 709-20. (Incorporated in *The Flower of the Chapdelaines.*)

Letter, "Mr. Cable as an Editor," *Critic,* XXII (February 4, 1893), 63-64.

"The Taxidermist," *Scribner's Magazine,* XIII (May, 1893), 679-88. (In *Strong Hearts.*)

"New Orleans," *St. Nicholas*, XXI (November–December, 1893), 40-49, 150-54.

"The Gentler Side of Two Great Southerners," *Century Magazine*, XLVII (December, 1893), 292-94.

"After-Thoughts of a Story-Teller," *North American Review*, CLVIII (January, 1894), 16-23.

John March, Southerner, Scribner's Magazine, XV, XVI (January–December, 1894), 53-68, 154-70, 380-93, 461-76, 554-64, 740-53; 49-62, 236-50, 371-88, 489-510, 634-56, 768-89.

Tribute to Oliver Wendell Holmes, *Writer*, VII (November, 1894), 162.

Letter, "Authors Who Ride," *Critic*, XXVII (October 12, 1895), 226.

"The Speculations of a Story-Teller," *Atlantic Monthly*, LXXVIII (July, 1896), 88-96.

"Gregory's Island," *Scribner's Magazine*, XX (August, 1896), 149-59. (In *Strong Hearts* as "The Solitary.")

"Extracts from a Story-Teller's Dictionary," *Chap-Book*, V (September 15, 1896), 411-23.

"The Brown Ghost," *Symposium*, I (October, 1896), 16-19.

"Thoughts and Views," *Symposium*, I (October–December, 1896), 36-38, 75-76, 125-127.

"To See Our Life As Romance Sees It," *Symposium*, I (November, 1896), 59-66.

"At the Edge of the Woods," *Bradley: His Book*, I (November, 1896), 3-7.

"A Visit from Barrie," *Symposium*, I (December, 1896), 99-102.

"Preface" to a new edition of *Madame Delphine*, 1896.

"The Portrait of a Life," *Book Buyer*, series 3, XIV (February, 1897), 65-66.

"A Curious Misdemeanor in Letters," *Book Buyer*, series 3, XIV (March, 1897), 184-85 (review of Richard Le Gallienne, *The Quest for the Golden Girl*).

"Editor's Symposium," *Current Literature*, XXI, XXII (April–September, 1897), 290-93, 386-89, 514-17; 1-4, 97-104, 193-200.

"Books of the Holiday Season," *Book Buyer*, series 3, XV (December, 1897), 479-507.

"Art and Morals in Books," *Independent*, XLIX (December 16, 1897), 1643-44.

"Introduction" to *The Eugene Field Book*, ed. Mary E. Burt and Mary B. Cable, New York, 1898.

"The Entomologist," *Scribner's Magazine*, XXV (January–March, 1899), 50-60, 220-27, 315-26.

"Children of Jesus: A Christmas Carol," *Ladies' Home Journal*, XVII (December, 1899), 23.

"Père Raphaël," *Century Magazine*, LXII (August, 1901), 545-61.
   (Separately printed in 4 copies, New York, De Vinne Press, 1901; in *Posson Jone' and Père Raphaël*.)

"Some of My Pets," *Youth's Companion*, LXXV (September 5, 1901), 427.

"The Clock in the Sky," *Scribner's Magazine*, XXX (September, 1901), 327-32. (Incorporated in *The Flower of the Chapdelaines.*)

"The Angel of the Lord," in *A House Party*, Boston, 1901, pp. 340-86.

Bylow Hill, Atlantic Monthly, LXXXIX (March–May, 1902), 293-303, 452-65, 588-601.

"Neighborly Gardens," *Good Housekeeping*, XXXVIII (April–May, 1904), 332-42, 419-21; 467-70. (Incorporated in *The Amateur Garden.*)

"The American Garden," *Scribner's Magazine*, XXXV (May, 1904), 621-29. (Incorporated in *The Amateur Garden.*)

Tribute to Henry Ward Beecher, in *Henry Ward Beecher As His Friends Saw Him*, New York, [1904,] p. 130.

Tribute to Mark Twain, in "Mark Twain's 70th Birthday," *Harper's Weekly*, XLIX (December 23, 1905), 1888-89.

"Where to Plant What," *Century Magazine*, LXXII (May, 1906), 90-98. (Incorporated in *The Amateur Garden.*)

Letter on Public Gardens, Northampton *Daily Hampshire Gazette*, June 6, 1906.

"The Home-Culture Clubs," *World's Work*, XII (October, 1906), 8110-14.

"How I Write My Novels," New York *Herald*, October 25, 1908.

"New Orleans Revisited," *Book-News Monthly*, XXVII (April, 1909), 561-65.

"Thomas Nelson Page: A Study in Reminiscence and Appreciation," *Book-News Monthly*, XXVIII (November, 1909), 139-41.

"The Northampton Prize Flower Garden Competition," in *Proceedings of the Convention at Which the American Federation of Arts was Formed*, Washington, 1909, pp. 144-59. (Revised and published in 1911 as "The Cottage Gardens of Northampton.")

"The Midwinter Gardens of New Orleans," *Scribner's Magazine*, XLVII (January, 1910), 58-70.

Tribute to Richard Watson Gilder, *Century Magazine*, LXXIX (February, 1910), 634-35.

Tribute to Mark Twain in a symposium November 30, 1910, in *Proceedings of the American Academy and National Institute*, New York, [1911,] III, 21-24. (Reprinted in the Academy Notes and Monographs Series for 1922, pp. 68-82.)

"The Cottage Gardens of Northampton," *Youth's Companion*, LXXXV (April 13, 1911), 190-91. (Incorporated in *The Amateur Garden*).

Anecdote in "The Story-Tellers' Hall of Fun," *Cosmopolitan Magazine*, LI (July, 1911), 282-83.

"William Cullen Bryant," *Encyclopaedia Britannica*, eleventh edition, 1911.

Tribute to W. D. Howells, *Harper's Weekly*, LVI (March 9, 1912), 33.

"Preface" to L. L. C. Biklé, compiler, *The Voice of the Garden*, New York, 1912.

Letter to *Monthly News Letter* (American Association of Teachers of Journalism), I (April 15, 1915), no. 3.

"My Philosophy," *Good Housekeeping,* LX (June, 1915), 628-33. (Published also as "A Novelist's Philosophy," in *Proceedings* of the American Academy and National Institute, New York, 1915, VIII, 41-44.)

Tribute to James Whitcomb Riley, *Writer,* XXVII (October, 1915), 149.

"A Prayer for Peace," New York *Times,* December 24, 1916.

"A Song for France," *Life,* LXIX (May 24, 1917), 896.

"The Tocsin," *Outlook,* CXIX (June 12, 1918), 254.

"Malvina: Song and Melody," in *Liber Scriptorum: The Second Book of the Authors Club,* New York, 1921, pp. 79-80.

II. Works Dealing with Cable

This list has been held to books and articles containing information or criticism relating directly to Cable or his works. Only a few major reviews of his books have been listed. Other reviews and works relating to his times and the times he wrote about, as well as manuscripts and documents, newspapers and magazines, have been cited in the text and the footnotes. For volumes having distinct chapters or sections on Cable, the appropriate pages are shown.

[Lyman Abbott] "Mr. Cable and His Church Work," *Christian Union,* XXXVI (October 27, 1887), 428-29.

Alden, Amelia D. "George W. Cable," *Literature, an Illustrated Weekly Magazine,* II (November 17, 1888), 25-29.

Anderson, Charles R. "Charles Gayarré and Paul Hayne: The Last Literary Cavaliers," *American Studies in Honor of William Kenneth Boyd,* Durham, N. C., 1940, pp. 221-81.

B——z. "Mr. Cable, the 'Negrophilist,'" *The Louisiana Book: Selections from the Literature of the State,* ed. Thomas M'Caleb, New Orleans, 1894, pp. 203-5.

Bacon, Edwin M. *Literary Pilgrimages in New England,* New York, [1902,] pp. 443-45.

Barrie, James M. *Letters,* ed., Viola Meynell, New York, 1947.

—— "Note," in *The Grandissimes,* London, 1898, pp. xi-xv.

—— "A Note on Mr. Cable's 'The Grandissimes,'" *Bookman,* VII (July, 1898), 401-3.

—— "Two Prefaces by Mr. Barrie," *Academy,* LIII (June 4, 1898), 604.

Bartlett, Rose. "How One Man Made His Town Bloom," *Ladies' Home Journal,* XXVII (March, 1910), 36, 80, 82.

Baskervill, William M. "George W. Cable," *Chautauquan,* XXV (May, 1897), 179-84.

—— *Southern Writers,* Nashville, Tenn., 1897-1903, 2 vols., I, 299-356.

Bentzon, Th. [Marie Thérèse Blanc]. "Les Nouveaux Romanciers Américains," No. III, Cable, *Revue des Deux Mondes,* LXI (January 15, 1884), 402-39.

—— *Les Nouveaux Romanciers Américains,* Paris, 1885, pp. 159-226.

BINGHAM, JOHN. "Home Culture Clubs," *Christian Advocate* (New York), LXX (April 25, 1895), 259-60.

BIKLÉ, LUCY L. C. *George W. Cable: His Life and Letters,* New York, 1928.

—— "Introduction to New Edition," *Old Creole Days,* New York, 1937.

BISHOP, D. H. "A Commencement in the Eighties: George W. Cable's First Public Address," *Southwest Review,* XVIII (January, 1933), 108-14.

BISLAND, ELIZABETH. *The Life and Letters of Lafcadio Hearn.* Boston, 1906, 2 vols.

BLOOM, MARGARET. "George W. Cable, a New Englander in the South," *Bookman,* LXXIII (June, 1931), 401-3.

BOLTON, SARAH K. *Famous American Authors,* New York, 1887, pp. 345-64.

BOWEN, EDWIN W. "George Washington Cable: An Appreciation," *South Atlantic Quarterly,* XVIII (April, 1919), 145-55.

BREWSTER, MARY. "George W. Cable," *Congregationalist,* CX (December 10, 1925), 816-17.

BRIDGMAN, S. E., "Northampton," *New England Magazine,* N.S. XXI (January, 1900), 581-604.

BROWN, STERLING. *The Negro in American Fiction,* Washington, 1937, pp. 64-67.

[BROWNELL, W. C.] "Cable's 'The Grandissimes,'" *Nation,* XXXI (December 9, 1880), 415-16.

BULLOCK, PENELOPE. "The Mulatto in American Fiction," *Phylon,* VI (First Quarter, 1945), 78-82.

BURLINGAME, ROGER. *Of Making Many Books: A Hundred Years of Reading, Writing and Publishing.* New York, 1946.

BUTCHER, PHILIP. "George W. Cable and Booker T. Washington," *Journal of Negro Education,* XVII (Fall, 1948), 462-68.

—— "George W. Cable and Negro Education," *Journal of Negro History,* XXXIV (April, 1949), 119-34.

—— "George W. Cable: History and Politics," *Phylon,* IX (Second Quarter, 1948), 137-45.

CARDWELL, GUY A. "The First Public Address of George W. Cable, Southern Liberal," in *Studies in Memory of Frank Martindale Webster,* Washington University Studies, St. Louis, 1951, pp. 67-76.

—— "George W. Cable Becomes a Professional Reader," *American Literature,* XXIII (January, 1952), 467-70.

—— "Mark Twain's 'Row' with George Cable," *Modern Language Quarterly,* XIII (December, 1952), 363-71.

—— *Twins of Genius.* East Lansing, Michigan, 1953.

CARNEGIE, ANDREW. *Autobiography,* Boston, 1920, p. 295.

CHESNUTT, HELEN M. *Charles Waddell Chesnutt: Pioneer of the Color Line.* Chapel Hill, N. C., [1952].

CHEW, SAMUEL C., ED. *Fruit Among the Leaves.* New York, 1950.

CLAY, CHARLES M. "George W. Cable," *Critic,* I (October 8, 1881), 270-71.

CLÉMENS, SAMUEL L. *Mark Twain's Letters,* ed. A. B. Paine. New York, 1917, 2 vols.

—— *Life on the Mississippi,* Boston, 1883, chapters XLI-LI.

—— *The Love Letters of Mark Twain,* ed. Dixon Wecter. New York, 1949.

—— *Mark Twain in Eruption,* ed. Bernard DeVoto. New York, [1940].

COLEMAN, WILLIAM HEAD, COMPILER. *Historical Sketch Book and Guide to New Orleans and Environs.* New York, 1885.

DABNEY, R. L. "George W. Cable in the Century Magazine," *Southern Historical Society Papers,* XIII (January-December, 1885), 148-53.

DART, HENRY P. "George W. Cable," *Louisiana Historical Quarterly,* VIII (October, 1925), 647-56.

DeMENIL, A. N. *The Literature of the Louisiana Territory.* St. Louis, 1904, pp. 216-19.

DENNIS, MARY CABLE. *The Tail of the Comet.* New York, 1937.

DONNER, STANLEY T. "Mark Twain as a Reader," *Quarterly Journal of Speech,* XXXIII (October, 1947), 308-11.

EGGLESTON, EDWARD. "Some Recent Works of Fiction," *North American Review,* CXXIX (November, 1879), 510-17.

EIDSON, JOHN OLIN. "George W. Cable's Philosophy of Progress," *Southwest Review,* XXI (January, 1936), 211-16.

EKSTRÖM, KJELL. "The Cable-Howells Correspondence," *Studia Neophilologica,* XXII (1950), 48-61.

—— "Cable's *Grandissimes* and the Creoles," *Studia Neophilologica,* XXI (1949), 190-194.

—— *George Washington Cable: A Study of His Early Life and Works.* Upsala and Cambridge, Mass., [1950].

ELLSWORTH, WILLIAM WEBSTER. *A Golden Age of Authors: A Publisher's Recollection,* Boston, 1919.

GAINES, FRANCIS PENDLETON. *The Southern Plantation: A Study in the Development and the Accuracy of a Tradition.* New York, 1924.

GARLAND, HAMLIN. *Roadside Meetings.* New York, 1930.

GAYARRÉ, CHARLES. "Mr. Cable's 'Freedman's Case in Equity,'" in Thomas M'Caleb, *The Louisiana Book: Selections from the Literature of the State,* New Orleans, 1894, pp. 198-202.

GILDER, RICHARD WATSON. *Letters,* ed. Rosamond Gilder. Boston, 1916.

[GILMAN, DANIEL COIT.] "Mr. Cable's Lectures in Baltimore," *Critic,* III (March 24, 1883), 130-31.

[GOSSE, EDMUND.] Review of *Madame Delphine, Saturday Review* (London), LII (August 20, 1881), 237-38.

GOULD, ELIZABETH PORTER. "Mr. Cable's Sunday-School Work," *Critic,* XI (October 15, 1887), 191.

GRADY, HENRY W. "In Plain Black and White," *Century Magazine,* XXIX (April, 1885), 909-17.

HALE, EDWARD EVERETT. "Mr. Cable and the Creoles," *Critic,* VII (September 12, 1885), 121-22.

HALE, WALTER. "George W. Cable's New Orleans," *Bookman,* XIII (April, 1901), 136-47.

HALSEY, FRANCIS WHITING. "Cable in Northampton, Massachusetts," in *American Authors and Their Homes,* New York, 1901, pp. 135-42.

HAMMERTON, JOHN A. *Barrie: The Story of a Genius.* New York, 1929.

HARKINS, E. F. *Little Pilgrimages among the Men Who Have Written Famous Books.* Boston, 1901, pp. 75-89.

HARRIS, JULIA CORA. *The Life and Letters of Joel Chandler Harris.* Boston, 1918.

HARWOOD, W. S. "New Orleans in Fiction," *Critic,* XLVII (November, 1905), 426-35.

HEARN, LAFCADIO. *Creole Sketches,* ed. Charles Woodward Hutson. Boston, 1924.

——— *An American Miscellany,* ed. Albert Mordell, New York, 1924.

——— *Editorials,* ed. Charles Woodward Hutson. Boston, 1926.

——— *Essays on American Literature,* ed. Sanki Ichikawa, introduction by Albert Mordell, Tokio, 1929.

——— "The Scenes of Cable's Romances," *Century Magazine,* XXVII (November, 1883), 40-47.

HOLMAN, HARRIET R. "A Letter from Henry W. Grady Regarding Southern Authors and the Piedmont Chautauqua," *Georgia Historical Quarterly,* XXX (December, 1946), 308-11.

HOWELLS, W. D. *Literary Friends and Acquaintance.* New York, 1900.

——— *Heroines of Fiction,* New York, 1901, 2 vols., II, 234-44.

JENKINS, C. N. "The Blue and Gray," *Century Magazine,* XXIX (March, 1885), 797.

JENSEN, GERARD E. *The Life and Letters of Henry Cuyler Bunner.* Durham, N. C., 1939.

JOHNSON, CLIFTON. "Home Culture," *Outlook,* LI (June 8, 1895), 952-54.

JOHNSON, ROBERT UNDERWOOD. *Remembered Yesterdays.* Boston, 1923.

——— Tribute to Cable, in *Commemorative Tributes to Cable, . . . Sargent, . . . Pennell,* American Academy of Arts and Letters Publication No. 57, 1927, pp. 1-6; reprinted in *Commemorative Tributes of the American Academy of Arts and Letters.* New York, 1942, pp. 178-80.

JOHNSTON, JOHN W. "The True South *vs.* the Silent South," *Century Magazine,* XXXII (May, 1886), 164-66.

KENDALL, MRS. JOHN S. "George Washington Cable," in *Library of Southern Literature,* Atlanta, [1907-1923,] 17 vols., II, 619-24.

KENNEDY, W. S. "The New Orleans of George Cable," Boston *Literary World,* XVI (January 24, 1885), 29-30.

KING, GRACE. *Memories of a Southern Woman of Letters.* New York, 1932.

KOWALEDSKY, WALDEMIR. "My Acquaintance with Cable," translated by

Charlotte Adams from the *Viestnik Evropii*, May, 1883, *Critic*, III (July 28, 1883), 316-17.

KREHBIEL, HENRY EDWARD. *Afro-American Folksongs*. New York, [1914].

LeBRETON, DAGMAR RENSHAW. *Chahta-Ima: The Life of Adrien-Emmanuel Rouquette*. Baton Rouge, La., 1947.

LORCH, FRED W. "Cable and His Reading Tour with Mark Twain in 1884-1885," *American Literature*, XXIII (January, 1952), 471-86.

McILWAINE, SHIELDS. *The Southern Poor-White from Lubberland to Tobacco Road*. Norman, Okla., 1939.

MACKAIL, DENIS. *Barrie: The Story of J. M. B.* New York, 1941.

MANES, ISABEL CABLE. "George W. Cable, Fighter for Progress in the South," in *A Southerner Looks at Negro Discrimination: Selected Writings of George W. Cable*, New York, [1946,] pp. 11-18.

MATTHEWS, BRANDER. *The Tocsin of Revolt*. New York, 1922, pp. 289-90.

MILLER, DORA R. "Mr. Cable as an Editor Again," *Critic*, XXII (March 18, 1893), 167-68.

MOORE, RAYBURN S. " 'Don Joaquin,' a Forgotten Story by George W. Cable," *American Literature*, XXVI (November, 1954), 418-21.

MORSE, JAMES HERBERT. "The Native Element in American Fiction, since the War," *Century Magazine*, XXVI (July, 1883), 362-75.

ORR, A. E. "Is It Sectional or National?" *Century Magazine*, XXXII (October, 1886), 961-62.

PAINE, A. B. *Mark Twain: A Biography*. New York, [1912,] 3 vols.

PATTEE, F. L. *The Development of the American Short Story*. New York, [1923,] pp. 256-59.

—— "George Washington Cable," *Dictionary of American Biography*, New York, 1929, 24 vols., III, 392-93.

—— *A History of American Literature since 1870*, New York, 1915, pp. 246-53.

PABODY, E. F. "Mark Twain's Ghost Story," *Minnesota History*, XVIII (March, 1937), 28-35.

PENNELL, ELIZABETH R. *The Life and Letters of Joseph Pennell*. Boston, 1929.

PENNELL, JOSEPH. *The Adventures of an Illustrator*. Boston, 1925.

POND, JAMES B. *Eccentricities of Genius*. New York, 1900.

QUINN, A. H. *American Fiction*. New York, 1936, pp. 345-51.

RIGHTOR, HENRY. *Standard History of New Orleans*. Chicago, 1900.

ROSEBORO', VIOLA. "George W. Cable, the Man and the Novelist," *Book-News Monthly*, XXVII (April, 1909), 566-68.

[ROUQUETTE, ADRIEN.] *Critical Dialogue between Aboo and Caboo on a New Book; or, a Grandissime Ascension*. [New Orleans,] 1880.

RUSSELL, MATTIE. "George Washington Cable Letters in Duke University Library," Duke University *Library Notes*, No. 25 (January, 1951), 1-13.

RUTHERFORD, MILDRED L. *The South in History and Literature.* [Atlanta, 1907,] pp. 501-4.

SMITH, CHARLES FORSTER. "Southern Dialect in Life and Literature," *Southern Bivouac,* IV (November, 1885), 343-51.

TINKER, EDWARD LAROCQUE. "Cable and the Creoles," *American Literature,* V (January, 1934), 313-26.

—— *Creole City.* New York, 1953, pp. 208-22.

—— *Lafcadio Hearn's American Days.* New York, 1924.

TOOKER, L. FRANK. *The Joys and Tribulations of an Editor.* New York, 1924.

TOULMIN, HARRY AUBREY. *Social Historians.* Boston, 1911, pp. 35-56.

TURNER, ARLIN. "James Lampton, Mark Twain's Model for Colonel Sellers," *Modern Language Notes,* LXX (December, 1955), 592-94.

—— "George W. Cable, Novelist and Reformer," *South Atlantic Quarterly,* XLVIII (October, 1949), 539-45.

—— "George W. Cable's Revolt against Literary Sectionalism," *Tulane Studies in English,* V (1955), 5-27.

—— "George W. Cable's Beginnings as a Reformer," *Journal of Southern History,* XVII (May, 1951), 135-61.

—— "George Washington Cable's Literary Apprenticeship," *Louisiana Historical Quarterly,* XXIV (January, 1941), 168-86.

—— "George W. Cable's Recollections of General Forrest," *Journal of Southern History,* XXI (May, 1955), 222-28.

—— "Mark Twain, Cable, and 'A Professional Newspaper Liar,'" *New England Quarterly,* XXVIII (March, 1955), 18-33.

—— "Notes on Mark Twain in New Orleans," *McNeese Review,* VI (1954), 10-22.

—— "A Novelist Discovers a Novelist: The Correspondence of H. H. Boyesen and George W. Cable," *Western Humanities Review,* V (Autumn, 1951), 343-72.

—— "Whittier Calls on George W. Cable," *New England Quarterly,* XXII (March, 1949), 92-96.

VEDDER, HENRY C. *American Writers of To-Day.* New York, 1895, pp. 261-74.

WARFEL, HARRY R. "George W. Cable Amends a Mark Twain Plot," *American Literature,* VI (November, 1934), 328-31.

[WARING, GEORGE E.] "George W. Cable," *Century Magazine,* XXIII (February, 1882), 602-5.

WARNER, CHARLES DUDLEY. "On Mr. Cable's Readings," *Century Magazine,* XXVI (June, 1883), 311-12.

WEBSTER, SAMUEL CHARLES. *Mark Twain, Business Man.* Boston, 1946.

WETHERILL, J. K. "George W. Cable in New Orleans and Northampton," *Critic,* IX (October 9, 1886), 169-70.

WILLIAMSON, KINNE CABLE. *George W. Cable: A Short Biographical Sketch.*
New Orleans, 1945.

WILSON, EDMUND. "Citizen of the Union," *New Republic,* LVII (February
13, 1929), 352-53.

WILSON, FRANCIS. *The Eugene Field I Knew.* New York, 1898.

WYKOFF, GEORGE S. "The Cable Family in Indiana," *American Literature,*
I (May, 1929), 183-95.

INDEX